THE PREFECT'S ROPE

A NOVEL OF THE LATE ROMAN EMPIRE

EMBERS OF EMPIRE VOL. IX

Q. V. HUNTER

EYES AND EARS EDITIONS

Sign up for future intelligence at:
qvhunter.com

Editorial queries to:
eyesandears.editions@gmail.com
c/o Editorial Dept.

ISBN 978-2-9701084-6-7

This novel is entirely a work of fiction. The names, characters
and incidents portrayed in it, while at times based on historical
figures, are the work of the author's imagination.
Q. V. Hunter has asserted the right under the Copyright,
Design and Patents Act, 1988, to be identified as the author of
this work.

TO P, 'OUR ROCK'

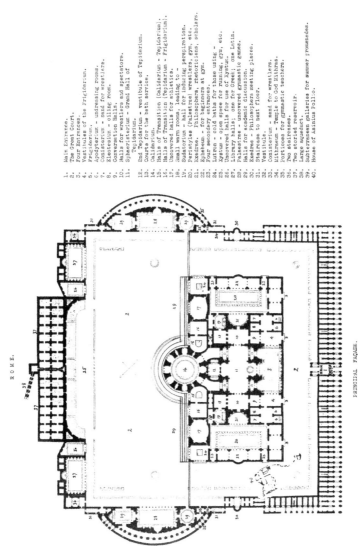

THE THERMAE OF CARACALLA

ROME.

PRINCIPAL FAÇADE.

1. Main Entrance.
2. The Great Court.
3. Four Entrances.
4. Vestibules of the Frigidarium.
5. Frigidarium.
6. Apodyterium - undressing rooms.
7. Coniisterium - sand for wrestlers.
8. Eleotesium - oiling room.
9. Conversion Halls.
10. Halls for wrestlers and spectators.
11. Sphaeristerium - Grand Hall of Tepidarium.
12. 2nd Tepidarium - vestibule of Tepidarium.
13. Courts for the bath service.
14. Calidarium.
15. Halls of Transition (Calidarium - Tepidarium).
16. Halls of Transition (Tepidarium - Frigidarium).
17. Uncovered halls for athletics.
18. Small warm rooms leading to -
19. Sudatorium - hall for inducing perspiration.
20. Peristyles (Palestrae) wrestlers, gym, etc.
21. Exedrae. Philosophers, rhetoricians, scholars.
22. Ephebeum - for beginners at gym.
23. Four secondary entrances.
24. Lutron - cold baths for those using -
25. Xystum - open space for running, gym, etc.
26. Uncovered halls for use of Xystum.
27. Library halls; one for Greek; one Latin.
28. Palaestrae - uncovered gymnastic games.
29. Halls for academic discussion.
30. Exedrae - Philosophers meeting places.
31. Stairease to next floor.
32. Vestibule.
33. Coniisterium - sand for wrestlers.
34. Mithraeum - Temple to God Mithras.
35. Porticoes for gymnastic teachers.
36. Two staircases.
37. Two storied reservoir.
38. Large aqueduct.
39. Subterranean galleries for summer promenades.
40. House of Asinius Pollio.

THE BATHS OF CARACALLA

URBAN PREFECTS OF ROME

Gaius Ceionius Rufius Volusianus (Lampadius)
(April—Sept. 365)

Viventius
(Oct 365—May 367)

Vettius Agorius Praetextatus
(Aug 367—Sept 368)

Quintus Clodius Hermogenianus Olybrius
(Jan 369—Aug 370)

Publius Ampelius
(Jan 371—Jul 372)

TABLE OF CONTENTS

Chapter 1, A 'Political' Illness

I didn't invite you here to wash, Numidianus. You're here to talk.'

'Talk? Here? Like this?' I sputtered from under a bucketful of water Amosis sluiced over my head and shoulders.

'What better place to converse? Everyone tries to eavesdrop, yet nothing can be heard.'

Prefect Olybrius was right. I could hear the city boss next to me all right—somehow. It was a question of attuning my ear to his cultured baritone through the racket.

Every splash, slap, and salutation echoed through the halls of Emperor Caracalla's gilded pleasure complex. The shouts of sportsmen bounced off the vaulted roof, between its marble columns, and off the colorful floor tiles.

It was just as noisy in the wrestlers' sand room and the *ephebeum* for exercising teenagers. Joggers circled the Baths' gardens on an outdoor track, plunged into the *frigidarium* pool, warmed up in the *tepidarium*, or sweated hard in the *sudarium*. Swimmers did their fifty-meter laps in the *natation* warmed by a sun reflected off bronze mirrors overhead. There were six thousand bathers a day and up to a thousand at any given hour.

Only the two dusty libraries for Greek and Latin in opposite corners of the complex stood silent. No one read anything of quality these days. Fashionable people entered libraries as eagerly as they visited funeral vaults.

We lay stretched out side by side on portable massage beds. Olybrius commanded a desirable alcove along the rounded wall of the domed *caldarium's* six shallow pools. His slave was trimming his toenails. My Egyptian Amosis dried me off and started to massage the wounded muscle below my left knee. Two surgeries had failed to return the damaged sinew back to complete flexibility.

From the distance of twenty feet, we two might have looked downright collegial. The city's ruling *praefectus urbi* Olybrius and myself, the *magister* of the department in charge of imperial post and road network—and spying.

But Quintus Clodius Hermogenianus Olybrius and I weren't two buddies relaxing from a morning's civic labors. We weren't even acquaintances. Up close our bare flesh betrayed crucial differences between us.

His rolls of muscle running to fat adorned a fifty-ish body accessorized by the sheen of perfumed oils and a gold-threaded linen towel tossed across one shoulder. Yet the nude Olybrius still seemed dressed somehow. One might say Olybrius was 'dressed' in civic titles past and future.

But even then, you'd miss the point. Olybrius didn't need to adorn himself with job descriptions. Long after the Julians and Claudians had died out, there arose two families in Roma—the Anicii and the Ceionii—to lord it over the other great houses. With fleshy arms akimbo and warm balls spilling over the edge of his bed, Olybrius lay decked out in the invisible vestment of any senior Anician.

My own torso advertised nothing so elite. A white hash of old whip scars webbing my shoulder blades might offend any noble eye. I lay here not just naked—but exposed. My difficult ascent from a noble Roman general's slave-bastard *volo* to the *agentes'* freedman chief lay carved in my flesh. That ugly map of corded skin made my claim to the rank of *vir clarissimus* seem tenuous— even presumptuous.

My ivory wool tunic thick with embroidered *orbiculi* and office insignia hung useless in the dressing room. I felt like an actor stripped of his costume.

The luxury-loving Olybrius scratched himself. Had he planned to put me at this disadvantage? After all, we weren't here for the steam. We could afford baths at home. Why not summon me to his city palace? Too welcoming? Why not visit my Castra headquarters? Too suspect and secretive?

Yes, an 'accidental' encounter arranged at the monumental Baths of Caracalla in the city's Regio XII was just right—close to the *schola*'s Castra Peregrina headquarters in Regio II and even closer to my new home near the Porta Capena in Regio I. Olybrius had made it downright impossible to beg off.

'More snacks! Fig pastries and cheesy puffs,' he ordered his slave away.

'Now, tell me, Numidianus. How was the East? You've been gone now four months? Five?' He admired his pedicure.

'Just over six.'

He wasn't listening. His gaze had fastened on a celebrity actor on the far side of the pools. We had this Roscius in our Castra files. He was a talkative type and reported to be desperate to escape the humiliations of the stage to which his parentage condemned him by law.

'You got an audience with Emperor Valens?' Olybrius tossed off 'emperor' as if it were an actor's casting for no longer than the current season.

'I even witnessed Valens' concession to Prince Athanaric. The Emperor consented to sign their peace treaty by meeting the Goth half-way, literally, on two boats in the middle of the Danuvius.'

'How did the barbarian manage that?'

'Athanaric claims he promised his father King Aoric never to set foot in the Roman Empire.'

Olybrius' slave delivered a tray of snacks and started combing neroli oil through the prefect's dyed hair.

'Valens is weak. A Roman emperor wading through muddy shallows to put down a savage? He won't last.'

'He's wall-eyed and clumsy but—'

'But who's really in charge? We hear rumors—'

'Valens hears those rumors too, even in his army camp at Marcianopolis or roving in and out of Antiochia.'

'Well, why doesn't he rule like a proper sovereign from a proper court in a proper capital?' Olybrius devoured his fig pastry.

'Was Trajan ever home?' I joked, then turned serious. 'Because Valens loathes Constantinopolis. And my agents report the capital's elites loathe him in return.'

'They'll overthrow him.'

I sat up so that Amosis could scrape my lower back clean. It gave me more authority facing Olybrius. 'Valens put down the usurper Procopius. He can do it again. I hope you haven't laid bets, Prefect.'

'No, no bets.' The city boss flopped onto his stomach like an oiled dolphin. 'I prefer the illusions of the theater to the delusions of the racetrack.' He watched Roscius chatting away.

'Exactly what our dossier says about you. *Not a gambler.*'

'Ha! I hope it doesn't mention my lovely new friend Cordelia.' Olybrius gazed at the well-endowed actor regaling his audience with backstage gossip. ' . . . You wonder how that man dares play a eunuch . . .'

After a pause, Olybrius asked, 'So you defend Valens?'

'You attack him?'

'That would be treason.'

'Our *schola* defends the Empire, East as well as West, Prefect. We're more than three hundred men strong now. Not quite what *Magister* Apodemius once commanded, but we hope to be useful. Imperial stability is essential.'

'Bah! I'd be happy just to get this city running smoothly. I suppose Sirmium's a useful hub?'

Why was I here? Even Amosis, trained to express nothing, passed me a fig tart with questioning eyes.

'It's essential to operations. If the center weakens, the ends won't hold. The brother-emperors work in tandem. A new law in Treverorum is prosecuted a month later in New Roma.'

'These imperial siblings must write a lot of letters,' he chuckled.

'We're adding riders in the East.'

'Don't bother. New Roma is full of useless *nouveau riches*.'

'Yet noble Romans move there for cleaner streets and bigger gardens. You hear the murder report every dawn—the Tiberis is clogged with fresh bodies. New Roma's a haven of civility.'

Olybrius growled: 'I'd like to see their idea of a well-produced play. No city will replace Roma. Not now. Not ever. We're eternal.'

So was Olybrius' delay in getting down to business. He watched the actor Roscius ostentatiously discard the towel encasing his impressive 'attractions'.

'You admire the celebrated thespian?'

'I admire credible facades. You know, his name Roscius is fake? He stole it from an actor from Sulla's day. But his revival of *The Eunuch* is very amusing.'

I noticed someone else who parted the crowd merely by glancing this way or that.

'Isn't that your cousin, Sextus Petronius Probus?'

'Consul Probus is now my son-in-law as well. You missed the wedding.'

A cheap shot. No one invited us despised *curiosi* to society weddings. Especially since these particular nuptials had elevated Consul Probus to *Aniciae domus culmen*, the 'summit' or chief of their gilded mob, and therefore the third most powerful man in the entire empire after our two Pannonian sovereigns.

This merger must have cost Daddy Olybrius a fortune, but it was well-spent. Now his daughter's vast inheritance stayed safe inside the sharp-clawed Anician family conglomerate.

I parried his barb: 'Well, if I missed your invitation, I can hardly claim mine got lost in the post.'

His chuckle died too soon. 'Numidianus, dismiss your man.'

'I trust Amosis.' But my slave was already sliding away as only Egyptians can—sideways.

'I trust no one, Numidianus, least of all his kind. And don't believe I confide this to you out of some "duty to the Empire." I have better reasons. I'm going to retire.'

'Why?'

'Illness. The former proconsul Publius Ampelius takes over in the new year.'

Olybrius looked just fine to me. Tomorrow's matinee would find him in his usual seat.

'Let me recommend our Castra doctor—a Greek, of course.'

'No thanks. As it happens, my malady is rather convenient,'

Olybrius' attention wavered. His cousin Consul Probus was abandoning a throng of well-barbered officials. A scintilla of acknowledgment shot between the two Aniciians. I was the only man among hundreds who noticed—but that's my job.

'While you were away, Numidianus, the official Chilo and his wife Maxima claimed someone tried to poison them. There were arrests of a trio of stooges straight out of a Plautus farce—but not enough evidence. We've jailed them in the Tullianum far longer than customary.'

'Release them.'

'I'd hoped Chilo would drop the charge.'

'Go to trial for dismissal?'

'Chilo filed a complaint up high. I must pass the investigation to a deputy to speed it up.'

What had this to do with my department?

'You see, Numidianus, the Chilo case has a few... loose threads. You mentioned those bodies jamming the river. Many of the corpses bear signs of poisons, spells gone wrong ... *magicium*.'

A sunbeam shooting from a high window caught Olybrius' flabby shoulders juddering away the illegal horror of sorcery.

'Who are these accused stooges?'

'An organ-builder Sericus, a wrestling teacher Asbolius and a soothsayer Campensis. Don't pretend you know them. Even Castra files couldn't scrape up filth that sticky.'

'Why poison Chilo? I hear he's an upright bore, tapped for the next vice-governorship of Africa.'

'Someone hired them, of course.' Olybrius scratched his plucked armpit. 'It's so annoying they don't confess.'

'If you're ill, your inquiry falls to your deputy, Senator Aginatius.'

'Yes. Well, no. Chilo requested Deputy Maximinus and I agreed over a month ago. That put Aginatius' nose out of joint, but how could I refuse? I'm sure Maximinus will clear it all up, but ... there may be more arrests.'

Those heavily pouched chestnut brown eyes searched mine.

Now I got it. This was bad news and not just for the snubbed Deputy *Vicarius* Aginatius.

The requested investigator was none other than Flavius Maximinus, Roma's newly-arrived *praefectus annonae*. Born to a humble accountant in the governor's office in Pannonia, Maximinus' family descended from the roughshod Carpi refugees Diocletian had transferred into an estuary of the Danuvius around the turn of the century.

Maximinus had washed off the river mud between his toes. He'd wangled work as a lawyer. Some said he was talented, others said mediocre. Somehow, he'd climbed to *corrector* or governor of

Corsica, then Sardinia, and finally of Tuscia. Now he'd graduated to running Roma's cumbersome welfare system.

Wasn't Olybrius' dilemma obvious? Maximinus wasn't one of *us*. Highborn, powerful, plump, and Christian, or lowborn, flayed, and pagan—Prefect Olybrius and I were both proud products of this crumbling city—for all its sins and sewers. Our beloved hometown might be frivolous, rotting, robbed of its court, and well past its heyday, but Roma was still the Mother of Cities, a society within a society. We answered only to ourselves.

Deputy Maximinus was one of *them*. He enjoyed close ties to the clique of Pannonian soldiers serving Emperor Valentinian's court far north in Treverorum. Sure, let Deputy Maximinus haggle with state-franchised bakers. Let him divvy up oil flagons and wine *amphorae* for Roma's poor; after all, the capital's machinery exploited talented bureaucrats of all shades and dialects.

But sooner or later, Maximinus should move on to greater glory somewhere else. He shouldn't meddle with our elites. What did a Pannonian know of Roman families and their entangled lives? Chilo's impatience for justice had vaulted the Welfare Manager into Maximinus, Investigator, Intruder, and Interloper.

Worse, Maximinus was ambitious in all the wrong ways. Olybrius was a confident Anician known for his easy-paced governance. He cared more for the belly laughs of *The Eunuch* than any real-life scandal. But Maximinus was on the make. He might turn this local farce of a failed poisoning into a show trial for his own gain. At whose expense?

More arrests—at last I understood. This was where *Magister* Marcus Gregorianus Numidianus came in.

We *agentes* managed the imperial mail and licensed use of state roads. But we had nastier responsibilities, like ferreting out secrets. Keeping files. Forging seals to copy mail. Auditing dubious prefectural accounts. And when necessary, carrying out politically-sensitive arrests of the most powerful and prominent.

Modern *vigiles* and the *cohortes urbanae* were hardly the high-ranked officials of old Caesar's day. They'd been reduced to registering the city's brothel districts along the riverfront and policing bathhouses. No respectable Roman took the job anymore. And no respectable citizen was taken into custody by them.

My service filled the gap. The Castra trained its cadets in the legalities of carting off the high and mighty and the diplomacy of detention. Address the victim by his full name and proper title. State the charges clearly. Avoid the use of ropes, chains, or shackles—if possible. Search a lady's purse, wig, or *mamillare* breast-band for concealed knives or razors without causing embarrassment.

Amosis offered me a cheese puff. But at the name Maximinus, I'd lost my appetite.

'You fear Maximinus will charge prominent Romans?'

'Oh, I've no idea.' Olybrius twisted one of his thick rings.

'You'd prefer arrests to be carried out under the strict protocols of *agentes* qualified to testify later in court?'

'It won't come to that, I'm sure. But . . . Maximinus is bound to be . . . well, surely you know the saying about Pannonians? Treat them like ferocious animals being transferred between their cages and the arena—with great care? Who knows what so-called leads Maximinus may torture out of his stooges.'

'But accusations are checked, tested, confirmed, or disproved in court.'

He scoffed, 'What good are lawyers under this crude regime? Who can restore an innocent Roman his ruined reputation? If Emperor Valentinian runs the Empire like one vast military camp, what can we expect of his deputies? We must ensure that decent citizens receive every possible legal protection before it's too late.'

'Aren't the wrestler and soothsayer citizens too?'

Roman Law was clear; an accused citizen must be tried and convicted in timely fashion or released. Punishments included fines, exile, life in the mines, or painful death. But endless detention in a sunless cell was perverse, uncivilized, inhuman, downright . . . Persian.

Olybrius relaxed back on his massage cot. 'You might soon find yourself working with Maximinus. But with you by his side, I'm no longer worried. You were raised by the Manlii, a noble house. We know you love Roma.'

Our city boss was ordering me, the *magister* of an imperial *schola*, to trot behind Maximinus' bouncing *sella* from organ factory to wrestling school? I'd had my bath, thanks, and was feeling more than soaked.

I rose to my bare feet. 'My *agentes* will observe all the regulations, I assure you.'

'No, no, no! I want you, Numidianus, only you.' Olybrius poked his thick finger into my stomach, 'not some hairy *eques* from Lugdunum.'

'I have the roads and post of an entire empire to supervise,' I said. 'And while I may not be *vir clarissimus* enough to witness your daughter marrying her illustrious consul cousin, I delegate sensitive arrests to my *centenarii* or higher. You're not the only busy man relying on deputies, Prefect.'

'But you'll keep an eye on Maximinus for me?'

'I'll do what I can.'

'I knew you were a real Roman!'

Affronted, I marched off to the dressing rooms with Amosis on my heels. If Prefect Olybrius admired Roscius' acting, surely he'd applaud 'Exeunt Numidianus and Slave.'

⚹⚹⚹

It takes time to escape the countrified magnificence of the Baths of Caracalla's vast grounds but I knew all the shortcuts. We crossed the stately geometric gardens to plunge into the clatter and clamor of the Via Appia's traffic racing for the Porta Capena in the old Servian Wall before nightfall.

Avoiding the Capena's notorious pick-purses, we veered away from the Circus Maximus to climb a steep lane leading into the Regio II.

Even halfway up the slope, the air hung fetid with the late summer stink of the city. But it felt fresher than the sweaty, perfumed steam of the Baths.

Amosis' black eyes darted up and down the side street where we paused. As head of an imperial department, I had the right to bodyguards from the Castra. But any official crossing Roma on foot with half a dozen *equites* in his party would draw attention.

Of course, I could travel in curtained obscurity like Olybrius and his fine ilk. But I couldn't work like that, hidden from view in a *lectica* teetering head-high over the sidewalks. I preferred to see any assassin before his blade rent the draped linen brushing my cheek.

My mentor *Magister Agentium in Rebus* Apodemius had survived into his arthritic old age. One of his secrets was to carry out his duties as discreetly as possible. Amosis was my accessory to this end. With his greasy black hair, narrow pointed feet, and dancer's frame, Amosis was a human placard reading, 'My master is an underpaid, overdressed, limping nobody requiring no serious protection whatsoever.'

The alley entertained the usual stray dogs, laundry vats of urine, and bread racks cooling flat loaves. The Egyptian extracted some snacks from his leather belt-purse. They were not Olybrius' treats. Amosis must have put his 'dismissal' back at the Baths to good use.

'What did you pick up besides anchovy grease?'

'The actor Roscius wears makeup to hide his pimples and takes a tonic for potency. The youngest son of old Senator Lampadius is collecting magic secrets for an anthology he hopes will be a bestseller. Victorinus Someone is finally dying. Who's Victorinus, *Magister*?'

'I can think of three without blinking. I keep telling you, always get full names. This isn't Alexandria. Anything else?'

'Prefect Olybrius isn't sick. His mistress Cordelia complains that for such a fat fart he makes "too many demands" on her.'

'Who said that?'

'A tribune complaining that Olybrius' wife, Tirrania Anicia Juliana, makes "too many demands" on *him* behind the cuckold Olybrius' back. At least I got the wife's full name.'

I left Amosis to his munching. It was the usual harvest of a lazy Roman afternoon—adultery, superstition, self-aggrandizing postures, petty rivalries. Did no one talk of civic duty? Did no one debate how to serve the Valentinian brothers' administrations East or West? Not in Roma.

Perhaps beyond Aurelian's ageing walls, our beleaguered, bankrupt empire had less time for gossip about property deals and advantageous marriages. The hard men actually running things were struggling to keep our frayed borders intact on the backs of an army speaking a Latin thick with foreign vowels.

I paused to rest my weak leg. Then Amosis and I skirted Vicus Honoris et Virtutis Street named after a temple and took the Vicus Statae Matris named after the protectress against fires. We were soon back on the familiar side streets that housed some of Roma's finest old families as well as the walled Castra Peregrina.

'Home, *Magister*?' Amosis mumbled through crumbs stuck to his lips. We weren't far away.

The lingering Roman light was settling into the delicious bronze-rose of a September dusk. The days were shortening and the heat was bearable again. Many of the small shops closed through August had reopened. Romans had returned over recent weeks from their country villas and resorts to their families' fashionable townhouses.

Apollonia would be serving the last tray of her own snacks to a party of ladies she entertained every week. My wife didn't enjoy public spaces or crowds. She didn't even enjoy private dinner parties. She preferred listening to talking. Her thick-walled garden sheltered many a confession. She deserved another hour of relaxation without my grumbles.

'No, I want some files at the Castra. Go home and tell my wife I'll be another hour or so.'

I admit I'd reached *Magister Agentium in Rebus* mostly on the strength of two decades of exhausting riding, spying, and fighting. But I flatter myself that the dying *Magister* Apodemius bequeathed the skeleton of his dismantled *schola* to me also because of mental persistence (all right, my Numidian slave mother called it mulishness) and quick recall. Even so, an intelligence service can't rely on one man's memory. Our archive of secret dossiers, saved by Apodemius from Emperor Julian's purge in 363, was a fearful legend to men with troubled consciences.

Tucked into the shadow of the looming Claudian Aqueduct, our overstuffed headquarters had been built by old Augustus himself. Two centuries later, it housed Hadrian's intelligence service, the *frumentarii*. Now the passage of a further hundred years had turned Augustus' spacious square of pounded ground and airy barracks for visiting soldiers—his *peregrini*—into my stony kingdom. The Castra was a claustrophobic warren of office buildings, classrooms, gymnasium with leaky swimming pool, canteen, a barrack-turned-prison, with competing altars for pagan and Christian *agentes*.

What was more somber than the Castra after the streaming sunbeams, shining marble floors, and refreshing waters of the

Baths? The *frumentarii* had been disbanded here by Diocletian for corruption. Our *carcer* had held many a chained barbarian or noble traitor since.

I never entered the Castra without noticing its tarnished and dented memorial plaques, mounted over centuries. Many names hid stories of betrayal or greed. These silent tributes whispered a warning; any Roman blinded by misplaced loyalty might bring about his own downfall.

Once through our guarded gate, past the tiny chapel fighting for space with the Temple of Jupiter Redux, across the flagstone courtyard, past the canteen noisy with riders on leave, and up the creaking stairs to my office, I asked my clerk Cyrillus to fetch our dossiers on Olybrius, Ampelius, Aginatius, Chilo, and Maximinus. As an afterthought, I etched onto his wax tablet the names Sericus, Campensis, and Asbolius.

The Castra didn't keep records on wrestling coaches or organ makers, but maybe Campensis? It was easy for a soothsayer to land in trouble under a pair of imperial brothers who trembled at any rumor of poisoning or fortune-telling directed against their joint reign.

Cyrillus returned with a pile of slim packets. I excused him for the night. Those rosy fingers had faded from the western sky. Our sunlit garden would be slipping into cool shadows. Apollonia's little salon must be breaking up.

I pondered Olybrius' request, lubricated by pastries and the privilege of lying next to his massage bed, that I work with Deputy Maximinus. But cheese puffs bought no favors from me. Of course, my *agentes* would follow the rules for arresting highborn Romans. But being an Anician, Olybrius assumed a single public appearance in his august company sealed the fealty of a half-North African freedman. But to what? For whom? For the love of aristocratic Roma? Olybrius hadn't told me half of it, I was sure.

I sighed a half-hearted apology to Veritas, Goddess of Truth. After all, I hadn't been honest with Olybrius either.

I had no intention of 'keeping an eye' on Maximinus. I wouldn't get any closer to Maximinus' Chilo case than a Frankish *laetus* flinging his axe at an enemy across the Rhenus.

After all, Deputy Maximinus hated my guts. I'd forgotten to tell Olybrius that simple fact . . . I guess.

CHAPTER 2, THE LIGHT IN THE GARDEN

—APOLLONIA'S WALLED GARDEN—

I trudged up the last stretch to the *compital* shrine serving our neighborhood. Sitting just at the crossroads of three narrow streets, the old shrine was a seedy affair, not more than a trickling fountain in a granite alcove festooned with sun-bleached figurines and tinkling charms left over from last winter's *Saturnalia*.

Our *vicomagister*, a freedman nicknamed Flaccus for his floppy ears, was napping. Centuries ago, such *vicomagistri* were powerful officials. They officiated over the *Compitalia* Festival. They kept the census of each neighborhood. They supervised local coming-of-age rituals, when new brides donated coins or local teenage boys offered up their outgrown *bullae* for protection by the neighborhood *lares*.

But we lived in dispiriting times, in every sense of the word. The snoring Flaccus sprawled along his stone bench. His unshaven face lolled against the chipped marble altar. The incense brazier was cold. The basin sat clogged with dead leaves so the fountain's dribble overran into a gutter.

A handful of *nummi* tossed into his moneybox always woke him up.

'How's the *vicus*, Flaccus?'

'Peaceful, *Magister*, peaceful,' he snorted, sitting up with difficulty. 'Your ladies are still there.'

He smirked at my bulging satchel. He knew what I did for a living. He knew everything about everyone on this street. I always 'offered' to the *lares* who protected our street. Flaccus spent my coins on wine as soon as I was out of sight.

Municipal slaves were lighting the street torches just as I reached home. A stray dog who hung out at the neighborhood laundry trotted past, her long ears as floppy and dirty as those of Flaccus. Four teams of *lectica* bearers in household livery waited along the curb outside my own door.

I tipped the poor sods for their patience as I guessed at my wife's visitors.

The chairs' finishing and draping varied, each marking the taste and status of its owner. I recognized the clean-lined, lightweight chair hung with pristine linen hemmed in dark red as the pale and slender Hesychia's.

The outsized show-chair of Charitas had carved gilt finials finishing the leather-padded handlebars and rich blue and gold damask curtains. It stood askew, almost tipping into the gutter. Her squatting bearers were playing dice with her house eunuch, the last a very trendy accessory for processions through town.

Now, the expensive (and heavy) oak-railed vehicle manned by hefty bearers in livery matching the chair's silvery drapery? That must belong to Flaviana, a lady of what passed these days for taste.

But who rode chair number four, with the worn-off handle varnish and faded brown brocade curtains? The chestnut wool cushions were flattened by years of wear. Its bearers crouched apart from the others and diced by themselves. They pocketed my tip without comment.

I heaved a sigh of relief on escaping the scorching street. Two feet into our *fauces*, I smelled stewed lamb and leek from the kitchen. Verus and Atticus plunged headlong into me, tugging on my tunic. Their childish jabber was like a tumble of cool stream water, an onslaught of innocence and energy that filled me with joy.

They'd been shy—too shy—for many weeks when I returned from my months in the East. They were too young for such extended separations to trust a *pater* who came and went. Or at least they required proof I really was the head of the household, proof in the form of toy boats and wagons, outings to the Manlius estates to play 'farmer', and lessons in *latrunculi* or other rainy-day board games.

They weren't as identical as they appeared. Verus was the deliberate one. He took a long time over each game move and studied his brother's reaction first. Atticus was bolder, too quick to move his pieces and impatient with rules. He had to conquer, one way or the other. Occasionally he cheated when he thought no one noticed.

Whatever the bribe in time or toys, I had to win my four-year-olds over again and again, because I was their competitor for the real prize—their mother's attention. They already knew they had her devotion. After losing our newborn Clarissa, Apollonia and I valued young life all the more.

This evening, our nurse Lavinia stood in Apollonia's place at the family shrine near the entrance to our atrium. She was lighting the evening *cyphi*, the Egyptian incense that eases men into tranquil sleep. It never subdued the children but worked a charm on the adult Amosis. I often worked through the night in my study while my personal slave 'in attendance' slept soundly.

Lavinia turned at the noise of me dragging the laughing barnacle-boys across the tiles. The evening's palm-lamps, wicks adjusted and oil refilled, were glowing at her elbow on the altar, like pottery ducklings in a neat row. She peeled the boys away and hurtled them at the kitchen.

'Good evening, *Magister*. Will you take your wine in the study?'

Lavinia knew garden parties and heavy satchels don't mix.

There was a burst of feminine laughter from the garden. 'I take it the distaff senate is still in session?'

Lavinia laughed and handed my *pilleus* and satchel to Amosis who headed off to my study. For a man of my high rank, we still ran a modest house, barely a dozen slaves. After so many decades in the Manlius townhouse, I was unprepared for starting from scratch with a family of my own. We'd spent a lot of savings on plumbing repairs and garden landscaping when we took up residence here. Retinues of idle slaves had to wait.

Anyway, I preferred our social obscurity. I was not a 'public man', for all my political reach. The *Magister Agentium in Rebus* must be discreet and I entrusted our home to an equally discreet *matrona*. The Castra was enough headache for me—I didn't deal with the head gardener, cook, seamstress, chambermaid, housekeeper and all their helpers and trainees. After a sequestered youth as *Magister* Apodemius' granddaughter, Apollonia disliked too many extra souls in her private domain.

But Nurse Lavinia and our tipsy *dispensator* Cornelius were exceptions. They'd been my helpmeets for decades. Lavinia and Amosis pretended that Cornelius was in charge but when it came to real authority, Cornelius came third, and the pecking order between Lavinia and Amosis was contentious. Amosis was my shadow outside the house. Lavinia prevailed the moment we crossed the threshold. All the more so during recent months while Cornelius was in Mediolanum, attending our Leo. The young Manlius heir was prosecuting a case involving corruption in the purchase of offices.

Lavinia was gray-haired and stout now, her once-pretty face deeply lined by decades of tending others. She'd joined the Manlius *domus* to help with baby Leo and then stayed to nurse Leo's wounded mother, our dear Kahina.

The years went by, poor Kahina left to worship her Savior in the North African desert, Leo grew into a promising lawyer, and Lavinia went to work for other families. So we were lucky she'd returned to our new house and a family with toddlers. She gave the twins no quarter but was more than an ageing babysitter.

My dear Apollonia was a resilient and intelligence Roman city girl—nothing like the wide-eyed country girl Kahina. But Apollonia had never known her own mother. Despite Lavinia's intellectual simplicity, Apollonia looked to the older woman with a trust and respect that touched my soul. Only Lavinia was allowed to help with Apollonia's ritual chores of replacing the fragrant cakes on the family altar every morning and refreshing the scented lamps and the laurel wreaths near the doorway at dusk.

'Marcus? Is that you?' Apollonia's voice sang out from the garden at the rear.

When I reached the rear of the house, I paused to take in a picture of complete Roman September serenity. The blooms of a fading summer—the tall purple tassle-flowers and scarlet, fuchsia, and gold gladioli—framed the quintet of ladies lounging in the shade in a silken rainbow of their own. Afternoon light slanting low through the tall trees lining the back wall dappled them with the dancing shadows of rustling leaves.

'Here are the regulars—Hesychia, Flaviana, and Charitas—to make me laugh,' Apollonia rose to embrace me. 'But you've never met Anepsia, I think.'

I gave a touch of greeting to Apollonia's younger companions. I knew Hesychia only a little. She was a shy young heiress, coiffured in tight ropes of mousey hair bound in blue cord. Tiny sapphires hung from her ears. She nodded hello and tightened her yellow linen *palla* protectively.

Hesychia spent too much time indoors. Even after a long summer, she'd taken no color. She'd entered Roman society, head high, as gracefully as any girl with three famous vineyards to her name and been married off to a man twice her age. The husband preferred his slave girls and her country vintage to the clamor and exposure of Roma.

Thus Hesychia was reduced to chose between the company of an ageing philanderer shuttling between Baiae and Sicilia versus an invalid grandmother residing in Roma. Hesychia chose the old lady. She was well-read and intelligent, but obliged to listen every morning to her grandmother's whitterings. Still, nothing was wasted: Hesychia used that gossip of families old and new as her social currency in private gardens such as ours.

Charitas was another story—as flamboyant and outgoing as her friend Flaviana was beautifully serene.

The fashion of this summer of 370 was to emulate a floating butterfly in transparent silks imported through Constantinopolis from the Seres lands, east of India. Reclining on a couch set against a bush of dark-pink hortensia, Charitas was wearing more float than fabric—the cheaper, thinner silk from Cos rather than the expensive weave from Seres. Her dark brown nipples lurked unbound beneath the apricot silk of her sleeveless *tunica*—she'd eschewed the sticky binding of a *mamillare* for her afternoon with other women.

Charitas rose to offer me a lingering kiss on my cheek. I hardly knew where to look but I was a healthy, curious man. My wife watched my diplomatic expression with amusement.

I fixed on Flaviana's sage blue-gray eyes as she told me from her couch, 'We're discussing divorce, *Magister* Numidianus.'

'What have I done now? Am I the last to know, Apollonia? Will you take custody of the boys—please?' I joked.

'Stop it, you ass.'

'If you're gossiping, ladies, I leave you to it. I've had enough at the Caracalla.'

Apollonia handed me a glass of chilled and diluted wine. 'Forget the dirty jokes of the Baths, Marcus. Here we're discussing theology and law.'

'I never doubted your parties were elevated, but divorce?'

'—the arguments for and against the Emperor's divorce from Marina Severa. Is his marriage to *Domina* Justina really legal or is it bigamous? Is it truly a Christian marriage? Is it legitimate under all the reforms since Constantine?

I didn't take the bait. Gossip travels in both directions. Always remember that, especially when a group of women with made-up eyes and fluttering hems await your pronouncement on the love life of your touchy soldier-emperor. Your opinion might shoot faster than a flaming *ballista* dart to the ears of an enemy official.

'And what are the arguments so far, Ladies?'

I addressed the stranger Anepsia, sitting upright in a dining chair next to Apollonia's bench.

But Charitas was too quick for the older matron. She wanted to show off for the only man present.

'As a widow and a virgin widow at that, Justina is blameless. The fault, if any, lays with our ruler. He divorced Marina Severa on accusation of her illegal property wheeler-dealing that brought shame on him. On balance, I say the second marriage stands.'

Hesychia said, 'But the Church disapproves of any divorce. They are both Christians. Therefore the imperial couple have risked the sin of bigamy.'

'There, Marcus, the case for prosecution and defense,' Apollonia said. 'Now, we need a judge. Anepsia?'

I knew my wife too well to think this guest Anepsia was of no interest. The stranger's amber and gold necklace spoke of old-fashioned wealth. Her multiple coils of thinning hair dyed tiger-gold were held fast by gold pins dangling from a fishnet of shimmering thread. But her old fashioned dress betrayed a reliance on refurbished finery.

If anything, this woman came to Apollonia's garden for sanctuary, not social stimulation. Her rouge was a bit too vivid. The flesh under her upper arms hung slack. Her hazel eyes had tired pouches beneath the black eyeliner.

Anepsia sighed. 'Marriage is hard enough without priests and lawyers weighing in. Isn't it most important that Valentinian is finally contented? And even if he isn't, he won't stray. The beautiful Justina is attentive and clever. Marina Severa took her husband for granted for far too long.'

'But to be exiled to the East!' Hesychia shook her head. 'I'd rather die than be sent away from society forever, like Marina Severa.'

Anepsia sniffed. 'She isn't a Roman of elegant tastes like us, Child. After Cibalae and Treverorum, any metropolis will do for Marina Severa. She'll enjoy life in New Roma. I believe their main entertainment *is* property speculation.'

Would Apollonia admit to being a trusted confidante of Valentinian's new wife? Never. Even among these close companions, Apollonia kept her access to *Domina* Justina to herself. I smiled at the way my wife was as guileful in gathering intelligence as her crafty grandfather. She had many of his features. Her light-hearted banter hid his sharp intelligence.

Hesychia jumped up. 'Was that the rattle of an oxcart? Oh, we've stayed past sundown! Now the streets will be jammed with cargo deliveries. I promised my mother—'

'—And I must go home to nurse poor Victorinus.' Anepsia also rose to her feet. A practical woman, she already wore closed shoes for the chill of autumn.

Victorinus? My ears twitched.

She continued, 'Let's all agree that *Domina* Justina will influence her Pannonian Minotaur for Roma's benefit. If the Emperor hates everything our city represents—and he does—at least he loves his new wife.'

'Justina's one of us,' Charitas shrugged, 'a true Roman noblewoman. Her blood runs straight back to Constantine, even if she is an Arian Christian.'

'Yes, Justina brings advantages to the court that a Pannonian sow like Marina Severa knew nothing of—support for new libraries and universities, religious tolerance between pagan and Christian, good poetry—'

I laughed, helping Anepsia to straighten her light cloak. 'Ah, good poetry. There I must dampen your hopes, *Domina*. Have you actually heard any poetry by the new court tutor, Ausonius?'

Apollonia grimaced. 'Oh, Marcus, must you?'

'I must. I must. For Valentinian's marriage to Justina, our imperial laureate cobbled phrases from the *Aeneid* into a pastiche entitled, *Cento Nuptialis*.' I began to recite.

'—*he snatches from his thigh his weapon hidden in his robe . . . and he strikes with his ivory plectrum. Now with the course almost complete, they approach the very end exhausted, rapid panting then and convulsing limbs and parched mouths! Streams of sweat flow everywhere. Bloodless she sinks, fluid trickling down her groin*—'

'That isn't the *Aeneid* at all,' Hesychia protested. 'That's pornography!'

'Stop, Marcus, please!' Apollonia wailed through her laughter.

'Sorry, but that's how the laureate from Gallia entertained the imperial wedding guests—with dirty pastiche.'

'Oh! My earrings!' Anepsia's hands flew up to her earlobes.

'You left them in the bedchamber when we tried that new hairstyle,' Flaviana said, making her farewell.

Apollonia called our slave Drusilla to fetch Anepsia's earrings. Charitas covered herself with a lightweight silk *palla* for her exit into the street. The blushing Hesychia slipped away through the atrium. I don't recall more than a murmured 'thank you' and a rustle of timid silk from her.

'Your husband is Victorinus?' I asked Anepsia. 'I'm sorry to hear he's ailing.'

She looked me square in the face. 'My husband is *dying*, *Magister* Numidianus. But I have consolations, like the engagement of my daughter Callista to a fine young man from a noble Roman family. Ample savings to cover my old age. And Victorinus has made influential friends who won't let me down after he's gone.'

I fumbled for condolences, but she waved a thin hand as I escorted her through the atrium and *fauces* to her waiting bearers.

'I take these things philosophically. Victorinus is my second husband. I don't mean offense when I say that you men are brave but we women are resilient. The women of this city particularly so. Your wife is a good example. I regret not meeting her years ago.'

Anepsia settled into her vehicle. Apollonia rushed out of the house, her face flushed. 'We can't find your earrings! Are you sure you left them on the dressing table?'

'They're loops—twisted gold ropes—dangling emerald *amphorae*. But I can't wait, Dear. Just send them over when they turn up.'

Apollonia was reluctant to let her guest ride off with bare earlobes. It was an awkward farewell. But Anepsia's *lectica* was already aloft, its old brown curtains drawn.

We bolted the great front door and retreated into the house. I carried a palm lamp to my study. Apollonia crossed the atrium to see that Verus and Atticus were tucked into bed. After an hour or so, Apollonia brought me a bowl of the lamb stew and pulled up a small stool to chat while I ate.

They say women dress for each other, but my wife had changed into a linen nightdress I particularly liked. Her hand toyed with the *stili* in a cup. I'd already opened the first packet from my satchel and spread out the papers.

'A lot of work tonight?' Her smile suggested a different kind of evening.

'Another hour, I'm afraid. Was it a good afternoon?'

'Passable. I still miss Sybilla.' She laid her chin on two fists on my desk and looked across at me. 'I wish Drusus had never moved them to New Roma.'

Drusus had been Leo's old *rhetor* and a close friend to me. Though not a member of the *schola*, Drusus had been a useful observer of social and political life in Roma. He was a frequent presence before and after our marriage. In the comfort of the Senator's old library, Drusus and I had often shared our thoughts.

His wife Sybilla had been just as welcome. She offered Apollonia witty and perceptive distraction from weightier concerns about our family's survival.

But Emperor Julian's idiotic ban on Christian teachers had lasted just long enough to shake Drusus' confidence in any worthwhile career in local Roman society.

Drummed away from Palatine Hill vestibules by fearful families, months of near-bankruptcy had shaken the pair for good. Their decision to try Constantinopolis came as no surprise.

I scooped up my stew. 'A Christian teacher with excellent Greek and Latin? You know Drusus was right to go. It's a new-built city with bigger gardens and fresh sea breezes—no summer fevers.

They have all the culture of Roma there, all the wealth and promise, but none of the blood caked into these ancient alleys and *fora*.'

'Whose side are you on, Marcus?'

'You have only yourself to blame for losing Sybilla,' I teased. 'Drusus was bound to attract dozens of pupils on the strength of your reference letter alone. Now, explain, who's Anepsia?'

'Hardly Sybilla. Anepsia's a bit heavy-going. But I want to be kind. Her husband has weeks, maybe days, to live and Callista will move to her new home after the coming wedding.'

'So Anepsia trusts her future welfare as a widow to Victorinus' friends in high places?'

'I'm afraid Anepsia expects loyalty where she will find none. Victorinus cultivated younger men he found promising—which is to say ruthless. But Anepsia can show a little ruthlessness herself.'

'A down-to-earth matron, then.'

'But attractive enough for a woman well over thirty. She already praises Senator Abienus a trifle too much for a woman attending her husband's deathbed . . . It irritates Flaviana who harbors soft feelings for Senator Abienus herself. Marcus, what did that amiable slug Olybrius want at the Baths?'

I scraped up the last soft morsel of lamb.

'First, he pretended interest in doings east of Sirmium, Emperor Valens, *et cetera*. Then he warned that the city's wave of poisonings and sorcery may reach into higher social circles.'

'Oh, dear, Lavinia must hide the boys' fortune-telling toy!'

'It's not a joke, Apollonia.'

'Oh, it is, Marcus! Take that poor mentor of Leo's, the famous lawyer Marinus. He's put it about that he's going to hire a magician to win the hand of my friend, the very pretty Hispanilla. Nobody takes it seriously.'

'Did you hear of an attempt to poison an official named Chilo?'

'Oh, that was ages ago, while you were gone! Nothing happened. Chilo and Maxima are healthy as horses, last I heard. He's tipped for Africa soon.'

'But three men accused of trying to poison Chilo are chained up in the Tullianum. Chilo wants the case investigated by someone more energetic than Olybrius.'

'More energetic?' Apollonia laughed. 'That could describe anyone. But then the case falls to, no, Marcus, no hints . . . to . . . Deputy Aginatius, right?'

'Oh, you'd keep my *biarchi* awake at morning briefings! Indeed, but Chilo asked for this man instead.'

I slid a papyrus file across my desk for her to read.

'Maximinus of Sopianae. Why that's—Apollo's Ass! Not him!' Her brown eyes flickered like the lamp flame.

'Olybrius wanted me to supervise any socially awkward arrests that Maximinus might request.'

'You'll steer well clear of him, won't you, Marcus?'

'Of course. I'll delegate it to Saturnus and his team.'

'Justina warned us about Maximinus after the Valentinus affair.'

'And so did Olybrius, in his neroli-oiled way. But Olybrius isn't worried about my welfare. He's worried that a Pannonian won't respect Roma's social barriers.'

'Are the Anicians involved?' Apollonia shivered.

'Not likely. Chilo's a nobody to the Anicii. Their new *culmen* Probus is imperial consul. Why poison a minor official who's leaving Roma any month now? No, it makes no sense.'

Apollonia was now reading over my shoulder, her finger running down another dossier. 'I remember this charge of immorality against Faltonius Alypius, here. But he got off without a trial. Now, let's see, Cethegus of the Cornelii Scipiones, here, he was really hot gossip for about a week. I wonder what happened to him?'

Apollonia wasn't authorized to read our secret files. But during Emperor Julian's purge she'd been the curator and protector of her grandfather's hidden trove of intelligence. And she recalled better than Olybrius why Deputy Maximinus was our enemy.

Our Emperor Valentinian was obsessed with threats to imperial borders, barbarian uprisings, and challenges to his rule. Barely two years ago, Maximinus' brother-in-law, the exiled Prefect Valentinus, had managed to wrap all three threats into his bid to break the diocese of Britannia away from imperial control to his own criminal control.

As part of an undercover surveillance mission to the chaotic island, I'd fingered Valentinus for treason. Within weeks, I'd seen the beheaded rebel's sightless eye sockets staring at me from the end of a sword.

I felt no pity or remorse. Valentinus had treated the Empire badly. He'd treated me far worse. I was lucky to see my wife and twins ever again.

The rebel's sister was still married to Maximinus, who publicly disowned Valentinus. Any Roman courtier would. Maximinus had a promising career up the *Cursus Honorum* to shield from suspicion.

And as every man understands—be he Berber, Goth, or Hun—you can't always choose your brother-in-law.

Prefect Maximinus and his wife couldn't fault me for doing my duty. I'd traced the conspiracy straight to Valentinus' signature and my service had won the new emperor's trust at last. I'd cut a direct channel to our sovereign's ear through all the rivalrous officials jockeying for his favor. Through our long acquaintance with Valentinian's new wife Justina, both Apollonia and I now enjoyed direct access to the Emperor whenever we wished.

Apollonia straightened up. 'Was that someone at our door?'

I listened with her. 'It's the boys jumping on their beds again.'

'No, Marcus.'

There was a polite, but insistent tapping of a boot toe. Her fingers on my shoulder tightened. 'Send Amosis to the door.'

I got up with a groan. With Cornelius in Mediolanum, it was easier to answer myself than to wake up Amosis. I went to the peephole which Cornelius had drilled into the oak when we moved in.

'You forget who you are and what you do, Marcus,' he'd said. 'I never do. I trust nobody.'

I expected a slave from Anepsia sent to collect the misplaced earrings. Instead, I opened the door to face an unarmed man in City livery. I didn't recognize his insignia by street torchlight.

'*Magister Agentium in Rebus,* Marcus Gregorianus Numidianus?'

I laid a cautious hand on the *pugio* dangling from my belt between the folds of my house robe. 'Yes?'

He handed me a folded piece of *Livia* papyrus tied in ordinary string and marched away.

'What is it, Marcus?' Apollonia was already behind me.

The blood drained from my cheek as I read:

'Please meet me in the first hour after dawn tomorrow at my offices, Deputy Flavius Maximinus, *Praefectus Annonae*.'

'His messenger didn't even wait to see if you were free. How rude!'

'More than rude. Maximinus should have sent this to the Castra gatehouse.'

'Then the Pannonian already knows where we live.' She pulled her *palla* tighter over her nightgown.

'That's my busiest hour at the Castra. I'll send Amosis tomorrow with my apologies.'

Apollonia reread the note with a trembling hand. 'No, offer no apologies. You are your own man. Suggest a better hour, so as not to appear hesitant or afraid.'

'You're right. I'll offer a meeting at the end of the day.'

'But promise me, you won't—'

'—No, no, I won't tangle with him. I'll just encourage him in his new assignment—no more.'

'I'll go now and lay out your best clothes for Amosis. You may have the authority to hold your ground, but tomorrow you have to look it too.'

'Don't worry. I won't touch the Chilo case.'

Chapter 3, The Prefect's Rope

—THE OFFICES OF THE ANNONA—

The next day was as busy as any other. The morning passed with a review of reports from Antiochia, the Gallia-Hispania border, and the Rhenus Delta, followed by decisions about the training school budget. I spent the early afternoon debriefing two *circitores* preparing for the winter *Mare Clausum*, the foul-weather slowdown in cross-sea shipping and its dampening effect on the Africa-Roma mail delivery. The annual hiatus threatened a reduction in our intelligence gathering on a gruesome increase in Austuriani tribal attacks on Romano-African towns.

I had almost forgotten my appointment with Maximinus when Amosis appeared in my outer office at dusk. He was delivering an armful of formal garments to replace my usual garb, no fancier than those worn by my *centenarii* or *ducenarii*.

The heat had hardly abated. I washed as Amosis banged the street dust off Apollonia's thick bundle with my ceremonial baton. She'd warned me, 'Tomorrow you must seize any advantage. You're a Roman, Marcus, at ease with such trappings. A Carpi Pannonian may swagger around in his official *chlamys*, but he's still a rustic. Let him wonder with whom you're spending tomorrow evening in these clothes. Nobody that counts in Roma invites him anywhere and we can be sure he knows it.'

Frankly, I didn't think *Praefectus Annonae* Maximinus deserved even this level of laundry expense. Twenty years ago, *Magister* Apodemius had hobbled everywhere in mended ivory wool and worn goat suede shoes distended by his knobby toes— when he wasn't in full disguise, that is. But even emperors had learned the hard way to fear old Apodemius, whatever he wore. I had yet to earn his comforts.

The other courtiers of my youth had observed Emperor Constantius II's extreme Eastern formalities. As a young *agens* in my rough riding gear, I would peer over the heads of scribes, churchmen, bureaucrats, and eunuchs to see the most powerful officials stretch out on the floor in their finery to perform the ritual *proskynesis* at the feet of Constantius' *cathedra*.

At least the Valentinian regime didn't impose such Persian-style indignities. Our current ruler was a soldier, born and bred. So now the fashion among civilian officials mimicked wartime wear.

But this afternoon I refused the centurion's baton—ridiculous to wield around the dock district, block after block of glorified bread and wine warehouses. Of course, by law my *spatha* couldn't be brandished through the city. Only my high-cuffed riding boots would have concealed the Castra-issue folding knife I used for protection on the road. But surely, today it was enough that I was armed to the teeth in sartorial splendor.

Amosis handed over a bleached, long-sleeved tunic with gold-and-red embroidered rectangular *segmenta* and matching trim at the hem to be pulled over spotless light wool trousers.

'Suck it in, *Magister*.' Amosis cinched and buckled my widest *cingulum*, its gold struts fixed with sapphire studs and its gold buckle crafted into a horse's head denoting my start as a humble postal rider.

He pinned a knee-length cloak of very fine weave at each shoulder with similar gold horses. He laced my stamped-leather *campagi*, polished to a jet-black shine, over fine-gauge socks. My best felt wool pilleus with the gold trim and cocked at a jaunty angle and my money purse and other accessories hooked onto links in the belt.

With everything but an eagle painted onto my forehead, Amosis judged me ready. I boarded a Castra litter to bounce the tedious breadth of the city to the riverside where the municipal distribution of the *annonae* was administered. Amosis trotted along beside my vehicle—even he had relinquished his slapping Egyptian sandals for laced shoes to protect him from the muck of the gutters. Down the Caelian Hill we plunged to navigate the slums of the Subura, the jam-packed Forum district, the markets, and cook-shops full of slaves collecting supper, and onward to the Tiberis quayside.

Despite the seediness of the warehouse district, the ancient offices of the *frumentationes* were huge and solid. Discolored and disfigured by numerous annexes, the headquarters stood as a testament to the Eternal City's largesse to its eternal poor. The marble buildings' worn edges and the cracked paving stones of their serried alleys spoke of centuries of foot and wagon traffic.

Apart from the product of the imperial estates, Roma collected tax grain from Sicilia, Sardinia, and the African colonies. With Constantine's reign, Roma's bellies had lost the Alexandrian grain supply to its new rival Constantinopolis. Still, collecting and distributing the *annona* between commercial interests and charitable networks was a huge responsibility for any ambitious man. Maximinus commanded subordinate officers in Ostia, Portus, and Puteoli overseeing the unloading of millions of units of grain, oil, salt, pork, and wine.

They watched for speculation or fraud on the market and gave legal support to private businessmen who distributed the grain to our state bakers, the Pistores. These in turn delivered it to distribution depots around the city. It was also Maximinus' job to ensure that these loaves, nicknamed *panis gradilis* after the steps of the depots, were given only to holders of welfare tiles or *tesserae*.

I indulge in this tedious digression because it was a tedious journey, which I heartily resented. I finally ascended the stone steps to Maximinus' airy office, half-shuttered against the setting sun glinting off the water beyond.

Maximinus wasn't in.

'He's a busy man,' said a junior official with well-brushed Gallic moustache and impeccably shined *campagi*.

'We had an appointment.'

Loaded down with invoices, he replied only, 'He'll be here,' and left Amosis and me alone in an office as vast as a small palace reception hall.

I'd wait no longer than ten minutes. So I was a bit deflated when Maximinus appeared in less than five. His work clothes were damp from the day's exertions and his rough shoes scattered a fleck or two of seed. He extended a hearty greeting.

'So sorry, *Magister* Numidianus, *mea culpa*! I must make the rounds of *horaria* three times a day. I'm wearing two or three hats now, but of course, you know all that, or you wouldn't be the *Magister Agentium in Rebus*! You know everything and everybody, don't you?'

I sat down in the wide-armed chair he offered. He settled some last bit of business with the impatient clerk and continued: 'I'm still waiting for the incoming Governor of Tuscia to get going, leaning heavily on Firminius here to get the bread and oil out on time. And now this Chilo case. I'm sure you've heard—'

So Flavius Maximinus was all hail-fellow, good will, and collegial intimacy. At that moment, I might have beheaded half his family and all his slaves and I think his wide, white smile would not have wavered.

'You look disconcerted, *Magister*. Ah, my brother-in-law Valentinus! Forget that ugly affair. The man's mind was already twisted, then embittered by exile. But then he deserved it, didn't he?'

'What was his original crime, exactly?'

'The details are unspeakable.'

Most Pannonians are very tall, but Maximinus descended from refugees as swarthy and thick-bristled as their black-haired Sarmatian barbarian cousins. His face was square, with a jaw as wide as his forehead over glittering, deep-set black eyes. He had wide, over-muscled shoulders but very short legs. He gave the impression of an inverted triangle powered by the springs that release *ballista* bolts.

'As you are so busy, *Praefectus,* and I have an evening appointment, let's get down to business. I know very little of this Chilo case from your superior Olybrius but I assured him my *schola* knows all the procedures necessary for legal and discreet arrests. Let's hope the case never comes to that. I'm sure it'll reach a swift conclusion in your capable hands.'

Maximinus' beetle eyebrows lifted a jot. Outside the door, Amosis lounged like a languid cat, soaking up the usual disdain of busy men like Deputy Firminius for indolent slaves. But the Egyptian was eavesdropping on my chat. Later he'd regurgitate every syllable for Cyrillus' transcription back at the Castra.

'You sound confident, Numidianus. Perhaps you know something of this case I don't? You *agentes* do know so much.'

'Not at all. I'd be hard put to name the suspects but after so long a detention, surely the answer is a swift trial or immediate release?'

He rested a hip on the corner of his desk and smiled down at me. 'No. I must break them first.'

Roman Law protects our upper classes from torture under questioning—except in cases of treason. I felt a tug of pity for the lowly organ-maker and his mates.

'They sound broken enough as it is. Chilo enjoys rude good health. Release them.'

'Oh, I can't let them go. Do you follow the local court hearings?'

'Not the petty cases—property disputes, divorces, burglaries—that sort of thing.'

'No, Numidianus, I meant darker, nastier doings.'

I frowned. 'You mean the scandals published in the *Acta Diurna*? I worry about logistics of state, not local bedrooms.'

Acta Diurna was a gossip sheet of 'daily events' distributed at various points around the city, including markets and public baths. 'Publicize and Propagate,' was its slogan. But most of its news was hardly worth even the cheap *taeneotic* paper it was copied on.

Our Castra Archivist, Zephyrinus, a crabby ex-priest who filed away our dossiers and agent reports, relished these tabloid confessions as only a former priest could. He spent his dawn hours sifting *Acta Diurna* for valuable nuggets. Occasionally, he produced something for our morning briefings, excavated from an endless seam of weddings, births, deaths, crimes, trials, astrology forecasts, announcements of Imperial Family appearances, gossip about the sex lives of the rich and famous, gladiator events.

There was even the odd children's feature: 'Fido, Lost from the Back of a Carriage on the Road Outside Arelate, Finds his Way Home to Roma' had enchanted our twins when Nurse Lavinia read it to them over the kitchen table.

Maximinus' smile fell. 'No, I don't mean gossip, Numidianus. I mean the spate of murders that have left dead bodies strewn along the riverbanks and ended in over twenty capital convictions this year alone.'

'I've been away six months. I had no idea our slums required such a Herculean purge.'

'Too many of these deaths are linked to poisons, spells, and strange rituals. Aren't you aware that a craving to communicate with the dead is spreading like an addiction through all classes of Roma?'

'*All* classes? I know there's a fashion for love potions and baldness cures. And maybe some of these co-called tonics turn out to be toxic. Judging by those bloated corpses in the Tiberis, a lot of these concoctions go wrong.'

'I'm not talking about baldness cures.'

'Communication with the dead? The pagans of this city know better and the Christians can't be that foolhardy. Emperor Constantius was a Christian and he condemned to death anyone who called forth the dead through magic spells—'

Maximinus leaned over, jabbing the air. 'And doesn't that prove how much Constantius himself believed in such powers, for all his Christian posturing? I start to understand the people of this city—'

'Do you? Perhaps you take local foibles too seriously.'

'You take them too lightly. Invoking the spirits who know our future can be a powerful lure, especially to the ambitious.' He smiled with a curious mix of disdain and lurid fascination.

'I prefer omens read by respectable priests.'

'I was even tempted once or twice myself while governor in Sardinia.'

'Really? I'd assumed you were a Christian.'

'Yes, of course, Valentinian favors Christians. But you're not, are you? You've never tried soothsaying? Out of sheer curiosity, of course?'

'No, I stick to the usual incense and prayers.'

'Well then, you're safe.'

'Safe from what, may I ask?'

'You see, Emperor Valentinian is passionate about reform. He's promoting lawyers who actually know the law and administrators who deliver results. There will be no more buying offices. No more leapfrogging up the *Cursus* over more reliable men on the strength of a fancy letter of introduction. And if such men are solid, they'll hold their office longer, long enough to make things better.'

'Most of those solid new men being Pannonian, I take it.'

'And some of the best from the Gallic aristocracy.'

'Ah, yes.' It was my turn to smile. 'I see the hand of our Poet Laureate in those promotions—the cream of his Burdigala graduates.'

'We need talented men—Pannonians or Gauls. The Constantines left the Empire a bankrupt mess.'

'And I applaud the new era. But what has Valentinian's laudable reforms to do with the Chilo case?'

'This isn't just about Chilo and you know it.'

'Do I?'

'Valentinian hates poisons and spells. And he hates men who tolerate them.'

'But he permits traditional *cultor deorum* practices within the law and—'

'I intend to eradicate the spiritual corruption that infests this city.'

'Then I'm afraid you'll spend the coming winter in districts even dodgier than this one. And you don't need our *schola* to arrest scum.'

Maximinus lowered his voice. 'Listen, Numidianus, I admire your loyalty to the class who educated and freed you. But the Chilo case leads straight up the leafy lanes of the Esquiline and Palatine Hills. So I expect your . . . unofficial help.'

I heard the squeak of reeds as Amosis shifted on his stool outside. The Egyptian was listening more closely.

'How . . . unofficial?'

'Help me get this Chilo case off my desk, so I can return to other responsibilities. Already my promotion has angered Deputy Aginatius. With your assistance, I can speed things up.'

'Arrest people faster?'

'I know my limits. In this crib of our empire, I'm a "new man", an innocent baby. Help me.'

There was nothing cherubic about the afternoon shadow of black bristles on his chin. He leaned over my chair.

'You're a freedman of the venerable Manlius *domus*. And whispers along imperial corridors always add, Numidianus is himself half-Manlius.'

He actually winked. My bastard birth was now our little secret? I would not give this insinuating Carpi an inch. But he bored ahead like a blind siege drill.

'So you're like me, aren't you? One foot in, one foot out, no more or less Roman than myself.'

This man from that two-temple-backwater Sopianae had insulted me and yet he beamed. But they say the definition of a true-born aristocrat is that when he insults a man, he does it on purpose—never by accident. I gave him the benefit of the doubt.

'We're all Roman citizens,' I replied. 'That's the glory of our empire. What is it you really want? I've already guaranteed my *schola* for any arrests of *honestiores*.'

'Right.' He clapped his hands together, a rug salesman settling the price tag. 'I need your dossiers—'

'My what?'

'—your files, the secrets of the top families that run this city: their incestuous marriages, their mistresses, their legal heirs and bastards, their slaves, their hobbies, vices, debts, devotions, ambitions—'

He caught my astonishment. With a slight huff of frustration, he collapsed into the chair behind his cluttered desk, hands in the air. He threw his final spear.

'Come now, Numidianus, how can I investigate Chilo's poisoning case—or others like it—without knowing who's protecting whom? These days I visit an elegant townhouse to find a gallery of ancestors' busts and *imagines* staring down at me. I don't know who they are. So if I hear an accusation against someone, is it credible? Or it is just slander linked to some ancient vendetta that started in the reign of Caligula?'

I smiled, apologetic for his situation.

'I can't help you, Prefect. Our files are sacrosanct.' I rose to my feet and offered him a small bow of regretful respect.

He laughed. 'Because the files hide dirt on your own family or your inestimable wife's?'

I laughed right back. This was a threat, an ominous offer to trade access to the *schola*'s secrets for my family's immunity. I thought of the twins' fortune-telling board, a painted wooden toy with suddenly deadly implications.

Of course, the Castra had files on every leading family in the city. Information was power, the only true power my department enjoyed. We guarded it closely—to protect our undercover sources as well as our own *agentes*. To give imperial courtiers and their rivalrous cliques free run of our archives would be to negate any independence we enjoyed to serve the Emperor and the Empire.

'Our archives are closed to protect the innocent. It's a question of defamation, Prefect. I admit a small amount of private information falls into our *agentes'* laps from time to time as we audit accounts and deliver state mail. But it's mostly negligible, unverified . . . unreliable. Not every rumor, however carefully noted, is true. Not every calculating error discovered by an *agens* auditing a provincial prefect's books signals intent to embezzle. To draw random tittle-tattle into an official context risks a lawsuit.'

Maximinus didn't believe a word. But what could he say? With a gesture of defeat, he tossed another threat.

'A very complete and correct explanation. Thank you. Your inability to cooperate will help me explain the inevitable delay in my work. No, no, I understand.'

'So will Emperor Valentinian. I knew him as a tribune serving Caesar Julian. He rose up through the camps where military authority can sometimes obscure justice. But if you have any intention of complaining about my "inability to cooperate", remind him to check with his new cadre of expensive Gallic lawyers.'

꛲꛲꛲

In a narrow space between the welfare buildings, Amosis was already waiting with the Castra bearers. One would never imagine he'd heard every phrase spoken, even that last volley of veiled threats.

Two men in nondescript tunics and sandals worked halfway down the shadowed alley. They were shouting up to an open window out of which a sturdy rope dangled, uncoiling like those cobras that spiral up from a pot in the Syrian markets. The thick twine bounced and flirted its way down the pockmarked brickwork until it reached the waiting hand of the taller man.

I jerked my head at my lead bearer. He straightened his Castra tunic and sauntered towards them.

'Want some help?' he called in a light tone.

'Sure, we're just getting . . . this thing . . . bolted down,' the shorter man said through grunts and tugs. He dragged a wooden box fixed with a padlock forward on a wheeled pallet. He half-hopped as he rounded the taller man so together they could lift and fix the sturdy box to the rope end. They were having trouble hinging the box by a sailor's boat hook to a stable's hitching ring hammered into the building's limestone side.

This sight reminded me of something familiar, but what? A rope hanging out of any window is sinister. It smacks of robbery or similar deceit. I was curious.

I nodded Amosis off to join the trio as I slipped into my litter and waited with the other bearers.

I'd been a slave. I know how it works. Let Amosis and my bearer joke and be rude about me, as lowborn men always are about the self-important. The fun of keeping a decked-out imperial official waiting a few minutes longer might appeal to the thuggish strangers. I trusted my slave and bearer could entice the two rope-men into explaining what that weighty box was for.

The river's evening lullaby of boat horns and wagons rumbling away with heavy cargo—all the stage business of any city docks—mingled with the cooling breezes. I sat through a tantalizing fifteen minutes or so, but I was not disappointed. We set off for home, Amosis puffing a little as he explained to me riding in cushioned estate.

'That box was lined with lead against arson and heavy as a casket.'

'Who are they?'

'Called themselves Mucianus and Barbarus, *Magister*. I ribbed Mucianus, the short one with the club foot. Asked him why he wasn't exposed at birth with that useless thing dangling from the end of his leg. He called me a filthy worshipper of the "Sun bastard Ra". Said he was a decent Christian of Christian parents who didn't go in for that kind of pagan nonsense, killing off a poor cub over a stubby foot.'

'Charming banter. What else?'

'We kept it up—a dirty joke about Jesus, a dirtier one about Jupiter, an offer to cut off my balls to make me a priest of the Cybele. Best of friends by now.'

'Who do they work for?'

'Your pal upstairs.'

'And the box?'

'To catch out pagans' "nasty" ways.'

That word again, *nasty*.

'Did the box have a slot in the lid?'

'Guessed it in one, *Magister*. Tomorrow every man and woman who reads *Acta Diurna* will know where to report illegal superstition and sin.'

'Tittle-tattle signed, From A Friend? Or Concerned Citizen?'

Amosis curled his lip. 'Even Egyptians don't go in for that sort of backstabbing.'

'Oh, indeed? You upright, foursquare Egyptians welcomed, betrayed, and beheaded poor old Pompey the Great five minutes after he landed on your shores.'

I uncinched my belt, loosened my tunic, and fell back on the cushions for the jostling ride across the city.

So Maximinus wasn't even pretending to limit his new mandate to the Chilo poisoning case or where it led. He was openly fishing for more dirt. But luring squealers, snitches, and scandalmongers is a treacherous art. Maximinus' slotted box-on-a-rope was a snare for baseless, indiscriminate slander.

Who knows better than a *curiosus* like myself? If you cast a wide net, you dredge up a lot of sewage.

The Castra trained its cadets to cultivate useful sources: office scribes, temple keepers, church sweepers, innkeepers, barbecue cooks, whores, and stable boys, all the invisible people serving the Empire's vast web of towns and roads. But even the greenest *tiro* rider was taught to know his informants and filter their reports for suspect motives.

I closed my eyes against the choking dust of the street. That elusive memory finally surfaced—of a similar gambit in the court of Caesar Gallus back in 354. The imperial half-brother of Julian and his cousin-wife, Emperor Constantius' sister Constantia, had reveled in 'cleaning up Antiochia' by ferreting out the dirty secrets of their licentious capital.

But Gallus and Constantia didn't use a slotted box. Their palace sat in the middle of a river on a narrow island connected to the teeming capital by a bridge to the east. There was a minor back door in their compound wall facing the water to the west, used by deliverymen and slaves. The imperial couple encouraged Antiochian citizens to slip in unobserved via this unimposing

depot to make a different kind of 'delivery'. To guarantee their
snitches' anonymity, the imperial couple replaced the previous
gatekeeper with a blind eunuch *domesticus*.

The rear door channel only led to more vendettas and
wrongful prosecutions. And the vicious traffic made the city jumpy
and mistrustful, until innocent men and women feared their
bedroom walls had ears of their own.

Sitting in Mediolanum, the rigid and upright Emperor
Constantius II finally despaired of Gallus as ruler of the East.
Scheming and paranoia had curdled Gallus' wits and left his
vindictive wife dying of fever in the wastes of Bithynia.

I personally escorted Caesar Gallus all the way from Antiochia
to his 'trial' in the fortress at Pola, a high-profile arrest indeed for
the young *agens* Numidianus.

I'd earned my promotion up a rank, completing a frantic drive
smuggling my maddened passenger across the Eastern provinces
to meet *Magister* Apodemius and a handful of jurists. I did not
enjoy the trip.

But then, neither did Caesar Gallus. And we all know how he
ended. Prefect Maximinus' rope only reminded me of how that
disaster started.

Chapter 4, Missing Earrings

—THE CASTRA BRIEFING—

I'd lain butt-naked listening to the noble boss of the Empire's greatest city cajole me as a trusted Roman insider. Then within forty-eight hours, I'd sat decked out in the formal attire of a Roman department chief only to hear myself cut down to share the outsider status of a Pannonian *arriviste*.

Scratch up one *solidus* to Momus, God of Irony.

But Maximinus' casual insult about my social rank was not what left a sour aftertaste as I set off again for the Castra the following dawn. Maximinus had claimed to feel no resentment over his brother-in-law's bloody downfall. But he'd made two warning swerves at my own family.

He'd sent his invitation to our house instead of my office. And he'd quipped that Apollonia might have something to hide. Misplaced manners? A joke? I couldn't take chances.

Magister Apodemius had always worked in darkness, in more senses than one. Yes, he was the keeper of the Empire's secrets, but he even scuttled to and from the Castra in the shadows. His office hours ran from dusk until dawn, when he hobbled on those swollen ankles out a small gate in the Castra's side wall to disappear under the arches of the Aqua Claudia into the twisting lanes beyond. No *agens* knew where he lived or with whom.

Returning from a marathon ride, the young *eques* Numidianus had spent many a sleepy midnight yawning and dozing on the bench outside his inner office until my debriefing session was called. And Apodemius' night owl hours didn't get easier when I was a *biarchus, centenarius,* or *ducenarius,* either.

I had served fifteen years as an *agens* before I understood why the old man lived such a furtive, nocturnal existence. In his long career, he'd made enemies galore—all his *curiosi* knew that. We accepted that social revulsion was our fate, provided we do our job right and rise up through the ranks.

But not until the end of his life did I discover Apodemius wasn't just protecting himself from a poisoned sweetmeat or sudden dagger thrust. He was the guardian of his clan's only other descendant, a victim of a bitter family feud. She'd survived a vengeful fire that reduced his great townhouse and all their relatives trapped within to ash and bone. She'd been raised in seclusion as a child and returned to Roma as a young woman whose features—so like her grandfather's—remained hidden by a long *palla* pinned across her lower face and thin veils drifting from her Vestal-like headdress. She hid away as a 'maimed burn victim' behind the shutters of a secret home.

Eight years ago, I hadn't just inherited the authority and secrets of the Castra. I'd also inherited a sacred duty—to protect Apodemius' sole heir, his granddaughter—my lovely wife. She lived free of those deadly threats now. The enemy family had died off and the lethal grudge was forgotten. She should never have to live in terror again.

But the habits of childhood persist. Other society women shopped all day, attended the baths and theater, and toured in groups to famous resorts and religious sites. Apollonia preferred a quiet existence of improving her new house and garden, raising the boys, and supervising a household expanding in tandem with my rising status.

Our house near the Porta Catena was her new domain in which she was empress, judge, priestess—and spy. For no woman listened better, delved deeper, and reasoned more quickly than Apodemius' granddaughter. She embodied what I loved most of Roma. She gave me hope that the true soul of Roma was not in danger.

⚜⚜⚜

The morning after my unsatisfactory confrontation with Maximinus seemed just another routine *dies Martis*. As I left the house, Apollonia was lighting the resin at the *lararium* where the two ivory figurines of the Penates stood before a modest painting of a priest in old-fashion toga with two snake-guardians at his feet.

The warming sky was clear, but I felt uneasy. So for extra favor, I tipped the *lares* at the corner temple.

'Beautiful weather, Flaccus.'

'Yes, *Magister*, but I fear the season of thin robes and loose underthings is drawing to an end.'

'Be careful watching the ladies, Flaccus. Remember the story of Coronis? One of these days some jealous Apollo will peck out your lustful eyes for staring too hard.'

He stretched a flabby thigh. 'Oh, I don't have to watch them at all, *Magister*, I know they're passing with my eyes closed. My big ears hear them coming, like chattering birds, and my sharp nose says they're close, so fragrant and fresh.' He scratched his balls.

'You need a woman of your own, Flaccus.'

'I do indeed, *Magister*! My ears may flop down but the best of me goes stiff as Trajan's Column! I just may have a girl soon.'

'Really?'

'And wouldn't you be surprised! Good day, *Magister*!'

It wasn't far on foot to the Castra with Amosis loping along at my side, finishing his breakfast flatbread rolled up in his fist, some last olives rolling around in his purse. My Egyptian dribbled crumbs and discarded stems round the clock—inelegant for the slave of a man of my rank—but I dared not complain. Every morning, noon, and night Amosis tasted any food not prepared by my own household, especially food offered by powerful, smiling hosts. I don't know where all this nourishment disappeared, for he stayed thin as a *stilus*.

For this same purpose, old Apodemius had kept a cageful of mice in his office. I'm not comparing a trusty Egyptian to a mere rodent, but Apodemius had been *magister agentium in rebus* far longer than I. His enemies were legion and his peril greater than mine. More than once, one of his beloved namesakes, his *apodemii*, had struggled with an anonymous gift of dried dates or shiny meat tarts to be discovered within the hour, four paws in the air.

I sent Amosis across the courtyard to ready my chambers for the briefing meeting but I lingered at the gatehouse to consult Ressatus, a Thracian *centenarius* on our security team.

'Until my *dispensator* Cornelius returns from Mediolanum, I'd like two *circitores* to guard my family. Anybody who needs a rest from hauling mail bags is fine.'

'Yes, *Magister*. Maybe Cotiso and Brasus? They came in off the Lugdunum circuit last week.'

'The gods, no! Those two belong in the arena.'

Ressatus laughed. 'So just anyone isn't fine?'

'They should look like they might belong to my household, discreet enough not to raise the neighbors' eyebrows.'

'How about Avitus . . . and Numa? They still do guard duty in a pinch.'

'Good. If it works with your rota, tell them to move over there this morning, hide their insignia, and keep their *pugiones* out of sight but handy.'

Ressatus was gray-haired and in his late forties. He was one of my better hires in the rebuilding phase after Emperor Julian's purge of the *schola*. My former superior Ahenobarbus had recruited Ressatus from decades of hard service against the Franks along the Rhenus. He was too old for riding or even spying but he appealed to the younger men as a sort of confidant father-figure behind my back. He had a proper cubicle near my offices but never used it, saying long years in camp gave him a taste for watching 'the palisade.'

'You expect danger at home, *Magister*?'

'Just a precaution. I might need outside witnesses in case of trouble. Tell them to insert themselves into the life of the house.'

'Bit of holiday for Avitus and Numa.'

'Holiday? You haven't met my twins.'

Soon some fifteen *agentes* were climbing the stairs to my briefing. There was just enough space to cram them in, now that I'd cleared out Apodemius' massage bed. On the wall behind my desk hung a fresh version of the imperial map the old man had punched and poked so long with pins and flags it had frayed into tatters of vellum. Apodemius might not have recognized my Empire, with many more mail routes crisscrossing in a web to the new capital in the East.

Before we convened, I scribbled a small note and called Amosis to my side.

'Deliver this to the Mons Oppius.'

He winced. 'The palace of Praetextatus? It'll take hours.'

'And you'll wait. This goes into his hand and no one else's.'

I never asked that all staff attend the briefings. Many of them, like the auditing and language teachers, the exercise and self-defense trainers, and the riding coaches were already in sessions with the cadets. And the crush of men on stools and benches, leaning against the walls, or squatting like roadside vendors on their haunches was uncomfortable enough. Even the most garrulous kept to the point.

But the meetings were popular, for which *Biarchus* Rubellius might take credit. He was a relatively junior officer, but I let this popular son of a second-hand weapons dealer in Sirmium kick off by sharing reports of any hiccoughs along the routes that had reached our gates overnight. As latecomers squeezed in, his comic asides reduced the tensions among competitive men of all stripes and strengths.

'So, we need two *equites* to rescue Julius and Crescentius. They ran into problems coming back on the Comum-Cambodunum, somewhere between the Cunus Areus Pass and Curia.'

'Oh, Neptune's Balls, what happened this time?'

'Not again.'

'The bloody Alpes. I hate that route.'

'Julius' horse hurt his hoof on broken paving outside the Clavenna *mutatio*. They doubled up on Crescentius' horse and limped to the *mansio* at Tarvessedum but the second horse gave up at the gate and the *stabularius* at Lapadaria—'

'No, no, not that dick!'

'Yes, our favorite, the "Dick of Lapadaria Stables" refused them fresh mounts, saying they abused horseflesh, and should be reported to us, which,' Rubellius rolled his eyes, 'they were. Meanwhile, Crescentius ate some bad lentils, got the runs—'

'I'll deal with it,' a voice muttered from the back.

'His backside?' another quipped.

'No, the replacement riders.'

Rubellius raised his voice over the laughter, 'Also, Senicianus riding the Rhenus route reports from Agrippina that the bridge repairs over the Mosella still aren't finished. That means until the winter snows clear next spring, keep using the ferry crossing upstream.'

Rubellius looked up from his notes, wiggled his hips with a wink, 'More business for the lovely Lintruda!'

He closed with a sobering item; 'Interference along the Naissus to Philippopolis route—Goths. Mail for those hubs delivered by Oreles continuing alone as far as the Serdica station. His partner Istros is resting from wounds at Bessapara station. He'll be transferred by wagon to Constantinopolis for surgery. Expect updates from *Centenarius* Benedictus on his condition.'

'Provided Benedictus' report even reaches us,' said one cynic.

That was my cue: 'Thanks, Rubellius. The junior officers can leave now.'

After Cyrillus had closed the door, we made ourselves more comfortable.

I resumed, 'The routes running eastward are insecure. I've decided to expand the Sirmium hub. I'm asking for volunteers, any rank, preferably with some Greek, to transfer out of Roma, Treverorum, Lugdunum, or cities to the south of Arelate. The pay will be better because the dangers are obvious.'

'If no one volunteers?' asked Saturnus.

I laughed. 'When Emperor Constantius ordered transfers from Gallia over the Alps to fight Persians, Julian's soldiers rebelled. I won't make his mistake. We won't force any transfers and we'll recruit *in situ* if necessary. But training takes years and money.'

'Recruit Goths?' Ressatus looked dismayed.

'I remember when Apodemius accepted his first Toxandrian *laetus*, a prisoner-of-war castrated in the East. He was one of the best men I served with. And in case some of you don't know, he was *Centenarius* Grifo's father.' I tossed a warning glance: jokes in this instance weren't welcome.

Finance Officer Ferreolus asked, 'Speaking of money, may I move the *donativa* strongbox into the archive rooms for a few weeks while they repair the prison floors?'

Zephyrinus agreed. 'We have more room now that the older files are out of the alcove. Put it there.'

I interjected, 'Don't leave the strongbox there too long. The archives aren't as secure as the prison cells. Where did you move Apodemius' old files?'

The archivist scratched his stubbly chin and picked a seed from his teeth. He had no family or life outside the Castra, so his bathing habits were irregular. 'Oh, they're six feet under, safe as a grave, in the repository under the Temple floor. They were blocking the window. We needed more space and light, too much new stuff coming in.'

It wasn't the first time Zephyrinus had grumbled about the flood of paperwork from Constantinopolis.

'Be patient, Zephyrinus. Benedictus wants to make a good impression. Don't forget—he started life as a scribe. Writing is his passion. It's just our luck that the emperors keep in such close touch.'

'As long as we don't have to read it all,' joked Rubellius.

'Well, you do, provided you don't get caught. The Castra needs to know immediately if anything's amiss. Keep our counterfeit seals up to date, right? Fine. Well, that's it for this morning—except for Saturnus.'

Ducenarius Saturnus kept his seat, his watchful hazel eyes unsurprised. He was one of my most senior recruits as I branched out from the handful of loyal stalwarts who resolved with me to rescue our *schola*.

Saturnus was around thirty-eight, a Christian cavalryman from Lutetia who'd proved his worth in the north. In two years, he'd restored the erratic postal service along the Rhenus threatened by repeated Alemanni incursions.

I'd promoted him on the success of his next, more subtle task, a year of intercepting Church correspondence moving across Gallia and Italia. He'd mapped out bishops' families and friends, their debts, favors, peccadilloes, and accumulated legacy properties. The Church was spreading its parallel web, an embryonic empire all its own, underneath our Roman state.

I was not going to make the mistake of my predecessor. Apodemius neglected useful intelligence on Christ's faithful. After that, I exploited Saturnus' political acumen more often than his administrative or riding talents. If I found the former horseman's wit slightly dry, he was certainly well-mannered and highly groomed—like so many men from that Gallic city obsessed with fragrant oils. He slid through the better echelons of Roma society without remark.

Officially, Saturnus ran a small team of *biarchi* entrusted with the most sensitive duties inside the city—delivery of private messages from Valentinian's or Valens' courtiers to top civil servants or friends, issuance of *diplomatae* to use the state roads for other-than-state business, and of course, making the rare arrest among the senatorial class, those *honestiores*.

Best of all, Saturnus was very discreet in front of the other *agentes* about acting as my sounding board.

'I'm going to warn you, there may be some high-profile arrests for your team. Any I missed during my time away?'

'A rather pathetic one. An official named Faustinus was arrested two months ago for killing another man's ass to make a baldness cure. He ended up losing more than his hair—lost his whole head.'

'Superstitious idiot. Saturnus, what do you know about a wave of murders, poisoning, magic killings, that sort of thing, sweeping around town?'

'It's rampant, but nothing new. Why?'

'Valentinian's *praefectus annonae* is investigating an attempted poisoning against that official Chilo and his wife.'

'Why bother? Isn't Chilo going to head up Africa?'

'Yes, but Chilo wants Maximinus to keep pursuing the case. And Maximinus isn't a guy to climb up from the sewer with only stinky hands. He intends to pass us bigger names. I promised Prefect Olybrius we'll do everything by the book.'

'Olybrius? He put his fat finger into this?'

'He seemed nervous at the Caracalla Baths. And as of yesterday, I realized why; Maximinus told me he views this Chilo case as only the start. He aims to root out more poisoners, sorcerers, and adulterers. I gather Olybrius has a new mistress, Cordelia.'

Saturnus shifted in his chair. 'The crime of adultery depends on whether this Cordelia is married or not.'

'Find out what *Domina* Cordelia's status is. If that explains Olybrius' worry, I'd be relieved.'

46

He nodded. 'Will do. I've heard of this Maximinus. A Pannonian trying to make his name too fast. But, *Magister*, all we have to do is follow arrest procedure, remind Maximinus of laws protecting senators from torture except in cases of treason, and fix the conditions for house arrest, right?'

'Right. Very discreet house arrest, unless we stumble over some senator selling poisons in Trajan's Market at noon.'

'Or casting spells at the Altar of Victory at midnight.'

There was the tap of a sandal at the door. Amosis slipped into our conference. He'd returned from Praetextatus' palace far too soon for someone seeking the ear of a nobleman inundated by hundreds of clients every morning.

'He returns from his country villa later this week. His secretary grants you an appointment of ten minutes the hour before dawn, the day of Veneris.'

Amosis slipped back to the outer office to resume his napping on the bench against the wall.

'I'm worried, Saturnus, and not about arresting idiots for cooking up baldness cures. Maximinus made a request along a very different line. I refused.'

'I'm sure you did the right thing.' Two long creases framing his thin lips gave his face a graven aspect.

'Your team indexes all the important correspondence that passes through the city. Look out for comments to the effect that our *schola* is "not cooperating" or "got above itself" or "not supporting the regime".'

'Of course we support the regime.'

'We support the Empire, Saturnus. But others might claim they support the regime better.'

'Who are you meeting on the day of Veneris, *Magister*?'

'The finest nobleman alive, Vettius Agorius Praetextatus. You're a good listener, Saturnus, but Praetextatus is a useful mentor—when he can spare me the time.'

'Praetextatus? Whew!' Saturnus puffed out his creased cheeks with a deep exhalation of doubt.

Yes, I know, but I rarely bother him unless I have a real problem. And I do. Maximinus asked me for access to our files.'

Saturnus' jaw dropped. 'That's what you refused?'

'Yes, but I'm not sure of my ground if he's investigating on orders from Olybrius. Happily, Maximinus termed it "unofficial help". I pin my defense on that.'

'What would Apodemius do?'

'No one would dare ask Apodemius such a thing. It's early days for us.'

Saturnus sighed. 'Sit the Pannonian out. These anti-vice campaigns come and go with the Christians. Maximinus was talking hot air if he thinks he's going to rid Roma of every last adulterer and fortuneteller.'

'Maximinus wants "to break" the Chilo suspects—an organ-maker, a wrestling coach, a fortuneteller—for names. And he wants to sniff around the great and good of the city by sticking his nose in our dossiers. He smells something—but what?'

'Well, at least he can't torture the great and good. That's against the law. *Maleficium* and other magic tricks don't amount to treason.'

'Still, I need Praetextatus to have my back. We're not powerful like we were. We need friends, not enemies. On what ground can our *schola* deny assistance? Who has the right to files paid for by state taxes? Am I stalling because I'm confusing serving the Empire with building a little empire of my own?'

Saturnus shot up from his stool. 'Now that's nonsense. You're doing your job, that's all.'

'Am I, Saturnus? Suppose Maximinus says that my refusal to cooperate is treason itself?'

'You're sure Praetextatus can put your mind to rest?'

'No, but he can defend me with unmatchable rhetoric when I find myself shackled next to the organ-maker in the Tullianum.'

⚔⚔⚔

Avitus and Numa were seated next to the atrium pool and playing some warrior board game with Verus and Atticus. My two sun-weathered riders—lanky legs folded under them in awkward twists to face off at the level of their little opponents—gave me some relief.

The boys stayed glued to their game, suspiciously docile, with no signs of boisterous outbursts or sneaky plays. Our slaves, such as I noticed them, were folding clean laundry and sweeping the peristyle garden walk with heads down and eyes averted.

The altar's *myrrh*, Roma's quotidian incense of noon, had burnt out. But I was arriving well after dusk and no evening *cyphi* burned its balm onto my troubled spirit.

I discovered Apollonia sitting on the edge of her bed, Lavinia at her side. The lamplight was low, the bright mural of flowers and birds over a painted balustrade circling our little chamber in shadow. Before they looked up at my footstep, I caught sight of them, heads bent low, their troubled murmurs inaudible from the doorway.

'Marcus! You're home! That's all right, Lavinia, I'll tell him.'

I took Lavinia's place on the mattress and put my arm over my wife's shoulder. She bit her lip. I took her trembling fingers in mine.

'What is it?'

'Marcus, we can't find Anepsia's earrings anywhere. Lavinia, Drusilla, Cook, Gardener Gavius and his little Beata, Apustia, Aucta, all the slaves—even the twins—everyone has searched the entire house now for days.'

The flame of the iron table lamp flickered in her dark eyes.

'Have you told Anepsia?'

'Of course not. I keep hoping the damn things will turn up. I didn't sleep last night. I woke up and suddenly I was sure they'd rolled under the chest in that corner, but no luck. I ran my hand around the cushions of all our couches again and crawled from end to end of this whole house.'

She done all this while I'd slept like a sailor on leave. 'Anepsia shouldn't have taken them off. Are you sure she was even wearing them when your slave dressed her hair in here?'

'Yes. Anepsia admired my hair and I offered to have Drusilla do hers the same way. Drusilla swears by the *lares* that she last saw both earrings exactly here.'

Apollonia laid her palm on the outer corner of her dressing table holding her unguent jars, scent vials, combs, and curling tongs organized in boxes and jars. They stood in unusually neat order this evening, each having been repositioned, one by one, after another desperate search.

'Why didn't you tell me before?'

'I just told Lavinia that I couldn't hide it any longer from you.'

'The baubles will turn up. They always do.'

'Lavinia said she's seen this happen before, in a rich house on the Palatine where she nursed. A missing bracelet had been stolen by a chamber slave who was severely punished. The household kept it quiet for the sake of their reputation as hosts.'

I glanced over my shoulder to see if any of our slaves was listening. Now I understood keeping the door ajar, but voices low. A door closed in conference was an open invitation for a curious ear pressed against the wood. I know. I was an eavesdropping little slave myself once.

'I've let you down, Marcus. You trust me to run our home well, with kindness and efficiency and honesty. What did I do wrong? I treat our slaves well. They have cubicles to sleep, good food, time to rest—'

'So you suspect Apustia? Aucta? Not Drusilla?'

'Impossible! Drusilla was our housewarming present from Leo! It was incredibly generous of him. They grew up together. She's been part of the Manlius *domus* since birth.'

I suppressed a smile. True, flirtatious Drusilla had been one of Leo's first playmates from birth. But when he grew peach fuzz on his chin and the lithe girl developed a buxom figure, their childish games 'matured.' More than once, their teenage fumbling made the older members of the Manlius household blush and wink.

Such were the ways of any adolescent Roman heir with tempting household slaves. But I noticed that, having passed Drusilla on to us, Leo's bride Aurea kept domestic slaves far less attractive. Aurea was a young *matrona* born and bred in Roma, which is to say, Aurea was no fool when it came to nubile women serving her virile bridegroom.

'So one of the younger slaves?'

'They're practically children! How could they expect to get away with it?'

'True, no thief can wear such earrings. So he or she will try to sell them. If we alert the right people, perhaps we can recover them. It might be easy.'

I squeezed her shoulder and kissed her cheek. A thief in the house was the nightmare of Roman matrons, but petty pilferage of food, a sip of wine, a discarded pair of socks—the wise mistress looked the other way for the sake of peace. However, Lavinia was wise to remind us that a serious robbery of a prominent guest tainted the reputation of the house.

Apollonia slipped her feet back into her sandals and adjusted her bodice drape. 'So I must do the honorable thing. Tomorrow I'll visit Anepsia to pay for her loss. Oh, Marcus, it might be a lot of money.'

'Were they very valuable?'

'Well, I noticed at the time that the gold loops weren't evenly matched and the emerald dangles were chipped. They weren't as nice as many of my own pieces.'

'And Anepsia didn't seem overly troubled. So, go now and light the *cyphi*. I'll take the boys off their hands outside.'

'Marcus, wait. Those two riders came here to help with what, exactly? How long will they be with us?'

She knew better than to ask about anything truly secret. And my physical safety was as much her business as anyone's. But I didn't have the heart to tell her right now that her own wellbeing had been threatened by Maximinus.

'Nothing to worry about. A few weeks, that's all. Maybe they can find the earrings. It may turn out to be quite simple.'

Apollonia sensed these were only consoling words. I had no idea who acted as the 'fence' for petty theft in our new neighborhood.

But of course, Flaccus the *Vicomagister* would know. Tomorrow Amosis should ask Flaccus—in a roundabout, guilty, Egyptian fashion—where he might offload a valuable item 'left behind by the former proprietors of our house.'

The important thing with intelligence is to gauge the reliability of your source. And so far, Flaccus seemed to know everything that passed by his temple at the end of our street. What harm could come of asking?

CHAPTER 5, SECURITY MATTERS

—THE CAELIAN HILL—

Y ou can be in the middle of a Roman army camp waiting for battle to begin and yet feel a great calm in your breast. The palisade is well-guarded. The tents run in perfect parallels away from the central command ground. It's nightfall and your fellow *contubernales* are stretching out on their cots or tallying up their dice winnings. The *cornicenes* are testing their horns in the night air and a few cavalry dandies are grinding sand to polish their face armor and sharpen their *spathae*.

Tomorrow any man's Fates might twist his rope the wrong way or sever it altogether—and he'll lie in agony from a wound by nightfall or never see the nightfall at all. But the Empire is as ever and everything seems in place.

Strangely, that's not how I felt when we retired that night. Apollonia had taken a mild sleeping draught and yet she tossed on her narrow bed. I was just dropping off at last when I heard footsteps and murmurs. Our two riders were crossing the atrium to answer a foot-tap at the main door. I pulled on a tunic and padded through the *fauces* on their heels. I admit, I grabbed my *pugio* from instinct as if only too ready to find an enemy on my doorstep.

But it was the young Atolitus from Gallia, one of our new Castra guards. I'd hired him as a promise to his father Cintu, a murderer condemned to a slow death in a Britannian gold mine.

The youngster was out of breath, helmet askew, and followed a pace or two behind by two other guards doing nightshift.

'—a break-in at the Castra, *Magister* . . . for the strongbox . . . You . . . have to come. Anthimus . . . got hold of one but . . . did him in hard . . . face and leg badly carved up. Bleeding a river . . . Zephyrinus was working late . . . got in the way . . . knocked the old man out cold.'

'Is the doctor with Anthimus? I'm right behind you.'

They raced away up our narrow, echoing street. Tousled and dazed, Avitus and Numa were pulling on their belts and boots, but I shouted, 'No! Nothing, *nothing*, removes you two from this post.'

Amosis and I were off for the Castra minutes later. Below the Caelian Hill, the city's heavy merchant traffic rumbled in towards the markets. Boat torchlights twinkled on the Tiberis beyond. But our neighborhood slept on in a darkness punctuated only by the *vigiles'* ancient torch sconces and the window lamp of a slave or two rising early.

I pushed myself hard, but my left leg protested, the tightly strung sinew pulling as I forced myself at double-pace to the headquarters. My mind raced unhindered. In my twenty years with the *schola*, I couldn't recall anyone trying to breach the old gates to rob us. Like every imperial department in the capital, we stashed away ready coin for salaries and expenses. It wasn't a fortune, but enough to stake a scoundrel for many comfortable years, providing he had some way of lugging away hundreds of gold *solidi* without getting caught.

The Castra archives sat on the eastern side of our compound behind the main office building. In Republican times, this building had been an armory for the weapons of the *peregrini*, the non-citizen soldiers visiting Roma from the provinces. Then it became the library, but the books were eventually moved to the cadet school in the southwest corner of the compound next to the gymnasium and baths annexed to the prison.

Finally, the tired little building had become the handiest depository for the mounting files moving in and out of the main offices. It was Zephyrinus's weary job to index and store anything I deemed useful and to check with me before his quarterly cull of outdated trivia.

I couldn't yet bring myself to chuck out the last six boxes from Apodemius' era—whether from sentiment or superstition, who could say?

I entered a Castra courtyard blazing corner to corner with torchlight, every agens out of the barrack and fully clothed, ready for orders.

But Ressatus' trusted men held the archive building off-limits until I arrived. His team must wait a little longer. My first stop was to the infirmary, a set of three rooms tucked above the ground floor gymnasium and baths. Our medicus Myron was hard at work.

'Zephyrinus is in the other room, unconscious. His pulse is weak and he's got a massive swelling on the head. Even if his body pulls through, I won't answer for his wits.'

'The guard?'

Myron shook his head. 'Next door.'

Young Anthimus was stretched out on Myron's surgery table. His face had been sliced in three places and his tunic, soaked red, lay discarded on the floor. His hairless young breast was covered in Myron's linens, also blood-drenched. Myron moved his palm lamp over the boy to show me that one thigh was a mess.

'I stitched up the *arteria femoralis*—that accounts for the blood all over the floor—but I can't stop the internal bleeding from his chest wounds.'

Three of us stood at Anthimus' side—Myron, myself, and his childhood friend Defendens. I'd come across these two robust stable lads shoveling horse dung and straw outside a *mansio* where the Mataurus River meets the sea south of Pisaurum. After cadet school, they'd just started their obligatory service as Castra guards before graduation to *equites*.

'Do something, *Magister*!' Defendens groaned.

Anthimus mustered his failing resources. I laid my palm on his wet brow.

'What happened, Anthimus?' I lowered my ear close to his pale lips.

'*Magister*? I almost held one but . . . couldn't . . .'

I straightened up and looked at Myron. He shrugged. I squeezed Anthimus' left hand. I felt little resilience.

'We're here, Anthimus. Just try to hang on.'

Defendens seized his friend's limp right hand. I prayed to the god of healing Aesculapius to grant Anthimus more strength. But tonight, the gods were deaf. So three helpless humans stood vigil to accompany the guard's journey until Myron held a copper mirror to the motionless lips.

'No! No!' Defendens cried.

I braced Defendens with one firm arm over his shoulders: 'The Castra will send his family a small pension. And I will provide the coins for Charon's Obol to cover his eyes as a sacrifice to ease his crossing.'

But the boy swallowed a sob to say, 'No, *Magister*, he wasn't a *cultor deorum*—we're Christians, remember? He was named after St. Anthimus buried near our home.'

'Of course, of course, forgive me. Then a Mass in the chapel. When you're finished helping Myron here, draft a letter to Anthimus' family and bring your tablet to my office by noon. We'll have Cyrillus copy it onto vellum and send it to Pisaurum with my official report. Wait with Cyrillus until I join you there. I'll have a few questions.'

I left Defendens with Myron and his slaves to clean the corpse and make himself useful through his tearful shock. Such face wounds no longer shocked me. I'd grown up in army camps. I'd slain men myself. But rebuilding the Castra meant recruiting many kinds of men, including boys who'd never seen a friend disfigured in battle.

The eastern sky was lightening to gray. I'd been in the infirmary longer than I realized. As I turned the back corner of the office building, Saturnus and Ressatus rose to their feet.

We three inspected the scene inside the archives.

'Watch your boots, *Magister*.' Ressatus lifted his torch over our heads. A drying puddle reflected its dancing flame. The blood was mostly in the central room where Anthimus' leg wound had gushed forth. The blood wended outwards, streaming along the runnels of the old flagstones' grouting.

'The guard Anthimus is dead,' I told them.

Ressatus cursed, 'Bastards. Zephyrinus?'

'Still breathing. Knocked out from a bad blow to the head from a sword pommel or some other bludgeon. All right, Ressatus, how did they escape your guards coming for them?'

'Through that high window at the center back there, then shimmying up the gutter and over the roof tiles to where the building skirts the outer wall. We found a trail of smeared blood outside on the street. It's probably how they entered as well.'

'The strongbox?'

The tall Thracian circled his torch through the air to illuminate the main room lit by that high, wide window flanked by two windowless alcoves lined with shelves for storing scroll boxes and file chests. Beyond the cooling blood, the strongbox sat, still padlocked, directly under the open window.

'They dragged it across the floor toward the window. See these scrapes in the flagstones?'

'Did they prop a ladder outside the wall?'

'No. These guys didn't want to attract attention, even at this hour. I suppose they brought ropes and hooks to grapple the strongbox up out the window and over the wall.'

'Who could do that?' Saturnus asked. 'Army vets trained to climb siege walls in the dead of night? Winners of the *Corona Muralis*?'

Ressatus frowned at his joke. 'Any professional burglars. Watch out! Don't cross that way. It's a mess of footprints.'

Saturnus crouched at the edge of the bloody pool. 'Anthimus must have fought for some minutes all on his own—how else would they have the time to escape before backup arrived?'

'Trying to be a hero, poor kid. They made a good pair, Anthimus and Defendens, *Magister*,' Ressatus said. 'Quick and willing.'

I skirted the messy evidence. The fight between Anthimus and his murderers must have been brutal, zigzagging between the central room and the alcoves on either side. Their struggle had sent file packets spilling off shelves and scrolls bouncing out of their wooden *arcae* to roll in all directions.

'So, the robbers tried to silence Anthimus and Zephyrinus and were forced to make a hasty getaway without the box only when they realized Anthimus' cries had drawn more guards and wakened up the *agentes* in the barrack?'

'Seems so,' Ressatus replied.

'Saturnus, you recall Finance Chief Ferreolus announced the move of the strongbox at the morning meeting? And I warned him it wasn't secure? In front of half our staff?'

Ressatus stared at my implication. He was in charge of Castra security, after all.

'This is obviously an outside job, *Magister*!'

'Nothing's ever obvious, Ressatus. Wait until daylight before you swab down these floors. Save anything dropped or torn off. And is there anyone who could make a reliable sketch of the room, including the blood traces and any useful footprints once we have full daylight? It might tell us more.'

'Sabazios?'

Ressatus wanted to allay any suspicion this was an inside job. Sabazios was Ressatus' fellow Thracian and fluent in both Latin and Greek. An army veteran like both my companions, he'd been pensioned off after losing half a foot to the blade of a Frankish *francisca* in a skirmish on the Rhenus. Now he taught written code and fire signaling based on army manuals to our cadets. But he seemed an odd suggestion to me:

'You think our killers left us a secret code?'

Ressatus gave a rueful laugh. 'No, *Magister*. Sabazios paints murals in his spare time.'

⚡⚡⚡

Poor Zephyrinus had sunk into a deep coma. But I had one remaining witness—the grieving Defendens who'd been the first to answer Anthimus' shouts for backup.

By noon, I'd briefed the entire staff on the details of the previous night. Our priest Natalius gave his plan for a Christian requiem ceremony. All the senior men of the Castra, pagans included, would squeeze into our small chapel to pay respects to the dead guard. The resident cadets and subordinate *agentes*, including riders in from their circuits, would stand in formation in the courtyard outside to honor him.

An exception was made for the shaken Defendens who'd assist the priest at the altar.

He was waiting in my outer office with his wax tablet of simple sentences etched in a wobbly, semi-literate hand. I nodded to Cyrillus to start copying.

'Come in, Defendens. Close the door. Take that stool.'

The boy faced me across my desk. His trousers were still caked in his friend's blood. He stared at the studded wall map behind me.

'This is the Empire as we *agentes* must learn it. Here in the center is Roma and our great sea.'

'It's so vast, *Magister*. I had no idea.'

'Yet you already know more of it than you think.' I pointed to a tiny green circle. 'That's your home, Pisaurum, there on the

58

coast. And that tiny gray square nearby is the *mutatio* where we met. And next year that will be part of your first mail route.'

'Without Anthimus.' I heard the monotone of shock.

I gave him a few seconds before asking, 'Now, what do you remember of these men? How many were there?'

'Three, maybe four? Anthimus called to me when I reached the archive door. He was fighting two men, but they'd got the better of him. They pulled him down or else he slipped. Then there was a terrible sound—he screamed again. They were just hacking at him—'

'You saw their faces?'

'No. I saw a light as I ran to the archives but it went out. It went totally dark. I wanted to save Anthimus, but I was terrified my sword would strike him by mistake. There were at least two more men, rushing past me to the window from the righthand alcove. So I went after them. I nearly got hold of the last one. But he slipped from my grasp and was over the windowsill before I could pull him down.'

'Then what did you do?'

'I slid and fell but got myself up. My eyes had adjusted so I took a good swing to help Anthimus, but I missed. His attackers shoved me right off my feet again and got out the window.'

'You went after them?'

'No. Anthimus was screaming for help. I held him in my arms until the others got there.'

'Did he say anything?'

'Say anything. You saw his face! Those butchers—'

'I know, but he was screaming. His lips and jaw still moved.'

'He . . . he asked me whether they got away with anything. And I told him, no, because he had fought them so hard.'

'But how did you know that?'

'Well, he must have fought like Hell to hold them off—'

'Yes, Defendens, but how did you know they left with nothing?'

'Because the strongbox was still there.'

'But how did you know? You said it was dark.'

'I don't . . . because . . . I heard them using it like a step to get up to the window. The metal lid made a buckling sound under their weight and the padlock banged.'

'Good. Now, what was Zephyrinus doing?'

'He arrived next but he went down right away. I tripped over his leg . . . Then I saw Anthimus . . .'

'Defendens, look at me, concentrate on my questions. Now, what did you smell or hear?'

'Smell?'

'Yes, smell. An *agens* uses all his senses.'

'Smell? . . . I don't know. Leather, wood, papyrus, you know, like a library . . . and blood.'

'Nothing else?'

'Maybe . . . spilled lamp oil?'

'What they speak? Any accents?'

'Just grunts, a few shouts.' Defendens squeezed back tears of frustration. Nothing could bring back his childhood friend.

'Oh, *Magister*! If only I'd got out of bed faster. I could have got in a good swing at those bastards before—' He collapsed into sobs.

I went around my desk and shook him by his shoulders. 'Stop it. Stop it! You were the first man to reach him. Next year, when you set off on your circuit, your reputation rides ahead of you: *Eques* Defendens, a Mercury who flies on bare feet to save his fellow *agens*.'

He shuddered and looked down. His naked feet were crusted over with his friend's dried blood.

'Before you start on your circuit, I'm doubling up your weapons training. Now, wash yourself, borrow some fresh clothes, and put on your boots. Come back at dusk to sign Cyrillus' copy of your letter in time for tomorrow's Porta Flaminia mailbag.'

He hesitated.

'What is it, Defendens? Have you remembered something?'

'I'll always remember one thing, even when I get to be as old as you, *Magister*.'

I smiled. 'That old? What will you remember?'

'Atolitus said your first question was whether the *medicus* Myron had got Anthimus to the infirmary.'

'Of course. Atolitus said Anthimus had been carved up badly—his very words.'

'Yes, *Magister*, but my old boss, the *manceps* back in Mataurum Station? First thing he would have asked would have been, did they get the money?'

'Oh, don't give me too much credit! A good agent costs the Castra a fortune—feeding, clothing, training, and arming. I know what you men are worth—each one more than a strongbox.'

And I saw my young self reflected in the determination, loyalty, and good humor of each and every one.

₽₽₽

Cyrillus copied the sad, short epistle from the boy's battered wax tablet onto a sheet of our best *Augustus* from the Castra's stock of papyrus. It took him less than fifteen minutes.

'Let me see that when you're finished, please.'

'Already dry. Have a look.'

It was more a wail of grief and apology than anything coherent: 'I got hold of one villain's cloak but he slipped my grasp and the others were too powerful and quick for me . . .'

The emotional outpouring of his private account made it easier to fill my own summary with something more than official facts. But by mid-afternoon, I still hadn't finished. I had never had to calculate such a pension before, nor explain how a handful of men had breached our security and killed a guard.

Ressatus sent one of his team to alert me before the final swabbing down of the archives. I descended the stairs back to the archives now awash in morning light. Our muralist, Sabazios, was busy sketching in one alcove corner.

'No new clues, Ressatus?'

'You were hoping for a severed ring finger? An initial daubed in blood on the floor?'

'Why was Anthimus alone?'

'You said at the meeting that the archives weren't as secure as the prison, so I shifted one of my guards over from the northern gate.'

'Anything missing, Olli?' I asked the young slave retying scroll ribbons and restacking their boxes. Olli was a clever scribe Zephyrinus had bought cheap for the Castra off an old Neronian family after reading in *Acta Diurna* that they'd fallen on hard times.

'Nothing missing, *Magister*. All the *Urbis Romae* files are all here in perfect order, except the files you requested this week.'

'You're sure?'

'Yes, *Magister*! I've cross-checked every file scattered on the floor against our index. They mostly disturbed the files over there.' He pointed to the opposite alcove.

'Which are?'

Olli crossed to run his scrawny bare arm across a long shelf with obvious pride: 'Constantinopolis, Egypt, and Eastern regions go here. Reports on Valens' court, here. Summaries of western provincial reports over three reigns—Julian, Jovian, and Valentinian—here. You edited them yourself, *Magister*. And Hispania, Sardinia, and North Africa at this end.'

'And you're sure they took nothing?'

'Not so far, *Magister*, though I'm not finished. In fact—they left something.'

The slave came from the back of the alcove carrying the broken pieces of an unglazed palm-lamp—no embossing or fancy handle—the kind you buy for a few *nummi* at any pottery stall.

'This isn't ours. Zephyrinus uses heavy desk lamps. They're all lined up on the side table over there for refilling and trimming, see?'

'So, our visitors didn't risk a torch—it would have been spotted right away,' Ressatus said. 'They only needed enough light to locate the strongbox.'

⚱⚱⚱

I'd got almost no sleep over the last twenty-four hours. I cancelled a routine review of the incoming mail reports from the hubs in southeast Gallia and called Finance Officer Ferreolus up to my office. He was a canny Gallo-Roman accountant I'd pinched off the Manlius cattle estates on the basis of his honest reputation.

'How much is in the strongbox?'

'Four hundred and nine-four *solidi*, *Magister*. Don't worry, I counted it this afternoon.'

'Move it back to the prison. Find it a well-guarded cell. Damn the floor repairs. We were luckier than I realized.'

'It's barely enough to hold the Castra and the western hubs until the next mint shipment. All the departments in Roma are ekeing it out until the imperial treasury schedules the next delivery. So, I suggest a few more economies . . .'

I listened to Ferreolus' budget suggestions, but my troubled mind wandered: word of the strongbox's re-location had leaked out of my staff meeting in mere hours to the wrong ears. Yes, we were lucky, thanks to the boy from Pisaurum. The screaming Anthimus' delaying action had made all the difference. Our Castra operations had come within seconds of shutdown for lack of funds.

I locked up my inner office and said good-night to Cyrillus with a heavy heart. Amosis and I were just starting down to the courtyard when the sweating coding master Sabazios hurried up to the offices, his leather *sagum* flapping back from his thick shoulders. He unrolled a peculiar painting across Cyrillus' desk.

The fine detail and perspective were worthy of a villa dining room. His expert rendering of the archives' recessed shelves, the side table with its rank of foot-long iron lamps, the two shadowy alcove wings, and the open window shutters in shades of gray and black only made the rust red of the dried blood smeared all over on the flagstones all the starker.

This was his best attempt to record the murder scene and it had taken the poor man all day. But the painting's forensic purpose had eluded him.

Disappointed, I said only, 'You're very talented,' to the eager artist. After he'd lumbered back down the stairs, I rolled the painting up and told Cyrillus to stash it with our official record of Anthimus' death.

※※※

Lavinia's face fell when she opened the door to see me instead of her mistress. It was now two hours after dusk and Apollonia had not yet returned home from Anepsia's.

I decided to dispatch one of our two lanky 'houseguests' to escort the family *lectica* back safely through the streets. Avitus had just changed into his boots when Apollonia arrived home.

I'd been angry at discovering she'd gone to honor her debt without any protection—not even a companion like Drusilla or Lavinia—but I forgot any scolding when I saw her. I wasn't ready for the lifeless expression in her eyes as she unpinned her light cloak and sank exhausted onto the carved bench at the entry of the narrow *fauces*.

I signaled the household to leave us alone. Helping her up off the bench before her pale features and limp posture alarmed the sharp-eyed twins, I escorted her through the atrium and into our bedchamber. This time I closed the door.

'I'm sorry, Marcus. I meant to be here hours ago. By the time I realized I should send a slave with a message, I thought it better just to race home by myself.'

'Didn't Anepsia offer an escort?'

'No, she needed everyone at home.'

'Were the earrings very valuable?' I sat down beside her and took her in my arms.

'I don't know.'

'Don't worry. Whatever she asked, we'll manage,' I whispered.

'You don't understand, Marcus. Victorinus died late last night. I didn't know until I got there.'

'Oh, that was a shock for you. So, the earrings were forgotten?'

'But Anepsia begged me not to leave. I tried to be useful. I kept an eye on the household while Anepsia and Callista received small groups of close relatives expressing condolences. They expect dozens more, mostly family clients and friends, all week. And there are so many things to be organized, people notified by letter—I did everything she asked—for hours on end. Then something—'

She stared at the wall opposite.

'What happened?'

'A furious row broke out, right there in a house of mourning.'

There was a tap at the door. Lavinia brought us a supper tray of cold pie and wine.

'Thank you. Take a sip, Apollonia. There's no rush. What row?'

'Do you know Deputy Prefect Aginatius, Marcus? I mean, have you ever done more than see him across a forum or riding in state to some dinner party?'

'Oh, Aginatius always makes himself felt. I spotted him leaving the Senate House a few weeks ago. He always wants so badly to be noticed, he rather defeats the purpose. Now he's been upstaged by Maximinus getting the Chilo investigation.'

'Well, now I've met the man. He stormed into the house and crowed over the body! He threatened to "expose" Victorinus. He said that through a deal with "the Pannonian bread dealer", Victorinus has been protecting powerful Roman friends from harm, selling acquittals even before charges were laid—for steep fees. Aginatius called Victorinus a blackmailing traitor to Roma's *honestiores*.'

'Charges? For what?'

'Poisoning, adultery, *magicium*—that sort of thing. While you were gone, a few months ago, there was a scandal—but Marcus, it didn't seem so important at the time!'

'Tell me, my love.'

'A group of senators—Tarracius Bassus, the one with the—?'

'—the loud red-headed wife, yes.'

'And his brother Alfenius Camenius and a certain Senator Marcianus. We might have met Marcianus briefly at Tarracius' reception last year? And Senator Eusaphius—they all faced charges of studying poisons under some charioteer named Auchenius.'

'More of this nonsense!'

'We thought so, too. Of course, all four were acquitted and everyone laughed it off. But this afternoon Aginatius raged until the whole atrium was echoing. He yelled at Anepsia that the whole scandal against Tarracius Bassus and the others was cooked up by Maximinus, just so their acquittals could be won by special pleading from Victorinus in exchange for secret payoffs.'

She whimpered, 'Marcus, can you follow? Am I making any sense at all? Victorinus blackmailing his own friends?'

'How did Anepsia take it?'

'I don't know how, but she held her own.'

'I'm sure she did.'

'She told Aginatius that he himself had been left a generous legacy by Victorinus and that now she only hoped she had the power to withhold the gift from such an ungrateful friend.'

'Was Aginatius surprised?'

'Yes. He didn't believe her at first. But then shouted he wanted nothing to do with dirty profiting off the misery of innocent Romans.'

'And everyone heard this?'

'He staged this scene in front of Anepsia's whole household and her grieving in-laws! With Victorinus' body laid out right there in the *tablinium!*'

'And then?'

'She ordered her *dispensator* to throw Aginatius out of the house. Marcus, how could she remain so cool?'

I could well believe Anepsia capable of facing down a legion of Gorgons. But I couldn't believe a deputy urban prefect would offend all notions of Roman etiquette. He'd ruined his social standing for good.

I urged her to eat and drink. We'd say no more until she'd rested.

She pushed her glass away and continued, 'Listen, please, Marcus. Aginatius fought off the *dispensator*. He refused to leave the house. He said it wouldn't be Anepsia's house for much longer, anyway. A stream of threats poured out of his mouth. He made absurd accusations against Anepsia's honor. He threatened lawsuits! Madness! Marcus, I still see all their expressions—the most distinguished members of Victorinus' *gens*—all of them hearing this man's bile!'

'You've got to rest now. We got hardly any sleep last night. You shouldn't have gone today.'

She pushed away my hand soothing her brow. 'Let me finish, please, Marcus.'

'Good gods, there's more?'

'Do you recall how Anepsia reassured you as she left my party?'

'She said she'd survive as a widow because Victorinus had made good friends she could count on. You think there might be any truth to Aginatius' accusations about Victorinus and Maximinus?'

Apollonia looked at me through the shadows of the little lamp Lavinia had set on the dressing table. My wife's pupils were wide with fear.

'Anepsia didn't say in so many words. That would be tantamount to laying the crime of blackmail on the deathbed of her own husband. But once Aginatius had gone, she rambled on, in a strange way.'

'Strange how?'

'Breaking from the stress, yet dangerous—like crackling firewood. She said Victorinus had always been gullible. And then she asked me, who would dare try to buy off Deputy Maximinus from pursuing justice? Victorinus held the Pannonian in high regard. Then she said she was sure that Maximinus would protect her.'

'Did Victorinus really leave Senator Aginatius a legacy?'

'No. I asked. Her answer shocked me. She said Victorinus had bequeathed Maximinus three thousand pounds of silver in his will.'

'*Maximinus*? No wonder you look horrified. A legacy or a pay-off?'

'*Both*, Marcus. I suspect Victorinus died owing Maximinus his cut of money from some acquittal deal. At my garden party, Anepsia had boasted that Callista's dowry included three thousand pounds of silver bequeathed by her first husband in trust for his daughter. Today Anepsia tried passing off that exact amount as Victorinus' bequest.'

'So in one breath, poor Anepsia confirmed *exactly* what she denied.'

How I'd underestimated the Pannonian 'bread dealer'! During my absence from Roma, Maximinus had enjoyed weeks to put the Chilo case to rest—time to release that wrestling coach and his friends or time to 'break them.'

Instead, Maximinus was prolonging the Chilo case as cover to intimidate Roman nobility for personal profit, like a worm driven by *avaritia,* drilling through the city's soft flesh. He wasn't only 'eradicating spiritual corruption.' He was making a bundle in the process.

The dangling box might be only one of his lures for building a case against potential victims. And once he had his prey in his sights, he won either way. He'd offer to withdraw scurrilous charges for a friendly fee, using Victorinus as his middleman. Otherwise, successful prosecutions included the confiscation of the convicted citizen's property for the 'state coffers' via Maximinus' own purse.

The missing earrings now seemed trivial indeed. And the murder of Anthimus by burglars was a tragic concern for only the Castra.

But tomorrow, one hour before dawn, I had an appointment with Vettius Agorius Praetextatus, to my mind Roma's greatest living nobleman. Could Praetextatus stem the corruption spreading out from Maximinus' dockside office? Of course, he could.

But would he be willing to try?

Chapter 6, Roman Deals with Roman

—THE PALACE OF VETTIUS AGORIUS PRAETEXTATUS—

Apart from the two emperors, Consul Petronius Probus of the Anician clan might be the most powerful official inside Roma and beyond. But Vettius Agorius Praetextatus occupied a terrestrial Olympus of high reputation all his own. This distinction might seem slight to many—all but true Romans, perhaps.

Praetextatus was currently between official posts and enjoying the leisure or *otium* of moving between country estates and his urban palace.

I knew the family, of course—what bright slave boy attending Senator Manlius through the Roman streets in the 330's would not have heard of their wealth, good looks, exceptional education, and virtuous conduct?

I've said that even nude, Prefect Olybrius wore his titles like robes. But Praetextatus exerted his influence from an even loftier vantage point—without reference to any title whatsoever. He'd held Olybrius' job running Roma in 367, but city boss was just one in a string of posts scrolling down his *curriculum vitae*.

He'd started very young. If I mention that at a beardless fifteen, Praetextatus served as *Pontifex Vestae* so that, with the Neo-platonic philosopher Sopater of Apamea, he officiated over the *polismós* ceremony setting the foundation stone of Constantinople—well, need I go on? His lifelong service as a priest of Roma's traditional worship wrapped him in an extra vestment of respect, even from Christians who otherwise loathed our old cults.

More telling is what his exquisite wife, Aconia Fabia Paulina, (daughter of Fabius Aconius Catullinus Philomathius, *Praefectus urbi* in 342–344 and Consul in 349) answered her parents when informed she was to marry the handsome young noble.

Any other lucky Roman girl would have skittered around the garden in delight and then dashed off to giggle over her good fortune with a gaggle of little girlfriends.

No, Paulina was different. For now Posterity would be watching her too. So the sober virgin replied: 'My parents' distinction does nothing greater for me than to make me seem worthy of such a husband.'

Or so they say. Praetextatus and Paulina had been inseparable ever since, producing children and tending altars, side by side. In a city of slander, libel, and malicious gossip, few marriages escaped so unscathed.

Over the year, Praetextatus had collected hundreds of clients and very few enemies—as far as the Castra knew. Praetextatus had been born to *gratia*, those political connections that set a boy off his *Cursus Honorum* along the smooth stretch of road paved with privilege. And you can bet your vineyard that Praetextatus would never once let his fortunate destiny down.

Otium or *negotium*, he was never idle. He kept busy, managing estates dotting the Via Appia and near the Napoli bay in Lucrina, Baiae, Puteoli, Bauli, and farther down in Sicilia, Apulia, and even Mauretania. He tended his sacred obligations to the gods and was famous for his expertise in divine rituals.

Praetextatus avoided all public baths, theaters, and sports arenas. If he had any spare time, he buckled down and translated Aristotle's *Prior and Posterior Analytics*—or something else in that worthy vein.

As prefect of the city, he'd managed to be dreaded and not disliked at the same time—no small feat. He quelled a nasty spate of rioting among the Christians and tore down the illegal balconies obstructing Roma's traffic. He demolished illegal private constructions grafted like barnacles onto the venerable walls of ancient, sacred buildings. He established standard weights through the district markets. And in the examination of legal cases Praetextatus earned the distinction which Cicero once extended to Brutus: he did nothing to gain favor, yet everything that he did was looked upon with favor.

In short, Praetextatus was the ancient Roman ideal, born four centuries too late.

Yet, for all my admiration, I found it hard to *like* Vettius Praetextatus. As the new intelligence chief reviving our discredited service, I'd filed a little note on him in 364, when he risked his political neck once and only once.

He'd been serving as Proconsul of Achaea—a pinnacle of prestige due to the glory of its capital Athens. In fact, Praetextatus stuck his neck out surprisingly far: he appealed against an edict by the new Emperor Valentinian forbidding night sacrifices during pagan 'mysteries.' Praetextatus argued that the Pannonian Christian ruler's edict made it impossible for devout pagans to observe their faith.

The temperamental Valentinian had grown up in rough army camps where subordinates followed orders. But to my astonishment, Valentinian backed off. He left capital punishment in place only for any rituals veering into magical spells tainted by treason. I noted this down as startling proof that, though battle-hardened Valentinian resented our city's educated pagan elites, the soldier was still too unsteady on his new throne to face them down.

After that signal victory, Praetextatus survived our new Pannonian brother-sovereigns by compliance and stealth. He thrived on 'strategic omission.'

So now you know the man as well as anyone limping down the Caelian Hill, through the valley of the Flavian Amphitheater and back up the Mons Oppius with the help of a walking stick to consult the nobleman. Before the sunbeams broke over our city's ancient walls, I led Amosis to our short but precious appointment, with a little hope but few assumptions.

We were hardly the only eager penitents loping across the Horti Vettiani, the dewy gardens that encircled the noble's urban seat and offered breathtaking views. Praetextatus' palace nestled on the southern spur of the Esquiline Hill plateau just inside the Severan Wall. We glimpsed Trajan's Baths, the Temple of Venus, the Amphitheater and perhaps less breathtaking, the crumbling palace of the faded third-century Sicinia family.

City officials, harried messengers, servants, slaves, and sycophants were trickling from all directions toward the great house, like water circling toward the center of a ritual basin. I braced myself to use my time with him well.

My consolation was that my urgent note had obtained a swift appointment. And my worry was that every other man here brandished yet more privileged invitations. Amosis and I could not get farther than ten feet outside the front door in a queue of murmuring arrivals standing three abreast, their features visible only by the flame of two torches shining from sconces in the wall overhead.

I sent Amosis to the front of the queue to assess the wait, but after a minute or two, the clever slave fetched me forward at the order of Praetextatus' senior private secretary vetting the clients.

'How much did that cost?'

'That's my affair. Slave deals with slave, *Magister*.'

Beyond the yawning bronze-bolted oak doors was a deep *fauces*, as long and cavernous as any public tunnels or *vomitoria* leading into a modest arena. We emerged into a grand vestibule. The palace's public atrium—for there were many *atria*, gardens, shrines, baths, and even an aviary and small temple on this estate— was a wonderland of murals. Classical scenes from tales of the gods were painted in saffron, sapphire blues, and ruby reds and framed in rectangles of rust-red trim sparkling with genuine gold dust.

Priceless Greek statues of the gods depicted ininl vivid colors ranked down both long walls. They reached out to welcome us but their open gestures and stares did not put me at ease.

I was led away, leaving Amosis behind. My bootsteps echoed down the fine mosaic floors—a handful of boy slaves in damask slippers swept behind me as I proceeded, like spirit-cleaners with feather brooms, appearing and vanishing between the shadowed columns.

What was that exotic scent that cleansed my nostrils? It floated through the cavernous space still cloaked in gray dawn. *Domina* Paulina lit no ordinary resin.

At the far end of the great space, these fumes of pungent incense poured from bright copper braziers flanking the family's mammoth *lararium*, a masterpiece of marble carving and gilt. Two ivory Penates, each holding a *rhyton*, watched over an ancestor-*genius* garbed in an old-fashioned toga. His head was covered priest-like for sacrifice. He held a *patera* or libation bowl and an incense box. A painted snake for fertility and prosperity coiled at the base of the *lararium's* altar wall behind the figurines. The shrine's *tympanum* showed an ox-skull, sacrificial knife, and another bowl.

Two junior secretaries now shepherded me beyond the echoing atrium. The impatient murmur of the other clients fell away. I filed down another long, windowless corridor, passed two dining rooms, caught a glimpse of the elegant *Domina* Paulina in discussion with her staff, and at last reached a dark and airless library that Praetextatus preferred to his more formal public *tablinum*.

The door closed behind me with a velvety hush. Only the sound of a trickling fountain somewhere interrupted the silent rehearsal of my appeal.

The nobleman had indeed given me the first opening in his schedule. He arrived a moment later, freshly shaved, anointed, combed, and plucked, wearing the spotless old-fashioned ivory wool of a religious man finishing his morning ritual of prayer and offering.

His expression was polite, his smile bland, his features unreadable, his teeth shining and even—but all that was nothing new to me.

Praetextatus descended from so many centuries of well-bred, hard-negotiated, drilled, and tested noble scions and virtuous virgin heiresses that his face and form offered no irregularity or interest whatsoever. A stranger might ride through Achaea and see a bust of the former Governor Praetextatus in a prominent alcove. To be polite, he'd comment, 'Now, there's the face of a noble Roman,' but he would have no clue as to his personality or even the century of his birth.

'What have you been reading lately, Numidianus? Still Suetonius?' We'd met over a love of reading and that, at least, was a common language.

'He offers useful lessons in how to change with our times and adapt to a variety of imperial personalities.'

'Then you must learn him by heart.'

We settled in wide-seated carved chairs under a pair of windows still shuttered against the fast-fading night.

'Now, Numidianus, what is today's business?'

'If a man who enjoys the Emperor's complete trust demands I open the Castra's sensitive files to him, do I have the right to refuse?'

'As *magister* of your *schola*, yes. Even I could not dance over to the Treasury and demand they open the state accounts. Ah—'

He'd rung a little bell and small glasses of diluted wine arrived, borne on a wide silver tray. As a former slave, I could only admire his staff for their silent, self-effacing movements. *Domina* Paulina's breeding surfaced in the graceful discipline of even her lowliest minion.

He sipped. 'On the other hand, Numidianus, as you offer the deep knowledge of the Castra for the benefit of the Emperor, why would you deny assistance to his delegate?'

'I can't allow strangers to rummage through our records.'

'Rummage, no. But research?'

'Our files include provincial audits, *agentes*' reports, unverified rumors, and secret information about the prominent and vulnerable. Don't quote me to our two sovereigns, but the use of intelligence can resemble a kind of sorcery. Skillfully interpreted, raw observations can reveal deep and hidden truths. On the other hand, they can be open to manipulation, distortion, and mis-interpretation. In short, I fear abuse, intentional or otherwise. Even criminal exploitation.'

'Oh dear. Numidianus, remember the lessons bequeathed by ancestors far wiser than ourselves. Our Senate once enjoyed real power—when it held together. A Roman with a sense of the collegiate can always count on allies later.'

'You can always count on me, Prefect.'

He smiled. 'And you should be able to count on me?'

I had presumed. We sat in silence. He hadn't endorsed my decision to refuse Maximinus or insisted I comply. He hadn't even asked for the applicant's name. My time with him was short and—

He spoke: 'Perhaps you guard your hard-won authority too closely? Please don't misunderstand me, Numidianus. I mean no offense. I'm not suggesting your personal history makes you unusually anxious.'

With that, he just had. So I was no more than an over-promoted freedman, a green *clarissimus*, clutching my position to my chest like an ageing virgin crossing her legs for no reason?

'Then you think I should allow a man to rifle through our dossiers?'

'No. I can guess the true reason you hesitate. And why you want me to endorse your refusal. In the old days, men of responsibility shared their roots in loyalty to Roma, the *paideia* of the classical curriculum, the reputation of their interlinked families, and pride in honors won. These days men of all varieties, provinces, learning, faiths, and flaws rise to power. They donate to the Church but leave our great buildings and bridges to crumble. They care nothing for our city's glorious history. Sadly, the only thing we all share as imperial officials now is ambition and perhaps . . . fear.'

'Then you see my problem?'

'Yes. We ask ourselves, do certain outsiders boast the discretion to match their curious purposes?'

'Where the oldest of Roma's surviving families are concerned, the answer might be "no".'

'Ah.' He sipped.

'Prefect Praetextatus, I've been in the East for over six months. In my absence, a few foolish nobles got caught up in Valentinian's interdiction against *magicium*. In reference to a pending case of attempted poisoning against the man pegged for next *vicarius* of Roman Africa, Chilo, I've been warned; more charges against the highborn and prestigious may follow. Of course, I've promised everything correct under the Castra's arrest procedures—'

'Of course.'

'But a suggestion that these investigations could be concluded more swiftly to everyone's advantage by using secret intelligence on Roman family ties and minor vices is hard to credit. In fact, Vettius Agorius, I fear the opposite for some of our top names.'

He chuckled. 'By not naming the *gentes* involved, even to me, you display admirable discretion.'

'Of course.'

'But think again, Numidianus. Your *schola* isn't trusted by the other departments. Refusing to comply with an honest request from Valentinian's court won't enhance the reputation of you *agentes*. You're already seen as too independent, too secretive, and too nosy. Even this instant, I remind myself that anything I say this morning, here in my own private study, may end up copied and stored beyond my control in your stony, dank headquarters.'

'I enjoy a reliable memory. It's not necessary for me to record every confidence.'

'Of course.' He pondered the stem of his gold-filigreed wine glass.

'You say you have a good memory? Then you recall the old Etruscan fable of the lowly baker who dabbled in spells? He woke up one morning to find himself transformed by the gods into a dangerous beast? No? Well, it's an ancient tale so, forgive me, I can't recall the storyteller.'

I waited. By the 'lowly baker,' Praetextatus meant the low-born, bread-distributing Pannonian, Deputy Prefect Flavius Maximinus. He'd known whom I was talking about from the start.

'This baker was so emboldened by his sharp new claws and long fangs, he took a swipe at one of the village's best hunters. Of course, he was clumsy and missed. But a meddling lawyer, outraged by the baker's new ferocity, advised this renowned hunter that he should take the animal's attack more seriously. The hunter should track down and kill the beast for his own good, as the beast had tried to wound him once and might try again.'

I listened, my impatience fighting curiosity and confusion.

'It's an interesting tale, but I'm afraid I don't know it.'

'Oh, you should. The hunter merely laughed and taunted the beast to his face, repeating the lawyer's warnings. Yet in his heart, the hunter was not so blithe. He guarded himself all the more closely when he ventured into the forest. Soon, he even left the village. Meanwhile, the lawyer had exposed himself to the wrath of the baker-beast.'

If the prefect of the *annona* was the baker-turned-beast, then who was the 'meddling lawyer' who urged a powerful 'hunter' to bring down Maximinus? And who was the 'hunter' who abandoned the village altogether?

'I enjoy such tales, Numidianus. They're written for children, of course, but only children ignore a fable's lesson.'

I couldn't follow the noble's riddling. He'd frustrated me beyond expectation. For all his friendliness and fine breakfast wine, he refused to back me up in keeping *schola* files from Maximinus' prying. Instead, he prattled on about bakers and beasts and lawyers and hunters. I readied myself to clear his inner sanctum for the next client.

He escorted me to a side door opened by a silent porter slave. Another visitor stood poised outside the main door.

'As for that former matter, Numidianus, there might be a better way to protect your *schola* files and serve our great city at the same time.'

I waited for his verdict.

'Keep your files to yourself but put them to better use. Demonstrate the Castra's collegiality to all of us who admire its resourcefulness. The best way to circumscribe any investigation and to limit its taint or exploitation from damaging wider Roman society—and given our neighbors' foolish superstitions, there's a definite risk to many—'

'Yes, Prefect?'

'Solve the Chilo poisoning case yourself.'

He laid his manicured hand on my shoulder.

'And quickly.'

Four rings as heavy as nuggets pressed down hard.

'The Castra will do its best.'

'We are in complete agreement, as always, *Magister* Numidianus. It's always best that true Romans deal with true Romans.'

ℛℛℛ

The sky was bleeding raw pink and orange into the gray dawn. I'd promised Apollonia I would never touch Maximinus' Chilo investigation. But I'd never promised her I wouldn't launch my own. Back in my office, I had one precious hour before the morning briefing to decipher what Praetextatus had said.

Why had Praetextatus used an allegory to warn me that Maximinus had attacked and failed to bring down a great man? Why had Praetextatus encouraged me to thwart the Chilo investigation from spreading too far? All I knew was that Praetextatus had advised me without implicating himself in any way. This—not some specious senatorial collegiality—was why Praetextatus sat inhaling imported incense in palatial comfort while the rest of the city's elites sat on edge.

The morning briefing began. Ressatus had re-enforced the guard shifts because of the attempted burglary. Archivist Zephyrinus' breathing and pulse were more regular but he still lay comatose.

The mood lightened a bit when *Biarchus* Rubellius ran down the previous night's update on roads and mail routes. After that, Rubellius handed me a second packet of sealed reports from *agentes* near and far on topics not meant for airing—even here.

I recall reporting as a young *eques* to this office late at night and finding Apodemius sorting through messages written on everything from the most expensive vellum and varieties of papyrus to the flimsiest pocket tablets framing cheap, crackled wax. Some information shifted pins and ribbons on his crumbling wall map. Other reports disappeared into the padlocked safe in the corner of the room or went downstairs to thicken files.

Imagine—I'd once thought of the weekly culling of imperial secrets as an enviable privilege. Had Apodemius felt as overwhelmed as I did by the flow of intelligence landing on this very desk? I was drowning in a sea of names and places, plucking at the flotsam and jetsam of strange observations, sketchy rumors, and dark, hard news for two Emperors facing off foreign threats on a bankrupt budget.

Apodemius' ageing files now sat untended underneath the temple floor. Was most of the information before me, so fresh and troubling, also destined to crumble and rot?

After a half hour of routine business, the majority of the men returned to their duties. I had decided to broach what was preying on my mind to four trusted deputies: the Castra's legal expert Clemens, the fighting coach Durans, *Biarchus* Rubellius, and of course, *Ducenarius* Saturnus.

'The Castra is going to investigate a criminal case here in the city. While I was in the East, an official chosen for next *vicarius* for Roman Africa, one Chilo, complained about a poisoning attempt on his life. Three low-class men were jailed—then nothing. Everyone agrees that this case has dragged on far too long. Urban Prefect Olybrius should have brought it to trial or handed it to his deputy Aginatius for closure months ago. Instead Olybrius begged ill-health and agreed to Chilo's irregular request to delegate the investigation to *Praefectus Annonae* Maximinus.'

'What's that to the Castra?' asked Clemens. His father had been a Gallo-Roman deputy *quaestor*, but Clemens preferred teaching us legal niceties in the Eternal City to arguing property rights in front of a backwater *curia*.

'I was warned by Olybrius from his massage bed at the Caracalla Baths that the Castra may soon receive some sensitive warrants for arrest. Olybrius asked for all protection due the *clarissimi* and their families.'

'The procedures are clear,' muttered Clemens, fiddling with his *stilus*. 'I'll answer for every single man I've trained.'

Durans murmured, 'We gather intelligence in secret. We carry out arrests in public. But we don't conduct open investigations like imperial *notarii*, right, *Magister*? I'm only the fighting coach. Is there something I don't understand?'

'We have to understand before it's too late. The three men accused of the botched poisoning have spent many long months in so-called "investigative custody"—which is a mystery in itself, given the law's preference for a swift trial.'

Clemens said, 'To be specific, if a governor or other high state representative initiates an action, the limit on detention is six months. If the complaint comes from a private citizen, the maximum is twelve months, unless the crime is very, very serious, in which case—.'

'The crime wasn't serious, Clemens. The murder never happened. Chilo and wife Maxima, hale and hearty, have left for some country villa to await their posting to Africa,' I said.

'So what's to investigate?' Saturnus asked.

'Everything. Maximinus hinted to me that the Chilo case is only his hook to catch untold schools of fish. He plans a purge of superstition and vice across the city. He dangles a slotted box outside his office to attract anonymous informants. This morning Prefect Vettius Praetextatus all but asked me to bring the Chilo affair to a swift end.'

'So where do we start?' Rubellius asked.

'With the three jailed suspects. We ask ourselves, what does a wrestling coach named Asbolius have in common with a soothsayer named Campensis and an organ manufacturer named Sericus? And why would anyone hire them to poison Chilo?'

79

'You're sure there's a mastermind behind them?' Rubellius asked. 'People do weird things these days for thrills.'

'Of course someone's behind this. Can you delegate your defense classes to someone for a few days, Durans? I want you and Rubellius to haunt the bars and brothels around the city's wrestling schools for information about Asbolius. Start with the *Ludus Magnus* of course, and fan out from there. You know fighting jargon, Durans. Our young Rubellius here enjoys a certain rough charm. I think you two will dig up what we're looking for—if only we knew what it was.'

Rubellius inhaled with pleasure. As long as he returned with hot information on Asbolius, the Castra would cover the expenses of all the drink and girls he needed for his 'exploration.'

'Now for the organ-maker. Do we have any man in the Castra who's musical?'

The officers fought back a snigger. There were always two or three soldiers in any Roman unit who could ripple a tune off his flute by the campfire. But standing in the corner of a gilded *triclinium* to warble a song or pump away at a hydraulic water-organ as tall as a legionary and broad as an altar? That just wasn't manly.

'All right, we'll come up with someone for the organ factory later. I also want any information on two thugs, Mucianus and Barbarus, who work for Deputy Maximinus near the river docks outside the Annona offices. It should be easy to spot them. One has a club foot, his right leg, and the taller man has a deep scar across his forehead, here.'

'Nasty,' commented Durans.

'Yes, he took a good swipe from somebody's *spatha*. These two strung up Maximinus' gossip box. But they don't fit the style of his rising station, so I don't expect they're allowed inside his chambers. They'll be lurking in some *popina* or *caupona* within his easy call. We need a man to befriend them.'

'Why don't we ask that rider, Mussidius, to join the team?' Saturnus asked. 'He's here for a few weeks for language and defense training before his promotion to *biarchus*. Built like a centurion and seems to have quite a collection of road jokes.'

'He sounds perfect.' Before Durans could scoff, I added, 'A stint making friends with gladiator lowlife and Maximinus' scum is just as important training as Frankish axe-throwing or Persian strangulation techniques. I ask our riders to collect everything they can on the road. A store of jokes and a good head for wine is as important for our service as an arm of iron.'

'That leaves the soothsayer?' Saturnus prompted.

'Yes, the fact one suspect is a *haruspex* suggests that the man wanting Chilo dead was a pagan. But given the current religious climate, any *clarissimus* would avoid open contact with a disreputable soothsayer.'

'Couldn't we just talk to the suspects' lawyer?' Clemens asked.

There was a ripple of dismissive chuckles. The ways of Roman lawyers fed many a joke along the lines of 'Three lawyers walked into a brothel—'

I cut off their smirks. 'We'll inquire. But I doubt any lawyer is still around if they've been rotting in those cells for months waiting for a trial date.'

'*Magister*, why not just question the accomplices directly?' Saturnus asked.

'Apodemius always said never interrogate a man until you have a pretty good idea of his answers. We don't know that these three *are* accomplices. We don't know if they're guilty. And we don't know if they even knew each other before Chilo's accusation. They've been tortured, so only the gods know what they've admitted to in hope of release. I want independent confirmation that they were even acquainted, much less working together.'

But I hadn't really answered Saturnus' suggestion and they all knew it. The long silence was broken by Rubellius:

'Where are the buggers chained up?'

'In the Tullianum.'

They grimaced and shifted on their stools. Unless they were delivering a new prisoner to the front doors of those black chambers, my officers had no authority inside the Tullianum.

Only I, as the head of our department, might get into the domain of the municipal magistrates and demand the guards present a prisoner. Only I could penetrate those pockets of Hades this side of the Styx. Only I could descend to the lowest levels of our ancient city and wend deeper down that lightless passage wracked with pain and the heavy weight of untold deaths, sordid and noble alike.

I broke the silence: 'Yes, Saturnus, of course you're right. I'll question them myself.'

I was about to set out a timetable for reporting back on what our explorations through the city's gutters produced when a cadet reporting to Saturnus got permission from Cyrillus to interrupt our meeting.

'They told me this was urgent, *Magister.*'

The sweating youth handed me a thick packet, its fold creased razor sharp under an ostentatious circle of jade green wax as wide as my palm. The impression was deep and determined, the seal unmistakable—Deputy Prefect Maximinus at work.

'The messenger warned our gateman not to delay delivery,' the cadet panted.

I cracked the seal open and read the neat block letters. The Pannonian was, after all, a trained lawyer; his formulation was impeccable and phrasing exact. But the name on the warrant sent cold shooting through my bones—Lollianus, the son of Gaius Ceionius Rufius Volusianus.

For a moment, I couldn't bring myself to read it out loud. Maximinus demanded we arrest the youngest child of the wiliest survivor of the powerful Ceionii dynasty. Gaius Ceionius Rufius Volusianus was a politician so formidable, he went by only one name throughout the entire Empire—Lampadius.

One of our empire's most senior living statesmen, Lampadius had started up the *Cursus Honorum* as a *praetor* in his teens thirty years and served as urban prefect in Roma only three years ago. That's a long career, even by the standards of Roma's most venerable. And Lampadius took his prestigious career for granted every day of his privileged life.

His father had been a prefect of Roma at the end of Constantine the Great's reign and his accomplished grandfather renowned for his devotion to our cults. If you want to understand the Ceionii crowd, you don't need a Castra dossier. Just turn your back on Constantine's great new Basilica for the Christian saint Peter and gaze instead at the temple of Magna Mater covered with plaques and inscriptions thanking the Ceionii for their generosity and devotions over centuries of Roma's glory.

Lampadius was no friend of mine. I'd watched him for years employ his arrogant, entitled wiles as the crafty councilor of

Emperor Constantius II. He was a vain, dishonest, slithery foe of far worthier men serving the stolid, devout late emperor.

Hidden in the darkest recesses of Lampadius' office in Mediolanum, I'd even spied on him one night in 355 drawing forged papers from their hiding place in a cold brazier. With *Agens* Gaudentius, I'd seen him slipping those forged papers to Emperor Constantius lying prostrate in prayer in the palace chapel. The forgeries had worked long enough to frame the rising General Claudius Silvanus on false charges of usurpation.

All this, so Lampadius could ascend another rung to Prefect of Gallia. When at last the cruel conspiracy against the Frankish hero who'd cleaned Gallia of Alemanni barbarians was exposed, Lampadius swallowed his temporary setback like the noble he was.

But once Constantius II was gone, Lampadius resumed his climbing. Nothing defeated him for long—except his own vanity. They said he was a man who took it badly if even his spitting wasn't praised for being better than anyone else's. As city prefect, he'd launched into a grand building spree dedicated to polishing his glory in the eyes of a million Romans. But he'd engraved his name as 'founder' on buildings he'd merely restored. He failed to pay the suppliers of the lead, bronze, copper, and iron he'd lavished on his showpiece restorations out of ready civic funds. Admittedly Emperor Trajan did the same and for that reason modern Romans jokingly call Trajan a "wall-wart".

But Lampadius was no Trajan. He was arrogant, mean, and shortsighted. Mobs of unpaid craftsmen protested, violent riots broke out, and finally one night, the honest plebeians of Roma's streets threw torches and fire-darts at Lampadius' grand new townhouse near the Baths of Constantine. While his terrified neighbors defended their street, Lampadius hid from the mob under the Milvian Bridge only to return later to a smoking ruin.

Since that debacle, Lampadius had lain low, bitter, and reclusive, in the oldest of the Ceionii clan's many city mansions.

As tempting as it was, I couldn't send Saturnus in my stead. As Praetextatus had said this morning, 'Roman deals with Roman' and *Ducenarius* Saturnus was the best of Lutetians—but no more. The arrest of so elevated a scion, even the sixth and last of Lampadius' offspring, demanded the *Magister Agentium in Rebus* himself serve as witness.

Well, Olybrius had warned me. Amosis had heard rumors about the kid that same day. Now Maximinus' game—whatever it was—had begun in earnest. There would no longer be any possibility of keeping the Castra aloof. I gave myself an hour to compose myself and review the protocols.

I didn't need that hour, but I confess to a strange fear. Certainly not fear of Lampadius' majestic ancestral line. I'd overcome the slave's nervousness around great names by the age of ten.

It was a different fear that clenched my stomach—the fear of Lampadius' personal *smallness* and his potential for meanness and harm. It seemed my trip to the depths of a fetid jail must make way for an ascent to the heights of ancient breeding.

The stooges in the Tullianum Prison must wait. A very different stench awaited me, but a stench all the same.

CHAPTER 7, A NOBLE THRESHOLD

—THE PALATINE HILL—

An hour later, our four-man team set off on foot from the Castra for one of the oldest residential streets on the Palatine Hill. We brought the minimum show of force required by state regulations. After all, we were arresting a fifteen-year-old Roman society brat, not the grizzled barbarian King Chnodomarius.

Still, I expected trouble. For the purpose of swift physical intimidation, Saturnus lent me the Dacian *circitor* Tarbus, the most Herculean *agens* available. Then I added a fast-riding *eques* idling between routes—an Umbrian named Vibius. It would be good training in case he had to make an arrest in the field one day. Vibius carried the required sack for collecting evidence that might be pertinent to the charge.

Almost as an afterthought—out of consideration for Lollianus' coddled upbringing?—I'd added the pale ex-stable boy Defendens. Despite the shock of the senseless murder of his friend, the young man from Pisaurum had stuck to his duties. But he was dispirited, expressionless, almost voided by grief. I hoped being included in the arrest party would motivate and distract him.

Until that moment, the weather had offered a lovely respite from early autumn's monotonous, sweltering skies. We'd enjoyed the balmiest of days set to the crisp rhythm of dying leaves swept into piles by city slaves.

But we'd scarcely crossed into Regio X when the first rain of the changing seasons dampened our progress. The drizzle spread a glistening sheen on marble and stone but lent our march a melancholy air.

We were headed to a rarified address at the western end of the Palatine, a narrow terrace north of the Temple of Magna Mater and south of the Temple of Augustus. The central *fora* and streets were very crowded. The spectacle of four armed *agentes* moving with such purpose through the market crowds and side alleys drew too much attention for my comfort. It was important that we give the House of Ceionius no warning and it was too risky to delay until nightfall for the same reason.

Although I took every shortcut a former slave boy raised in Roma knows by heart, we were still a little winded by the time we marched past a tall wall of ageing travertine limestone and stopped outside two great oak doors bolted in bronze fittings. I sent Defendens down the remaining length of this elegant fortification, unbroken by the usual vulgar shopfront or food stall, to make his way around and up the slope to the rear of Lampadius' house. Republican architecture preferred there should be no back exit, but my knowledge of such old residences assured me otherwise. After three centuries of habitation, there'd be some modern access cut for slaves' traffic with vendors and domestic vehicles.

We waited a few minutes for Defendens to take position.

'Go ahead, Tarbus.'

The Dacian gave a polite tap of his mammoth boot on the door. We waited a few minutes. I nodded again. This time Tarbus knocked with the hilt of his *spatha*. Again, there was no answer. He had to pound three times before one of the tall, twin doors creaked open.

'The hour for receiving *clientes* and *consultores* is over,' said a *dispensator*. He made to slam the door in our faces but Tarbus' boot blocked the threshold.

I stepped to Tarbus' side. 'I am the *Magister Agentium in Rebus,* Marcus Gregorianus Numidianus. We come from the Castra Peregrina to speak to one Lollianus of this house, sixth son of Gaius Ceionius Rufius Volusianus, known as Lampadius.'

'Lollianus is too young for any business with your kind,' he answered, pushing the door against Tarbus' foot.

'We bring a warrant for Lollianus' arrest from the Magistrate of the Urban Courts acting on a complaint from the Deputy Prefect of the *Annonae*.'

The *dispensator* twitched a little smile, saying, '*Annonae*? Any boy of this house hardly needs to steal bread. Besides, the boy's not at home.'

'Please call the head of the house.'

'*Praefectus* Lampadius is a very busy man. He's seen clients all morning. Write to him for an appointment.'

Tarbus' hobnailed boot didn't budge. We waited, meeting the *dispensator*'s mounting insistence with silence. Finally, the *dispensator* tried to push Tarbus' boot aside again but the resulting scuffle left the *dispensator* leaning hard on the door, but powerless to dislodge Tarbus' limb.

'What's going on?'

The *dispensator* made way for a man about thirty. The Ceionian family features—pointed jaw, close-set eyes, tall brow— were obvious. I recited the reason for our appearance, as required.

'I'm Publilius, eldest son of the house,' he answered. 'There must be some mistake. There has been no summons for my brother and no communication of charges from any plaintiff. Show me this so-called warrant.'

I held the document up for his scrutiny and pointed out the particular court and magistrate's name for reference. Publilius wanted to take it from me, but I didn't relinquish it. The elder brother dropped his waiting hand and masked his frustration.

'Our family's legal advisers will make our answer known to the magistrate in writing without delay. I believe we enjoy that right?'

He displayed natural authority, this Publilius. It was the best of bluffs, delivered in impeccable Latin carrying a whiff of Palatine dining rooms. Few would challenge the scion of the Ceionii when faced with such a reasonable guarantee. If I hadn't been confident of my procedural protection, I might have hesitated. If the charge had been a minor misdemeanor, I might have even relented.

'Please do record your objections for the magistrate. In the meantime, the law requires we take custody of Lollianus. The charge of *maleficium* is too grave to leave him here.'

'Of course, there's the law,' Publilius said with a knowing smile, 'but there's also the unwritten custom of Roma observed by civilized men. Out of respect for this great house, surely you understand, we can't hand Lollianus over to just anyone.'

I'd brought my identity papers with me and now held these up for Publilius' scrutiny. At my nod, Tarbus and Vibius did the same, all the while with Tarbus still balancing on one boot. We risked moving from drama to farce.

'Who's at the door?' shouted a voice from within the *fauces*. Another Ceionian, a few years younger, appeared behind Publilius in the doorway. He needed a bath and a shave. I suspected a long night out on the town.

'*Curiosi* come for the kid,' Publilius muttered.

'Little Lolli? That's ridiculous! Tell them he's busy,' barked the younger man. 'I'm Caeionius Albinus. State your business and be done with it.'

'What a relief! Your little brother's at home, after all,' I said with a patient smile at the lying *dispensator*. Despite myself, I admired their swift and confident good brother-bad brother defense of a silly sibling.

I turned my back and murmured to Vibius, 'They're playing for time. Go warn Defendens.' Vibius sauntered away along the terraced wall.

'Where's your man going?' Caeionius Albinus asked.

'We'll be waiting here some time, I expect. I don't need him.'

The two brothers conferred with backs turned. The rain turned from drizzle to downpour. We stood our ground, water streaming off the old gutter above onto our felted hats. Tarbus kept his boot fixed like a stake.

Finally, without any warmth, they gestured Tarbus and myself to come in. The Dacian kept one hand on the hilt of his *spatha* and the other resting on the *pugio* hanging from his belt.

Caeionius Albinus muttered to Publilius, 'I'll fetch Hatarius.'

The two brothers abandoned us in the public atrium where the rain cascaded down from the *compluvius* in the roof overhead into a large square pool at our feet. Its bottom was a dirt-crusted, cracked mosaic of Neptune surrounded by dancing goldfish. Two tines of the god's trident had broken away and been filled in with cheap grout. The aquatic god was left holding a long black toothpick.

A whiff of cheap frankincense coming off an imposing resin-caked and soot-coated *lararium* battled the damp air. The heavy scent mingled with the lingering aroma of old-fashioned chamber pots and ageing slaves. This must have been a luxurious residence centuries ago, but now the great reception hall felt uncleanable and irreparable. Small wonder Lampadius had planned a new showpiece in a less dilapidated neighborhood for his retirement.

I told Tarbus to block anyone's exit down the *fauces* tunnel leading to the front doors. I filled the waiting time by strolling alone down the length of the atrium's high walls. It was like walking the edge of a stage before an audience of silent faces; every available space had been filled with *imagines* of Ceionii ancestors. They'd run out of wall space decades ago and my tour was impeded at regular intervals by granite pedestals supporting the busts of more recent antecedents.

And what a mob they were! Here was the death mask of Lampadius' father, Gaius Caeionius Rufus Albinus, born 290, and his grandfather, Gaius Caeionius Rufius Volusianus, born 255 and great-grandfather, Marcus Caeionius Varo, born 225 and Roma's urban prefect in 284 and 295.

There was some relief for the visitor in a small reclining statue of Varo's mother, Flavia Postumia Varia, a comely young matron of Roma, born during the golden reign of Septimius Severus, and wife of—yes—another Caeionius.

Consul in 106, Lucius Ceionius Commodus Verus was too important to bunt right up to the ceiling, where his own Republican father Lucius Ceionius Commodus and grandfather Ceionius Commodus—that final mask where the family tree reached its towering apex of illustriousness around ten years before the birth of the Christians' 'Savior'—hovered like the supervising *genius* of the clan.

So the stern Consul remained, yellowed and sour-lipped, just at the level of my eyebrows, squeezed in between Caeionius Caeionius of 150, Caeionius Caeionius of 175, and a third Caeionius bigwig born in 200. Caeionius Plautius born in 102 had been shunted higher to make way for his son, Marcus Caeionius Silvanus.

Dozens upon dozens of painted eyes, graven cheeks, and unsmiling lips bore variations on that sharp jaw, high brow, and a certain droop of earlobe. And if there'd been any doubt, here were the names repeating themselves in dizzying variations: the Caieonii, Lolliniae, Lampadiae, Albinae, and Plautiae.

And after twenty tedious minutes of reading plaques, dates, and dedications, I realized I'd been neglected here for this very purpose. I'd been granted enough time to study and learn who I dared take on—enough time to realize my mistake and depart.

But this gambit didn't work on me. I'd arrived at a very dull plaster face when a cultured baritone boomed behind my right shoulder, 'Prefect Lampadius declines to see you, *Magister*. I am Secretary Hatarius. I must copy your warrant for the family lawyers' reference.'

He must be a very senior secretary to Lampadius—that much was obvious in his grizzled hair, round-shouldered comportment, unadorned but impeccable long tunic covering bare legs, and gnarled fingers bunioned from decades of pressing *stilus* into wax.

'I have no choice, Hatarius. We cannot leave without the boy.'

'The youth left the house some time ago in the company of his mother, *Matrona* Caecinia Lolliana.'

'Please tell Lampadius it won't work. Every soul hanging on this wall would second my advice—to flee is unworthy and un-Roman. And besides, it's futile—'

A woman's shriek echoed through the hall. Defendens and Vibius were coming toward us from the peristyle garden behind the far end of the atrium, hauling a girl forward by her *palla*, her white legs kicking and flailing, one sandal missing. She was wailing herself hoarse.

To one side of this chaotic trio flew a Fury in dark red brocade. Her claws were working at Defendens' neck while her other hand was pulling him away from his captive by the loose *baltea* dangling from his belt.

Defendens' face streamed with the sweat of fending off two desperate females at once. It was with relief and triumph that Vibius took control. He pushed the girl, her makeup streaked by tears and rainfall, to the floor in front of me like a gangly, wet wool sack. Vibius held her down while Defendens bent over double, hands on knees, and fought for breath.

'Get your hands off her!' screeched the mistress of the house. I could tell by the slaves' expressions, they'd suffered such a tongue-lashing often enough themselves.

At the sound of his wife's screeching, Lampadius at last showed his face. He lurched on stiff legs down the long, enclosed corridor that ran down the side of the house from his private chambers.

Vibius addressed me alone: 'He dropped out of a tree hanging over the wall and gave me quite a chase down the street but then he doubled back and Defendens followed him back over the wall and brought him to ground in the slaves' latrine.'

The father's embrace and the mother's shrieking curses confirmed that the girl fumbling inside the unfamiliar folds of a borrowed *tunica* and *palla*, was our boy Lollianus.

'Seen enough, Castra Dogs?' Lampadius shouted. 'Yes, of course, I recognize you, Freedman Numidianus. Your insignia mean nothing here. I would have expected that you, of all people, so lowborn in the House of Manlius, would have divined your true position under this roof and accepted our terms.'

He pulled the *palla* off the boy's brow. 'Look! Peach fuzz—no more! Now get out of here, all of you! I'll deal with this Pannonian prefect myself. Go to your room, Lolli.'

But Defendens kept pressing the kneeling boy firmly down by the shoulders while Tarbus bound the boy's wrists behind his back. It was a matter of seconds for me to repeat the charges for the third time.

Lampadius grabbed my arm. 'Come, now, Numidianus, stop this. You risk a charge of *calumnia* on yourself with these ridiculous accusations! Someone's fallen for envious gossip! Slave's tittle-tattle! And you know something of that, right?'

Lampadius glanced around his gathering household as if a traitor was hiding among the clusters of gawking slaves.

I held my temper. 'It's too late, Prefect. The boy compiled a book of superstition: poisonous concoctions, curses and spells, the application of black magic, etc. I expect the magistrate already holds a copy of his compendium as evidence. Lollianus will stand trial for the crime of *maleficium*. Read the details of our warrant.'

Turning white-faced, Lampadius managed only a weak chuckle. 'How sad that for the head of your particular department, you're so misinformed. *Magister* Apodemius would never have committed this error.'

'Error? Then an open trial will provide justice and exact the correct punishment on his accusers.'

'I should think so! *Maleficium*? Who calls it *maleficium*? Who dares? Some ignorant, upstart Christian, right? My boy was only studying *haruspicina*, the rituals of our ancient cult.'

And the old man looked to his household for some reassuring laughs. He got none.

'Save your defense for the magistrate, but there's no point denying it, Prefect. Everyone in Roma knows of it. My own Egyptian slave heard about your son's book at the Baths of Caracalla. Let's go, Tarbus.'

'But it wasn't even finished!' Lollianus sobbed.

'Shut up!' Lampadius wheeled around and kicked his son.

We'd moved back from farce to tragedy. I was keen to bring down the curtain.

'Vibius, take the evidence sack to the boy's room. Collect any pamphlets, vials, measuring spoons, wax tablets, papyrus notes, distillations, tokens—whatever he might have used as reference tools for his book. They'll probably be concealed—but not very well. Take his chamber slaves with you. They'll know where to search.'

Old Lampadius started wheedling:

'But it was just a parlor game, Numidianus! You're half-Roman. You grew up among us. You know our entertainments to survive a hot summer evening! Who would take his childish hobby so seriously?'

Actually, it was a good question. He knew his browbeaten slaves were guiltless. Who indeed had contributed this adolescent's name to Maximinus' list of criminals? Could there be any connection between the three goons suspected of the poisoning attempt against Chilo and this gullible idiot's hodgepodge of *magicos apparatus*, magic recipes, or wicked prayers, those *nefarias preces*?

Certainly *Pater* Lampadius had made many political and commercial enemies over his long career. And there was that tempting slotted box dangling outside Maximinus' dockside offices. Perhaps Maximinus himself didn't know the identity of his informant against Lollianus.

Caecinia Lolliana burst out. 'Stop being so weak, Lampadius! They're going to torture our child! The pain of *cruciatis tormentorum*? No! Not my son! Never! Never!'

I stepped around the cowering youth to face his mother.

'No, *Matrona*, Lollianus is a member of the senatorial class. He's protected from interrogation under torture, *majestatis immunitas*, unless suspected of treason against the state under the *lex majestatis*. Grave as these charges are, there's no accusation of treason in this warrant. I would not fear torture. But I would prepare for a thorough trial that might include further accusations of *stellionatus*—trickery or fraud—and the like.'

Lampadius pulled me away from his frantic wife. 'That's not good enough, Numidianus. You mistake our objection. We have no reason to fear a hearing that teaches the boy a needed lesson. But as you well know, the old days of Roman justice are over and juries a thing of the past. There can be no true and fair trial. We shall appeal this, *Matrona*, we shall appeal this, before it's too late!'

The sniveling boy was on his feet at last. A house slave presented trousers, a grown man's traveling cloak, and a pair of street shoes.

'Clean off his face,' I ordered his hysterical mother. 'And he'll need a warmer tunic.' She went off with a slave to prepare a basin of hot water.

Lampadius seized on his wife's absence to double down on his pitiful bargaining. He gripped my arm like a man clinging to wreckage in a roiling sea of pride.

'Have pity on his mother's distress,' he whispered. 'Leave Lollianus here until his trial. We'll find a *fideiussor* as guarantor this very day. But no chains or shackles—no *vincula*—for the boy, I beg of you, Numidianus.'

Publilius weighed in: 'No chains! The disgrace, the *infamia*, for all of us, is unthinkable. Only *custodia libera*, we beg you.'

Custodia libera, house arrest, was a way for the senatorial class to protect its standing in society's eyes from the shame of incarceration. It was always applied to highborn women. They awaited trial under the supervision of a *fideiussor*, a guarantor from another noble house making a gesture of *amiticia*.

But in helping the boy attempt escape, Lampadius' family had compromised its *honesta*, the honor system on which *custodia libera* depended.

I hesitated. Lampadius saw his opening and grabbed it. He drew me deeper into the atrium, out of the earshot of Defendens, the wailing boy, his two brothers and dozens of slaves.

'You're a true Roman, Marcus Gregorianus Numidianus. I knew your master, Commander Gregorius. In my own youth, I even heard his father declaiming in the Senate. The Manlius House was great once, with a long memory. Surely, its freedman knows who we Ceionii really are.'

Lampadius stretched out his arms to direct my attention to the atrium walls where hundreds of dead Romans awaited Lollianus' fate.

Who we were, echoed the *imagines*. It was their ancient cry of privilege, honor, *Romanitas*, but it sat ill on Lampadius' shoulders. Remember, I'd witnessed him, Constantius II's trusted councilor, pass those forgeries that killed General Claudius Silvanus. Yes, I knew who Lampadius really was.

'You hesitate, *Magister* Numidianus! I see you understand us.'

'I'm waiting for my man Vibius to return with the evidence and your Hatarius to finish his copying.'

'Listen to me. If not *custodia libera*, then *custodia* under a state-appointed guarantor. Give us time to appeal to Treverorum.'

'An appeal to the Emperor?'

'It's our only chance. I confess, I'd consulted the new *Praefectus Urbi* Publius Ampelius before this—in confidence, of course—about the risks of my foolish boy's scribblings.'

So the fearful Lampadius had tried to rig an absolution before any arrest. Yes, that was the Lampadius of 355.

'Ampelius has hardly assumed office. What did he advise?'

'He's a lightweight! All Ampelius cares about is laying curfews on street sales of grilled meats! Says the better classes shouldn't be seen eating in public! But when I bring him a real problem, what does he do? Recites precedent; *humiliores* in possession of magical books are beheaded, but *honestiores* are stripped of all possessions and exiled. Beyond that, he begs off, says only Valentinian himself could acquit Lollianus. I should have acted sooner.'

'Perhaps Ampelius knows that the power of Prefect Maximinus is growing under the Emperor, not diminishing.'

'But an appeal to the Emperor is worth a try. Give me ten days, no, two weeks at least. Have your fastest rider carry my appeal without stopping. I'll pay, I'll pay for the white feather of urgency in your rider's *pilleus* and I'll pay for any other . . . expenses. You do understand me.'

'I understand you very well.'

A bribe . . . Roma's most notorious miser was desperate now.

'Whatever you ask, Numidianus. Valentinian can't let this pass. Not to the House of the Ceionii. He's not that secure. And when he saves my son from this serpent of a Pannonian, he'll thank you for the chance to redress this injustice. Please, *Magister*, you have sons of your own, do you not?'

Notice how I was no longer 'Castra Dog? Freedman? Half-Roman?' I was now '*Magister*,' the head of an imperial *schola* with a warrant to arrest his quivering sprig-in-lipstick. The old scoundrel felt no shame trying to buy me. He showed no regard for the *Romanitas* due his illustrious lineage—or mine.

'I offer you this, Lampadius. We'll hold the boy in the Castra under *custodia militaris* pending the Emperor's reply. This will keep him safe from illegal mistreatment and give you time to prepare his defense. This much the *Schola Agentium in Rebus* will do for the House of Ceionii.'

It would also give me time to find out if Lollianus' black magic had links to the Chilo case.

'Thank you, thank you, *Magister* Numidianus. I'll go tell his mother the hopeful news. Hatarius will prepare our letter to Valentinian. Yes, that's better. We'll send it by our own means and it will fly like Mercury to the court, faster than any *agens* on wings!'

He'd realized nothing he sent with my riders would stay secret. I was sure he intended something desperate. We left that unhappy stately home and plunged back into the pounding rain with the weeping Lollianus in tow. The towering Tarbus cleared the usual throng for Vibius and myself but Defendens trailed behind. The young guard slowed his own pace when the shocked Lollianus stumbled over a square boulder bridging a gutter at the base of the Caelian Hill. From time to time, he adjusted the oversized cloak back over the boy's thin shoulders.

'*Magister*?' Tarbus grunted with a glance over his shoulder.

'I spotted them.'

Two men in hooded cloaks lanolin'ed against the rain marched exactly a block behind us. They dodged between clusters of pedestrians and carts to keep a steady, safe distance, always within sight but never too close. No insignia or *orbiculi* signaled their rank or department. Their faces were scarfed against the weather.

I wasn't alarmed. It was the natural precaution of such an important clan. So what if Lampadius wanted to make sure his son went safely past Tullianum Prison and all the way to the Castra? He judged all men by his own wiles. And I didn't doubt his affection for 'Lolli'.

Who could predict how my own sons Verus and Atticus might turn out? A privileged upbringing held pitfalls. In my lifetime in Roma, I'd seen the pastimes of good reading, healthy sport, and a love of nature give way to frivolous fashions and dangerous party games. The temples were silent. Roma's book stalls had closed. The libraries at the Baths gathered dust. The Manlius house had been lucky to find Rhetor Drusus for its heir Leo and to send him off to Burdigala to study under the poet Ausonius, now tutoring Caesar Gratian. I intended to do as well for our twins.

But modern times were against conscientious parents. Why or how had Lampadius and Caecinia Lolliania let their sixth child, one of four sons, fill youthful idleness with a fevered obsession with darkness and evil?

The rain softened as we passed through the Castra's old gates. Lollianus was installed in a locked cell overlooking the courtyard. I dismissed Tarbus and Vibius with thanks, but took Defendens upstairs to my office and summoned Saturnus to join us:

'Now, listen carefully, Defendens. For the next two weeks, you'll be Lollianus' personal guard. Make friends. Gain his trust. Get him to talk about this book of his. Act impressed with his hard-won expertise in magic.'

'But I'm a Christian, *Magister*.'

'You're a *curiosus* first, aren't you? So, for the gods' sakes, act curious!'

'Why pretend interest in that gibberish?'

'Because a good *agens* is not only a tough rider and keen watcher, he's a sympathetic listener—with a purpose. Lollianus doesn't strike me as a creative genius kissed by the Muses. He didn't make up his spells and poisons out of thin air.'

Defendens' features relaxed with relief. 'So you think he didn't write the book himself? You think he's innocent?' It was obvious the youngster believed in some innocent-until-proven-guilty ideal.

'No, Lollianus wrote it all right. Find out his sources. Remember every name you can—soothsayer, gladiator, charioteer, potion-maker, and especially, listen for a fortune-teller named Campensis or a wrestling coach named Asbolius. And wait— there's one more name—'

I fished out my notes on that magic trial during my absence, tossed out of court thanks to the late Victorinus' intervention: the brothers Tarracius Bassus and Camenius with two pals Marcianus and Eusaphius—all of them senatorial rank. After Apollonia's comment, I'd fished up what information the Castra had on it.

'Here it is. There was another case a few months ago where four senators employed a charioteer called Auchenius to teach them the art of poisoning. See if Lollianus knows Auchenius.'

'But don't let him see you taking notes,' Saturnus warned.

'Why would he tell me anything? I'm a stable boy, a nobody compared to his great family.'

'Because you're not much older than him. And precisely because you already know who you are, whereas he's only the runt of a great litter. He craves attention. He wrote this book to earn celebrity in the kind of society his elders hold in esteem.'

'Well, it's better than standing night watch without Anthimus,' Defendens sighed.

Saturnus saw the fatigue weighing on my face. He explained to our country recruit what he would be dealing with.

Roman gladiators and charioteers enjoyed a lurid reputation and not just for living fast and dying young. Any athlete who survived the blood-soaked circus past his thirtieth birthday was rightfully suspected of attracting more than natural luck. These popular slaves ruled the world of lucky charms, incantations, and *defixiones*, those violent texts hawked by all the athletes and traded among superstitious fans and rival teams.

This created a lively market in powerful spells endorsed by any thug sporting laurels, even if *defixiones* made for disgusting reading—calling on daemons to crush the bones of an opponent under a horse team or to lacerate and dismember a driver.

Defendens' eyes widened. Lampadius had been right to consult Prefect Ampelius. Lollianus had been flirting too long with this vicious community's commerce that barely skirted criminal *veneficium*, the most polluting category of black magic.

Many of the bloated corpses clawed out of the Tiberis River tide each morning were casualties of this sordid world. But the dead weren't all victims of poison and spells. At least a few were blackmailing middlemen. They would frame an innocent citizen with accusations of how he'd employed a charioteer's illegal skills and then collect the hush money—only to be murdered by the charioteer himself to pocket all the profits.

Sometimes the victim was merely an inconvenient witness to such dirty transactions. Sometimes he was a disgruntled customer threatening exposure after an overpriced spell or poison turned out to be useless fakery.

After this sordid briefing, Defendens muttered, 'That boy's lucky still to be alive.'

'Do you think we'll learn anything?' Saturnus asked me as the young guard's footsteps faded down the stairs.

'When Lollianus sees how much Defendens wants to think well of him, he'll talk. He'll want to make a friend.'

I hoped there was a link to the Chilo case. We had about two weeks while Lampadius' appeal traveled to Valentinian. Saturnus would bring Defendens to our Chilo debriefing a few days from now to share the confidences of his new 'friend'.

I had Cyrillus draft a notice to the urban magistrate that the Castra would hold Lollianus pending the result of his father's appeal to the imperial court. Then I started for home with Amosis at my heels.

At first light tomorrow I'd go to the Tullianum to question the wrestler, organ-maker, and soothsayer. I certainly did not think well of them and I did not expect to make friends. I just wanted to learn what Maximinus had tortured out of them without another day's delay.

CHAPTER 8, THE SENATE'S REBUKE

—THE CURIA IULIA—

As a *volo* bastard slave attending Commander Gregorius in the North African field, I'd been talent-spotted by one of Apodemius' retired *agentes*. Leontus was a prosperous Roman colonial merchant and landholder in Numidia. At a summons to his study, I'd been tested by Apodemius himself, disguised as an elderly visitor. I had a lot of faults as a young *agens*—I still have them as a middle-aged man—but my quick eyes and sharp memory had won me a chance to join the Castra service. And over many tough missions, those eyes and memory had often saved my life.

Crafty old Lampadius had made his own error in leaving me to study the family tree. Because I was, as he so rightly reminded me, a former child slave and a survivor of many tedious evenings in a Roman society dining room. And now, by comparing memories of those long-ago gossipy stories with the *imagines* on the wall, I'd made a connection.

Two of the men the late Victorinus allegedly got off— Tarracius Bassus and his brother Alfenius Ceionius Julianus Camenius—were members of the Caeonii Julianus branch. That meant they merged with Lampadius' branch about five generations back. They were all great-great-grandsons of that Urban Prefect Marcus Caeionius Varo, himself a grandson of Caeionius Caeionius of 175.

Was this significant? Or just inevitable coincidence? After all, Roman elites intermarried for centuries. Not everyone was a Ceionian or Anician, but it wasn't hard for any snob or social climber to scrounge up a connection somehow, somewhere, to the Reburri, Falvonii, Ragonii, Ferasii, Pammachii, Vitrasii . . .

At the street corner I tossed a few coins at the *comital* shrine and bid good evening to Flaccus. The rain had left his perch more bedraggled than usual. He was pulling faded garlands off an overhead arch.

I sidestepped a huge puddle to dive under the shelter of the enclosure. 'Did you ask around for us, *Vicomagister*, about the missing earrings? I'd be happy for any information, even via a middleman, no questions asked, of course.'

'Nothing, *Magister* Numidianus,' he shrugged. 'There's not much market these days for the kind of bauble you described. People like the newer fashions I guess. Don't they, Venus?'

He patted the dog settled at his feet. Venus was our neighborhood bitch, collarless and unwanted. Her matted fur stank of the urine of the laundry vats down the street. Today she looked pregnant and hungry.

I was back to mulling over the 'coincidence' of the Ceionian cousins all dabbling in sorcery when I found the *circitores* Avitus and Numa huddled over a bench in the privacy of the *fauces* just inside the front door. They were enjoying a discreet game of dice but my first reaction was one of alarm.

'Any reason to guard the entrance so closely, Avitus?'

'No, *Magister*.'

'No one restricted your movements inside?'

The two young men glanced at each other in embarrassment.

'I see. The twins are too much for you?'

'Well, they're a . . . playful pair, *Magister*.'

'You mean rambunctious and spoiled. I completely understand.'

'How much longer are we assigned here, *Magister*?'

A burst of boyish laughter came from the kitchen wing. My brooding over sinister dangers in the twins' future dispersed as lightly as that afternoon rain shower. My fears for the household seemed exaggerated. Should I send Avitus and Numa back to the Castra?

Apollonia was checking the table setting in the garden where the wet flowers released their perfume and lanterns cast flickering shadows against the tall walls that gave us privacy. She wanted to eke out every last evening in the summer *triclinium* before moving our meals indoors.

'I'm sorry, my love. Still no lead on who might have fenced those earrings. Flaccus just implied they were worthless.'

'The stones weren't, even if the settings were . . . but perhaps he's right. Anepsia still refuses to let us pay.'

There was only a half-moon and the garden lanterns caught her brow furrowed with discomfort rather than relief. For the reputation of our house, we both would have felt better to have the episode settled more honorably, at any cost. To have it dismissed too publicly reflected badly on our standing, financial and social.

'Perhaps one of your other friends, that Charitas, for example, could hint that we're not so grateful to be left in her debt? In my position, it could backfire.'

'I haven't seen Charitas since the garden party,' she murmured. Was there a rift between the two women?

'If you have to know,' she said after a telling silence, 'I've long suspected Charitas is having an affair. And before you try to sniff it out of me, my darling *curiosus*, I don't know the man's name.'

I sat down on the same bench Charitas had lounged on that sunlit afternoon. I reached out for my wife. She settled into my lap and nuzzled my neck.

'I don't want anyone to be unhappy,' she said. 'So I don't judge others. But I lived too long, safe and hidden by Apodemius to take such things in my stride, as if sophisticated, modern women laugh off *stuprum* like naughty children who think they're clever.'

'Is her marriage very unhappy?'

Instead of answering, she kissed me. I understood. She didn't want to dwell on her friend's misfortunes or waste time on the floundering love lives of others. We must cherish our own good fortune.

I must have kissed this woman now a thousand times but tonight Charitas' waywardness made our own time together seemed fresh, urgent, almost furtive. As Apollonia reached with a familiar hand to loosen my belt, I murmured Catulo's love invitation to Lesbia in her ear, '*Nox est perpetua una dormienda, da mi basia mille, deinde centum, Dein mille altera, dein secunda centum, Deinde usque altera mille, deinde centum.* Our night should last forever, a thousand kisses and a hundred more, a thousand more again, and another hundred more, let us lose track . . .'

I wasn't very original in my seductions, resorting to another man's tried-and-true phrases to moisten my wife's thighs, but it worked. We lost track of time and even forgot the waiting meal.

When we emerged from our chamber, hungrier than ever, the household had given up on us and retired to their own beds. The half-moon had gone behind a cloud and the garden lanterns had burnt out. We made do like slave children thieving behind the cook's back. Apollonia rustled up cold pigeon in garum sauce and some dried fruits and nuts. We ate by the light of a palm lamp in the kitchen. I smoothed the loosened coils of her hair and pulled the soft blanket covering her shoulders a little closer against the chill of the bare stone walls. At that moment, it was as if Roma itself was forgotten. There was no one in the world who counted for me but Apollonia.

꘎꘎꘎

'You from the family of the accused?'

Two Tullianum wardens on duty chuckled. They were chewing on long sausages, like dogs gnawing at raw sheep legs. The idea that any of their prisoners still had family who claimed them seemed hilarious.

'No.'

'Well, you can't be legal either, 'cause we've seen their *causidicus* once or twice, haven't we, young Pinnius? You see, this one here and I got the same name—Pinnius. Coincidence, ain't it? When was the last time their advocate visited, Pinnius? July?'

Pinnius the Younger shrugged. 'More like June, I reckon. Complained about the stink below, remember?'

The Guards Pinnii sneered at that, too.

It was the busiest hour of early morning, when the city took advantage of the cool weather to get business done. But these two seemed at leisure, their line of work not requiring even a shave or bath. Yesterday's rain had left puddles in the broken paving around the ancient prison entrance. The two guards had set out stools facing the Curia to watch the world pass through the imperial *fora* of Nerva, Vespasian, and Augustus. Between the jail and the neighboring *Tabularium* housing the Republic's ancient records, ran the Gemonian stairs ascending the northeastern slope to the Arx of the Capitoline Hill. To think this grimy, shabby setting had once been the very heart of the world's greatest empire.

'So,' Pinnius the Elder said, 'If you're not family bringing food and medicine or some kind of lawyer trying to save them from their very, very, very obvious fate, then you can't get in, *Magister*.'

'That's absurd. I'm the head of the *Schola Agentium in Rebus*.'

'Well, ain't that my point? I'd say your *schola*'s job—arresting and all that—your job's done once they're in our hands.'

He was not the fool he looked and he pressed his point.

'Them's the rules, *Magister*. You see, supposing these prisoners had enemies—and that's a healthy theory, ain't it? Or they wouldn't be rotting down below, would they? Even enemies as respectable and important as you, *Magister* Numidianus? And supposing we let those enemies into our cells? And supposing we discovered our prisoners next day not so much better off for your visit? Supposing we found them a little, say, short of breath? And who'd have to answer to the magistrate who put'em there? And who'd have to answer to the plaintive who asked the magistrate to put'em there?'

'You would.'

'Well, we would, wouldn't we? Pinnius Junior and myself.'

I reached for the money purse concealed inside my baldric, but he laid a rough hand over mine, saying, 'Thank you, *Magister*, but I'm smarter than that. It's not worth my weight in *solidi*. I like to lock the shackles, not wear them.'

'So whom do I need to see?'

'Well, if I remember right, those three are here on charges of *veneficium* and attempted murder on the request of *Praefectus Annonae* Maximinus. Go ask him for permission. I just seen him heading for the Senate. They're hearing the appeal of Proconsul Hymetius today.'

'Not likely to see the likes of Julius Festus Hymetius in here,' said Pinnius Junior with a smirk. 'We don't host many proconsuls here, do we, Pinnius?'

I headed through the Arch of Septimius Severus to the Curia Julia in the corner of the Forum. Vendors and beggars blocked the steps up to its great bronze and oak entrance doors.

I took my time. How could I request access to Maximinus' key suspects in the Chilo case without tipping my hand? The

Pannonian would ask why I interfered. He'd refuse—no—worse—he'd bargain his scruffy stooges for access to the *schola* files.

Even before I passed the Niger Lapis, I heard the rhetoric of a prosecutor thundering away inside the hallowed hall. I produced my insignia and crossed the threshold so familiar to me as a slave child carrying the belongings of the blind Senator.

The prosecutor, a pompous man with thin curling strands pommaded flat over his balding pate, was midway through the state's case against Hymetius. I squeezed myself on a bench near the rear between senatorial scribes, *lictores*, *apparitores*, and slave-runners. Prefect Maximinus was seated many rows down front of me, next to the new *Praefectus Urbi* Publius Ampelius who famously worried about upright citizens eating barbecued ribs in the street.

'. . . find yourselves here, as Julius Festus Hymetius wastes his time, your time, the Senate's time, only because a cheap appeal to a busy sovereign has won him a few more weeks of life.'

I spotted the noble Praetextatus, buffered from importuning colleagues by two secretaries and two liveried attendants, in the uppermost corner of the opposite benches. His eyes were half-closed, as if Senate attendance was an easy solution to a nap. I myself could not have dozed through this prosecutor's shouting:

'. . . and we know how, when Hymetius was governing Africa, he took grain intended for the bellies of decent citizens of this city and sold it instead to the hungry Carthaginians. How he deceitfully restored supplies only once the harvest was in? How he thought no one in Roma would notice his profiteering?'

'But Carthago was starving!' shouted someone in the front—the defendant Hymetius?

The prosecutor boomed back, 'Oh, yes! The Carthaginians were starving, so Hymetius bought thirty bushels for one *solidus* and for the same price sold the locals only ten bushels and thus produced magnificent "profits" for our imperial treasury. But justice was swift! Emperor Valentinian investigated! And for Hymetius' double-dealing, Valentinian fined our "illustrious" friend a part of his property. Was that not lenient enough for this crook, my colleagues?'

The Senate stomped a few feet, as required, but they seemed impatient for the proceedings to move along.

'No, the defendant Hymetius was not satisfied. But that, my esteemed Senators, is not where the crux of this morning's story lies, that is not why we must hear this despicable Hymetius' appeal for yet more mercy today. The grain fraud case is closed. We gather to hear his appeal because the man before you stands convicted of *veneficium*, of heinous dabbling in the blackest magic.'

There was noticeable discomfort on the benches at hearing rumors confirmed.

'Hymetius employed the soothsayer Amantius to perform forbidden sacrifices on his behalf. And of course, Amantius denied this with all the oaths under Olympus, even when he was bent and broken on the rack, but even as he was denying his wickedness, the state discovered papers hidden in his house—papers in the accused's own handwriting. Hymetius' letter begged the foul sorcerer to prevail on the Deities and use forbidden blood sacrifice in order to mollify the Emperor—note, Hymetius wrote our "cruel and excessive" emperor—yes, my friends, Hymetius' treasonous words in his very handwriting . . .'

An odd undercurrent swept across the room. Was it my imagination? Or was the senators' reaction to this invective—so criminal on the face of it—pretty sympathetic?

Maximinus glanced at Ampelius. Had he caught this frisson crossing the benches, too? Were the two officials worried? They'd hidden their initial hearing of Proconsul Hymetius in the suburban hills of the Ocriculum magistracy, some thirty miles safe from the city's heart of political sentiment, where they'd felt free to condemn Hymetius to death, yet here . . .

' . . . so, my friends, is any senator surprised that, when the Emperor heard this report from the judges, he demanded another thorough investigation? And then, what was discovered?'

He took a theatrical pause. Hungry stomachs were growling.

'Hymetius' personal adviser, *Conciliarius* Frontinus, was charged with drafting a treasonous prayer to accompany this blood sacrifice. Of course Frontinus denied it until he was mangled with rods and exiled to the very edge of our civilized world, that sunless island of Britannia. And their sordid partner in all of this, that practitioner of foul spells, Amantius, was executed.'

The prosecutor paused for breath so all of us in the audience could digest the rack, the rods, the forbidden *sacrificia funesta* of blood sacrifice, the execution, and exile to the gale-tossed butt-end of the Western Empire.

'Oh, I've heard enough! I'm hungry! Let's hear the Defense!' chomped a toothless, grizzled senator on the front bench facing Maximinus and Ampelius. He belonged to the Petronii clan.

At the presiding magistrate's invitation, the Defense, such as he was, took the floor. I'd met him years ago as an apple-cheeked law student friend of Leo's. He looked not a day older.

'Magistrate, elders, and statesmen, I am too junior among you to waste your time—'

'Good! Get on with it,' grunted the Petronius codger.

'So I pass over the fact that Hymetius' only so-called "crime" as proconsul was devising a way to save the Empire's citizens in Carthago from famine while at the same time relieving some of our state treasury's grievous deficit—all in service to our esteemed emperors, Valentinian and Gratian. I also pass over that for his so-called crime, your colleague Hymetius has paid dearly already. And I'll omit to recall that those good souls who have tried to assist his return to imperial favor by an appeal to our ancient gods—not entirely a bad thing—have paid a little more dearly indeed.'

Praetextatus opened one eye and allowed himself an indulgent smile. The nervous youngster shouldering this open-and-shut case of the doomed Hymetius was so green from the classroom, he was trotting out every device in public speaking learned at the knee of his classical *rhetor*. He'd imitated Cicero in 'passing over' and 'omitting' the very details he wanted his audience to recall, not to mention the humorous understatement at the end, that *litotes* of 'not entirely a bad thing.'

The youngster wiped his brow with a small linen handkerchief, a classic gesture that drew smiles from more practiced speakers. But this debutant's sweat looked genuine. Was this his first public defense?

'And now Proconsul of Africa, Julius Festus Hymetius, stands on the very edge of death. *Death*! DEATH! Oh, gods, but why?'

Well, you had to admire that repetitive *epizeuxis* with each 'death' delivered in a fresh tone—first authority, then hushed shock, then horror. And before the trembling graduate had finished his turn, our jaded senators had relished alliteration, allusion, amplification, *antanagoge*, and on down the gamut of speaker's tools from his dogeared rhetoric textbook.

'But all poor Hymetius sought was to convert the Emperor's ill regard to clemency. Clemency for supplying a two-hundred percent profit to the imperial State Treasury, clemency for saving Romans in Carthago from starvation, and clemency for putting his fate in the hands of our eternal gods through sincere prayer and sacrifice.'

Praetextatus leaned forward on one elbow. After all, it was he who'd restored the right to traditional sacrifice in the face of Valentinian's wrath.

'Senators, did Proconsul Hymetius err? Yes, the Defense does not deny it. But what harsher verdict do our historians deliver to any emperor than *saevitia*, cruelty? And what greater compliment do our historians record than an appeal to that same emperor's inner *humanitas*? Fathers of the State, I learned as a schoolboy—'

'—last Tuesday?' barked the cranky Petronius. But the old fart enjoyed being called a 'Father of the State'.

Our nervous Diogenes rallied, 'Actually three weeks ago Friday, *Domine*.'

Well done. Over a ripple of appreciative chuckles, the youngster persevered through a beautiful ending, complete with *epanalepsis*.

'I learned that three centuries ago, in this very chamber, the great Cicero stood defending Ligarius before Julius Caesar. He pleaded *deprecatio*, an appeal for mercy. As Ligarius stood charged with treason, the *rei publicae utilitas*, our public good, was at stake. But Cicero found a way around that. He trusted, "Not so much to the strength of our case as to Caesar's *humanitas*." Yes, Cicero relied on Caesar's *clementia*, *misericordia*, and *humanitas*. So, are we still caesars? Or hyenas? The Defense for Proconsul Julius Festus Hymetius today appeals to the virtue that distinguishes all Romans from beasts, *humanitas*.'

He bowed his head and whispered, '*Humanitas*.'

Praetextatus stood and clapped. The old men of the Curia burst into applause. The magistrate nodded approval. The Petronius coot pulled himself to his gnarled feet with his walking stick and croaked up at his fellow senators. 'Exile, not death. Now, can somebody get me to the toilets?'

A man sobbed near the front—Hymetius himself?—through the magistrate's sentence, exile to the Dalmatian island of Boae.

Prefect Maximinus shot to his feet and rushed past my bench before I could ask to see his jailed suspects. He stormed out through the tall double doors. So I lingered as far greater names, eager for their midday meal, filed out behind a defeated Ampelius. Only Praetextatus acknowledged me as I waited just inside the doors.

'Life at the Castra must be tedious, Numidianus, for you to waste your time here.' A rebuke for not yet solving the Chilo case?

'I thought there might be a link between Hymetius' soothsayer and the Chilo case.' I could hardly admit I was here to beg a favor of Maximinus.

'Amantius had nothing to do with the Chilo *haruspex*.'

'Let Campensis tell me himself. I can't get into the Tullianum.'

'A note from an ex-city prefect will open those chilly depths. I'll send it to the Castra by nightfall.'

I thanked him as we emerged into the sun.

'You're right. I detected no connection to the Chilo affair. So why has Maximinus seized this Hymetius case to his bosom?'

'The heart of this case wasn't sorcery, Numidianus, it was Hymetius calling Valentinian "cruel and excessive".'

'Yet Hymetius survives. Because the Senators also think Valentinian "cruel and excessive"?'

'Oh, come now, Numidianus,' Praetextatus laughed, 'You were practically raised in that chamber at the hem of Senator Manlius' robes! The Senate's only a theater. The prosecutor was a clod, while the defense gave a bravura performance. "Death, *death*, DEATH!".'

I laughed. 'It was a pretty stylish debut.'

'Wobbly in bits, but the closing Cicero parallel was a masterstroke. We still appreciate that sort of thing in Roma.'

'Hymetius was lucky to find a *tiro* so fresh out of law school that he'd take on a lost cause.'

'My dear Numidianus, our canny *tiro* guessed that any senators with a shred of breeding left in them must reward him for flattering them as caesars. That's just basic good manners.'

We trailed southeastward behind a column of senators dispersing into the crowds of the Forum. Praetextatus' secretaries and bodyguards, natty in matching gold and maroon, kept a polite distance in two pairs.

Maximinus and Ampelius had met up some twenty feet ahead, so Praetextatus slowed our pace. Through the mingling of pedestrians, *lecticae*, and vendors' carts, they were wrangling over how their easy victory in the obscure suburbs had skidded off-track in the face of an appeal downtown.

'Maximinus doesn't share the Senate's love of oratory?'

Praetextatus' easy smile faded. 'Valentinian is waiting to hear that we executed Hymetius. He'll be outraged to hear Petronius and the other old boys overturned Maximinus' conviction.'

'But Valentinian tossed the appeal to the Senate, right?'

'He'll be furious all the same, Numidianus.'

'Furious with Maximinus? Or furious with the Senate?'

'Both. When the Emperor hears that Hymetius is sunning himself on Boae's rocky shores, Prefect Maximinus will deflect the blame on us Romans, like that shopper over there inspecting a mirror at the glass stall.'

'But Maximinus must be weaker now. When Victorinus died, he lost his most faithful apologist in decent Roman society. This morning he lost a judicial appeal in the heart of the Empire.'

Praetextatus looked me in the eyes, 'No. Maximinus is more dangerous than ever before. He will double down on his anti-vice campaign using his authority from the Chilo case. Until that's pulled out from under him, good Romans cannot sleep soundly.'

That afternoon I double-checked our files: Hymetius' wife was named Praetextata. Of course, of course. Now I understood the great noble's rare appearance in the Senate. It was never about encouraging classical rhetoric in the next generation.

He was just there to look after family. And his fellow senators took note.

CHAPTER 9, THE SHRINE IN THE DARK

—TULLIANUM PRISON—

An hour after dusk, two men in Praetextatus' livery arrived at the Castra gates. They delivered sealed instructions on expensive vellum in the lettering unique to government scribes ordering: '*Magister Agentium in Rebus* Marcus Gregorianus Numidianus be given access to the Chilo Case detainees Asbolius, Sericus, Campensis.'

So far, so good, but as one of my noble mentor's 'good Romans', I didn't sleep well that night. I'd wake up to Apollonia's soft breathing from her bed and the trickling of the atrium fountain outside our chamber, then realize my mind had been churning through questions for the prisoners. My pillow was damp with sweat.

I might get only this one visit to make headway before our Castra team of 'Chilo investigators' compared notes. To ensure the best chance of using my pass from Praetextatus, I traveled as anonymously as possible by Roma's lesser arteries. The *lectica*'s brocade curtains muffled the sound of sweepers, laundry workers, delivery men, market vendors, and messenger slaves taking advantage of the half-empty streets to cross town with speed.

It was not yet a social hour and mine was not a social call.

I'd prepared better than the day before. I carried a bladder of wine, four long Sicilian sausages, and fresh flatbread. The summer sun was rising overhead and the warming flagstones passed under my chair, but the morning felt haunted. Lingering nightmares—one minute I was the interrogator and next the tortured victim—shadowed my soul. My restless night clung like a sticky tunic.

Shivering, I emerged from the *lectica* full of foreboding. Was I so susceptible to the shades of the notorious dead whose last sight on earth was this very same view?

I must be too full of the stories I'd read aloud to the blind Senator Manlius in his dusty study. Despite my imposing garments and comfortable vehicle, I felt suddenly that child again, wide-eyed as my eyes and lips revisited our forebears' primitive horrors.

That great historian of the Republic, Titus Livy, said the Tullianum Prison was built a thousand years ago by Ancus Marcius, the fourth king of Rome.

What a strange man Ancus must have been, adapting an old cistern in ancient rock into an inverted conical prison lined with tufa stone. Ancus dropped his condemned through a hole in the floor into a narrowing black pit where only the original spring provided sustenance for their final days.

Four hundred years ago, my Numidian compatriot King Jugurtha had been tossed into the pit to starve to death, his royal robes stripped from his body and his earlobe torn off by the mobs attending Gaius Marius' triumphal procession through the streets behind me.

Three centuries ago, Vercingetorix, who led the Gauls in revolt against Julius Caesar, wasted for years in the Tullianum before being paraded and strangled.

Cicero executed Publius Cornelius Lentulus Sura and other co-conspirators supporting Lucius Sergius Catilina in that same pit to protect his beloved Republic and Senate from their plot.

Emperor Tiberius dropped his Praetorian, Prefect Lucius Aelius Sejanus, down this hole as well.

Today's Christians say their holy man Peter was thrown into the stench and foulness of the pit. But I must warn you, this is not part of any reliable history.

A sudden scream pierced the quotidian rattle and chatter of the morning crowd. Was it a prisoner within? No, it was only the squawk of a seagull circling overhead for scraps. I hurried ahead, determined to get the truth and escape the cursed place.

'We told you yesterday, *Magister*, no one allowed but family and lawyers for the case.'

I smiled at Pinnius the Elder. 'But I bring the necessary food.' I handed him the sausages. He took them, then stopped me with the flat of his hand.

'You ain't family.'

'Who's to say I'm not?'

'Who's to say you are?'

'This.'

Seconds after showing him Praetextatus' seal, I was bending my head under the low entrance to a set of small grimy rooms ending with a set of winding stone stairs lit by one faint torch.

A sudden, powerful stench sent me reeling.

'Feeling all right, *Magister*?' Pinnius called.

I steadied myself with one hand against the wall with revulsion. Even Roma's greatest sewer, our Cloaca Maxima, was flushed day and night by runoff from the city aqueducts. But here, history stuck and grew, alive and spongy on the walls like rotting flesh clinging to a corpse—terrifying to the touch.

'Make good use of your time, *Magister*, the younger guard barked as he followed me down the steps. 'The Bishop's due soon.'

At the foot of the steps was an irregular, almost circular room under a roof too low for me to stand straight. At my elbow was a neglected shrine—its altar bare and foundation cracked. There was no *vicomagister* in attendance here.

'What *lares* belong here? Military or municipal?' I asked.

'Oh, that's from a long time ago, *Magister*. Only the bishop says prayers, at that altar over there.' Pinnius Younger lifted his torch to shed light on a granite Christian altar flush against the opposite wall.

His torch revealed something worse than a neglected shrine. Lying, leaning, groaning, sleeping—bodies that were once free citizens—spread across the floor—all men awaiting trial. In the center of the room was a hole scarcely wider than a single man— the notorious pit.

'It's impossible here,' I said. 'I'll take Sericus first, but upstairs.'

'I'll find him for you. He sure ain't out behind in the courtyard. The law requires fresh air, bread, and water. We always follow the law, *Magister*,' Pinnius the Younger said, kicking a sleeping man hard in the small of his back to clear his path. 'But not with those legs, not Sericus. He's over here, I think.'

He kept on kicking, lifting heads, and pushing sleeping bodies over on their backs until he'd roused a slumped figure with a punch to his shoulder. 'Wake up, Sericus! The organ-maker, right? Come on. The *Magister Agentium in Rebus* wants you.'

Sericus opened his eyes and made to answer my summons. He crawled forward on his arms, dragging two sliced and broken legs behind him.

'Can't you help him?'

'His friend is strong enough. C'mon! You! Help your mate.'

A man, as tall as myself and twice as powerfully built, stood until his head scraped the roof. He lifted Sericus into his arms to carry him upstairs.

'You're Asbolius?'

The bare-chested coach grunted.

'Bring him upstairs, then leave us until I call you.'

Asbolius' ascent was slowed by heavy *prolixiores catenae*, long chains linking his ankle shackles to the wall. Most of the prisoners weren't chained but his strength and reputation must have made Pinnius the Elder nervous. We yanked the chains free from torsos and limbs in our way. We finally got Sericus settled against the wall upstairs and Asbolius clanked his way back to the cellar, his chains slithering down behind him like twin snakes.

'Give him some of my wine,' I ordered the elder guard. Sericus guzzled down two full goblets. I pushed the bread at him and let his eyes adjust to the light. His prosperous factory manager's clothes—thick trousers and good wool tunic—were filthy.

'That's enough. I don't want you drunk. I want the truth.'

'*Agentes*? You make empty promises, too?'

'Who makes empty promises?'

'Prefect Maximinus. If I told him everything I knew, he promised I wouldn't be touched "by flame or sword." He promised. But I'm still here. And these legs won't heal.' He began to weep.

'I make no such promises. But I need the truth.'

'More wine.'

'In a minute. Did you try to poison Chilo and his wife?'

'Course not. I've said it hundreds of time. Broke my legs, but I'm telling the truth. I never heard his name until they arrested me.'

'So why are you here?'

'They asked me, did I know anyone expert in dark things, things that change a man's Fates.'

'Who asked you? Who?'

He wiped his mouth and blinked at me in the light, like he was seeing me for the first time.

'I did a commission—organ big as a shed, finished in cedar and gilt. Latest in pumps and pedals. Needed six men to lift it onto the wagon. We got there just in time for some party. Shifted it into place. Waited for cash payment.'

He grabbed my wine and drank it down to the dregs.

'Get more wine,' I ordered Pinnius the Younger. 'And enough for the two others.' I gave him coins but Pinnius just stood there.

'But he's not shackled, *Magister*.'

'Oh, for the gods' sake, he's never walking again.'

I shoved the idiot off on his errand. Pinnius the Elder stayed at the main door, already halfway through a sausage and watching the street.

'Now, name them, Sericus, name the clients.'

But Sericus would tell the story his own way.

'They noticed my team, still strong enough to lift and carry but crippled or stupid from the arena.' He tapped his head with a grimy hand. 'I get'em cheap once they're finished like that.'

'Get who cheap?'

'Wrestlers, run-away gladiators—any scum with muscle.'

'Who noticed your team? Then what?'

'Led me out of the dining room and into the garden. Got me alone. Asked me questions. Did any of my men still mix with their old crowd? Keep up with the shady stuff? You know, the black *magicium*, the trade in curses and poisons? They wanted to know—did any of it actually work?'

'And you said yes?'

He broke into a hacking cough. I ordered Pinnius the Elder to fetch us a pitcher of water.

Panting, Sericus resumed: 'I said, sure I did, but for a price, if you get me. After the party, I asked around our factory. And one of our men has a brother who does construction work. He's always on the lookout for strong men hanging around the wrestling schools or gladiator training grounds.'

'And sooner or later you passed these organ clients the name of Asbolius? Then what?'

'Nothing! Nothing until I was hauled in here and they broke my legs, saying I was guilty of trying to poison some turd I never heard of. And that's all I know, I swear by Jupiter and Minerva and—'

'I believe you. What did Asbolius tell you down below?'

'He can tell you himself.'

'I want to hear it from you.'

'He does the trade, all right. In it up to his ears. If he still had ears.' Sericus gave a hoarse chuckle. 'He sent them to that other one, Campensis.'

'He's down below, too?'

'Oh, yes, but don't expect much out of him. He's crafty. If anybody could magic his way out of here, he'd do it. Can I have more wine now?'

I believed Sericus' short, sad story. I knew Maximinus' promise not to touch him with 'flame or sword' in exchange for this meager information wasn't going to save his life.

'The house you delivered the organ to was whose, where, exactly?'

I wanted to shake it out of him but I was too late, even for that. His head lolled on his chest and a dribble of vomit spurted between his lips. The wine had rushed to his empty, starved head. He'd passed out.

'Take him down. Send me Asbolius before the Bishop gets here!' I shouted to old Pinnius. I was sure Maximinus had got the name of the client family—the key to the whole story.

Asbolius halted at the top of the stairs. He straightened up, flexed his mammoth chest, and let me see his pleasure in flexing his spine again. Where once he'd kept his body hairless and oiled, black stubble was sprouting over his shoulders and breast like a beaver's pelt. He stank worse than any beaver.

His shaven head was half-covered, not with a battered *pilleus* of faded wool, as I'd thought glancing at him in the dark, but with a brown-crusted bandage. Where the earlobes should have been, the bandage lay flat against the skull.

The battered stool was almost too flimsy for his heft. His black eyes watched me check the entrance before I took the other stool.

A small smile escaped his lips as he noticed I favored my right leg. He must have been a formidable fighter once—he'd just registered my vulnerable side out of professional habit. Now anger or resignation were all that remained.

'I'm from the Castra Peregrina. Can you hear me through that bandage?'

The younger jailer returned with a cheap plonk from the nearest stall. I handed a cup of wine to the fighter. His wrists were shiny red, raw from shackles worn too long.

He emptied the cup. This man would hold three or four full pitchers of wine without fainting on me.

'Asbolius. You're Greek? Named after the mythical centaur, right?'

He looked at the pitcher. I poured him a second cup. This time, he took barely a sip.

'I've got nothing to say to any *curiosus.*'

'If you think talking to me will ruin your chance of escaping "the flame and the sword", don't count on it.'

His black eyes flared, then turned dull again. So far, he'd trust Maximinus over me.

'So, what was your specialty when you were a star? Before you had to coach? Boxing? Wrestling? Or were you one of those all-in-one experts of the *Pankration*?'

'Cut the small talk. I'm innocent.'

'You found them a poisoner.'

'A good *haruspex* isn't a poisoner.'

'How did you know Campensis?'

'I owe him a lot.'

'Wrote your lucky *defixiones* for you?'

'The spells worked all right, didn't they? I'm still alive.'

I was tempted to say, no, not really, Asbolius, you're not alive any longer. You're a doomed man shackled to the God Mors. Instead I asked, 'And every time you won a bout, you sold Campensis' lucky charms to your fans. You two split the profits?'

The fighter hesitated. Obviously 'split' was too generous a word for their deal.

'Who were your clients?'

His lips curled tight. I'd just made a mistake. If Sericus hadn't given me the crucial name, why should he? His shoulders relaxed. Now he finished off the cup of wine and poured himself a third.

'I was only a go-between.'

'So why haven't they made more arrests? Whatever you told Maximinus, your clients are getting off, while you're in here.'

He savored his wine.

'You see how they all stick together, Asbolius, even your lawyer? I should know. I fought that type myself once. I struggled to survive.'

I stood up, unbuckled my belt, and raised my tunic to expose where the whip of my Castra recruiter had cut me to ribbons twenty years ago. If these old scars devalued me in front of City Prefect Olybrius at the Baths of Caracalla, they might be solid currency inside the Tullianum.

Asbolius' dark eyes flickered. 'Who did that?'

I pulled my tunic back down. 'A big landowner in Roman Africa. I was a slave. I was nothing, worse than dirt, to the *clarissimi*. I fought hard for my freedom.'

'So what? That garlic-breathed bastard Pinnius called you *Magister*. You're one of them now.'

'But I think some of them went too far. Maybe they were your clients? I'm going to make them pay.'

His maimed head flew back as he laughed. 'How did you get into the *curiosi*? You should know already, no one touches men like that. All a man can do is bargain away others to save himself.'

'Whom did you bargain away? Who hired you to find Campensis?'

Too pleased that he knew a secret I needed so badly, he chuckled to himself and poured another drink.

I taunted him back. 'Or can't you think clearly any more? You need a tablet written by somebody like Campensis? Lost your wits in the arena? Memory gone for good?'

He slammed his cup down. I was lucky he didn't toss the wine in my face.

'I remember just fine, you cunt. The name was Warty Paphius. Face like a bed of mushrooms.'

Suddenly I was close. Unless the wrestler was toying with me out of piqued vanity, he'd handed me the key. Could I trust him? Torture rarely gives birth to truth but sires many desperate lies.

'Did Warty Paphius tell you why he needed an expert in the black arts?'

'Said it was woman trouble. Easy to believe, with that ugly mug. If I'd known it was murder, I'd have shoved him into a sewer.'

Pinnius the Younger appeared, a half-eaten sausage dangling from his belt. 'You better finish up. Bishop Damasus is making his rounds any minute.'

Damasus! This was bad luck. I couldn't afford that gossipy social-climber to alert half of Roma to my visit.

I held off Pinnius with an upturned palm. 'Quick, Asbolius. Did you know the gladiator Auchenius?'

The wrestler shrugged. 'A little. The charioteer Hilarinus—now I knew him a long time. He hired a poison expert to train up his son in private, so as to keep the business nice and quiet at home. But he got caught. He was a donkey's ass—fled to a Christian altar for sanctuary, but they beheaded him anyway.'

'Listen, Asbolius, that Hilarinus case didn't involve any top dogs, any *clarissimi*. I'm interested in Auchenius, the charioteer from that trial last summer. What would Auchenius be hawking to the Ceionii—Tarracius Bassus and the three other senators?'

He shrugged. 'Offering a contact in the underbelly of things? Auchenius was blackmailing debtors until they paid up and taking his cut from the lenders.'

'Blackmailing how?'

'Accusing the borrowers of messing with the dirty stuff, even if they didn't.' He stretched his chained legs.

'The Ceionii don't need money from debtors. What would they need from Auchenius?'

He shrugged. 'All I know, Auchenius is luckier than me. Some hotshot got Auchenius and his customers off. Just like that fat city boss who won his son exile instead of the sword.'

He leaned forward. The reek of dried blood came off his bandage: 'And that's how Prefect Maximinus will get me off.'

'Maximinus promised you no "sword or flame"?'

'That's right.' Asbolius leaned back and smiled. Half his teeth were missing.

'The Pannonian lies, you fool, he lies!'

Asbolius spat in my face.

I told Pinnius the Elder, 'Take him downstairs. The *haruspex* won't do business with any bishop. There's still time for me.'

Asbolius rose to his bare feet and stretching his great arms wide, gave a wistful glance out the window near the ceiling where a square of open Roman sky was visible.

The senior Pinnius pushed him back downstairs. It took a minute for the long loops of his iron *vinculae* to snake down the steps behind him.

I waited, thinking of the forgotten shrine in the darkest corner of that fetid room below. No candles, no lights, no offerings . . .

'Bring up the *haruspex*.'

'He stays down there, *Magister*.' Pinnius the Younger looked frightened.

'Then I'll go down before Bishop Damasus gets here.'

So it was back to the stench and the barely breathing bodies. I passed a scowling Asbolius. Sericus was sleeping off his stupor.

'This is him.' Young Pinnius pointed his torch at the fortune teller.

Or what was left of him. Campensis' two hands lay, skinned, maimed and useless, in his lap. His sightless eyes, with lids burned by irons until the orbs sunk inside inflamed skin, oozed the foul pus of untended wounds.

'Campensis?' I crouched down on my haunches at his side, though it pained my bad leg.

He jerked his head. 'Who's that?'

'Marcus Gregorianus Numidianus, *Magister Agentium in Rebus*.'

'The Castra? Oh. I'd hoped for a friend. What do you want?'

'The truth.'

'Why?'

'To end a purge of the city by officials using your practices as an excuse. How long ago did you tell Prefect Maximinus that Warty Paphius hired you to kill Chilo?'

He stared into nowhere. 'You know Senator Paphius?'

'Why did Paphius want to kill Chilo?'

'They all did. Chilo had to be shut up. Chilo isn't stupid. Is he safe, off ruling Africa by now?'

'He's left the city. Were all your clients as illustrious as Senator Paphius? Is that why they wanted to hire only the best?'

'Oh, you try to flatter me, *Magister*? There's no need, no need now. *Magister*, give me a drink.'

'Wine?'

'Water or *posca*.'

I signaled to Young Pinnius to fetch a cup of water from the public fountain gushing outside.

'Tell me everything, Campensis. You know you won't leave here alive.'

He gave an unnerving giggle. 'Oh, I know, *Magister* Numidianus. I'm not uneducated like the others. You forget, I can see into the future.'

'Of course.'

'I saw my death in an omen. So why talk? I'm going to burn. I saw it.'

'Why burn when you cooperated?'

'Yes, they had all the names anyway.'

'Did Asbolius give Maximinus the names?'

'Yes. Asbolius is a musclebound idiot. He named them months ago: Senators Paphius and Cornelius of the Cornelii Scipiones.'

'They hired you to poison Chilo?'

'Not poison, no. To cast a powerful spell, that's all. Asbolius made up the poison threat.'

'You took their money. But your magic failed.'

He shivered. 'My magic would never fail. Asbolius ruined the scheme. He'll deny it, but blackmail is that cretin's true trade. He warned Chilo. Said that if Chilo didn't come up with a sack of *solidi*, he'd be poisoned before he could tell what he knew.'

'What *did* Chilo know? Why was he their target?'

'Our clients never told us, of course. Or Asbolius would have blackmailed them too.'

It was a convoluted mess of a crime, but perhaps Campensis the Soothsayer was not a complete fraud.

'Campensis, what else have you seen in your omens?'

'The same thing his own father saw. That he'll rise to a great height and then die by the executioner's sword.'

'Vice-governor Chilo will die a criminal?'

He gave a small shake of his ghastly head. 'No, no, *Magister*, I mean the Prefect Maximinus, who left me to die like this.'

'You knew Maximinus' father? His own father predicted Maximinus' execution?'

'His father was an honest *haruspex* like myself. He prophesied his own son's ugly fate. And you bet all your dice, Maximinus didn't like that!'

I fell back against the wall. The Pannonian official's father was a practitioner of Roma's traditional rituals? The soothsayer must be wrong.

'But . . . Maximinus' father was a clerk in Sopianae.'

'So he was, so he was. He was a Carpian, humble in birth but blessed in calling, renowned for his skillful reading of bird flight. That man was worth knowing. Can't say the same for his son.'

'Emperor Valentinian dislikes the old ways of the spirits. Does Prefect Maximinus want you dead for knowing his father read the world beyond?'

The poor man winced, expelling fresh pus down his cheek. 'Not just the father.'

'Who else?'

'He'll deny everything.' He gave a bitter chuckle.

'Campensis, are you saying *Prefect Maximinus* is an augur?'

'He tried divination, once upon a time. Tried hard and failed hard. Because our wise gods withhold their gifts. Our great divinities know that a man like that misuses whatever they let him see.'

'You must have confused him with someone else, Campensis. Your torturer Prefect Flavius Maximinus is a Christian official in Emperor Valentinian's Christian court,' I whispered.

'Some Christian! You doubt my word? You ask that necromancer in Olbia.'

'Necromancer? Necromancy's a foul crime.'

'But why ask a dying man? The Castra already knows! Your boss . . . that old man with the wispy white hair? You ask him . . .'

Pinnius the Elder was leading Damasus, the self-regarding Bishop of Roma, down the winding steps. Keeping his ornate hems clear of the muck on all sides, Damasus held a linen handkerchief drenched in rose oil to his nostrils and announced he would now pray for their souls, 'as the law prescribes.'

I'd passed this Nicene cleric in the street. I knew him only as one rumored to have hired gangs to thwart his Arian rival, Ursinus, by staging a three-day massacre in the Julian Basilica while I was away on a long mission in Britannia. And wasn't it worth rioting over, the chance to parade around the city in elegant robes, accepting the offers of rich matrons, and attending to the sins of high society over their groaning banquet tables? I doubted this Damasus would have awaited the return of his Lord in some dreary desert cave.

Praetextatus had been the *Praefectus Urbi* of the city during the riots over this bishop's seat. He'd restored order only after the corpses of one hundred and thirty-seven dead 'faithful' were scraped off the sidewalks.

On my return to Roma, I'd congratulated Praetextatus on his successful term as city boss. He'd joked that 'he might be tempted to convert to Christianity, could he live like Damasus.' In fact, Praetextatus had only contempt for the morals of the promiscuous bishop. He called him an *auriscalpius matronarum*—a ladies' ear-scratcher—which was pretty crude for Praetextatus, who takes pride in more literary turns of phrase.

This morning Damasus took scant notice of his tortured flock and no notice of me crouched next to Campensis in the shadows. A junior cleric, no older than thirty, in a plain black gown followed. Once his eyes adjusted to the sight of the 'congregation,' the second man shuddered. He quoted under his breath in the accent of a rustic Illyrian, '*On all sides round horror spread wide; the very silence breathed a terror on my soul.*'

I slipped over to whisper, 'You cite the pagan poet Vergilius. What's your name, Priest?'

'Jerome,' he whispered. 'Oh, these poor suffering souls.'

While the Bishop bent in his stiff ruby brocade over the altar and droned prayers no one could hear, the trembling Jerome bent over the broken bodies, offering sips of water. This devout young man seemed the sort who'd either die young of some contagion or endure into the next century as a holy saint in the desert.

I paid the Pinnii duo for their services and slipped out. I'd try Campensis again later, knowing Damasus had done his weekly duty.

Outside, the my *lectica* bearers sat on their heels, waiting under a fraying post for the play, *The Eunuch*. I gave a thought to theater-fan Olybrius and his favorite star Roscius as I bounced away from the prison.

What jumbled facts I'd learned from the condemned men! A 'fat official' had got his son off a charge of *veneficium*. More than one branch of the Ceionii was hiring experts in black arts. And Campensis linked Maximinus to a necromancer in Olbia, Sardinia.

But why did Chilo have to be silenced. Who was the 'fat official'? And if Maximinus had solved the Chilo case, why hold these three in 'investigative custody' and leave the accused senators Paphius and Cornelius still at large?

When a sharp turn to start the climb up the Caelian Hill sent the curtains of my *lectica* swaying, one of the rear bearers chanced to look back down the street.

'Two men tracking us, *Magister*,' he whispered.

I parted the curtains a sliver. The elder Ceionii brothers still monitoring the Castra's care of their poor brother? I was no longer so sure.

A sudden question occurred to me, thanks to the blinded soothsayer. I decided to lose my twin shadows and perhaps get answers fast—all at the same time. With a quiet word, I ordered my bearers to reverse direction and carry me back into the morning's bustling throng.

'Then where do we leave you, *Magister*?' the panting head bearer asked me. He was covered in sweat but would zigzag all day if necessary. Our bearers were long inured to the irregular requirements of Castra work.

'I'm sorry. I just remembered some important business. Take me back through the city to Regio IX—The Theater of Pompey. Let me slip out in the shadows of the interior garden columns, well out of street view. Then keep carrying the closed *lectica*, low to the ground as if I'm still in it, all the way to the Gardens of Pompey. Treat yourselves to a good long lunch. Maybe by then, our two friends will realize they've wasted their morning and give up their game.'

CHAPTER 10, BACKSTAGE
SHADOWS

—THE THEATER OF POMPEY—

I confess I have no time for the mimes and farces of our modern drama. Not because I'm influenced by moralizing Christians trying to shut down the theaters—far from it. Nor because my adolescence in military camps left me with nothing but a hardened soldier's disdain for idle city pleasures. Nor am I one of those outdated moralists—you know that bore at dinner—who idealizes some purer Ancient Roma, before our empire was 'corrupted by the decadence of Greece and the luxury of the conquered East.'

And I can't argue that I was always too busy at the Castra or riding the vast network of roads, supervising the expansion of our service and staff. There were some lulls from time to time.

No, I'm the very worst kind of snob, especially for a freedman. As a child, I'd read aloud the best of Greek drama and Roman adaptations on many a hot, mote-dusted afternoon to the blind Senator. Reclining on his battered couch, the old man murmured his favorite lines of Terentus and Plautus to himself. I stumbled through the falsetto of the simpering *virgo* and her nagging mother, the wheedling insinuations of the pimping *parasitus*, the bass baritone of the old *senex*—the whole cast of predictable characters. All the while, the reading slave boy wondered why these silly adults were so confused about their true identities and inevitable fates. The only plot mystery was whether my meager supper would come before or after I reached the last act of the play.

Even those obvious stories have been downgraded for the modern stage from dramatic originals to their rudest, most lubricious versions. Thank you, no. I'd seen every kind of violence and licentiousness in real life, from the dockside brothels of Londinium to the execution ground of Chalcedon, not to mention the massacre at Mursa. Imitation sensations at the circus or theater hold few amusements for me.

I scrutinized the crowds around the theater entrance. The *lectica* trick had worked. I was no longer shadowed. I left the safety of the colonnaded gardens to melt into the comings and goings of the audience. A crowd of lowlife hangers-on blighted the entry to the theater. They'd been paid by the actors to cheer one performance or hiss another. In between key scenes, they came outside to pay a few *nummi* here and there to recruits to amplify their mob voice over twenty thousand other fans.

Dodging them, I couldn't avoid the heat of an open grill of rotating spits. An animal of dubious identity jerked and circled, its foulness blackening off its greasy bones. The stench of meat and men, marinaded or massaged in oils, was intense. I was eager to get in and out.

Though I paid top price for a good seat, I didn't intend to stay any longer than necessary. The three-story-high stage, its stately columns flanked with dead statues and live musicians, was busy up front with mimes and whorish 'actresses' making a mockery of the playwright's original version.

I submitted to the theater staff's cursory inspection for signs of disease and was waved in with a perfunctory 'enjoy the show.' Even before I'd checked the seat number scratched onto my wooden token, I was deafened by the drone of a mammoth organ at the foot of the audience. Proximity to the stage was not only costly but painful.

But I wasn't here to enjoy the reduction of *The Eunuchus* to a bedroom farce. The bellowing music was nearly drowned out by the raucous shouting of the spectators: here was the long-awaited scene where the returning soldier, Chaerea, passing himself off as a eunuch bodyguard, rapes the virgin Pamphila, slave girl and sister of Thais, the love object of—

But surely you know the story. Today the 'acting' promised to be violent and explicit.

Meanwhile, I spotted my prey. With his eyes fixed on Roscius' crude and mechanical 'seduction', the retired Urban Prefect Olybrius wouldn't notice me in time to escape. With apologetic smiles and ingratiating gestures, I eased my way down the benches between the other spectators until I was directly behind his well-plucked nape.

I whispered into his ear so that he couldn't help but hear my greeting, 'You recommended this production. So here I am, Prefect.'

Startled, he recognized me only after a glance at the insignia on my tunic. He knew me better nude.

'Oh, it's you, *Magister* Numidianus.'

He went back to enjoying the show.

'I see you're not so ill as you feared.'

He muttered, 'Surely the chief of the Castra is neglecting his duties?'

'Well, you did warn me of high-profile arrests to come. But you know, it's odd. I find that instead of a rash of high-profile arrest warrants overburdening my staff, we get too few.'

'Too few?' His puffy eyelids flickered but he kept his attention on the frantic thrusts of Roscius and the flailing 'virgin' whose ineffectual 'resistance' probably came from long experience backstage.

'Chilo's would-be assassins confessed weeks ago. Yet no one has been arrested for hiring them.'

'You must tell the investigator Maximinus.'

'Oh, Maximinus knows. You've known for some time, too, haven't you? The wrestling coach Asbolius confessed right away as part of a deal to spare his life. He named the instigators—including Senator Cornelius of the Cornelii Scipiones and a Senator Paphius covered in warts. Paphius shouldn't be hard to locate.'

He shrugged. 'It's Maximinus' affair now.'

'Yes, but why did you pass the job to a Pannonian who hands out bread and oil? Why not to the *Vicarius Urbis Romae*? Senator Aginatius was more senior. You put his nose out of joint for no reason.'

'I told you, Chilo demanded it.'

'I should confirm that with Chilo himself. Where is he?'

Olybrius began to rise, but I pressed his shoulder down with a 'friendly' hand. His attendants reached to stop me, but he shook his head. Too many people were watching. He didn't want to give a better show than the one on stage—though that wouldn't take much effort.

'Don't be clever. Just do your job, like I said at the Baths.'

'My job? Always eager to do so. But I think you asked for my supervision in particular because a freedman from the Manlius House—a clan just getting back on its feet after a fatal political mistake ten years ago—well, that freedman wouldn't ask too many questions, would he? Not where the almighty Anicii and Ceionii might be involved. He'd just make sure the rules prohibiting torture of the highborn were observed.'

'Your job is the arrests. Leave the rest to Maximinus.' His voice, so placid and amicable at the Baths, turned curt.

'Indeed. So why doesn't the Pannonian dispatch me off to arrest Paphius or Cornelius? Like he sent me off to nab that spotty brat Lollianus from under *Pater* Lampadius' nose? Moving on the boy was some kind of warning, wasn't it?'

'Mind your own business, Numidianus.'

'I'm trying. We have two senators, or four, all suspected murderers on the loose. Think of the danger they pose. Shouldn't I arrest them? Chilo was lucky, because the wrestler's specialty was blackmail, not poison. Chilo was warned in time to pay for his life and escape Roma.'

'I don't know anything about that.'

'But you should. You were the original investigator. How did you find those three losers in the first place? Someone betrayed their part in the plot to you, so you had no choice? Or Chilo fingered the blackmailing wrestler himself? But you held off pushing deeper. Chilo got fed up waiting—'

'Chilo's a troublemaking fool.'

'Then Maximinus wrenched the truth out of your suspects— the hard way. But instead of closing the case and prosecuting Cornelius and Paphius, he's still holding those miserable men in the Tullianum as "investigative witnesses". That makes the *clarissimi* all over town nervous and rightly so. It seems I can't go anywhere these days without tripping over Ceionii and Anicii with a fascination for *veneficium*—spells, poisons. Why? What are you all practicing for?'

'I have absolutely no interest in dark magic. Now leave me alone, Numidianus.'

The actress on stage was mock-weeping. She'd finally realized her 'eunuch' bodyguard was no eunuch.

'No, Prefect, you wouldn't go near black magic. You know the risk of crossing that line too well. Perhaps because there was an Alypius on trial for "immorality" some months ago. Faltonius Probus Alypius is your own son, right? Now, wasn't he arrested around the same time as Senator Cethegus of the Cornelii Scipiones on charges of adultery? I wonder, why does your lucky little kid still wear his head? Was your son's crime adultery as well? Or was it . . . messing with forbidden magic?'

Olybrius kept glued to that ridiculous performance on stage, as if he hadn't seen the nearly naked Roscius go at it half a dozen times already. But his shoulder flesh trembled under my grip.

'My son's affair had nothing to do with the Chilo case,' he muttered.

'I know. Because Alypius was charged many months ago. But you made a deal with Maximinus.'

'A deal? Didn't I implore you myself, in person, at the Baths of Caracalla, to curb that Pannonian's excesses? How could I make any deal? The Emperor appointed Maximinus himself!'

'I'm not buying that any longer, Olybrius. It was you—not Chilo—who requested Maximinus take over. You shoved Deputy Aginatius aside to give Maximinus a job well above his station, because Maximinus does deals. And the deal was, if you promoted Maximinus, your son Alypius would be released into exile.'

'Leave my family out of it or you'll regret it.'

'But Prefect, why did the senators try to silence Chilo? What does he know? Why delay issuing the warrants that would bring the case to a close? If I don't deliver Senators Paphius, Cornelius, and the others to justice, they might silence someone else who knows this secret.'

The 'rape' scene on stage ended. Olybrius' shoulder softened with resignation under my fingers as some tedious dialogue now ensued between the maid Pythias discovering the raped Pamphila with her 'lover'. The febrile excitement coursing over the bleachers subsided.

'It's over, Numidianus. Forget it all. It was foolishness, just a silly idea . . .'

Olybrius' excuses were lost in the braying groans of the water organ signaling a new scene. Spectators around us rose to fetch fresh snacks and gestured Olybrius to let them pass. Instead,

Olybrius seized the confusion to jump up and dash away, pushing past whomever blocked his escape to the exit.

He moved on the agile feet of a schoolboy caught peeking at exam questions. A 'convenient illness' indeed! My first theory was wrong. Olybrius' skittish resignation had had nothing to do with his tawdry adultery and today his lovely Cordelia was nowhere to be seen. She might well be a fling already relegated to the past.

No, Olybrius had recommended entrusting the Chilo case to the ambitious Maximinus instead of the logical deputy, the indignant Aginatius, in exchange for Maximinus promising leniency for his son. Culpable of double-dealing, at least noble Olybrius had done the honorable thing. He'd 'fallen ill' and resigned.

All in all, Olybrius was a man who'd missed his calling. He'd been a mediocre city boss but would have made a great actor. He'd mastered the art of playing the artless and showed a talent for dramatic exits. Now I was determined to penetrate what he was still hiding backstage.

⚎⚎⚎

As soon as I reached the Castra, I collared one of our gate guards, a slim young man swimming in borrowed armor, named Emygdius.

'I want you to slip down after dusk to the Tullianum. Make sure you're not followed. Give a verbal message to the warden named Pinnius—the older one, not the younger one.'

'What's the message, *Magister*?'

'Tell him I'm returning tomorrow with more questions for Campensis. Ask him the best time to avoid any interruptions.'

I crossed the courtyard and loped up to my office where I found Cyrillus sorting the day's incoming road and postal reports.

'Give that a rest for a minute. Fetch me any file we have on an exiled "Alypius". Probably an Anician listing.'

I handed Amosis all the official finery I'd worn to penetrate the innards of the Tullianum. The Egyptian saw I was in a bad mood but knew better than ask why.

As soon as I'd recalled the wrestler Asbolius referring to a 'fat city boss,' while I was riding back in the *lectica*, I'd acted on a

130

dangerous impulse to confront Olybrius. Olybrius had scoffed at me. I might have made a powerful enemy with a wrongful accusation.

When our paltry records for Faltonius Probus Alypius landed on my desk, they hardly seemed worth Cyrillus' trip to the archives. There were only a few notes extracted from our thick volumes on the Anician clan. The exiled culprit was of a younger generation and there was no doubting his powerful protector. There it was: 'Son of *Praefectus Urbi* Q. Clodius Hermogenianus Olybrius.'

Beyond that I found only Zephyrinus' note referring the reader to recent municipal court archives for Alypius' conviction for an 'error' involving '*maleficium*' the very month I'd left for the East. The note reminded me to pay a visit to our archivist who was still in the infirmary.

I found Zephyrinus lying, semi-conscious, in a small room within reach of Myron's supervision. Our *medicus* had detailed one of the Castra's laundry slaves to sleep on a pallet at the foot of the patient's bed, to slip spoonfuls of broth between the old man's lips three times a day, to keep him clean and shaved, and to alert Myron to any changes in his condition. Sadly, no change seemed likely.

'How long do we keep him here?' Myron asked me.

A perverse wave of affection for the old man washed over me. Many a meeting had dragged on too long while the ex-priest produced his harvest of trivia and scandal to compete with *agentes*' serious reports of violent incursions along the border, disruption of mail service between provincial capitals due to weather or brigandage, or scraps of sensitive political intelligence.

'As long as it takes. Anyway, where would he go? The Castra is his home.'

Myron gave me a warning glance. 'You'll need a new archivist. It's a miracle he's lasted this many days.'

'A miracle? Well, maybe even failed clerics get special breaks from their Savior. That broth looks pretty weak. Could he take some wine?'

Myron shrugged. 'Perhaps, if well diluted, but it seems a waste—'

'I'll send up some of my personal stock, the best vintage, from the canteen stores. And get a slave to read aloud to him. Nothing too improving—just the *Acta Diurna*. The juicy bits may raise the old boy from the dead.'

☩☩☩

A late-afternoon sun broke low in the sky, relieving the city of a week of drizzle and cloud. After okaying the vintage for Zephyrinus, I lingered in the canteen for a midday meal with some training school cadets. Some we'd picked out of the streets and stables—like Defendens and his dead friend Anthimus—while others came to us festooned with elegant recommendations. They all seemed so unmarked, so earnest, and so unprepared.

Was the young Marcus Gregorianus Numidianus ever so green? I don't think so. After all, I'd been a slave and any young slave sees too much for his young years, especially one carried by his master into the army at puberty.

But the older we get, perhaps the kinder we feel toward our impetuous, over-confident, stubborn, and ambitious selves?

After the meal, I settled down to comb through Ferreolus' latest ideas for stretching our budget until the Imperial Treasury's next coin shipment came through the gates.

Emperor Valentinian had introduced drastic measures to purify gold and silver coinage, a measure against longstanding corruption in tax collection by the dirty practice of coin dilution.

Now only coins bearing OB for *obryzum*, pure gold, or PS for *pusulatum*, pure silver, were to be used for government business— they'd gone through a clearing process of melting down collected coins into certified ingots checked by the *comes* in charge of the *sacrae largitones* of the imperial residence or *comitatus*.

Implementing Valentinian's tax reforms and coin regulations of last year into actual deliveries this year from the authorized mints caused delays. But it couldn't stay a headache for much longer.

After an hour, I turned with relief to reviewing *agentes'* reports. I took quiet pleasure in these scruffy missives off the circuit. I recognized the whiff of leather mail bags and the creases or grease stains suffered at the state *mansiones* and *mutationes* where our riders ate and grabbed fresh mounts. They'd been trained to scribble down anomalies, obstructions, observations, rumors, coincidences, and even popular jokes. Don't snigger— jokes warned us when a corrupt provincial governor became the butt of public resentment or when border villages toyed with comparing the attractions of barbarian freedoms to irksome Roman taxation.

As I finished with two piles, I felt my twenty years with the service settle back on my shoulders. Those cadets in the classrooms and gymnasium downstairs—were we preparing them for what our far-flung provinces would throw at them? I'd rebuilt the school as best I could. Their earnest heads bent over lessons in self-defense and weaponry—illegal and legal, formal arrest procedures, seal tampering, road guide usage, regional tongues, accounting, and auditing. I had yet to find another eunuch expert like the late Eino, the man who'd prepared me for work in eastern courts. But good eunuchs are hard to find. They're Nature's natural spies but Eino seemed unique among his brethren in sorting the truth of what he observed from fanciful mischief.

I updated the movements of *agentes*, informants, army units, and imperial camps on the wall map behind my desk. I'd improved on Apodemus' system of flags and pins. To anyone who could read my coded colors and symbols, it was rich with intelligence. Drawing on my slave boy Greek, one might call it my *panochronic* view of the Empire—an incomprehensible word to anyone who hadn't seen my map.

Our Chilo meeting was scheduled for sundown. As the shadows lengthened across my wall, I etched onto a workaday tablet the questions that plagued me:

Why silence Chilo? What did he know?

Was there any connection between the plot against Chilo, the arrest of Lampadius' Lollianus, the cases against the Ceionii brothers and their friends (dismissed thanks to the late Victorinus,) and the case against Alypius that won reprieve because of father Olybrius' intervention?

Was Maximinus' reluctance to close the Chilo case only a means of prolonging his extortion racket without Victorinus? Was he extending his crackdown to earn another promotion as

Valentinian's loyal 'Christian' courtier? What might the necromancer of Olbia tell us?

And what of that outburst of *Vicarius* Aginatius at the deathbed of Victorinus? What had outraged the senator more—being overlooked for the Chilo case? Roman repugnance at judicial corruption? Or was there something more?

And what was the meaning of Praetextatus' fable about the baker, the hunter, and the 'meddling lawyer'?

The Castra fighting coach Durans was trudging up the stairs behind our giant 'centurion,' the rider Mussidius. I rose from my desk to wave them onto the waiting stools around my desk. We'd have to begin without Rubellius, probably still crossing the city from the river wharf districts. Saturnus arrived a minute later.

I hadn't spent much time with this Mussidius. His talent as an *eques* able to re-open neglected or dangerous mail routes with a scowl and clenched fist had meant we sent him onto distant and difficult roads as soon as we could. He'd quickly advanced to *circitor*, and could afford little time at the Castra school while we were so short of powerful riders. It was high time for Mussidius to catch up on subtler skills before promotion to *biarchus*.

Durans settled, lithe and confident, on a bench against the wall. Saturnus always took a sturdy chair near the righthand corner of my desk. Mussidius sat down slowly, fearful that the rickety old stool in front of my desk would give under his bulk. It did. We lost a minute or two while Cyrillus fetched a better stool. With a little sigh, I watched as the splintered wood was cleaned away. That was the relic on which I'd quivered as an *eques* before the stern Apodemius.

I gave them an abbreviated account of my Tullianum interrogations.

'Anything from you, Durans?'

'Nothing, *Magister*, sorry. But Mussidius hit gold.'

'What can you report, *Circitor*?'

Mussidius began: 'I roamed a bit around Asbolius' school, watching the coming and goings. It was hard to keep inconspicuous. Finally, I spotted an older trainer giving orders. When he quit for the day, I followed him to a rundown *taberna* called *The Sons of Diagoras*, not far from the Circus.'

'You got to him?'

'I wanted him to make the first move. He didn't drink much. He keeps himself in shape.'

'Was *The Sons of Diagoras* his usual hangout?'

'They all meet there. The walls are covered with paintings of famous bouts and hung with souvenirs.'

We let Mussidius relax into his story.

'He didn't talk to anyone else, just ate slowly, kind of brooding.'

'Did he meet anybody?'

'No. Finally, an opening came. Two older guys, fighters down on their luck, I think, started bickering. First it was over a whore who waits tables there between tricks, then over an unpaid debt. They were pretty well-matched—flabby and drunk—and I thought it might fizzle out until one of them drew his *pugio*. It got ugly fast. The second man wasn't armed. All the other customers moved away, jeering, laying bets—you know how fast it can happen—'

'Yes, Mussidius, go on.'

'Well, I just used that wrist trick Master Durans here taught us. You know, how to disarm someone moving forward with a short blade. I kept the *pugio* and shoved its owner out of the place, took the girl under my wing into the corner, and paid for fresh drinks for everybody in the house. Shouted out it was my last coin and I was looking for a job but happy to be alive.'

'You laid your bait and waited?'

He nodded. 'The girl got to be a nuisance. Too grateful, if you know what I mean. I didn't want to follow her upstairs and lose the coach. It was close, but then—'

'He joined you?'

Mussidius nodded. 'Sat down at my table, told the girl to get lost, and gave me an earful. A few of his men were still making a living but o business was down overall. They're feeling the Christians' disapproval of bouts. It's not much of a career any more, not for men with a chance for anything better. Recruitment is scraping up real dregs.'

Durans looked bored but Saturnus kept his attention fixed.

'Well, when I said I'd been fired from my job as a bricklayer, he offered work on the spot. He must be desperate.'

Mussidius showed a sense of humor, which is always good in an *agens*.

'Did you get anything off him?'

'This trainer was a Thracian named Dimoluk. He asked if I could read and write as well as I fought. Most of his fighters are runaways and freedman—pretty illiterate.'

I didn't remind him I was myself a freedman and formidably literate.

'Since when does a fighter need to read poetry"?' Durans prompted.

'Ah, well now, management of Asbolius' school, including heavy debts, has fallen on Dimoluk's shoulders. He needs a reliable man fast—strong and honorable, but also educated. You see, the school is only a small part of the business—just a front.'

'Their real business?'

'Selling incantations, *defixiones*, good-luck spells endorsed by champions.'

'Asbolius was waist deep in it,' I told the others.

'So I acted all keen. Said I'd heard of that stuff, but wasn't it something you needed a *haruspex* to do?'

'Dimoluk laughed. Said I was a naïve bugger. Said that real *haruspices* only attracted trouble these days, what with Christian priests breathing down everybody's neck. It was easier to just copy out old spells and invent new ones. That would my new job, you see, giving a few fighting classes in the morning and forging curses the rest of the day.'

'Anything else?'

'Yes. He said sometimes important people paid off without a peep if a fighter threatened to accuse them of using *maleficium*.'

I nodded. 'The blackmail racket. Asbolius again.'

'Well, *Magister*, I insisted I didn't want to get messed up in anything illegal. I kept playing the honorable bricklayer. He smiled it off. It would be my hard luck later if I was caught profiting from rubbish incantations behind his back.'

Durans nodded with approval from his perch behind Mussidius' shoulder. We'd chosen a man who might look cumbersome and dull, but Mussidius had an instinct for the deceits of any good *agens* in the field.

'We kept drinking and eating and he said he knew his boss was done for at the Tullianum. Said he'd got himself caught up in circles way, way above his head, something to do with the Ceionii and when the Ceionii call, you go—nobody refuses that family. But you already know that, *Magister*. Well, maybe here's what you don't know. Asbolius had a friend who got caught out, too, but he got off all charges. A gladiator called Auchenius.'

'We know that case.'

'Yes, but do you know who Auchenius really is? As a Greek slave his name was Arsenius. He changed it to Auchenius in tribute to his former owners—the Anicii clan. It seems Auchenius is a favorite *prenomina* that runs in the family—'

'Jupiter!' Saturnus blurted out. 'Then Auchenius wasn't just some random celebrity to them.'

'Well done, Mussidius,' I said. 'This links Roma's two great clans—Ceionian family elders hiring an Anician freedman gladiator for their dirty business. But what business? It never came out because Victorinus leaned on Maximinus to get those four acquitted of charges just time.'

Rubellius' footsteps pounded up the steps. The officer plunged into our conference panting as he pulled off his *pilleus* and bobbed in apology.

'Take a drink from the pitcher there and catch your breath,' I told him.

He glanced at Saturnus and the others and then wasted no time.

'Right. I started in the alleys behind the *annona* offices down by the river. The box is still there all right, swinging at the end of the rope from the window above. I played dice with some of the river boatmen up from Ostia waiting for fresh cargo to be loaded overnight, then some drinking games in a *caupona* next door, then a meal at a rough fish grill—that sort of thing. I acted like I was in off a boat, idle, maybe looking for a dock job or a way to spend my earnings.'

'Your earnings? You mean Castra accounts, don't you? Some girl got lucky,' muttered Saturnus.

'Go on, Rubellius.'

'Right, *Magister*. So, yesterday morning, I pulled myself off the pillow where I woke up and circled around the same spots, made myself friendly-like, remembered the names of the girls—all of them, yes—and minded my own business with the men. People decided I was harmless and horny and relaxed around me.'

Saturnus said. 'I hope you didn't waste our time or money.'

'Well, as a matter of fact, I didn't. The dice players took a few *nummi* off me over breakfast and then they had to shove off for Ostia. I rejoined the drunks down the street for a midday meal—totally liquid—the roughest *merum* I've ever forced down my gullet. Right, well, I planned to move on to the fish grill, followed by a dark hole of a bathhouse catering to sailors when your two thugs ducked under the canvas.'

'Sure it was them?'

'The clubbed foot? The cloven forehead? The two demons all right. They took a bench across the room. I watched them over my drink. They seemed intent on some kind of business between themselves. Didn't take them long to make a decision, so after some of that awful *merum*, they set off.'

I prayed to Mercury our Rubellius had found a way to follow them without being conspicuous. But he'd done better.

'I couldn't track them—they would ditch me after a few blocks. So I grabbed the big one by the elbow and asked him if they were heading into the city. Said I was new in town and needed to find an address in the Subura slums.'

'They believed you?'

'Better than that. They took me for a rube fresh in from Sirmium. Said they were going into a better end of town "to test their acting skills." The cripple said they could use me.'

I glanced at Saturnus, who shrugged.

'Right. This is the deal, *Magister*. They roped me in to help Prefect Maximinus. They were to put it about that Maximinus had fired them without pay—but he hasn't really, if you follow me. They were instructed to stage a very public fuss at markets, grills, and bakeries at the feet of the Palatine and Esquiline, anywhere the slaves and vendors serving the best houses would overhear them.'

'And what was behind all this play-acting?' Durans asked.

'They should act bitter and angry at Maximinus' ingratitude—to wail and warn everybody within earshot that this Pannonian bread dealer Maximinus was a nasty, tough-ass official. And if they had a mistress or master who'd been dabbling in any of the dirty stuff, they'd better look out for themselves first. They should make a friend of Maximinus so their household would get off lightly in exchange for turning in their neighbors. They drew quite an audience in some of the *tabernae* and especially in front of the southern stalls below the old *fora*. We must've played the same scene over twenty times.'

'Whew!' Durans threw his head back. 'You? Working for Maximinus!'

'That's melodrama indeed,' I said. 'Did you pull it off?'

'Can't say this soon, *Magister*, but I did my best.'

'What did *you* do, exactly?' Mussidius couldn't help asking, a little miffed his success had been upstaged by the latecomer.

'Right. Well, I had to play the innocent bystander and pester them with a lot of skeptical questions.'

'Their prompter?' I said.

'That's it. I've just spent the whole day trailing them from one *regio* to another, interrupting their moaning and bewailing so they could drop heavy hints that a city-wide purge is coming and clever people should move fast to get on the right side of Maximinus' list.'

'And now what?' I asked him.

'Well, I reckon the word will be out before not too long, maybe even reach your *domus* this very nightfall, *Magister*.'

'No, I meant, now what for you?'

'Oh, right. I should meet tomorrow to finish off the districts we didn't cover today. Should I go?'

'It seems our Deputy Prefect of the Annona isn't satisfied with the crumbs of scandal dropped into his anonymous box,' Saturnus observed.

'Oh, I learned a couple more things about them, too, *Magister*. Did you know that Barbarus, the one with the head wound, was a gladiator in Terranova, northern Sardinia?'

'Interesting,' I said. 'Maximinus was the governor of Sardinia before this. Rubellius, did they say why he *supposedly* tossed such loyal attendants off his payroll?'

''Cause he's quitting the bread line, Barbarus said. He's promoted to nicer municipal offices in the city center where there's no place for the likes of them.'

'Promoted to what? And where? Somewhere there's no place for his hanging box,' I mused. 'That's a little too crude for the upper crust. So he's advertising by new means.'

There was a tap at the door. Cyrillus ushered in the gate guard Emygdius. The young man was pale.

'I've come straight from the Tullianum, *Magister*.'

'You told the guard Pinnius I was returning tomorrow?'

'Too late, *Magister*. I arrived as the guards carried out the bodies of two men, your Asbolius and Sericus.'

'Are you sure? What did the bodies look like?'

'Their heads were bashed to pulp with a lead pipe.'

After a silence, I said, 'So Deputy Maximinus kept his promise to those two after all—no "flame or sword". What about the soothsayer Campensis? I wanted to see him.'

Emygdius said, 'Carried out, still alive, right past me, *Magister*, blind and bloodless as a ghost. He was headed for the execution grounds across the river. They burned him alive.'

'Thank you, Emygdius.'

Saturnus added, 'Go rest now. Take dawn shift at the front gate.'

As the door closed behind the shaken Emygdius, I let his news sink in before resuming.

As much as we'd learned, we still weren't much closer to reading the background story of the Chilo case in full. But Rubellius added rumors that Maximinus' persistence was winning him political favor at the distant court. I could imagine Senator Aginatius' foaming rage. We'd also confirmed that, when it came to soliciting know-how in the black arts of *maleficium* and *veneficium*, Roma's most prestigious *gentes*—those untouchable Ceionii and Anicii—were mixing with the filth and fraudulent of the capital at great risk to themselves and, now it seemed, in collaboration house-to-house.

'You think the executions' timing is a coincidence?' Saturnus asked.

'Of course not. The Tullianum guards told the Pannonian I'd be back tomorrow so he sacrificed them early. I was getting closer.'

'Suppose there's nothing to get closer to?' Durans spoke up from the wall bench. 'Maximinus knew the true culprits' names—those senators—for weeks and weeks. Yet he never moved on them. Maximinus just realizes you've caught him out, terrorizing the town, stirring up rumors without justification. So he covers himself.'

'I've been stupid. The noble Praetextatus asked for my help in closing this case down. He trusted me to erect a palisade around that man's ambition to trample over our city. Now the Emperor may lift him even higher.'

'But what's his next move?' Saturnus asked.

'More defensive action to protect himself. In the meantime, we do our jobs.'

I rose to my feet. 'The Pannonian's long-delayed warrants to arrest Senators Paphius and Cornelius, etc. may arrive at our gate any minute now. Saturnus, ready two teams. Take Tarbus. Mussidius, you go too. You need experience in arrest protocols. No, Rubellius, you look worn out from your . . . investigations.'

But I spoke too soon. We'd need Rubellius and half a dozen more. There weren't two warrants waiting at the gate or even four. There were six.

Chapter 11, Hunt and Capture

—THE CASTRA PEREGRINA—

I stood left alone in my office, its thick stone walls closing in on me. A whiff of Apodemius' stinky liniment lifted off the furniture when I shoved the stools and chair back against the walls. The old man's shadow wagged a gnarled finger from across the black waters of the Styx. He chided me, Numidianus, you were always dogged and brave on the road. But here in my old office, you're too clumsy and plodding. The Pannonian is always ten steps ahead of you.

A bell in the courtyard downstairs summoned the cadets and teachers to their evening meal. The Castra's working day had ended. For me, another shift began.

I bolted the shutters against the November chill and told Cyrillus to light more lamps. I sent Amosis to the canteen for a tray—anchovies, flatbread, some olives, dried fruit, and a small pitcher of whatever *medicus* Myron had left of my opened wine after measuring out generous portions for his patient and himself.

Then I opened Maximinus' packet of warrants.

As I'd expected, the first two charged Senators Paphius and Cornelius with *veneficium* including 'attempted use of murderous poisons.' We could expect trouble carrying these out. Neither senator was a pimply adolescent, disguised in a slave girl's *stola*, scurrying up a tree.

Saturnus and Mussidius would read out these charges and bring in Chilo's would-be assassins with the aid of four guards. Hoping for the least possible resistance, they'd go forearmed with meticulous copies of the charges and well-sharpened *spathae*.

At least these arrests would settle the Chilo affair. I'd kept my promise to Praetextatus and played my part. If my trip to the Tullianum had precipitated the end of this sad saga, then the details that eluded all of us were bound to surface during the coming trial, unless Paphius and Cornelius were made of marble. A charge of attempted murder of a high official was too heavy to qualify for *custodia libera* for very long. Sooner or later, they would sleep in the Tullianum.

The two senators might derive some comfort knowing they couldn't be tortured for the truth.

Then I shook my head at my own naiveté. Maximinus would be very wily in exploiting the senators' terror. He'd promise some elusive reprieve for full confessions—then eliminate them just as cruelly as their pawns Asbolius, Sericus, and Campensis.

Amosis arrived with the tray, then left me to my deliberations over the remaining four warrants. Cyrillus would stay on to usher my officers in and out through the long night while Amosis dozed on the long bench outside my inner door.

I smiled at the telltale nibbles Amosis had left in each dish. Being poisoned myself was the least of tonight's headaches.

The next two warrants offered far less resolution than the first two. They had nothing to do with the Chilo case nor with any political hysteria over *maleficium* and *veneficium* that could be vaguely linked to the poisoners. Senators Abienus and Eumenius had been linked to 'improper conduct with a certain lady of high position.'

I didn't personally know Abienus or Eumenius, nor much of either man's reputation. But hadn't my wife said recently that both the stylish Flaviana and the older Anepsia fancied him? In his convert's enthusiasm for Christian *mores*, Old Constantine Senior had made *adulterium* a capital offense decades ago. But Roma's sophisticated society observed this more in the breach. Our great, late emperor didn't like meddling in domestic policy. It was getting caught that brought shame on all the nobility. He'd limited possible accusers to the cuckolded husband, not just any old official or prosecutor.

What explained Maximinus' sudden rash of high-minded prudery? Was this an effort to stretch his Chilo brief by pleasing the Christian Emperor Valentinian, so scrupulous himself in sticking to the bed of his wife of the moment?

If so, then Maximinus had gone too far. These charges wouldn't stick against such venerable citizens. Senator Abienus came from the privileged *gens* of the Valerii Messala Corvinii.

Eumenius was equally respected. The Castra must be careful. I'd instruct my *agentes* to transfer them to the custody of whomever among the other great families would step forward tonight as guarantors.

I took a long swig of the wine Amosis had diluted for me just the way I liked it. But I almost spit it up when I read the frightening, legalistic words on the last two warrants.

The Pannonian had fixed his glistening serpentine eyes on two of the most prominent society women in Roma—and my wife's close friends. I felt the chill of his hand reaching into my private garden. The highborn Hesychia and flamboyant Charitas were charged with *adulterium*.

I read these warrants twice. The lamps flickered and sputtered low. Cyrillus refreshed their wicks and oil reservoirs while I sat immobile in half-darkness and recalled their girlish banter in our garden not so long ago.

Cyrillus noticed my expression as he removed the tray. 'Something wrong with your meal, *Magister*?'

We must find the best guarantors for these two women. But no—these warrants ordered the Castra to deliver Hesychia and Charitas into the residential custody of two different *apparitores* already alerted by the magistrate to stand by. The names of these poor civil servants of the city courts meant nothing to me. Their addresses were in dowdy suburbs occupied by minor officials of modest respectability.

I thought of the Tullianum and thanked Mercury that such accommodations must be the worst that awaited Apollonia's friends.

I would delegate the socialite Charitas, in her flimsy silks and airy insouciance, to Rubellius. His kind and flirtatious manners might distract the poor woman. He should enlist Avitus from my foyer as an excuse to deliver the bad news, leaving Numa and Lavinia to console Apollonia until I got home.

As for Hesychia, I anticipated the profound shock of the pale young woman. She'd struck me as high-strung on the best of days. No one could imagine her as anything but innocent.

I must shoulder that arrest myself and alone. Hesychia wouldn't put up any resistance. Her absent husband and invalid grandmother could hardly pose difficulties. And I could reassure the sensitive lady that the charge of adultery could not be investigated through torture of a woman of her class and breeding. That was the law. Whether Maximinus liked it or not, we still had Roman Law standing between decent citizens and the harsh avidity against our elites that was driving this Pannonian madman.

It promised to be a long night punctuated by scenes sad or ugly or ridiculous—and for me, a wrenching duty toward Hesychia that as a true Roman, my honor dictated I could not shirk.

ℛℛℛ

Saturnus and his men moved quickly through the shadows of dusk. Senator Paphius was not at home. After an hour of delays made worse by purposeful misdirection from his slaves, they tracked Paphius to ground in the closing hour of the Baths of Traiani on the Oppian Hill. He was undergoing an Egyptian wart cure.

But he was not to be hauled off just like that. Hearing the charge read out before a dozen curious bathers gathered around, Paphius fled his private treatment room. Dropping linens and dignity alike, he raced past my *agentes* through the *tepidarium*, the *caldarium*, the *frigidarium*, and finally across the *gymnasium* into the changing rooms.

He almost escaped through the subterranean honeycomb of passageways used by plumbing and heating engineers to service the baths' hypocaust heating system. But an unwitting slave's cart of dirty laundry blocked his escape. Thus was a sobbing 'Warty' Paphius tied up in half a dozen soiled towels and hustled away. Saturnus marched him across the *fora* district to the Tullianum where Pinnius Senior received him with a cold smile.

It proved harder for Mussidius' team to collar Senator Cornelius. The *honestior* had already got wind of the warrant via that invisible grapevine of gossip and rumor that twists and circles the city of Roma, *regio* to *regio*, bath to alley to slum, across the *fora*, and hill to hill.

But Mussidius had his orders—to track the aristocrat as far and long as necessary. Where Paphius offered a farce, Cornelius required a marathon. Senator Cornelius and companions had fled the city for a secluded villa estate set a mile or more behind cypress trees and vineyards off the Via Nomentana. Perhaps Cornelius thought a low-born *agens* would find the manicured drive running through the sheltered setting of his grand estate too much to breach without a formal introduction.

My Dacian wasn't deterred. His team penetrated the elaborate grounds and imposing house with patience and politeness, working their way through as many layers of slaves, domestic guards, servants, secretaries, and family lawyers as an onion has skins.

By the time the agents announced themselves under the archway opening to a sheltered garden, Senator Cornelius acted startled, then amused. He finished conversing with his clients over their evening supper in the *triclinium*, then gave leave to *Circitor* Mussidius to read out 'his little message' to the background music of a tinkling fountain.

The senator answered that he was forearmed with neither grandiose speech nor physical defense—which proved his total innocence. It all seemed so *infra dignitatem* for a man of his reputation to entertain a lowly postman—'the Castra sent a mere *circitor*!?'—delivering unsolicited mail at such an unsociable hour.

Everyone laughed.

Unfortunately for Cornelius' admirable sang-froid, his screaming wife entered the garden. She accused her husband of criminal idiocy and fainted into Mussidius' bulging arms.

Senator Cornelius' clients called for their cloaks, each man declining Mussidius' invitation to serve as his legal *guarantor*. Of course each fleeing guest offered the name of a good lawyer.

At this Senator Cornelius gave a bitter laugh. He didn't need such 'friends'. He'd be guarded by a cousin working for the municipal treasury. Thus Mussidius' last chore was to deliver Cornelius to the horrified cousin's doorstep.

Senator Eumenius had been in bed on the Esquiline Hill. He presented neither resistance nor gallant face. His servants dressed and shaved him with care while our *agentes* waited. They read out the charges twice, at his request, and then watched him bid good-bye to his wife, sons, and household gathered by lamp and torchlight.

The charge of adultery hung oddly on this man, my agents commented.

Senator Abienus had disappeared.

It was long after midnight before young Avitus returned from arresting a shocked Charitas.

'I sure learned a lot about procedure tonight,' Avitus said. 'Rubellius even shed tears himself.'

Rubellius had assured Charitas that no man would believe she was anything but a model of chastity for all noblewomen. He bribed her slaves to dry her tears and get her brushed, pinned, made-up, and shod. He helped her choose what clothes to pack.

Our ladies' man was now escorting Charitas to the *apparitor*'s address north of the river. Avitus headed back to my house with a head full of ladies' undergarments and curling irons.

These accounts took us through the small hours of the night. Cyrillus recorded all the details in shorthand on a wax tablet. He would transcribe full reports at daybreak for the city's judicial secretaries. One by one, my tired *agentes* left for bed.

One warrant remained. The reluctant winter dawn would break within the hour.

'You're stalling, *Magister*,' Saturnus said. 'Shall I take her?'

'No, Saturnus. That would be cowardly. Hesychia should present no problem. But I've never had to arrest a family friend before.'

'Then I'll do it,' Saturnus said. 'The gods only know, we've all had enough practice tonight.'

'No, you've done enough.' The Lutetian smelled of sweating horse from zigzagging around the city after Paphius. His tunic and boots bore the stains of spilled bath oils.

Cyrillus provided me with Hesychia's address. I saw with a twinge that she resided only a few blocks from my childhood home, the stately *domus* of the Manlius family now occupied by Leo and Aurea. The two households even shared the same ancient *compital* shrine.

A shudder ran though me, a frisson of danger creeping closer and closer to those I loved. Could the arrest of Apollonia's two friends be a coincidence? I must write to our Leontus Manlius before the new day ended. He must not return to the Eternal City when his casework in Mediolanum concluded. He must take up a new case, inspect the Manlius family estates—make any excuse to stay clear of the wild accusations coursing through Roma's best neighborhoods.

Soon enough I stood across the street from Hesychia's double oak doors. The sun rose. The bakery opened. The laundry man unhinged his storefront shutters and rolled his urine vat outside to collect pedestrian contributions. A gaggle of schoolboys marched past me in pairs, arguing the score of the last *harpastum* game.

Still I didn't budge. I would give the poor young woman one more full night of sleep.

After dawn, I imagined, she'd check on her bedridden grandmother, tell her maid to coil up that flat, mousy hair, apply the minimal makeup of a wife whose absent husband never notices even when he's home, and ready herself for a day of unremarkable social duties.

But I should not leave it too late for fear her neighbors might witness her humiliation. A door-to-door vegetable vendor began his sales to kitchen slaves at the far end of the street. Traffic would only get busier. I could delay no longer.

I announced myself at the door. The *dispensator* recognized my name. Of course my wife was always a welcome visitor, *Magister*. News of my arrival wafted down the *fauces*, across the atrium, and into the private rooms beyond.

Hesychia flew toward me from the kitchen wing.

'Why, Marcus Gregorianus Numidianus! It's so early! I just finished with the *lararium* and was settling today's menu.'

Her face still bore the creases of her pillow but she was presentably robed and eager to make me feel welcome. An instant later, her easy expression turned quizzical. She seized both my hands and tilted her head like an attentive kitten.

'Oh, the gods, forgive me! Is something wrong with Apollonia? Am I wanted? Am I needed? Of course, of course, why else would you be here?'

She dropped my hands and gestured to a chamber slave to fetch a cloak and street shoes. I'll cancel my—'

I led her out of earshot. '*Domina*, is there a more private place? I bring bad news which concerns yourself.'

A wary expression crossed her eyes. Her mouth gave a wry twist.

149

'Of course. Of course. I was half-expecting it. I've lived with this for years—always waiting for the other sandal to drop.'

She settled on a nearby bench and her modest skirts pooled over her bare feet. 'I always knew that sooner or later there would be something truly bad—not just ugly gossip. Well, I'm glad you're the messenger.'

I sat down next to her.

She took a deep breath. 'Well, break it to me, please. If you're the messenger, Lucius must be under arrest. Has he defaulted on his gambling debts? Am I to lose my house, my estates?'

There was no Castra training for this. Oh, where should I begin?

'You don't answer? So it's worse than debts? Is Lucius dead? Murdered by a jealous husband? An angry gambler who caught him cheating?'

'*Domina* Hesychia, the Castra received this warrant for your arrest on the charge of *adulterium*. Read it yourself. Take all the time you need. If there's any possible error, tell me now.'

She unfolded the warrant with shaking hands and read out softly—in Latin more impeccable than the hand that drafted it—the magistrate, the *regio* of the issuing court, her name and *gens* in full, and the date of a trial fixed for a few weeks' time. That firm date told me that Maximinus already had enough witnesses to carry his case. But I said nothing to upset Hesychia further.

She refolded the warrant and handed it back. I waited for the Vesuvius of indignation to explode from her narrow breast as she found fault with the warrant or protested that the charge was false.

'So, Lucius has finally found a way to rid himself of me and keep all my property.'

'You'll fight in court?'

She gazed around her ancestral home, with its cracked marble altar sending whirls of burning resin to clear the winter fug and her whispering slaves eavesdropping from pillars and doorways.

'What's the procedure now, *Magister*?'

'I must read the warrant out loud myself in case of any misunderstanding and answer your questions.'

She gave a rueful smile. 'You mean, in case your detainee is only pretending she reads well in front of her slaves? How well-trained you *agentes* are, how tactful. No, thank you, I understood every word.'

'Now you must prepare your personal things. I'm afraid I must examine your bag and person for weapons—to prevent harm to yourself or others.'

'My deadly eyebrow tweezers? My toxic hair oil?'

'Forgive me, *Domina* Hesychia.'

'I forgive you. Where are you taking me?'

'The magistrate assigned the private home of a married *apparitor* attached to his court. I've copied the name and address for your *dispensator* so that he can send you messages and supplies. Everything you receive will be examined first by your host or his wife.'

'You think of everything. May I travel in my own *lectica*?'

'Yes, of course, in my company.'

'Thank you, *Magister*.'

Magister . . . I was no longer a family friend. Her formal comportment made my job easier.

Hesychia mustered the dignity of an ancient Hera. Dry-eyed, she gave instructions to her staff, spent twenty minutes in farewell with her grandmother, and returned to the public rooms with a succinct letter of appeal drafted for the family's lawyer. I checked the pathetic mix of necessities in her inlaid cedar toilet box meant for outings to the baths. Finally, she prayed at the altar for a safe return as her slaves wept.

I waited out on the curb as her bearers, their family's summery linen livery swapped for a wintry wine red, brought the *lectica* to the front doors.

Hesychia emerged wearing a heavy cloak, thick socks, and sturdy country shoes. I helped her into her seat and watched her drained features disappear behind the curtain.

We set off down the Esquiline Hill—passing within sight of the old Manlius fig tree and front gate—as we made for an obscure neighborhood northwest of the *fora* district that would be her temporary home.

I struggled to maintain a neutral countenance as I lurched along, using my walking stick to keep pace with her bewildered bearers. This dreaded duty was almost over. Thank the gods she kept possession of herself.

Almost an hour later, we reached the residence of an officious midwife and her taciturn civil servant spouse. They'd set a small, windowless bedroom aside for Hesychia's detention. No brick-red trim or pastoral mural broke the monotony of walls freshly whitewashed with lime.

There was no table, only a stool of woven reeds and a very narrow, low bed made up with threadbare blankets. Washbasin, oil lamp, and water pitcher sat on a unvarnished shelf nailed to the wall. It was the clean, decent room of a slave.

As spartan as it was, I felt relief. A court *apparitor*'s space could be far more cramped than this. Sometimes the accused even shared his jailor's bedchamber. I recited Hesychia's legal rights to regular meals and supervised exercise to her 'hostess.' We were shown the rough toilet and walled garden behind the kitchen.

Hesychia moved with slow deliberation, her eyes taking in the limits of her cell. Her mind was elsewhere—the coming trial or her estranged husband? She spread her heavy cloak like a coverlet over the thin mattress. She set her toilet box on the shelf.

'Am I allowed a pillow?' she asked. The midwife fetched a thick cushion.

Everything complied with regulations. I reminded the *apparitor* couple of the absolute discretion required under the rules of *custodia libera*.

It was time to leave. In a dull voice, Hesychia murmured, 'Good-bye.' Part of her had died between the Esquiline Hill and this shabby suburb.

♙♙♙

I had no time to dwell on Hesychia's dilemma. As busy as the Castra had been all night, I plunged into a midmorning Roma in even greater turmoil. I crossed one forum after another teeming with gossiping servants, pushing-and-shoving porters, chattering housewives, and consulting officials. The pedestrian crowds heading for the public baths looked triple the usual number—and already clean enough as they were. I slowed to listen to the hubbub and finally grabbed a copy of *Acta Diurna* still damp with smudged ink and dozens of fingerprints.

The morning's items were earthshaking, even to one who'd spent the night coping with the early tremors. The city was agog. Maximinus had entrusted our service with the most notable and politically delicate of the night's warrants. But while Saturnus and his *agentes* were trundling back along the Via Nomentana with the disdainful Senator Cornelius in tow, Maximinus had been even busier. He'd seconded half a dozen teams of officers and guards from the municipal judiciary to haul in lesser victims by the dozens.

I was racing down the lines of the gossip rag, hunting for familiar, famous, or notable names for any clue as to what this wave of detentions meant, when my reading broke off at an explosion of jeers and shouts.

The crowd ahead of me parted. A woman bound at the wrists by a rope was dragged forward by a cluster of coarse men. She staggered and stumbled between hundreds of gawking strangers. Her hair showed vestiges of a braided coiffure. Her eye makeup coursed down her wet cheeks in black streaks. She'd lost her *palla*, and *stola*. Her bare feet were bleeding.

Worse, it looked as if the poor woman was dressed in discarded banners, not proper garments. A blade had sheared her flimsy night tunic into pieces fluttering free from shoulder to hem. Her stark white thighs were exposed to the mob's leering gaze. Her heavy breasts, torn free of her silk *mamillare*, jerked right and left, their nipples hardened to cold pebbles.

She struggled against the two escorts flanking her sides. She tugged at the rope in a futile effort to cover her loins with her bound fists. She cursed their abuse and chided the onlookers to be decent citizens and look away—or be ashamed of their nasty jokes and barbarian lusts. Her eloquent outbursts betrayed good education.

It was Flaviana.

What was the charge against her? The mob passed like a churning river within three feet of where I stood. And I overheard the telltale names Abienus and Eumenius. I couldn't understand what was happening; Flaviana was already on her way to trial. Execution must follow swiftly.

One of her captors grinned through broken teeth and waved a rag of her undertunic in the air to whip the horde into greater frenzy. He hopped past me on a club foot. His buddy with the dented skull could not be far behind.

The grotesque circus of Mucianus and Barbarus moved past. I limped up the long avenue to my home. I felt it my duty to make my first report on Hesychia to Apollonia before heading back to the Castra. I prayed there were no more warrants waiting on Cyrillus' desk.

At least I now had the excuse of our completed arrests to confront Maximinus myself. I would demand to know under what mandate and by whose authority had he ordered his parallel wave of arrests?

How did this grandson of Carpi savages once barely tolerated inside the Empire by Emperor Aurelian dare run roughshod over our empire's greatest and oldest city? Did Maximinus not know the laws regulating abuse of Roman citizens? Surely this naked, bleeding woman's public humiliation qualified as torture?

Apollonia's distressed state was awful to see. She'd lit incense and prayed for her friends until she collapsed in exhaustion on a couch in the *triclinium* where I discovered her. She'd suffered nightmares full of omens and fiends brandishing pincers and shackles.

I washed and asked for fresh clothes. She stroked the furrowed scars crisscrossing my back as I bent over the basin. She handed me a clean towel to dry off. I warned her of my plan.

'Yes, yes! You must challenge Maximinus. You have all my support! We're not nobodies in this city, Marcus! We can't wait any longer for Praetextatus and the so-called highest nobility to do what they should. Cowards! Cowards! And I must go straight to Anepsia,' she said, her brown eyes red with exhaustion.

'Anepsia? Apollonia, my love, stay out—'

'We must silence the gossips! Protect reputations!'

'My dear, who could stop up the mouths of those fishmongers and beggars down in the Subura? They act like beasts—'

I'd keep details of the ugly attack on Flaviana to myself.

'Of course they do. But who cares about the slums? We must find a way to warn decent families to curb their tongues.'

I saw I couldn't change her mind. 'I don't know about Flaviana or Charitas. But at least Anepsia can make it clear to decent Romans that poor Hesychia is innocent.'

Apollonia busied herself emptying the basin. How my wife's set jaw recalled her grandfather at his most determined!

I added: 'Her husband can't get away with using a vice campaign for his own greedy ends.'

Apollonia folded up the towels and put away my shaving kit.

'Apollonia? Hesychia is innocent, isn't she?'

Apollonia paused, then said, 'No, Marcus. The Pannonian's not that much of a fool. Lucius must have used that nasty hanging box to tattle on her—'

'Good gods—!'

'Oh, don't judge her, Marcus! Lucius treated her worse than his most abject slave girl. He squandered her inheritance on vice, bad investments, and other women. He beat her when she complained. But he never gave her grounds for divorce. I never knew a wife so lonely.'

I slumped down on the end of my bed, reviewing Hesychia's bitterness toward Lucius, then her rueful resignation, her dignity, and finally, her eerie calm.

'Don't look like that, Marcus! Don't begrudge Hesychia the only hours of affection she ever knew.'

Then, perhaps because Apollonia had shocked me, I shocked her back. I described the wild swarm torturing the naked Flaviana, the flood of taunts and insults, and the harried frenzy with which she fought them off. Why shouldn't I tell Apollonia after all? She would hear of Flaviana's humiliation before she reached Anepsia's door this afternoon.

And sadly, so did Hesychia. When I arrived at the Castra, Cyrillus passed me a terse message from the *apparitor*'s midwife in a gouging scrawl across a schoolboy's two-*nummi* wax tablet.

Domina Hesychia had suffocated herself with the pillow, the midwife recorded, so who would cover the expense of whitewashing their detainee cell—the magistrate's court or the Castra?

CHAPTER 12, A DOG IN JEWELRY

The Castra's courtyard waterclock trickled into the afternoon hours as our search for the fugitive Senator Abienus intensified. Saturnus and his men now coordinated with the municipal office of *vigiles*, their deputies, and slaves. They offered a reward for Abienus' whereabouts. We needed the *vigiles'* help. It was an irony of the *Schola Agentium in Rebus* that we learned more secrets about the vast Roman Empire through the postal, road, and *mansio* network we supervised, than we did about the Eternal City's dark gutters and bleak slums under our noses.

There were now enough eyes on all the city gates and suburban arteries to catch Senator Abienus on the run. But it took all day to set our traps and spread our nets. We'd find him in the end, even if it took weeks until the accused surfaced like a shit-covered rat from the *Cloaca Maxima*.

But my resolution to confront Maximinus hit an unexpected wall. I led Amosis across the city and into the riverside warehouse district at sunrise the following morning to demand an audience. I told the guard I was there to report the results of our senatorial arrests. On that ground, Maximinus could hardly refuse to receive me. And once I had one foot in his door, he dared not deflect my own interrogation.

I was admitted, but only to find his subordinate in full command of the week's bread and oil distribution across the city. In fact, Firminius gave me the impression of being only too well-versed with welfare procedures—the name of approved oil suppliers, feedback on some substandard baking ovens, etc.

It became obvious that the officious young Gallo-Roman had assumed the tasks of the *Vicarius Annonarium* some weeks, even months, ago.

No wonder Maximinus had been so free to pursue the Chilo case.

Firminius said I should send my written reports to the magistrates named in the warrants and consider the matter closed. There would be no more business for us *curiosi* coming from this building. He turned his back to correct a slave-accountant tallying '*Amphorae* Received.'

Firminius' insignia of office did not recommend he use this insulting nickname for my agents to my face. Did such insolence reflect Maximinus' past outbursts of contempt or frustration behind my back?

'No more arrests for our *schola*? How can you be sure?'

He gave a theatrical sigh: 'Because immediately after issuing that batch of warrants two days ago, Flavius Maximinus delegated management of the *annona* to me and left Roma.'

'Where did he go? When does he return?'

'None of my business. Possibly none of yours, though I'm too junior to decide such things.'

'Indeed, you are. Entrusted with the city's hungry, yet too junior to know your superior's schedule? Surely, he mentioned where he went? Well, I can guess. And you're very loyal to protect him. We senior men all need a holiday from overwork from time to time.'

Firminius kept his eyes fixed on the strings of X's, V's and I's numbering the week's deliveries.

'A rest cure at some luxury spa?' I persisted. 'I do hope Maximinus isn't sick. The city so recently lost the services of *Praefectus Urbi* Olybrius to ill health.'

'If you must know, *Magister* Numidianus, he's not sick at all! He's gone to consult Emperor Valentinian in Treverorum. He told me that much.'

I tried to winkle or provoke more out of Firminius. But for all his vanity, he wasn't careless. He recovered his temper and refused to discuss his boss any longer. He was far too busy feeding the city, thank you.

Amosis and I emerged from the old stone building into a dim winter sun. We rounded the corner to find the informers' slotted box and rope gone. Amosis and I split up for half an hour in search of the Pannonian's henchmen but there was no sign of Mucianus or Barbarus anywhere in the district's disreputable dives.

Our long trudge back across the crowded city and up the Caelian Hill gave me time to think. Had the arrests of the Senators Cornelius and Paphius truly closed the Chilo file? Was it possible that Maximinus' brief swagger over old Roma was actually over? Is that what explained his last-minute rush of detentions roiling the middle classes and their slaves, the unhappy souls not enjoying the legal privileges that would protect Senators Paphius and Cornelius from torture? Had Maximinus pushed his luck too far? Was he being disciplined? Recalled and replaced?

In short, were his dreams of the promotion that his two thugs boasted about to Rubellius already dashed?

Back at the Castra, more news sat on Cyrillus' desk; a judicial directive that we provide an escort of *agentes* for the transfer of the youth Lollianus of the *gens* Ceionii to a trial in Baetica on charges of *veneficium*.

I hadn't forgotten the boy, though I'd temporarily lost interest in him. Now I was curious. Did this shift of his trial out of Roma prove that the likes of old Lampadius still exerted some political clout over the new Valentinian regime?

Since the guard Defendens had looked after Lollianus, he should be the one to escort the boy to the Hispanic province. Cyrillus sent for him. I gestured Defendens should take the stool.

He sat upright and attentive, but still bore that melancholic air I attributed to the murder of his childhood pal. Tarbus had overheard Defendens saying he might quit the Castra to work near his family at a *mutatio* on the road to Pisaurum.

I would not encourage any thoughts of defection. I'd seen valuable qualities in this recruit, especially loyalty and perception.

'Defendens, tomorrow you leave before dawn to escort Lollianus to'—I doublechecked the name on the directive— '*Consularis* Tanaucius Isfalangius of Hispania Baetica who will preside over the boy's trial on charges of *veneficium*. Here, have a look at the legal language to learn something.'

'Hispania?' His smooth cheeks blanched, as if I'd suggested he tour northern Armenia solo on a lame mule.

'It's time you started riding. And Lollianus trusts you. That'll make security during the transfer easier for all of us. You look dismayed. You haven't grown fond of that little creep?'

'Sorry, *Magister*, but Anthimus and I always looked forward to riding our first circuit together.'

'For the gods' sake! You two thought you'd spend your whole lives in some kind of parade pair? We'd have split you and Anthimus onto separate routes within a year.'

'Oh, I didn't realize . . . Hispania is so far away.'

'Hardly! It's the rich birthplace of our great Emperor Traianus! Mining fortunes, olive-growing gentry growing fat on shipping oil to our troops in north Gallia—'

'The older riders say boats make you retch nonstop, like old Emperor Commodus in his *vomitorium*.'

'I'm a pretty bad sailor myself. Luckily, no boats for you during the winter *Mare Clausum*. The roads are safe as Hera's Bosom. Come here to the map.'

He rounded my desk with obvious reluctance.

'Now, Defendens, follow my finger. Roma to Cosa, Luna, Genua, Forum Iulii, Aquae Sextiae, Arelate, Nemausus, Narbo, Emporiae, Barsino, Tarraco, Dertoso, Sarguntum, Ad Aras, Mariana, and Castulo. Then you arrive in sunny Corduba by the Via Herculea.'

I resumed my seat. 'Don't worry. You'll be issued a road guide, like they explained in training.'

'How long will it take us?'

'About three weeks. You can't race a spoiled brat at relay pace, but I'll send Tarbus with you—nobody slows down Tarbus.'

'Oh, *Circitor* Tarbus, good. But why is the trial in Baetica?'

'You tell me, Defendens. What have you heard? Start from the beginning.'

'Yes, well, Lollianus was terrified at first. Then his family sent him sweets and trashy books—dirty pagan poetry—and he boasted his father would get him off.'

'How, exactly?'

'Well, he didn't mention bribes—'

'I hardly think so. His father is notoriously mean.'

'I don't know about that, but he praises his old man all day. You know, how powerful Lampadius was once as senior counselor to Emperor Constantius. He says the Ceionii don't get pushed around by *a bunch of Christian Pannonian upstarts nobody heard of until Emperor Julian croaked*—sorry, *Magister*—perished in Persia. He says his family still knows the right people.'

Our poor Christian stable hand had suffered a crash course in Old Roman snobbery.

'From what Lollianus told me, the Ceionii only speak to one other family.'

'Oh, do let me guess, Defendens. The *gens* Anicii?'

'That's right, *Magister*! To hear Lollianus talk, forget Romulus and Remus. The Ceionii and Anicii built this city with nothing but their bare hands and a folding spoon.'

'That would be news to the great Octavian Augustus, Marcus Aurelius, and Trajan. What did you say to this?'

'I wanted to kick his pimply face in, but I acted impressed.'

'So our prisoner relaxed after gifts from the Palatine Hill. Any messages from his family?'

'Yes, sticky with honey, hidden under the lining of the pastry boxes from his doting *mater*.'

'Defendens, tsk, tsk, tsk,' I clucked with mock outrage. 'You read *Matrona* Lolliana's most personal correspondence to her son?'

'But . . . the trainers taught us—!'

'Good boy! Well done! Does Lollianus know you read them?'

'Of course not, *Magister*!'

'Even better.'

I hadn't mistaken Defendens' potential. The guard had seen for himself the majestic Ceionian townhouse with its walls of *imagines* and busts. He'd endured days of whining condescension from their entitled scion ever since. And yet, he'd spied on their intimate communications without blinking.

'Go on, Defendens. Mummy's messages?'

'I memorized every one. Most were short lines, like "Model yourself on our great ancestors," and "The Ceionii family holds up Roma like noble human pillars"—that sort of crap. But they bolstered his spirits.'

'Anything about Baetica?'

He shrugged. 'No, just instructions to stay healthy, get lots of sleep, and be ready for a long journey south.'

I nodded. 'A journey south. It fits. So that was Lampadius' appeal to Valentinian—not for mercy, but for a rigged provincial trial. The family lawyers advised that getting Lollianus out of the Roman municipal judicial circuit was their best move.'

'He boasted his *pater* was pulling in favors.'

'Well, the mist begins to clear, doesn't it? Lampadius' appeal to the Emperor suggested an official his family has leverage over. The father is praying to the Goddess Clementia that Baetica's Governor Isfalangius will show mercy with an acquittal. But I bet Lampadius is relying on more than prayers. For whatever reason, he thinks he can lean on Isfalangius.'

Defendens glanced up at the map with brighter eyes now. I envied that impatience of any *eques* leaving the Castra's training school. Defendens had learned the life of the *mansio* and *mutatio* as a child. He'd brushed and harnessed the *agentes'* wet, snorting horses as weary riders loped indoors for food. He'd saddled fresh horses and stood ready to sling up heavy sacks of imperial mail as they remounted with a last swig of wine. At last Defendens himself would travel the Empire's never-ending *viae* promising fresh adventures at every junction and layover.

I continued, 'Lampadius' lawyers might be right. Some of our old Roman colonial families have lived along that southern coast for centuries. They stick to themselves, polishing the legacy of Traianus. They may supply their oil and gold to Treverorum. But they send their sons to marry the noble blood of this city.'

'I can't imagine anyone wanting to marry Lollianus.'

'Get packing and tell Tarbus to see me.' I escorted him to the door. 'By the way, did Lollianus teach you any useful magic?'

He laughed as he put his guard's helmet back on. 'No. But you were right, *Magister*. For his book, he consulted a famous gladiator, Auchenius. He seems confident that if Auchenius got off all charges in his trial, he will too. Who was Auchenius?'

'Auchenius' acquittal was months ago. That was when the powerful Senator Victorinus was still alive to traffic in pardons. But it confirms that the Ceionian Lollianus was hanging around with an Anician freedman.'

'Well, Lollianus is pretty cocky, at least during the day. I'm not sure he even realizes he's afraid.'

'How's that?'

'When he's awake, he's all bluster. But asleep, he tosses and sweats, moaning and muttering about some letter.'

'From his mother?'

'No, no. He keeps saying, *that letter's not my business. Nothing to do with that letter.* And a name—Anatius? Aganius?'

⚜⚜⚜

Defendens had listened well: the Ceionian heir had consulted a henchman of the Anicians and might have overheard more than how to recite a few *nefarias preces* of doom. The inner spirit of the boy was terrified, not of composing silly magic texts, but of being connected with a letter and Senator Aginatius. Why?

I scraped a handy wax tablet clean of my notes from the robbery attempt and began a fresh summary of questions that hung unresolved, unclear, or disconnected:

First, there was that fable Praetextatus told me; I wasn't imagining some kind of intrigue in Roman society. *Magister* Marcus Gregorianus Numidianus had merely been warned of deeper waters, but left in the shallows.

Why? Because Praetextatus was all too aware of my humble birth and mixed loyalties to the Valentinian court in Treverorum and the noble houses of Roma.

The head of the *agentes in rebus* was to be used by Roma's great families, but not trusted.

Which led to Item Two, Prefect Olybrius' warning that I should take special care of illustrious detainees. He'd bargained his own son's life in exchange for handing power over to Maximinus, so someone reliable must remain on watch—myself.

But I was to know little else. Olybrius had always known who hired the 'stooges' from his early investigation. But perhaps Olybrius still concealed *why* the Senators Paphius and Cornelius needed Chilo silenced?

Third, there was that trial of Hymetius which lured the watchful Praetextatus out of his vast palace. To protect the interests of a female cousin? Or because he feared Hymetius' successful appeal would trigger the volatile Valentinian to lash out harder at Roma's disdainful senatorial families?

Fourth, we had the sudden arrests of dozens of highborn citizens, including the ladies Charitas and Hesychia as well as the public ruination of lesser-born Flaviana, flailing nude and sobbing through the brawling crowd because of her alleged link to two prominent Roman senators.

What was the point of the Christian emperor's representative demeaning these all-too-human Roman ladies? With the Chilo case closed, Maximinus should have relinquished his temporary position by now.

There was the fifth element: four senators had been caught dabbling in spells under the tutelage of the Anician family's freedman gladiator Auchenius. Those senators had escaped death by paying off Victorinus and Maximinus. But why risk execution for some dubious spells in the first place?

Which led to six: I hadn't forgotten Senator Aginatius' outburst at the widow Anepsia and her attempts to bribe Maximinus with silver from her first husband's legacy meant for his daughter Callista. This was strong evidence that the 'upright' emissary from Valentinian's court, the Pannonian Maximinus, could be corrupted by any chance to pocket money—from the dying intermediary Victorinus, his widow Anepsia, or the property of other rich Romans he could ruin with accusations of vice.

Six reminded me of seven: the arrest and imminent trial of Lollianus, the vulnerable runt of the Ceionian clan, the same clan who were waist deep in the Auchenius business. What was young Lolli's night terror about Senator Aginatius and a letter about?

I'd almost forgotten item eight—the most tantalizing. The blinded soothsayer Campensis had begun to confide to me on the Tullianum's freezing floor:

Maximinus' Carpian accountant father moonlighted as a respected *haruspex* who read the passage of birds. He'd predicted his own son's death by the executioner's sword. And a necromancer in Olbia knew even more about Maximinus' past interest in divination.

Prayers to the ancient gods? All true traditional Romans still offered those, *pace* the rapid spread of the Christian cult outside our city walls. Interpreting the flight of birds in the sky? There was no law against that. Raised a *cultor deorum*, I myself believed in the power of prayer, the guidance of the gods, and the wisdom of souls who'd crossed ahead of me over the River Styx.

But I shuddered at the word *necromancer* or any mention of the forbidden practice of communicating with *animulas noxias*— toxic spirits—by reanimating corpses and skulls to learn their knowledge of the future.

Necromancy rituals were downright foul—not just using the blood of sacrificed animals to prepare a libation, but consuming decayed food, donning the clothes of the dead, and even mutilating and eating their corpses. Such means of coaxing prophesies from the Underworld deluded the practitioner into thinking he could shortcut the normal struggles our Fates deal every human being. Consulting the Dark became addictive.

And things could go terribly wrong. Instead of raising the shade of a deceased human being, the necromancer might arouse horrible, destructive daemons. The Christians knew this as well as any pagan. They warned that their God sent such daemons to test the faithful.

Whatever your religious persuasion, there was great danger in toying with the world of the dead through dirty means. Any decent Roman knew better.

⚜⚜⚜

Amosis and I only reached the corner of the *compital* shrine well after dusk. After traversing the wide city all morning, I'd toured the Castra classrooms, prison, barrack, and gymnasium with Ferreolus looking for ways to economize until the fresh Treasury funds arrived. My bad leg ached and I slowed my pace to ease out the overworked tendon.

The evening mist pressed down on a thick fug of smoke from thousands of streetside braziers and grills. It blanketed the far end of every block as we climbed.

'Long day, *Magister*. You should have eaten properly instead of working through midday without stopping.'

'You mean you didn't get enough from my tray to taste, you rascal?'

The swirl of city smoke sank to our heels as we reached the top of the Caelian Hill. Two strangers were talking to Flaccus. The lop-eared *vicomagister* wasn't paying them much attention. He was too busy sorting out the good coins from the chipped for his accounts to the municipal priest.

'Aren't those the same men who followed us away from the Lampadius *domus*?'

'I wasn't with you when you made the arrest, *Magister*.'

'Of course.'

'They could be anyone, couldn't they, under those cloaks?'

It was impossible to make out their faces from twenty paces. It might be the Ceonii brothers again, lurking uncomfortably close to my home. But why? Their brother Lollianus was off to his trial in Baetica. By the time we'd crested the sloping road, the two strangers had passed on.

'Greetings, Flaccus! Is that all for you or will the *Pontifex Maximus* feast tonight?'

'There's no respect, no respect at all, *Magister*,' he mumbled. A fistful of coins dribbled through his fingers into a hemp sack.

'Look at what people dump on our deities! Rubbish from years past, dated even before the reform. All clipped and chipped and sweated until nothing's left but base rubbish. Why should the gods reward such offerings?'

He couldn't pass off this junk at the *popina* down the street.

'We just saw two respectable worshippers. Weren't they as generous as they looked?'

'Got rid of them. Rude fucks. Think mocking a holy man in service of our great gods is fair fun.'

I tossed a decent coin into his pile.

'Goodnight, *Magister*! Blessings on the Numidianus household! But remember, the gods can't be everywhere at once! Lock up your doors! Lock up your women! Lock up your children and slaves!'

I'd done better. I had Avitus and Numa back together on watch, though with Maximinus at least two weeks' ride away in the north, they seemed redundant. Perhaps they felt superfluous as well, helping Apollonia, Lavinia, and the rest of the house decorate our atrium for Saturnalia.

The foul smells and coal-burning haze of the street faded as we passed through the *fauces* to smell the evening *cyphi* burning on the altar.

I'd totally forgotten the coming year-end festivities. They would be modest in our new home compared to the old days of the Manlius celebrations on the Esquiline. For one thing, Apollonia had been raised in such reclusive and modest circumstances that she found the holiday ritual both exciting but exhausting.

Our Saturnalia feast was nothing compared to the heyday of the old Senator Manlius leaning on his handsome son, the Commander, as he clowned and joked with the ranks of slaves and servants. And I recalled how both Manlius men would admire the beautiful mistress of the house, *Matrona* Laetitia, sweeping back and forth, laughing and glancing at her hero husband in the days before his mutilation in battle and her wasting illness set in.

And on the wonderful 'Day of Reversal', I'd been one of the slaves allowed to play 'master'. I can still feel the affectionate fingers of the Commander in my curling bronze hair as he instructed me, his unacknowledged bastard son, to gambol on his couch while he performed the tasks of my 'slave'. He cut up my meat and served me olives and rich wine.

Perhaps in my old age, I'll emerge from my study to clown with a boisterous hall of slaves and attendants 'playing master' at my expense. And I'll play their comic *pocillator*, pouring my slaves glasses full of intoxicating *conditum* mulled with coriander, anise, pepper, cinnamon, as a gray-haired Apollonia urges them to abuse my couch, my side table, and my best glasses without embarrassment.

'Marcus! Home at last! Come and see! Do we have enough boughs and garlands? Will this be enough or should I send Drusilla out to the market for more?'

Apollonia's skirts swept behind her as she rushed toward me, beckoning me to admire her day's work. The atrium was alive with fresh color, light, and scent. How much our new home marked a fresh start for her, turning away from the weight of Manlius tragedies and nostalgia to something all her own!

Avitus stood on a packing box to hang a garish wreath over the *lararium*. Numa was handing him ribbons and wooden *sigillaria* dolls from the street stalls.

'But Saturnalia is weeks away,' I protested.

167

'Yes, but once the house is done, I can start planning the food, buying and decorating the gifts—oh, Marcus! This is the first year the twins are old enough to have fun.'

'Those two have nothing but fun.'

'I want them to recite the prayers this year and get lots of presents. I have such a list! Look!'

She unfolded some cheap *emporitica* on which she'd scribbled the God Plutus' own cornucopia of treats—writing tablets, footballs, pipes, wooden boats, tin chariots, dice boxes, and 'knucklebones' sets—and this was just for our twins! Moneyboxes with tiny padlocks and keys, carved combs and toothpicks, an embroidered leather *pilleus* and hunting knife for Cornelius, jokey pottery lamps and perfumed oils for friends, cups, spoons, new underskirts and *pallae*, tabletop statues, masks, a parrot—'

'A parrot? Apollonia, who in Hades needs a parrot?!'

She clapped her hand over my mouth. 'Shhh! The cook. She confided to Lavinia that she's always wanted one. And she put up with so much during the kitchen repairs.'

'I replaced the ventilation shaft for that woman! It cost us—.'

'Well, if you think it's too much . . .'

Her happy expression faded. She was once again the intelligent and wary Apollonia I'd married. She'd remembered her doomed acquaintances. So I kissed her cheek and said, no, no, it was going to be wonderful. The whole of the city might rise to a dawn bleaker with each passing winter morning, but the Numidianus household would greet the year of 371 dizzy from incense, tipsy with Manlius wines, and driven to migraine by two little boys teaching a parrot to recite nonsense.

Later, when the atrium was almost festooned and the household was still quibbling about what garland looked better where, Apollonia drew me into the quiet corridor outside our own chamber.

'Marcus, I finally visited Anepsia this afternoon.'

'You talked about Hesychia and the others?'

'Yes. The city's full of pitiless gossip. The secret of Hesychia's unhappy marriage and the shame of her suicide is everywhere. Anepsia says no Roman matron is safe here.'

'What's keeping Anepsia in the city?'

'I don't know. She hinted I shouldn't visit again.'

Apollonia fidgeted with a loose thread of embroidery on her tunic. I knew better than to prompt her story. She didn't like being questioned—it was a reminder she was married to the chief *curiosus* of Roma.

Finally, she continued, 'She received me in her garden. It was too cold, but we sat there, wrapped in our heavy cloaks. Her fried snacks congealed on the plate. The servants dragged out braziers until we were surrounded by half a dozen grates and grills, all smoking away, but it was ridiculous not to go inside.'

'You didn't say anything?'

'No, but something was wrong. I stayed just long enough to be polite. I thought she was angry over the earrings, but she wouldn't hear talk of them.'

'You drew her out?' My wife was more skillful than I at interrogations, although she hated such comparisons.

'Marcus, the Pannonian has asked for Anepsia's daughter Callista to marry his son Marcellinus. He's been in Roma for what? Five minutes? And now, imagine! To marry off Senator Victorinus' stepdaughter to a Pannonian nobody!'

'But Callista is already betrothed.'

'And I thought Callista's three thousand in silver would be enough to lay that dirty business between Victorinus and Maximinus to rest forever.'

'Has Callista met Maximinus' son?'

'Never laid eyes on him. She still loves her Roman fiancé, a very nice, well-educated boy whom Victorinus approved of before he died. Even Victorinus—who was low enough to do business with Maximinus—wouldn't marry his stepdaughter into the snake's nest! And now the girl's expected to drop an excellent engagement like a hot coal for this boy Marcellinus on a posting a thousand *stadia* away!'

The maid Drusilla emerged from the twins' room and lingered, observing her mistress' obvious distress. Apollonia asked, 'Is there anything, Drusilla?'

'No, *Domina*. Do you need me?'

'Not now, thank you.'

I let the slave clear the narrow passage, then asked, 'Now that Victorinus is dead, Anepsia must stay clear of Maximinus.'

'She's so afraid of him. I left the house as soon as politely possible. But, Marcus—'

'What, my love?' I smoothed her furrowed brow.

'It was almost as if Anepsia were afraid of *me.*'

'Apollonia, promise me not to return to that house until—'

'Until?'

I was about to say, *until the Pannonian has left the city*, but after all, he was already gone. He'd left his threatening shadow hanging heavy over Roma like the winter's brazier smoke. Apollonia seemed more lighthearted now that she'd shared her discomfort with me. We returned to the atrium, happy to rejoin plans for feasting and games.

'*Magister*, may I have a word with you?'

I followed Nurse Laetitia out of the happy confusion to the kitchen to discover a convocation of sorts. The cook was standing, feet apart, at her grill. Numa and Avitus were behind the worktable. Lavinia invited me to take a stool. I realized all the lower slaves had been left fussing with boughs and ribbons in the atrium on purpose.

'What's wrong?'

As the most senior of our household domestics, Lavinia addressed me, much as I might open the morning meeting at the Castra. The shelves holding etched bowls, glass goblets, and stacked of redware plates in ranks bestowed a hint of the authority my map lent my own briefings.

'We're all worried, *Magister*,' Lavinia said. 'Cook has something to show you.'

Cook's fleshy lower lip jutted out. Something was about to boil over. She thrust a pudgy hand deep into her enormous bosom of draped wools and sweaty linens and then extended her closed fist under my nose. When she unfolded her fingers, there was a piece of battered gold.

'This was hanging from the collar of that pregnant mutt, the laundry dog Venus. The twins keep feeding her my scraps. And I asked the laundry folk what they were thinking, dressing up a hound like that. They said it was just gutter trash.'

'So it might be.'

'But whose gutter? They found it with the rubbishy coins tossed out by Flaccus at the corner. The clipped stuff.'

'We think it's one of the missing earrings, *Magister*,' Lavinia said.

'Did you show your mistress?'

Lavinia shook her head. 'We don't want to worry her yet. She relies on the girl, night and day.'

'Did you ask Drusilla to identify this? It doesn't add up to much.'

I turned to Avitus and Numa. It was annoying to have Castra staff mixing in domestic squabbles. 'What are you two doing here, listening to this?'

Cook said, 'I invited them. They've got proof something's afoot.'

'You've seen something?' I asked Numa.

Numa looked at Avitus. Avitus looked at his boots.

'Tell him!' Lavinia barked.

Avitus blurted out, 'We both had an eye on that Drusilla, *Magister*. We know it's wrong—she's your property—and there'd be Hades to pay if we damaged something that belongs to you—but it was getting boring just sitting around, doing nothing.'

'She's a tempting little bit,' Numa said. 'She led us on. It seemed like a harmless game.'

'And?' I waited for one of these healthy, strapping young men to confess he'd sullied my slave. I'd brought this on by not keeping a closer eye on things at home.

'She refused us both!'

Lavinia's eyebrows shot up at me, full of meaning. 'These days Drusilla goes off to market in a new *palla*, *Magister*, pinned with a nice set of new *fibulae*.'

And as I'd known Drusilla all her young life, from her first sultry games with the adolescent Leo in the Manlius library, to her sullen bitterness when Leo's bride Aurea discarded the lubricious young woman on us, I got their point. Drusilla's eye had wandered elsewhere, but so what?

'Drusilla needs a husband,' I said. 'Keep an eye on her, but if nothing worse happens, don't dampen my wife's holiday spirits with petty rows.'

CHAPTER 13, A NEW VICARIUS

—THE AERERIUM—

Over the following weeks, the Numidianus household gave itself over to festivity, frivolity, and occasional insolence. Our slaves and servants reveled in the Saturnalia ritual of playing master and mistress at our expense. Apollonia proved herself better than our cook at preparing many traditional dishes—which put that hearty woman's nose out of joint.

The pouting slave cheered up only when I poured some of my best *mulsum* down her gullet with a consoling pat on her chubby shoulders and presented her with the colorful parrot. We named him 'Cicero' in the expectation of many speeches.

I observed my boys during the endless visits Apollonia arranged with other mothers from our neighborhood. Verus ranked his new wooden soldiers in a corner of the atrium and shied away from interference. Atticus swapped his toys—at noticeable profit. He ate too many honeyed pastries and got sick.

Apollonia seemed content. But the most interesting and educated ladies from the oldest families on the Palatine and Esquiline, those perfumed society ladies in flimsy silks who'd made decorous visits to our garden until last summer, they were 'away,' 'indisposed,' or didn't answer Apollonia's invitations at all.

We heard that some had fled the city on short notice. Others had just 'disappeared.'

And all this time—under December's drying boughs and fading leaves, amidst the scattered crumbs and ready tears of two exhausted little boys—Lavinia, the cook, and our two guards watched Drusilla from under their suspicious brows. If the saucy young woman was abusing her mistress' trust, I would leave the investigation to them for now.

I needed a break from intrigue and sought refuge in my study. But even there, an air of uncertainty seeped in from our foyer, through the atrium, kitchen, and slaves' quarters. Perhaps the indefatigable Drusilla felt the chill, because she grew prickly and even more provocative.

But at least the Numidianus family felt safe behind our thick walls. It was more dangerous out on the streets. The swirling mist of December thickened into a brown fog suffocating the city as we welcomed in the new year and new consuls so long foretold. The 'senior' consul would be the Emperor Valentinian's son, twelve-year-old Flavius Gratianus Augustus II. While the 'junior' consul was that boulder of wealth and connections, the Anician clan's boss of bosses, Sextus Claudius Petronius Probus.

Where was he now, the Empire's Praetorian Prefect of Italy, Illyricum, and Africa? Where was that sleek and rapacious man I'd spotted so briefly last September in the Caracalla Baths?

Benevolent to allies and pernicious to enemies, servile to the two imperial brothers just above him, and pitiless to everyone else, Probus parlayed his boundless wealth for the high offices he craved. I had too many reports of his irrelevant attributes, like his generous sponsorship of that Gallic teacher-turned-court toady Ausonius, and too few analytic memos on his policies and practices. One thing emerged, however. Probus was insecure and petty, even at the height of all possible power. As the new consul, he'd probably get worse.

Such sour thoughts! Clearly, I hadn't been refreshed by my short break. I wished to linger in my comfortable corner, unrolling old texts and delving into unfamiliar authors. The foul fog wrapped the city so tightly, it was as if the year 371 was reluctant to rouse itself.

After a week's respite, Amosis and I returned to the Castra. Each dawn, the *vigiles* and their slaves dragged in bloated corpses bobbing in the eddies and shallows of the Tiberis. We followed our noses each morning, using the greasy aromas of familiar *tabernae* and urine-filled laundry vats as markers through the fug.

Blind turns made every narrow alley or curving path a possible haven for pick-purses and molesters. It would have been unseemly for a man of my station to carry more than a ceremonial weapon through the city streets. But Amosis was armed with a *pugio* and I resumed the affectation of carrying my carved walking stick with its razor-sharp blade concealed within.

At last a week of breezes swept away the fog, leaving the Eternal City to drier, chilly days under crisp skies studded with high clouds. One dawn as we marched up to the Castra, Amosis stopped twice in my wake to adjust his bootlaces. The third time, I was about to reprimand him when he muttered behind me, 'They're following us, *Magister*. Those same men talking to the *vicomagister* weeks ago.'

I never broke step and kept my face forward, but asked in a low voice, 'You're sure? Got a look at their faces?'

He caught up. 'I think so. Same height, same boots, same stride.'

We didn't change our direction or pace until we were nearly to the Castra gate. Amosis sped ahead to warn Cyrillus I was on my way upstairs and would expect the first paperwork of the morning sorted on my desk. I lingered with the night shift preparing to hand the gate to a fresh team. I glanced up and down the street.

The two cloaked strangers had gone. Had Amosis been mistaken?

The following mornings saw the same charade. Under less requirement than me to carry himself with any dignity, Amosis found one excuse or another to fall back a few steps—a snack, a stumble, a passing acquaintance. He loitered at a stall, flirted with a street whore, patted a cat, or chased away a beggar child just long enough to register the same two shadows behind us.

And for at least week, the two trackers kept their distance but lost interest just before we reached the Castra. And I'd almost lost interest in them when a messenger from our gate arrived in my outer office at the end of a particularly long morning meeting.

'A summons to the *aerarium Saturni, Magister*.'

'Signed by whom?'

'Didn't say, *Magister*.'

'That must be our funds for the year and none too soon. Why deliver our share to the old treasury house?'

As a rule, our *schola* coins arrived from Emperor Valentinian's financial department, the imperial *fiscus*, via Mediolanum. The dilapidated Republican treasury house in the

Temple of Saturn, adjacent to the Tullianum and the ancient *Tabularium*, had fallen in stature over the centuries. It was now just a dusty clearinghouse for local veterans' payments, city tax collection, and the like.

I stretched my legs and escorted the guard past Cyrillus, who was busy, and Amosis, who wasn't.

'Tell Ferreolus I want him to go right away.'

The guard hesitated. 'But the messenger said the summons was for you, *Magister*.'

'Of course, as I'm head of the *schola*. But it's for the financial officer to collect—'

'But, the summons specifies you by name. Look.'

The youth reached under his leather armor and handed me a packet of smooth, expensive folded paper, sealed fast with an unfamiliar insignia pressed deep into midnight blue wax.

It was indeed for me. I retreated back into my private office before cracking the seal.

Flavius Maximinus requested *Magister* Marcus Gregorianus Numidianus to come without delay to his temporary new offices in the *aeraerium Saturni* to report on the Castra's recent arrests.

The flamboyant signature was offensive enough, but the second line turned my stomach: '*Praefectus Urbi (Acting).*'

I dropped the summons on my desk and listened to the clatter of boots and slave carts crossing our courtyard below. The city's eerie interlude, that holiday suspension from care, no matter how illusory to anyone past the age of twelve and toy boats, had truly ended.

'Shall I tell the messengers you're coming or say you'll be delayed, *Magister*?' the guard asked.

'I'll be with them in five minutes.'

There was no time to buttress my morale with the finery of high office.

I read the summons again. There was no courteous phrasing or scintilla of respect. I felt its sender reach up from the thick paper and encircle my neck with his cold hand.

How well I knew the quirk of imperial hierarchy! The acting city prefect was not the *praefectus urbi*'s deputy. On the contrary, Maximinus now enjoyed complete freedom from all municipal oversight. Ampelius, Olybrius, Praetextatus—none of them could touch him now. Maximinus reported directly to Valentinian's court.

That vulgar signature told me that the new Acting Prefect for Roma, Pannonian Flavius Maximinus had for all intents and purposes seized complete control of our city.

⚷⚷⚷

Waiting for me at the gate were none other than the two dogged 'strangers'. They positioned themselves on either side of my *lectica* as we descended the Caelian Hill. Up close, these two men were nothing like the two Ceionii brothers. They were tall, yes, but graceless as they pushed through the crowds. They marched more like rustic Pannonian soldiers than urbane Romans. Only when one adjusted his heavy *chlamys*, did I realize with a start that their tunics bore the insignia of low-ranked *protectores* seconded from the imperial court.

I chastised myself for ever mistaking their gait as well-bred.

We arrived at the ancient Temple of Saturn, restored for the third time after a fire eleven years ago. There was a new engraving—*Senatus Populusque Romanus incendio consumptum restituit*, 'The Senate and People of Rome have restored what fire consumed'—on the pediment of the front porch. But this boast sat buried under a mess of tattered posters for last season's elections, plays, and games.

Only the gods know what the Temple first looked like seven hundred years ago. Perhaps it would outlive the city itself, always rising again and again, from worn out brick and marble.

The entrance at the back led into battered, echoing chambers denuded of gold and silver stores and denied the muffling comforts of archives long removed. I was told to wait on a marble bench with stone feet carved into lions' paws.

I stood.

After twenty insulting minutes, a stranger in fantastic court array—brushed and embroidered felts, gleaming pelts, shining brocades, polished leather, and a parade baton—emerged. He would escort me to Prefect Maximinus. I didn't ask who he was. I would not give this parade ground martinet that satisfaction.

At first, Maximinus seemed unchanged to me, except for a higher bounce to those short, bandy legs.

'Congratulations on your promotion,' I said, although I choked before getting out the new title. 'Why a temporary office?'

'Senator Aginatius is slow to clear his office for my use. My appointment took him by surprise.'

'He can't be happy.'

'Aginatius has more to worry about.'

Maximinus called for more light. When fresh torches arrived, they only illuminated better how sudden and temporary his occupancy was.

It was a shabby place from which to work—filthy and badly ventilated. The flames caught the draft with a roar, then settled, showing Maximinus' beefy torso pressed against a new and even wider *cingulum*. Its buckle linked to a bunch of golden grapes. His polished black *campagi* were embossed with eagles. A new flame-colored *chlamys* with gold bands swept across the broken stones of the sloping floor.

Not a fleck of flour or a splash of oil survived from last year's stint in the *annona* offices. Those leering henchmen, Mucianus and Barbarus, were gone.

'You've met my new man, down from the court? This is Leo, of the regiment of Valentinian's *notarii*, an expert at *notae Tironianae* shorthand. He will act as chief marshal of the municipal Roman courts, if need be. It was, in fact, *Notarius* Leo here who delivered the Emperor's imperial patent of promotion to me. Here you see it, properly laid out on blue cloth, as custom prescribes.'

I ignored the pretentious display of an imperial document on a new, overwrought ceremonial inkstand bedded in a waist-high bronze tripod. These new props only underscored the parvenu's gloating over his odious promotion.

I acknowledged his notary Leo, so different from our own beloved Leo of the Manlius household.

This soldier-turned-civil servant had waxed his black locks down hard on his skull with a reptilian sheen. He'd abandoned ordinary army garments to take up this powerful post in Roma. But any true Roman would spot him as a Valentinian courtier across a crowded forum. Emperor Valentinian preferred rough-hewn veterans over educated men in more tasteful dress. Acquired for Roma's unfamiliar dining rooms, Leo's new getup managed to be both unfashionable and vulgar—and the fashions of today's Roma were already vulgar enough. He made me think of that stray dog Venus wearing scavenged scraps of gold.

Worse, the newcomer reeked of cheap bath oil but seemed to have skipped a week's worth of baths.

'The *Schola Agentium in Rebus* will endeavor to fulfill its duties to this office, as ever,' I told them both.

'You'll do better than that, *Agens*.' Leo's accent marked him as a rustic Pannonian indeed. And he displayed the manners of the military camp.

'Our reports should satisfy you both.' I laid down the written summaries Cyrillus had copied from our arrest records. Maximinus ignored the excuse he'd used to get me down here.

'Our *augustus* Valentinian isn't happy with the management of this city,' Maximinus said, toying with his new ceremonial swagger stick mimicking a centurion's *vitis*.

I bristled at his dismissive *this city*. Did he mistake our Eternal City for Lutetia or Lugdunum or that soggy backwater Londinium?

'For one thing, Emperor Valentinian is livid that Proconsul Hymetius wasn't executed as my personal judgment decreed. Prefect Ampelius had agreed with the sentence. How dare the appeal court reverse our decision!'

'Hymetius' only crime was to seek imperial favor. I hear the Africans are raising money for a statue to Hymetius as thanks for saving them from starvation.'

Maximinus kept thumping the baton into his other palm.

'The Emperor doesn't like being crossed.'

'No one does.'

'He especially doesn't like using spells to win back his favor.'

'I observed Hymetius' appeal. Hymetius' only magic was hiring an eloquent lawyer too junior to understand the shadow of politics over justice. I wish the same luck for Lollianus, now on his way to trial in Baetica.'

'So I heard.' Maximinus tossed Leo an unnerving chuckle. 'Old *Pater* Lampadius will discover his sneaky suggestion of a judge he considered a faithful crony was a fatal error. Consul Isfalangius is now a great favorite of Valentinian's, for both loyalty and severity. I myself endorsed his selection in my *relatio* to the Emperor.'

Ten steps ahead . . . I had to disguise my horror at young Lollianus' bad luck. I pointed to my reports in Leo's hand.

'All the accused senators are under house arrest, except for Senator Abienus. But he'll be stopped at any gate if he tries to flee the city.'

'I trust your reports include the locations where private guarantors are holding the senators? We're going to move them to less comfortable abodes.' He grinned at Notary Leo.

'With respect,' I said. 'I observe some irregularities that keep these senators in detention. Where are the full and detailed written charges as required under Constantine's reforms? There can be no lengthy detention without accusation in writing being provided to the accused and their advocates. And two ladies of my own acquaintance were detained—'

'Oh, we'll observe the formalities, won't we, Leo?'

'It's too late for *Domina* Hesychia. She suffocated herself in despair.'

Maximinus slapped his baton against his meaty thigh. 'Then the lady knew herself to be guilty.'

'Valentinian can't possibly approve your methods. You detain wellborn women from families of *honestiores* on minor charges, threatening torture for allegations with no link to treason?'

'Minor charges? Adulterous sluts in imported silks? And what if their partners in vice are traitors? Information must be obtained, Numidianus. Questions must be asked. Answers must be found. Don't worry. More detailed charges will be filed.'

'Will they be anonymous slanders fished from the bottom of a wooden box? Or substantiated accusations a decent witness would dare put his name to?'

'Oh, the accusations come from reliable sources. I confess, I was shocked but perhaps you wouldn't be. You grew up in this depraved city.'

The *Notarius* Leo glanced up from my reports. 'Yes. You were a slave here. And slaves hear things, don't they?'

Maximinus continued, 'Even highborn women must be made to talk.'

'But not tortured.' I slammed my palm down on his thick marble desk, the only polished furniture in this morbid gallery of antiques.

'Yes, tortured, tortured until they cooperate. *Custodia libera* is not appropriate in these cases. There will be interrogations.'

'Interrogations, but no torture. I saw what you did to those wretched *humiliores* in the Chilo case. No torture for the Senators Eumenius, Paphius, and Cornelius—they enjoy senatorial privilege under Roman Law.'

'Not in cases of treason. An arrest warrant is going out now for Senator Aginatius on charges of treason'

'Maximinus, the accusations against these senators have nothing to do with treason. Vice, perhaps, adulterous misbehavior to be proven in court, surely, but not treason, not *maiestas*! Have you misled Valentinian for the pleasure of extorting tortured Romans who openly despise you?'

'Misled?' Maximinus took a seat behind his battered desk. He gazed at his ceremonial promotion display to boost his morale. 'I simply informed the Emperor that the offences which many men and women have committed here could not be investigated without taking severer measures. The Emperor understood. He gave me one general judicial sentence to cover all these cases by linking them to the design of treason. Read it to him, Leo.'

Leo reached for the hallowed document on the blue cloth and read aloud, 'All those whom the justice of the ancient code and the edicts of deified emperors have made exempt from inquisitions by torture should, if circumstances demand, be subjected to torments.'

'You tricked Valentinian!'

'Hardly, Numidianus. Given his recent brush with fatal illness and the suspected poisoning attempt on his brother and himself before that, the Emperor is terrified of betrayal by any vicious means—and rightly so.'

'You solved the Chilo case! You intend to go further? Have you no compassion for simple human frailty?'

'Compassion? Why so forgiving, Numidianus? Are you a Christian drunk on mercy, by any chance? No, I didn't think so.'

'This has nothing to do with Christian mercy. *Veneficium* isn't treason. Adultery isn't treason! Fraud, trickery, any kind of *stellionatus* may be disreputable, but not treason. There can be no torture for love affairs.'

'You needn't shout at me, Numidianus.' The torchlight caught the bright shine of Maximinus' white smile and the steely flicker in his deep set eyes. 'This city's a sewage drain.'

'Valentinian's regime is upright, virtuous, and law-abiding,' Leo added.

'So yes, Numidianus, there will be torture. There must be torture. Notary Leo and I are empowered to employ all tools at our disposal to root out the political and spiritual malady coursing through this city.'

I was wasting my time. Maximinus thought so too.

'Don't worry about Senator Abienus, Numidianus. We'll make sure someone turns him in eventually.'

Leo walked to the door and opened it. I'd been hauled across *this city* like a minion, but I wouldn't leave like one. I reached across *Notarius* Leo to slam the door back shut.

'You're new to court life, Leo. I once knew a man who employed torture to advance favor with an emperor—*Notarius* Paulus Catena. Emperor Constantius limited torture to investigations of treason, cases of *maiestas*.'

'Of course I've heard of Paul "The Chain". Pannonians aren't ignorant fools, Numidianus,' Leo said.

'But Catena also stretched the definition of treason to breaking point, just like he stretched the limbs of innocents until they popped from their joints. He enjoyed it—'

'We hardly enjoy such duties!' Maximinus struck the desk with his baton.

'But you share one failing. Catena learned, at least for a while, how to buffer his sovereign from the ugly side of security. To allay a nervous Constantius, he dredged bloodied confessions from the basement of Mediolanum Palace. But Catena never learned one important thing from his pile of broken bodies.'

Leo asked, 'Learned what?'

'That torture produces more lies than truth!'

'Calm down. You overstep yourself, Numidianus, *again*. You were already wrong to question my prisoners at the Tullianum.'

I laughed at him. 'If you're right and I'm wrong, how could I possibly learn more with a cup of wine than your vicious methods had already produced?'

He laughed, yet he was frightened of something. I'd spotted fear in his eyes. Had I discovered exactly how long ago he'd solved the Chilo case, yet kept it simmering for his own ambitions? Had the blinded Campensis told me of Maximinus' father's prediction of death by an executioner's sword? Had Campensis hinted at the foul world of necromancy?

Perhaps Maximinus was merely frightened of displeasing his powerful sovereign in Treverorum.

'Catena terrorized his way from one end of our empire to the other. He destroyed whole families, great families of this city all the way to Britannian colonials, innocents caught up in the Magnentius' rebellion in 350. Then he tortured allies of General Silvanus in Mediolanum in 355 and went on torturing all the way to the East.'

'Emperor Constantius appreciated a man who the job done, Numidianus.'

'Appreciation? Constantius was a pious, squeamish man who craved the approval of bishops and saints. He never appreciated Catena's barbarity.'

'Valentinian's made of tougher stuff.'

'So am I, Prefect, I shared Catena's death cell in Chalcedon. He finished very badly.'

'We all have to go sometime.'

'Catena's legs were broken. He crawled around his cell. He begged me to kill him but I refused. I saw him tied to a stake and burned alive, screaming as his own feet swelled and exploded under his own eyes. A man who acquires so many enemies can end no other way . . . by a torch set to straw . . . or the executioner's blade.'

Maximinus' dark eyes flickered. The baton was very still.

'You can go now, Numidianus. Expect a flood of arrests, a river of interrogations as wide and fast as the Tiberis.'

'We'll follow normal procedures, no more—'

'From now on, your *schola* won't be used. The Emperor no longer trusts this city—or its departments. He's lent me a team of imperial *protectores* to carry out arrests ... *et cetera.* You've already met two of them.'

'*Et cetera* being the torture of senatorial citizens that I remind you is illegal?'

'The crime of treason protects no one! And when you hear your precious *honestiores* and their wives and clients and slaves screaming like Catena for an easy death, remind yourself—Prefect Flavius Maximinus is only doing his duty to protect his sovereign. He wouldn't need to resort to such lengths if Marcus Gregorianus Numidianus had helped him save time from the start.'

'I never stood in your way.'

'I needed those files! I needed to know the connections, the marriages, the relationships, so as to spare the innocent harsh questioning. You've wasted my time.'

'Stop before you destroy yourself, Maximinus. The Chilo case is closed.'

'The Chilo case? Ha! You really think this was about Chilo and his silly wife? That was a consequence, not the cause. I no longer need any Chilos to carry on my investigation. Remember, Numidianus, it isn't always the crime that condemns people—it's the cover-up.'

In a cloud of gaudy red damask and bad breath, *Notarius* Leo threw me out.

☙☙☙

'*Magister*?'

A mere whisper from the outer office floated through the evening shadows. Cyrillus had gone to bed.

'*Magister*?'

Amosis kept snoring on his bench.

'Is that Myron? What is it, Myron?'

'Oh, it's lucky you're still here.'

I gave a wry laugh. 'This was the hour that *Magister* Apodemius opened up his shop.'

'But you look tired, *Magister*. You need one of my tonics. Perhaps my news will cheer you. Your generosity has worked a miracle. Thanks to your good wine, old Zephyrinus has recovered his wits.'

'What? Impossible!'

'Yes, yes! He's sitting up and asking for you!'

I crossed the courtyard many yards behind Myron, already leaping up the steps to his infirmary.

'Hurry, please, *Magister*, in case the miracle doesn't last!'

The old librarian, kept alive on soup and wine, was a bundle of stick-bones under his coverlet. But his eyes were clear and his mind alert. Had my vintage revived him? Or the intervention of the great deity who protects us all at the Castra, pagans and Christians alike? Or was it the drivel of Roman hearsay from that ragbag *Acta Diurna* read aloud at his bedside?

For Myron, his tireless nursing slave, and myself, the attack on Zephyrinus seemed the event of a past season. But for the old crock, it had happened just the night before. So, with some impatience, I dragged my thoughts back to that failed burglary— to hear it all from the librarian again.

' . . . no, no, it wasn't completely dark, but they needed a lamp. That was what had alerted me to their intrusion.'

'But the strongbox could be located right away. Why not douse the light to avoid detection?'

'Because the man in the cloak was digging furiously through my archives. He needed that little lamp to read, obviously, while the others stood guard.'

Now I recalled the report of Anthimus, Defendens' dying friend.

'What man was that? Did you see him?'

'His hood hid his face. The others in the band were bareheaded scoundrels, but the man who was reading moved carefully under his hood.'

'You saw the fight that killed Anthimus?'

'Anthimus ran in. He tackled two of them. Then I was knocked out.'

'But what about the strongbox?'

'They weren't bothering with the strongbox. It wasn't a robbery for money, *Magister*. It was a violation of the Castra's true treasure—*my* precious files. *My* archives! How did they dare? My life's work!'

Myron winked at me. I'd almost forgotten Zephyrinus' implacable conceit that the Castra's collection of centuries-old imperial information—maps, political dossiers, mission reports, provincial audits, road maintenance and mail hub budgets—they all belonged to him alone.

Zephyrinus complained he was starving. The canteen should provide him a decent meal—for the gods' sake! Grilled fowl! Pork balls! Anchovy pastries! More wine! I promised him a fresh pitcher of my best *conditum*.

Myron said the old man's beverages should be well-diluted. Zephyrinus was very weakened. But not so weak that he hadn't resolved the mystery of the strongbox full of silver left untouched.

For far too long, I'd resisted making the obvious link that would inevitably plunge me into greater danger. Perhaps because it was *too* obvious and I knew something about my assumptions felt wrong—but what? Hurrying from the infirmary back to my office, I warned myself—don't make connections where there are none. I had no proof. None at all.

So now, how could I get it?

CHAPTER 14, ZEPHYRINUS AND CLEMENS AT WORK

—THE CASTRA PEREGRINA—

Maximinus had relegated *Magister* Marcus Gregorianus Numidianus to his list of enemy 'Romans'. All possible uses of ambiguity lay behind me.

Brooding and powerless, I threw myself into routine duties through the deadest weeks of January. The cold wet weather filled the city streets with charcoal smoke and mud. Our prison's gutter spilled rainwater until a lagoon spread across the courtyard's cracked paving stones. The barrack toilets backed up and the stench drove our unrulier cadets to pissing against the back wall.

I'd been beaten by a man I loathed, a ruthless provincial with a brother-in-law beheaded for treason, a man reputed for extortion and law-bending whose own father had predicted he'd die by an executioner's sword.

I just couldn't accept my *agentes* had been shoved right off the course by such a man to be replaced by crude teams of *protectores* seconded from outside Roma, not after so many years of getting back on our feet. Aided by half a dozen trusted secret allies, I'd worked like a mule since Emperor Julian's purge of our service nearly a decade ago, With the Castra shuttered, we'd bided our time, squirreled away Apodemius' dossiers, and slowly trained new *agentes*. It had taken years just to reopen our gates and more years of struggle to regain imperial trust and financial backing. We were almost back up to operational strength. I mustn't give in to the Pannonian so easily.

My staff was no more resigned than I was. Eager to prove his recovery was no short-lived miracle, Zephyrinus crawled from his sickbed to scour 'his' dossiers. After two days, he staggered up my stairs on the arm of Myron's nursing slave. His quavering voice demanded that Cyrillus admit him to my inner office.

When gentle Cyrillus said I was busy, the old man rang out, 'Tell the *Magister* I bring buried treasure.'

His discovery was actually modest but real enough. The newly-arrived *notarius* Leo appeared twice in our records. First, he'd switched from civil training as a mere accountant to serve as General Dagalaifus' *numerarius magistri militum*—hardly a post for heroes. But Leo had worked his way by degrees to the right place at the right time more than once. In his second appearance in our files, he'd secured Emperor Valentinian's personal gratitude by one very lucky stroke.

'So I missed something—?'

'Yes, *Magister*, I believe you did.'

The report clutched in Zephyrinus' spider-veined hands had reached the Castra only in 365, while I was caught up thwarting the Procopius usurpation attempt on Emperor Valens in Constantinopolis.

'Perhaps our informant delayed sending it in, *Magister*. Perhaps he didn't know whom to trust at the Castra—what with Apodemius and the rest of you gone.'

'Fair enough. Is his information that sensitive?'

'Very. The author's a wine wholesaler. He delivered bulk orders to army staff officers traveling the Nicaea-Ancyra route to the Persian front and back. That's where our friend takes deliveries—the port of Nicaea.'

'That's probably why Apodemius found him useful. Any guy delivering the booze to the barracks is as invisible as the barber and bootmaker.'

Zephyrinus lifted the folded paper up to his weak eyes. 'He writes he was in the town of Dableius, west of Dadastana, Galatia where poor Emperor Jovian dropped dead. He hastened eastward to see what he could learn for the Castra. He talked to the landlord of a *mansio* at Ceratae, close to Dadastana. And the landlord told him how the top officers, including "that Germanic old wolfhound General Dagalaifus," were huddled in a panic, "all day and all night in frantic debate" over who should be the next emperor.'

I broke in: 'I know *Magister* Aequitius, then of the First *Schola Scutariorum*, pushed his own name forward. I met that bastard during the Procopius uprising, Zephyrinus.'

The old man nodded, 'That's the one, because it says here, the landlord told our wine dealer that the other generals judged that Aequitius could never be emperor. He was too *asper et subagrestis*—'

'Bitter and aggressive? Believe me, that's the polite version.'

Zephyrinus mopped his pale brow with the hem of his sleeve. I must stop interrupting. I was tiring him out.

'The point is, *Magister*, in 364 our new friend Accountant Officer Leo was serving in Illyricum under General Dagalaifus and Commander Aequitius. So, let's see . . . back to the debate. Oh, yes, here it is. Someone nominated a Jovian relative for the diadem instead, one Januarius. The others refused him too, because Januarius was posted too far away. They couldn't risk the same kind of delay that followed Emperor Julian's death.'

'Ten days with no emperor. I remember it well.'

'The wine trader writes that they wanted a new emperor as fast as possible, someone near at hand. So then, someone suggested Valentinian.'

'Who? Does he say?'

Zephyrinus ran his finger across the faded lines of the wine dealer's forgotten report, discolored from neglect.

'Well, listen to this: "Commander Valentinian, son of the disgraced Pannonian general Gratian, was directing the Second *Schola Scutariorum* in Ancyra. He seemed a possible candidate. While Valentinian was being fetched, Commander Aequitius and a Pannonian *numerarius* named Leo "ensured" that the army officers would not nominate another candidate from those present until Valentinian could reach Nicaea to claim the throne. The landlord heard rumors of bribes to buy off any rival candidates which I have tried to confirm . . .'

'*A Pannonian numerarius named Leo . . .*'

'Yes, yes!' Zephyrinus' wattles flapped with excitement. 'You see, Numidianus? Maximinus' *Notarius* Leo was there, *right there*. He helped Commander Aequitius tie up the throne for Valentinian by—'

'—bribery to silence Valentinian's rivals. An ugly business, indeed. Well done. You have dug up gold.'

Zephyrinus broke into a hacking cough from hours spent unwrapping 'his' dusty treasures.

'You must go back to bed, now. But first, are you sure no one disturbed our files on the leading families—the Anicii and Ceionii—the night of the attack?'

'No, *Magister*. Anyway, you'd taken my files on those two families home. I presume they're still safe?'

He left me to make use of his discovery. So *Notarius* Leo was no innocent shorthand whiz. Maximinus' sinister right-hand man belonged to Valentinian's innermost cabal of Pannonian army veterans. I was dismayed but not surprised. I'd heard nothing about Valentinian's emergency roadside election in 364 to win my support to their rough club's inner circle. Their warrior rules went against the very system by which I'd earned high office.

The late Constantine had reformed the imperial government into two strict career paths—civil and military. Though the modern fashions of civil servants had long mimicked the panache of military dress and even our *schola* adopted the rankings of the cavalry for convenience, the separate lines of civil servant and fighting man had stayed clear.

Constantius II and his family had for the most part kept Constantine's practice alive; civil and fighting men rose separately, kept their authority and responsibilities distinct, whether in court, in provincial capitals, or even as they thundered on horseback behind his eagle standard as part of his roving *comitatus* crossing from province to province.

This was one way the Constantines kept power evenly balanced, healthy competition alive, and career priorities well-defined.

Valentinian had grown up in army camps. His talents began with clever sketching and ended with armor design. His idea of literature was vulgar pastiches of Vergilius which young Gratian's tutor, the Burgundian poet Ausonius, was happy to oblige with dirty puns and salacious allusions.

From the start, the court of Valentinian had been little more than a camp of ruthless soldiers scrubbed up for high office. They might exchange their scratched and dented *spathae* for ceremonial weapons and vinewood batons, but their methods came straight off the battlefield.

And ... Secretary Leo was one of this Pannonian circle advising, flattering, and often corralling Valentinian's moves.

So who was really in charge of our city? The 'senior' man, the ambitious lawyer Maximinus? Or his 'junior,' this Leo who knew the underhanded secret of how Valentinian had bought supreme power?

⫷⫸⫷

Valentinian's permission to link virtually any vice with state treason and torture seemed to have lifted Maximinus' boots off the ground with the pleasure of those legendary sages of far off India who walk through air.

His promotion ate at me like a festering wound. It soon seemed as if Maximinus and *Notarius* Leo had sought unfettered powers to bring down every aristocratic house in the city. With each disappearance of a Roman citizen or slave into the bloody jaws of Maximinus' redoubled purge, I felt more powerless.

For one thing, I'd failed Prefect Olybrius. He'd made his pact with the Emperor's demon courtier to save his son Alypius' life. But he'd salved his conscience that day at the Caracalla Baths by entrusting Maximinus' other targets to the rigor of my Castra's protection.

Far worse—somehow, I'd failed Roma itself. Of course we had procedures and laws by which *honestiores* and *humiliores* alike conducted their lives but the Roman Senate had long lacked any true authority to check intemperate emperors. Their repetitive, empty acclamations at the unveiling of a new regulation handed down from a distant court, their rhetorical charades debating the hours of barbecue sales in residential neighborhoods—these pantomimes rivaled the performances of that greasy actor Roscius parading the boards at Pompey's Theater.

Where was the judiciary? Where were the city's finest advocates? Was mine the only remaining imperial department ready to halt this madness?

With a chill, I observed Roma's most expensive legal teams, summoned by shattered aristocratic families, fade away and then vanish. Soon the more prudent advocates just slammed their doors against the wailing relatives of the accused.

They'd heard—no doubt from Prefect Maximinus himself—that the defense of the exiled Proconsul Hymetius had enraged the choleric Valentinian. The Emperor had wanted Hymetius' head—literally—but it was still attached to the ex-Africa official's shoulders in the coves of Dalmatia. To taint a legal practice by defending against charges of *maiestas* was so undesirable, it overrode any interest in testing even well-honed rhetoric.

Of course, the Castra wasn't idle. As *magister agentium in rebus,* I had more than enough to distract me from Maximinus' horrors passing outside our gate.

The imperial treasury convoy with our *schola*'s shares of taxes arrived at last. I held painstaking budget meetings with Ferreolus to marry road maintenance costs and state *mansio* accounts to our fresh supply of coins.

Privately, I digested constant updates from the Empire's harried fronts—all of them rich with details of Emperor Valens' victories over roving Gothic bands or senior brother Valentinian's forays against the Alemanni tribes along the Rhenus.

I had hundreds of spies in the field still to manage, the unwieldy coordination of intelligence to discard, relay, or archive. And I had to ensure that my own condensed reports to the two distant emperors—my single cherished victory over a fortress of bureaucratic obstacles—were of strategic use.

These duties offered a respite before the end of each morning, when our senior officers delivered their harvest of the latest horrific developments right under our noses. My frustration was hard to contain as I listened: the Castra could monitor the most intimate state correspondence in Treverorum or Constantinopolis but in our own city, we were hardly better informed than the *Acta Diurna* posted down on the old *fora* billboards.

Slaves—boys and girls—disappeared from the well-guarded townhouses and suburban villas of our finest families. They were snatched up while running market errands or retrieving garments from public baths, or simply lured into the street on some feeble excuse, never to return except as mutilated corpses washing up under the Tiberis docks.

Their masters cowered from society, too shocked to claim the remains of their property. Even as they sought deeper refuge in unheated summer retreats or the unfamiliar estates of hesitant friends, they murmured—who was next?

Anyone might be next, depending on the family's tawdry secrets confessed by their slaves. Their 'crimes' of telling fortunes with a pendulum hanging from a tripod swinging from letter to letter, or repeating a lucky charm in public, or conducting a furtive affair during the lazy doldrums of Sicilia's summer shores—such ordinary pastimes were suddenly state crimes, social poisons to be squeezed out of their servants' bodies.

There was the sudden cancellation of a business meeting with a long-standing client, whose beautiful wife was not so much unfaithful as indiscreet about your flirtation at the Bay of Baiae resort. Yes, that coward might talk, would certainly talk, if strapped naked to the *eculeus*, the torturer's 'little horse', and pulled apart with a twist of a wheel or lacerated by the *flagellis et verberibus*, his scourges and whips.

With some of our cadets, Rubellius coursed every pre-dawn hour in conversation with the *vigiles'* riverside slaves netting and hooking bodies to land.

' . . . You can see the gashes of the *sulcantibus ungulis*, the iron claws they're using. And there are deep cuts to the bone from the fetters and cords from the rack, not to mention the bruises of the scourge. It's not pretty, *Magister*.'

'You found out yet where they're doing their dirty work?'

Rubellius nodded. 'My "good friends" Mucianus and Barbarus showed me a warehouse near the docks where Leo's men can do their work without decent people fainting. But even with the noise of the boat traffic, I heard screams from inside and somebody yelling, "Tighten it up! Hand me the torch." I won't sleep tonight, I tell you.'

'Take a break. Go get some breakfast.'

'No, thanks. My stomach's inside out.'

The great public baths dotted across the city suffered a sharp fall in custom. High-ceilinged halls built for the deafening sound of hundreds of swimmers, sweaters, masseuses, gossips, and fitness fans now echoed to the occasional slap of a servant's slipper or the rustle of a handful of bathers crossing the vast tiled floors in wary silence.

I drew up lists of the missing, overheard private appeals for intervention before an inevitable midnight arrest over which I no longer had control, and witnessed intentional degradation of respected city leaders dragged in fetters through the widest streets.

I insinuated our most inconspicuous *agentes* into the city's choicest corners of gossip. Later, we analyzed the rollcall of terror and noted down the names of the tortured corpses—if there was enough of a body left to identify—for their anguished families.

But we were cut out of any official role in these nightmarish developments. Public panic unrolled before us, like a lurid carpet of horror. What could I do?

One morning, some weeks after Zephyrinus' discovery, my morning meeting shared news of three more tragedies:

First, Senator Cethegus, of the *gens Cornelius*, descended from noble Republican consuls and senators and a grandson of the governor of Flaminia and Picenum no less, fell at last under Leo's torturers' scourges and iron claws. He'd languished in a prison outside the city for at least half a year. Whatever Cethegus said or didn't say, his usefulness had come to an end. He was beheaded for adultery.

Second came that state lawyer, Marinus, who'd been accused of seeking spells to win over Apollonia's pretty acquaintance Hispanilla for his wife. (And hadn't my wife scoffed last autumn when we talked of such things as worrying?) This noble Marinus finally fell to the executioner's sword. The flimsiest evidence against him was barely mentioned and never cross-examined during his trial. This omission was a complete contravention of law under old Constantine's reforms. To think a prominent *honestior* like Marinus, a renowned defense attorney—*defensor causarum*—couldn't even save himself from illegal capital punishment.

And then, the morning Marinus died, the head of Roma's mint also lost his head—without any charge being publicized or any trial held whatsoever! No magic or adultery charges were even rumored. A shiver of revulsion went through our Castra staff as Rubellius muttered, 'Another one.'

It was more than a footnote to me. I found the black curtain over the mint chief's demise the eeriest mystery so far.

There was one fast rule over centuries of Roman history; state mints provided coins, and coins confirmed imperial authority. Control of a mint was part of making—and breaking—imperial legitimacy. Our unpresuming mint chief—hardly a Roman outside his offices and residence could even name him—had simply disappeared. Why?

'That's it for now.' I closed that morning's briefing. 'Clemens, you stay.

Quaestor Clemens stayed behind. I ordered Cyrillus to bring us fresh *posca* and snacks.

Clemens nodded. 'I did what you asked, *Magister*.' He tapped the tablet onto which he'd etched precise notes.

I lowered my voice: 'Do we have a case? I don't want to waste the time of anyone—least of all Praetextatus.'

He fiddled with his *stilus*. 'I couldn't say for certain, *Magister*, but I'm trained to argue anything you want.'

'As I'm always reminded by our young lawyer in the Manlius household.'

He tapped his *stilus* on the tablet's wooden frame. 'This is pretty dry stuff. But I might see an opening. What you do with it is up to you.'

'All right. Release your darts, Advocate.'

He cleared this throat.

'Well, all treason law still refers back to the *lex Iulia maiestatis* of 48 BC . . .'

I closed my eyes as Clemens traveled back three centuries. '. . . the *Leges Corneliae* under the dictatorship of Sulla specifying only that the torture of *honestiores* is warranted in cases of *maiestas*, that is, treason against the state. Under *Ad legem Iuliam maiestatis* of 48 BC, we find the crime of *maiestas* is that which is committed against the Roman people or against their safety, or exactly; *Maiestatis crimen illud est quod adversus populum Romanum vel adversus securitatem eius committitur*.'

He looked up at me, 'Our noble ancestors were thinking mostly of military offenses.'

'Yes, of course. Please get to the point, Clemens. You're paid by the year, not the hour.'

Yet it was another ten minutes, after Clemens had run through a veritable marketplace of treasons—raising an army without imperial permission, questioning the emperor's choice of a successor, murdering hostages or high magistrates, attending public gatherings or city meetings with weapons or stones, releasing prisoners justly confined, falsifying public documents, and the failure of a provincial governor to quit his province at the expiration of his office or to deliver his army to his successor—before I cut him off.

'Yes, yes, Clemens, but treason against the person of the Emperor? How far can Maximinus stretch that accusation?'

He scratched his scalp with the point of his *stilus*. 'Tacitus wrote, "Emperors are as gods." Thus the crime is called *laesa maiestas divina* in law. But I have found nothing longstanding that says it's treason to commit adultery or the black arts. They're capital crimes, but not treason.'

'Nothing longstanding. But now?'

'I admit, things have grown murky this century, *Magister*. You see, treason's useful. It's special.'

'How? I need to know the law, exactly.'

'For one thing, any citizen—even women or scoundrels—can trigger a charge of treason, while the accused loses his normal rights to fight back for malicious prosecution. He loses protection from torture. He loses protection from seeing his slaves tortured if they testify against him.'

'I see. What else?'

'The accused loses all his civil rights, including the right to leave a will. The state confiscates all his property.'

'That's key. The more Romans Maximinus can link by one charge or another to treason, the more prime real estate he scoops up for the "state".'

Clemens wiggled his *stilus* like a haggling rug trader down at Trajan's Market. 'Once treason comes into play, it's more like a pick-up game of *harpastum*. No referees or limits.'

'So now, my legal eagle, the question is, how did Maximinus get permission from Emperor Valentinian to mix magic and adultery under the same rules governing treason?'

'I'm coming to that, *Magister*. The law only became confused quite recently. Constantine, our great reformer, ruled that magic used for good—let's see here—the health of crops or weather or a loved one, should not be punished—'

'Yes, but?' My patience was exhausted. I would never have lasted one week in the law courts.

'Constantius II took a fatal misstep. He made the first exception for torture against a senator during a case of magic discovered at his court. Perhaps he felt personally threatened?'

I leaned back in my chair. 'Constantius was the most jittery ruler I've ever served. So there it is. The breach in precedent. The damage was done. That's Maximinus' loophole.'

'Not quite, *Magister*.'

'But surely—?'

'Now, we come to our current crisis. On July 8, 369 to be precise, Emperor Valentinian wrote to Prefect Olybrius that torture was permitted in cases of *maiestas*, "the same law for one and all," but no other charges *without consultation of Valentinian himself*. So there's a net underneath the loophole.'

'Consultation with Valentinian? Maximinus will claim he's obtained that already. That's our best opening—?'

It wasn't much, but I didn't want to disappoint Clemens.

'But you know, Valentinian ruled just after his acclamation—reversing himself under pressure from noble Praetextatus no less—that traditional divination, which Christian Constantine accorded in earlier legislation, remains protected. Valentinian only prohibited "wicked prayers" and "magical fraud".'

'Your point—?'

'That in his rulings a few years ago, Valentinian did *not* lump adultery or stupid baldness cures together with treason allowing the torture of *honestiores*.'

'So how did Maximinus do it? What did he say that won him this blanket permission to rip apart the world's greatest city?'

Clemens tossed me a sharp glance. 'I'd like to see the wording of his new commission from the Emperor. Could I get it copy?'

'I saw it with my own eyes, but—'

'*Magister*? Are you all right?'

'No, I'm an idiot!' I pounded Apodemius' desk again and again, shot to my feet, and swore to the gods.

Cyrillus flung open the old door. 'What's wrong?'

My clerk saw me there, bulged-eyed at our legal officer cowering on his stool. My mind raced back to my angry confrontation with the two Pannonians at the old Treasury. I inhaled once or twice to calm myself and nodded to Cyrillus who disappeared with a gentle pull on the door.

I sat down, shaken.

'I've made a stupid mistake, Clemens! For over a month, I've assumed Maximinus went north to Treverorum to consult the Emperor *in person*. Simply because that pompous ass of a clerk for the *annona* told me so. The thickest cadet in the school downstairs would doublecheck.'

'But we know Maximinus was absent from Roma over Saturnalia.'

'Yes. We know that. But did we confirm his passage along the northern routes? No. Did we get any reports from our informers at court of his presence? No. We didn't check. *I didn't check.*'

'Is that all?'

'No. In his eagerness to boast how he'd sent that poor kid Lollianus Ceionius to a rigged trial, Maximinus let something slip. He boasted that he'd nominated the deadly judge in Baetica himself in a written *relatio* to the Emperor.'

'Written? So . . . he didn't advise Valentinian in person?'

'No.' I paced back and forth behind my desk.

'Maximinus even preened over his new commission, saying, *Notarius Leo here delivered the Emperor's imperial patent of promotion to me. Here you see it, properly laid out on blue cloth, as custom prescribes.* And there it was, Clemens, propped up on a fancy tripod next to its ceremonial inkstand.'

'So, Maximinus sent his *written* version of events to court. And Leo rode alone back to Roma, delivering a commission to shoehorn every vice into a treason investigation?'

'Exactly, Clemens. Every vice, whether it was directed at the person of the Emperor or not. Which begs two questions: how well does Valentinian understand the true situation in Roma if Maximinus did not submit himself in person for the *quaestores* to examine the legal position?'

'Especially *Quaestor* Eupraxius—that great Moor honors the very letter of the law.'

'A legal mind to be feared. No, instead Maximinus sends a *relatio* to a very busy emperor who's terrified by the idea of another poison attempt on his person. We have a sovereign who's still weakened by his illness three years ago and waging war with the

Alemanni. The Emperor despises and shuns anything refined and noble that Roma still stands for. Maximinus exploits our foolish recreations and moral frailties. He wraps it all up in a terse battlefield request to investigate suspected treason and associated vice, he requires the necessary arms.'

Clemens flipped his *stilus* and caught it in the air like a precocious schoolboy. 'Hail *Notarius* Leo, delivering the ammunition!'

He turned serious again. 'But *Magister*, you can't be sure. You have no proof. I would not place your arguments before a magistrate. You still want to consult Prefect Praetextatus?'

I stood up. 'We must try, Clemens. The biggest magic trick of the year may be Maximinus conning Valentinian. Please draw up a neat, penned version of your notes. We're going to Praetextatus immediately.'

Gathering up his ink-stained leather case and battered *pilleus*, he asked me as he reached the door.

'You said two questions. What was the second, *Magister*?'

'Oh, the second question is blacker than your blackest ink, Clemens. Maximinus lied to his assistant, Firminius. If he didn't go to court, where did he spend December?'

I ordered Saturnus to pull a dozen riders off the mail circuit. They were to fan out through the city gates and check with every *mansio* until they picked up a trace of Maximinus' December journey. Maximinus had ridden alone to avoid attention. But along the way, he'd have needed a fresh horse, a snack, a bed, or a bath. And use of the *Cursus Publicus* meant he must produce his *cursus diplomatae* that guaranteed such services.

While Saturnus selected our Castra 'hounds' to sic on the prefect's faded trail, Cyrillus looked up the registration number of Maximinus' road permit.

I smiled as I watched my *agentes* gear up for departure. Maximinus might have ridden unseen, but my men would pick up his trail. The Pannonian had given himself away every time he stopped to use a *Cursus* toilet.

CHAPTER 15, SLAVES, LOYAL OR NOT

—THE HIDDEN ESTATE—

The ambitious Maximinus had tricked the Emperor—I was sure of it. But to overturn his reign of violence, I needed more than the authority of my department—I needed the support of the Eternal City itself.

Roma's noblest pagan had not appeared in public for weeks. Locating the aristocrat would take hours of polite and insistent inquiries. The Castra's officers started at the grand double doors of Praetextatus' palace on the Mount Oppius, then spread out to various municipal offices and lesser residences.

It seemed Praetextatus and his virtuous Paulina had escaped the daily atrocities in the streets: respectable men and wellborn women, loyal clients, retainers, and slaves—beaten, fettered, and dragged bleeding past the jeering rabble to overflowing jails and *ad hoc* detention centers.

Who among Roma's comfortable classes wouldn't escape the hysterical city, given the chance? But old families that had served the Empire for centuries deserved more than abandonment from their terror. They needed standard bearers and brave witnesses to their persecution. It wasn't the first time in recent weeks I'd registered Praetextatus' convenient absence from the city's turmoil. Was this his secret to surviving our puritanical Pannonian Christian regime—strategic retirement to a life of bookish *otium*?

And where were the city's other 'leaders'? My roving *agentes* reported back: After his courtroom failure against Proconsul Hymetius's appeal, Urban Prefect Ampelius had hunkered down to supervise 'routine' city administration. His 'ailing' predecessor Prefect Olybrius was always at the theater. And Roma's foremost uncrowned power? The redoubtable *culmen* of the Anicii clan?

Consul Sextus Claudius Petronius Probus was very busy as Praetorian Prefect of Italy, Illyricum, and Africa and reportedly on an inspection tour out of his current base in Sirmium.

None of these men wore shackles. The survival of Roma had become an option only for Romans within reach of a prestigious posting, a hidden sanctuary, or a luxurious villa beyond city walls.

'Where's Senator Aginatius?' I asked Rubellius as we gathered up the team reports. Hadn't he shown himself in Anepsia's atrium to be Maximinus' first public opponent months ago? The indignant and volatile Aginatius had so far eluded arrest—yet was not reported missing or dead.

'One informant said he was hiding out on a rural estate,' the *biarchus* said. 'A second source said it too, so that confirms it.'

'Always be careful with so-called confirmations,' I warned Rubellius. 'Apodemius taught us they often confirm nothing more than that your second source heard the same baseless rumor as the first.'

It was midmorning when my young Gallic recruit Atolitus raced upstairs to Cyrillus' desk. He produced on his cadet's wax tablet the address of an obscure rural district. The directions—a tangled sequence of *viae privatae* and *viae rusticae*—added 'for the sole use of *Magister Agentium in Rebus* Marcus Gregorianus Numidianus.'

I resented forswearing the protection of Amosis' quick eye and alert ear just to flatter Praetextatus' fetish for privacy, but saw no possible objection to taking Clemens as my legal expert.

The February rainfall drove down like piercing needles. Under the protection of lanolin'ed riding cloaks, we rode out of Roma into the silent suburbs. But at least the endless wailings of the city were muffled by stately groves and the congealed blood draining into street corners gave way to garden pools circled by statues.

At a fork in the *Cursus Publicus*, Clemens and I took a *via munita*, its cracked paving hinting at declining county funds. I checked Atolitus' tablet instructions before continuing down a *via glareata* of well-combed gravel. And it was nearly dusk when we reached an unmarked *via terrena*, a plain drive of leveled earth marked by the fresh ruts of a carriage.

I would have suspected a wrong turn, except that our approach was interrupted no fewer than four times by small parties of private mercenaries in Praetextatus' livery posted at junctions en route.

Were they expecting us? They brandished no weapons nor did they seem disconcerted by our appearance.

We hit a short broad drive paved in marble. Parallel rows of towering cypresses guided us toward a walled two-story villa on the crest of a slope flanked by rows of olive trees, each in its own tiny, low-walled plot.

Farm buildings, stone enclosures, a separate bath complex wreathed in a spiral of steam—Praetextatus enjoyed deep and comfortable seclusion here indeed. It was the hour for lighting lamps and torches. One by one, dots of gold flickered from elegant windows. Our arrival would be noted by anyone gazing from the upper floors.

Given all his precautions, I imagined no conference would be more discreet, but I was wrong. Even here, it seemed, we must bide our time in a queue of clients. We handed the reins over and our horses were tethered between a jumble of city carriages. An old-fashioned low-roofed vehicle with pommels bearing the bronze crest of the Ceionii stood at a tilt closer to the inner gate, as if abandoned in haste. Six slaves in faded tunics with frayed embroidery crouched near a wheel. They sheltered from the relentless downpour under a blanket.

Clemens and I were escorted through the *fauces*, emerging into a long reception area. The sienna-red walls featured murals of that predictable country scene—the Theban hunter Actaeon transformed into a stag and captured by his own hounds as punishment by the goddess of the hunt, Artemis.

We continued down the columned walkway of a drenched peristyle garden, arriving at a choice of rooms. The slave attendant indicated we should continue along the right-hand corridor. We approached the threshold of a comfortable book-lined study.

How I was wrong about the quiet refuge of suburban life! A howling that would rend the hearts of the gods filled the room ahead. I gave an apprehensive glance at Clemens as we crossed under the archway to take in a painful scene. I felt like one of those embarrassed and shushed theater-goers ushered to his numbered seat after a tragic performance has already started.

'—been betrayed! And he's dead, *dead*!' A man groaned, swallowing deep sobs. 'Our precious youngest—*beheaded*! The most innocent of our illustrious line, *slaughtered* like a common criminal!'

'Common criminals don't qualify for beheading. At least the way of his death showed you respect.'

'*DEAD*! And his poor mother has nothing, no keepsake, no ashes, no body to bury! How are we to mourn him? How are we to honor him? I tell you, Praetextatus, my wife will not survive her grief. Mine is nothing to hers. That boy was her last and favorite. *Do* something!'

'Come, come, stand up. It's too late—'

A nobleman standing next to Praetextatus tugged at the agonized human heap in chestnut brocade clutching at his host's knees. Only as the miserable parent was peeled off Praetextatus' pristine robes could I recognize the former Prefect for Gallia, former Prefect of Roma, the forger of fatal papers framing General Silvanus, that duplicitous *consistorium* adviser to Constantius II, Gaius Ceionius Rufius Volusianus—that duplicitous old fox, Lampadius.

The weeping father must have arrived mere minutes before us. How long had the two others been here? I hesitate to call them 'guests'. I now recognized them by the powerful torchlight illuminating the scene from ornate wall-sconces. Such men had no time for idle salons or languid leisure. They were here on business.

'Stand up, I said. You demean your station, Lampadius,' Praetextatus muttered. But he made no effort to extricate his hand from the desperate elder's claw-like grasp.

Lampadius choked on his bitterness. 'My station? Did I claim consideration because of high station? Did I receive it? I am a citizen of this empire. Did I not merely claim the fair trial that is the right of any Roman citizen?'

'He had a trial.'

'A trial? I asked for a trial under someone trustworthy, someone I thought honest and impartial. I argued that my child's youthful folly would pass with time—as it does for all men of decent education and good upbringing.'

'But Roman Law says—' broke in the taller of the two officials.

'Oh, I put my faith in Roman Law,' Lampadius spat out, 'and for that, the Fates leave me a broken fool.'

He slumped on the gold-flecked mosaics of Praetextatus' priceless 'rustic' decor. At last his fingers released the expensive white wool of Praetextatus' long tunic.

The shorter official tried to pat Lampadius' shoulder. 'Faith in Roman Law is a luxury of the past, my friend. You're not the only honorable Roman to have made this fatal mistake when dealing with the Pannonians.'

The quartet spotted Clemens and me in archway.

'Yes, yes, what is it that you needed, Numidianus?' Praetextatus made it clear he respected Castra business but did not regard its *magister* as deserving any preliminary courtesy.

'I'm sorry for your loss, Lampadius. I believe that Roman Law is still there for the protection of—'

'Don't you dare address me, you freedman! You carried him off yourself! Roman Law has become a hollow farce when a noble Ceionian boy is beheaded over a book of silly spells!' Lampadius fought to regain his dignity on wobbly legs, his red and swollen eyes blinded by tears.

I raised my voice to be heard above his groans, 'Roman Law can only be rescued in person, at the court at Treverorum. The Castra's *Quaestor* Clemens has drawn up the legal arguments that must be presented immediately in person to Emperor Valentinian.'

Praetextatus looked unimpressed. He handed Lampadius over to the care of two sturdy slave women. They settled the old man on a couch with a goblet of wine. Meanwhile Praetextatus smoothed his crumpled tunic and collected his *dignitas* to deal with my interruption:

'You waste your time and ours, Numidianus. Emperor Valentinian enjoys the services of the finest jurist alive, Eupraxius the Moor—our *Quaestor Sacri Palatii.*'

'Precisely, Prefect. Please, stop and think. Does this blood-soaked abuse of longstanding senatorial protection against tortured inquisition bear the mark of the Moor's expertise? No! I do not—I cannot—believe Maximinus' new authority passed through Eupraxius' careful hands.'

Clemens piped up: 'The laws that come to the Castra from Eupraxius' desk are invariably fair, often erring on the side of moderate. And always based on sound legal precedent. Maximinus' commission is not.'

Praetextatus blinked at my upstart Clemens. His companions also stared, shocked that my junior had addressed the great nobleman without permission. But frankly, don't all lawyers—and doctors for that matter—love advertising their expertise over us mere mortals?

'Please forgive Clemens here. He has studied the situation hard and given me reason to believe you can act—'

'I? You're suggesting I—that I do what, Numidianus?'

His coyness angered me. 'Who else, Praetextatus? You reversed Valentinian once before.'

'And we have legal grounds!' Clemens started unbundling his briefing papers. I took firm grip of the young man's wrist.

I continued, 'We believe Emperor Valentinian has been pressured or tricked—through twisted information, inattention, or calculated miscommunication—who knows? But we can say for certain, the Emperor has been misled into fearing a political uprising from Roma.'

Praetextatus' eyes penetrated me like a *spatha* thrust. I faltered, then added, 'The Emperor has been confused *on purpose* as to the application of torture in cases of adultery and magic, versus treason.'

His high brow furrowed. Strategic suburban retreat might protect his household and intimates, but his political reputation was at risk if the Manlius House's freedman, that half-Numidian *magister agentium in rebus* was ready to fight for the ancient city and yet won no support from the most powerful pagan in Roma.

The two officials glanced at each other. I knew the taller as Volusius Venustus, Emperor Julian's former vice-governor of Hispania, and the other as consular governor Tiberius Victor Minervius. I'd captured their sympathy and so plowed on:

'*Quaestor* Eupraxius could rein in the Emperor. Like yourself, Eupraxius hasn't flinched in the past. Remember how he saved the lives of three Pannonian decurions from Valentinian's killing temper four years ago? I'm confident that Eupraxius will argue to rescind the authority abused by Maximinus.'

Minervius spoke up: 'If it means we form a delegation to Treverorum, I'll go with you, Praetextatus, as Treverorum is my birthplace. And here in Roma, I have friends or I *had* friends I cannot locate. We all do. I fear for their welfare.'

Venustus cocked an eyebrow at his friend, to which Minervius nodded, 'All right, then, I admit it! I fear for my *own* welfare. But what Roman guilty of some venial error in love or superstition doesn't?'

I pushed on: 'Praetextatus, you told me it would end with the Chilo case but instead—'

Venustus finished for me: 'Instead all Roma's *honestiores* tremble for their lives. Praetextatus, don't tell us you're waiting for Prefect Ampelius—'

'Ampelius!' Praetextatus scoffed. 'Ampelius presided at Maximinus' side over the conviction of Proconsul Hymetius. Hymetius would be dead today if left to Ampelius.'

I seized on his welcome disgust: 'And Maximinus told me himself that the exile of Hymetius enraged Valentinian. No, Ampelius will do nothing to put himself at further odds with the Emperor.'

Venustus nodded. '*Magister* Numidianus is right, my friend. Few Romans dare challenge this Pannonian serpent. The freedman *curiosus* and his young lawyer put us to shame.'

A long, discouraged silence followed, set to the dirge of rainfall overflowing the marble *pluvius* in the garden, runoff coursing through gutters overhead, and the muffled tears of Lampadius staining a priceless silk-upholstered couch outside.

Praetextatus ran his hand over a shaven pate smoothed with fragrant oil.

'I agree to nothing, Numidianus, nothing. But I'll hear your *quaestor*'s brief—alone. Take that young man's cloak. He's dripping all over the Persian carpet.'

He led Clemens away to an even more private study and closed the paneled door behind them. Clemens wouldn't falter, so diligently had he combed through the inconsistent history of state torture. Anyway, this was not a test of Clemens' erudition. It was a test of my choice of agents and their training.

I settled on a cedar bench and discreetly studied its carved lion-claw feet to allow the two senators to confer in private. It promised to be a long wait, marked only by the departure of Lampadius, supported by two of his household cortege, for the lonely trip through the wet night back into the city. He faced an anguished matron and those walls of dead-eyed Ceionii *imagines* condemning his failure to better preserve their illustrious line.

A tray of cold meats and flat bread traveled across my eye line to disappear into the little study. With a regretful nod to me, Venustus and Minervius went to dine in the family's private *triclinium* with *Domina* Fabia Aconia Paulina.

An ornate green glass of diluted wine and a bowl of olives arrived at my lonely bench. It was more than an hour before Praetextatus emerged with Clemens. Nervous sweat circles marked the lawyer's tunic.

'Your young man has argued well. As soon as the passes clear, we ride to Treverorum,' Praetextatus announced.

No, I couldn't let him delay. A month from now, Praetextatus would have tested the political waters, sent out feelers, and heeded arguments for greater caution. I wished Venustus and Minervius had stayed to bolster my plea.

'Prefect, my *circitores* don't let imperial mail wait for melting snow. And saving our city is more urgent than any letter. We must take the winter postal detour up the western coast and around the mountain passes to Forum Iulii, then straight north along the Rhodanus River valley to Lugdunum, Andematunnum, Tullum, Divodurum and straight to Treverorum.'

'But the harsh weather on our carriage wheels—'

'If you're prepared to ride a saddle under my escort, we'll make far better time than any carriage. We should leave this week.'

Praetextatus straightened his shoulders and adjusted a gold *fibula* on one shoulder. He saw the die had been cast as soon as he'd admitted in principle that only he could carry our appeal. He would have to stop translating Aristotle's *Analytics* for some weeks.

Chilled to the bone, Clemens and I slogged our way back into the city and up the Caelian Hill to the Castra gates. The barrack windows were alight with cadets and riders settling down for the night. The canteen and classrooms showed a candle flame or palm lamplight where slaves were cleaning. The soft slosh and slap of our busy laundry—the road dust and sweat of riders being a constant of our service—rose over the high wall. A lamp glow from the floor above the gymnasium said Myron was grinding medical plants or distilling oils.

'Clemens, wait,' I laid a hand on his arm. A dark figure trembling with cold under an oversized cloak stood at the guard post outside the gate. A pick-purse too lame to hide himself? A beggar who'd given up harassing the traffic along the street?

He spotted us and raced pell-mell to seize me before Clemens could step in between.

Amosis! The Egyptian slave been standing vigil under the gates' high torchlight for many hours. His long black curls lay matted flat by rain and his sallow complexion was the gray-white of a cod's underbelly. He pulled me away from the sentry post as he croaked:

'Hurry, *Magister*! Hurry! Hurry! Trouble at home! A foul Pannonian notary is interrogating our mistress!'

We'd left our horses for grooming at the city gate stables commandeered by our *schola* for all Castra riders heading east. How fast could I run on my bad leg? Would we go faster by *lectica*? Which men were the speediest bearers?

But Amosis was already half a block ahead of me, not even turning back, assuming that the fear surging through my veins would force my middle-aged legs up and down the familiar alleys and through the thinning crowds huddling and hurrying over their duties in the last hours of the evening.

I ran blind through the rain behind the flying slave. As I stumbled up the slope toward the junction where the *vicomagister* Flaccus should have been closing his temple, I felt a sharp, agonizing reminder of the left leg's wound. It threatened to fell me with each lunge past clumsy carriages and cloaked pedestrians.

I had become a winged but wounded thing, panicked and panting, screaming inside.

That creature Leo was inside my home.

⚔⚔⚔

Our gardener's little Beata had been posted at the *compital* shrine. She crouched, invisible to indifferent adults, under Lavinia's green blanket. We were all *agentes* now. The tiny sentry saw Amosis coming up the hill and dashed ahead in her laced winter street shoes to warn the house. Amosis was through the front door well ahead of me. I flew through the *fauces* as Avitus and Numa bolted the front door behind me and resumed watch.

My household had turned from a family sanctuary into a nest of guards. I raced through a silent fortress under siege. Our slaves had retreated to their quarters. No cooking smells came from the kitchen. No comforting whiff of *cyphi* wafted off the *lararium*. Most terrifying, no racket of sticky little boys greeted my arrival.

Lavinia stood like a centurion under the atrium arch, arms folded, eyes narrowed, and mouth set in a grim line.

'Where are they?'

'Gone, Magister. That *notarius* left only minutes ago.'

I screamed, 'He took her?'

'No, no, *Magister*. He tried. But Numa and Avitus demanded a warrant. He carried none and they stood their ground as witnesses against illegal detention with daggers drawn. But the *Matrona* is shaken. She's locked herself in the bedchamber.'

'The boys?'

'Aucta and Apustia took them to neighbors. Shall I fetch them?'

'Not yet, not yet.'

'Apollonia!' I tried the door handle.

'Marcus! Are you alone?'

'Yes.'

She unbolted the door and retreated to a high-backed wicker chair in the corner of our room. It was her favorite 'reading chair' with flattened feather cushions covered in bleached linen and a matching foot rest. She clasped her hands in her lap, her knuckles white, and looked up at me.

Her eyes were sad and exhausted but dry. Whatever her ordeal, she hadn't wept. Leo hadn't broken her.

My panting slowed.

She looked not resigned or distressed, but hard as granite and as removed from me as some hidden oracle.

I knew my beloved wife. If she'd retreated behind her former veiled and stoic courage, she'd been frightened beyond tears or trembling. I hadn't seen this Apollonia since the dangerous days when we first met trying to smuggle a dying Apodemius to safety from Julian's purge of the *schola*. Apodemius raised her from childhood in seclusion and deception for her own protection. It had taken years of marriage, motherhood, and social freedom to thaw her defenses and lighten her spirit.

Now that joyless Apollonia was back, the Apollonia that once eluded the *schola*'s enemies by denying herself normal life itself.

'Leo ordered me to accompany him for questioning "in a formal setting." But Numa demanded to see his warrant—'

'The gods bless him—'

'—and Leo didn't carry one. He hadn't expected any resistance. You see, Marcus, he timed his intrusion only too well! He said you were out of the city!'

'I was, but not far. Why didn't Avitus and Numa refuse him entry?'

'They know how things stand. They might be charged with obstruction. You might be charged yourself, for all they knew. But you've trained them to know their warrants. And they stalled him in the *fauces* long enough for Lavinia to get the twins to the Oclatinii family down the street.'

'Priceless woman.'

'And Numa never let him near enough to touch me. Avitus ordered Drusilla to fetch a tablet and *stilus* to record everything he said. The delays enraged Leo.'

'What did he want?'

Apollonia gazed up at me through the faint lamplight. 'Marcus, Maximinus' *protectores* discovered Senator Abienus hiding in Anepsia's house.'

'The gods save her!'

'Abienus was led in chains straight to the Tullianum. Anepsia was taken under *custodia libera* to a friend of her first husband. He stepped forward as *guarantor* just after dawn.'

I shrugged off my wet cloak. 'What's she accused of?'

'Adultery with Senator Abienus.'

'But Abienus is accused of sleeping with poor Flaviana!'

'Anepsia also dropped Abienus' name in jest.'

'So you knew Anepsia was sleeping with Abienus?'

'No, Marcus! I assumed she was joking along with Flaviana to brush away her fear of a lonely old age. But I'm not the wife and granddaughter of the Castra for nothing. Apodemius raised me to be watchful.'

'What are you saying?'

'Well . . . you know how you can guess the back of a coin from the profile on the front? And how you teach your cadets that the absence of something can say more than the most glaring clue? Well, I knew Anepsia admired Abienus. And now he was on the run for his life, with the whole city searching for him. During my last visit to her house, she was noticeably jittery and brusque. But one thing was missing; she didn't seem worried about Abienus' disappearance at all.'

'That raised your suspicion?'

'Not that same night, but later.'

'I recall you felt she was afraid of you.'

'She *was* afraid of any visitor who might notice something amiss. A slave carrying a tray to her stowaway might catch my eye. I might overhear a word that prompted my curiosity.'

'But later you deduced why Anepsia hustled you away from her freezing garden? Because Abienus was hiding there? Don't you trust even me, Apollonia?'

She shot to her feet, flushed with anger.

'Your Castra holds a warrant for Abienus. Suppose I was wrong? Suppose Anepsia was innocent? She wouldn't be the first ageing female to pretend a flirtation where it didn't exist.'

'But deceive me—?'

'Hush, Marcus, they'll hear us outside. I couldn't tell you, even on our pillow with the lamps out, because I had no evidence, much less proof. You would be obliged to act—and then?'

'I understand. Who needs proof these days to destroy another noblewoman?'

I took her place in the chair. Her almond fragrance rose off the cushions.

'So Leo suspects you of being Anepsia's accomplice?'

'Worse, Marcus. He accuses me of being Senator Abienus' co-conspirator. He thinks I've known where Abienus was for weeks. That I visited *him*, not *Anepsia* at the house. That I connived in his eluding arrest.'

'How did Leo even know you'd visited Anepsia?'

'I don't know.'

'Who betrayed Anepsia and Abienus?'

'Oh, Leo boasted about that. One of Anepsia's slaves, Sapaudulus, was taking his revenge. Anepsia had flogged his woman. So he slipped out after dusk and reported Abienus to Maximinus' team. He must have reported my visits, too. They raided Anepsia right after midnight.'

Like the dangling rope-box outside the *annona* office, a sudden arrest under cover of night was against all protocol—just another tactic to terrorize the city further.

What's more, slaves' accusations of adultery never led to trial—that was Roman Law. Slaves couldn't be interrogated by prosecutors to testify against their masters. And disloyal slaves making unprovable charges were to be burned alive and their stolen evidence burned with them—except in cases of treason.

'Leo holds nothing against you. You told the truth.'

'But I still made a mistake, Marcus.'

'You couldn't, my love. You are *veritas* itself. What was your mistake?'

'That vicious man hammered at me for over an hour, listing exact dates I'd met Anepsia. Shouting, insinuating, and threatening, it went on and on—'

'But what was your mistake?'

'When he asked me if I'd suspected anything was wrong at Anepsia's house, I hesitated. And he noticed.'

'He saw you'd suspected Anepsia was guilty of something.'

'Yes. He smiled to himself as if I'd walked into a trap and it was only a matter of time before he snapped it shut.'

'He mistook the doubt in your eyes for guilt.'

'Is that surprising? I'd already been disillusioned by Anepsia three times. First, she didn't deny that Victorinus solicited bribes for acquittals of trumped-up charges laid by Maximinus. Then she gave Callista's dowry to Maximinus. And finally, she even promised Callista to his son!'

'So Leo hopes there's only one step between alleging you suspected Anepsia to proving that you plotted with Abienus. But he'll need a better witness than a vengeful slave. You never told this to anyone?'

'No, only you.'

I rose to my feet. 'You're leaving Roma tomorrow morning.'

'With the boys?'

'No, they'll be decoys. Lavinia will disguise herself in your robes and take them for walks to the little market down the street every day. No one must suspect you've left Roma.'

'Where will I go?'

'To Leontus in Mediolanum—no, we mustn't involve him or Aurea. One of the Manlius farms?'

'Where the good Cambo Catorix will hang me, safe and sound, on a smoking hook in the dark? No, not across the Alps—not so far from you. And I'd be too conspicuous at the oyster farm—the resort bays are empty of good society this early.'

'So the apartment in Ostia. It's out of season but always crowded.'

'And it's where I've always been happiest—when I have to be away from you, that is.'

We looked at each other, both thinking something too awful to say out loud. Like a snake in the foliage, our fear had lain dormant but was always lurking there—every morning Apollonia lit the *lararium* resin to protect our home and every evening we relaxed in the summer garden at the back of the house.

Since the day of our marriage, we'd hoped that the wife of the imperial intelligence chief could live a normal life. Despite what we knew about society's contempt for us *curiosi*, we'd trusted that my professional enemies would respect the innocence of those I loved. We'd lived as if Apodemius' radical ruses to safeguard Apollonia from vicious retaliation belonged to Roma's dead generations and forgotten feuds.

But we'd been fatally naïve. Could Apollonia ever feel safe in Roma again?

CHAPTER 16, TWO DEPARTURES

We had only one week to ready our separate departures from Roma.

First, I instructed our *circitores* heading up the coastal mail route through Genua into Gallia to alert all the state *mansiones* and *mutationes* to prepare for Praetextatus' delegation to pass through. The redoubtable noble said he'd ride with his own protection— half a dozen *bucellarii*, mercenaries wearing his livery and supervising his supplies and spare horses. But our party would still need beds, baths, and food. The Castra issued road certificates for Praetextatus' cohort as well as more modest packets of permits for the Senators Venustus and Minervius and their few attendants.

We made no secret of our mission to Valentinian's northern court; all the lost glory of ancient Roma's senatorial authority would be on parade in the blinding leather polish and bright gleam of man and horse, the colored standards of house and office, and the inevitable public deference expected as we moved along the *Cursus*, station by station. Cost was no object when speed and influence were the objectives.

Meanwhile we prepared Apollonia's stealthier escape. Numa and Avitus were to guard the house as if she remained in residence. Disguised in Apollonia's hooded winter cloak and street shoes, Lavinia was to sally to market daily with the noisy twins in tow They were stuffed with sweets and pastries to keep their little mouths shut.

The morning after our decision, I gave a private note to the Castra's *circitor* riding the Florentia-Bononia-Parma-Placentiae route to Mediolanum. It was an urgent summons for the return of Cornelius, the Manlius *dispensator* attending our Leontus. I'd known Cornelius since my first days as an *agens*, long before he joined the late Senator Manlius' townhouse as the all-purpose majordomo, master of the gate, and general fixer.

A veteran of many battles, Cornelius could be thick-skulled and not always rigorously sober. But his deep loyalty to our extended clan made him a weathered and dogged foe. When it came to the safety of my wife, he would be the ideal escort. He would die in her defense, if necessary.

The rider needed three days to deliver the summons to Cornelius who would race back to us in another three. While we waited, Apollonia consulted with the cook and staff on managing the house in her absence. She was happiest when she was busy and I worried about her drifting alone through idle days in the out-of-season port.

'I'll take Drusilla, of course,' Apollonia said as she folded her *pallae* and *stolae* into a leather carryall. She wrapped her toilet box into a cocoon of bleached night tunics.

'Take Drusilla? No, leave her here—' I thought of my Saturnalia conversation in the kitchen with Cook, Lavinia, and the two guards. To be fair to Drusilla, nothing had come of their scrutiny since then and we'd agreed not to curdle my wife's relationship with her most trusted slave.

'But I may need her.'

'The neighbors might notice her absence.'

'I doubt it. Most of her duties keep her in the house. And she rarely goes out in such wet weather. Lately she's kept to herself whenever she wasn't needed.'

'Exactly. She's turned morose and slow. She might become a burden.'

We handed her heavy luggage to a waiting slave.

Apollonia insisted, 'I'm sure Cornelius will cheer up Drusilla. They haven't seen much of each other since she came to work for us.'

I said, 'It's time we married her to someone. She has sulked over loss of her intimacies with Leo for far too long. They were pimply adolescents then but she got above her station. It's hard, but that's life. A slave has to accept such things. It was my mother's fate.'

'I have a feeling that Lavinia and Cook will be glad to see Drusilla gone for a while. Oh, Marcus! I've tried to keep the house contented. I've tended the altar and been generous with food and drink—rests and holidays. But whatever I do, there's still too much tension.'

Drusilla stayed sullen right up to the morning of farewell. I reminded her she had no choice where she went, not if her mistress wished it.

'Yes, *Magister*.'

'My wife won't be seeing anyone. Cheer up. You'll enjoy a lot of free time in Ostia. Use it well, Drusilla.'

If she suspected she was on probation, Drusilla only nodded and finished her packing. I was dissatisfied with her ingratitude. I'd always been kind to her from childhood, but her lively humor had vanished. She flaunted a pouting indifference that soured the atmosphere.

Cornelius arrived at the end of the week. He looked well-fed and ruddy from constant recreation and hearty drink. All his reports of Leo's progress in the courts of Mediolanum glowed with avuncular pride in our young lawyer. The Manlius heir was fulfilling all the promise of his bloodline, in which I enjoyed that secret part, a part that became less important as the years nurtured his talents for rhetoric, analysis, and even-handedness.

Cornelius didn't burst into our atrium alone—he'd recruited his wife Delicia into the Ostia party. I suspect Delicia had invited herself when she heard the well-endowed Drusilla was going. Apollonia was unlikely to while away her hours in the chatty company of a former 'bargirl,' but she was happy to think Cornelius' outsized thirst would be supervised by his patient consort without extra effort on her own part.

My last night with Apollonia was anxious, passionate, and wordless. The hour for her flight came too fast for my desire and not fast enough for my peace of mind. Would the Pannonians try another stab at questioning her? Arrive with an arrest warrant at the last minute?

We couldn't delay her getaway another second. Cornelius had hired a four-wheel leather-covered *carruca*, complete with travel bed. It waited in the wet shadows beyond the street torchlight.

Drusilla saw the carriage and balked, making one excuse after another about forgotten chores and mislaid effects. I took it for guilty regret. Delicia finally resorted to tactics not necessary since her days as a *taberna* wench. With a swift pinch of one ear and a sudden twist of the maid's plump arm, Delicia muscled the girl through the *fauces* and onto the curb.

Our cook and Lavinia watched with relief. They'd grown tired of watching the slave for proof she'd sold Anepsia's earrings.

I hoped that petty incident was behind us. How familiar the eternal story of slave theft was to a freedman like myself! The child slave Marcus watched many a squabble from his corner in the kitchen or dining room of the old Manlius house on the Esquiline.

In any Roman *domus* these little grievances subsided over time, but they didn't always resolve or disappear. Sometimes they remained like cooking grime rubbed into the pores of kitchen granite.

No two dramas were the same, of course. Slaves varied as much as citizens. Some slaves seized what they could from the Fates' chances. I carried the physical scars and conflicted emotions of my manumission from the Commander, but I'd fought for my liberty and never regretted its cost. Other slaves just resigned themselves, worsening their bad luck into a life of misery.

Drusilla shrugged herself free of Delicia's grip and boarded the carriage. Apollonia kissed our confused and sleepy twins good-bye. She pulled Lavinia's drab cloak over her dark curls. Cornelius folded up the wooden steps behind her. She gave me one brave wave as he shuttered their window against the fading night.

'Oh, please, may the gods protect them,' I whispered, watching the *carruca* roll down the rutted stone street until it turned at the corner shrine and was lost in the mist.

The gray sunrise spread its faint pink glow over the city two hours after their escape. It was time I bid a far more ostentatious good-bye to the Mother of Cities.

⚞⚟⚞

Having been a high-ranking provincial governor required to tour his domain, Prefect Praetextatus proved an able rider. But poor *Quaestor* Clemens was a more modern creature—an educated Roman bureaucrat who'd never served on horseback. He'd have to stay at the Castra, trusting Praetextatus to argue our case.

Such a trip took Castra relay riders about eight days in good weather, changing horses at *mutationes* but resting little themselves. Praetextatus' carriage would have taken a month. We compromised on ten to twelve days. As I outlined the route—the Via Julia Augusta to Arelate and then the Via Agrippa to Lugdunum and Treverorum, the nobleman said he planned a rest outside Lugdunum at the villa of a good friend.

'You do not mind remaining at a *mansio* with the two senators, Numidianus?'

'No, no, of course not, Prefect, but time is precious.'

He tossed me a cool glance. 'So is our health and composure when we confront the Emperor.' He didn't name his host nor why he wanted to pay a social call during our crucial mission. My curiosity piqued, I bided my time.

No one chats during marathons like these. As it was, Venustus and Minervius were only in good enough shape to canter in discomfort with attendants refreshing their bladders of *posca* and warmed wine.

For my part, I breathed with deep relief up the first leg in view of the coast. Even in middle age with a bad leg and thinning hair, I hadn't lost the young *circitor* Numidianus' taste for the freedom of the *Cursus*. I could inhale the fresh breeze and forget the city's charcoal fug, the heavy duties of the Castra, the horrors of the Tullianum, and the naked Flaviana whipped through a jeering crowd. I could relive, hour by hour, station by station, those carefree years racing like Mercury himself from one postal hub to another.

The spell broke when we dismounted for a few hours' rest at a *mansio* in Arelate. This was my first chance to tell Praetextatus that my own wife was under suspicion of abetting Senator Abienus' seclusion at Anepsia's townhouse.

'Who would believe the wife of the *magister agentium in rebus* could be accessory to a crime against the state?'

'Thank you, Praetextatus, but under Maximinus, innocence is never assumed. I've sent my wife away until Valentinian has reversed his scourge of a policy.'

He was handing his heavy travel cloak and damp *pilleus* to one of his minions when he turned, struck by a thought. 'Did you frighten Maximinus somehow, Numidianus? If one knows a rock is sheltering a viper, one doesn't kick it over.'

When I dropped Campensis' allusion to 'an executioner's sword', had I hit a nerve? I said nothing.

Praetextatus took my arm. 'Maximinus knows your Apollonia to be a woman of the highest virtue—or he would, if he cared to study our society as thoroughly as he seeks to destroy it.'

'Yet his deputy gave her a hard going-over. *Notarius* Leo waited until I was visiting your country retreat to make his move. They knew where I was.'

'Maximinus was careful to frighten you a little, but not provoke you in person. Reflect, Numidianus, on how you made a dangerous enemy.'

'You recall, last September Maximinus asked me to take sides—Pannonians against Romans—and I refused assistance beyond the requirements of my office.'

'I try not to take sides, Numidianus. Already I fear our coming audience with Valentinian may be going too far.'

'It's too late to change our minds.'

'There's always time to reflect in Lugdunum,' he said.

I sighed to myself. Praetextatus was still capable of turning back.

We were within hours of Lugdunum, waiting in deep fog along the Rhodanus River, when we detoured to deposit Praetextatus and his cohort at the suburban villa of his mystery host, some son of a friend of his father's. Praetextatus would be a welcome guest, he explained too firmly to be polite, but he did not want to impose our large party of strangers—even for a single night—on a private home.

I was not offended. I suspect Minervius and Venustus were, though they said nothing disrespectful as we continued onward to the delicious local food and soft beds of Lugdunum. Here we would enjoy a full night's rest before tackling the second half of the journey. We spent a profitable hour in the city's 'Baths of Apollo' rehearsing Clemens' advice.

Praetextatus should cite the centuries of legal protections against torture. He should argue that Valentinian himself had recently limited such torture unless and until the specific case was referred to him alone. The noble should argue that Constantius II might have had grounds to apply torture in that single case of magic linked to a court plot against his person. But Praetextatus should stress that this instance did not lay down a broad principle covering everything from gladiator spells to fleeting love affairs in a city so remote from the imperial presence.

If that didn't work, Praetextatus might be forced to challenge Maximinus' *relatio* without knowing its contents—a tricky proposition, Venustus warned. Instead, shouldn't he disclose that Maximinus was abusing the vice and magic convictions to confiscate estates for his personal enrichment?

'Better not,' Minervius said over supper later. 'Don't forget, Valentinian inherited an empire bankrupted by Julian's Persian war. Show him easy money and—'

'He has a point, Venustus. Valentinian is frugal in his person but greedy for the state treasury,' I said.

Venustus relented: 'You're right. To tell Valentinian of the riches he might claim for his coffers might be too tempting.' And as we rode off the next morning for our rendezvous with Praetextatus' party, I realized Venustus had grown fearful for his own vast holdings in Tuscia.

The skies promised a storm later in the afternoon and we reached the first *mutatio* outside Lugdunum without delay. Minutes later, two of my *eques*, covered in mud and sweat, burst into the *triclinium* to toss down their mail sacks. They'd finished a night dash from the west and warned me that we should hurry northward if we hoped to keep to our schedule.

I would have to cut short Praetextatus' comfortable sojourn with his family friend. I rode out alone to fetch the great man, leaving the two senators—both suffering in spirit and rump from long hours in the saddle—to tend their blisters for an extra hour.

The rambling estate looked comfortable, with barns, workshops, and a bath annex. But the main house, though expanded over at least two centuries, was indeed too small for all of us. As it was, Praetextatus' *bucellarii* had slept in an unheated workshop.

When I asked for Praetextatus, a black-eyed Gallic hunchback slave led me past a *lararium* carved with images of the Celtic god Gobannus at his smithy and through an atrium muraled with palm trees and gold river fish. This led through a rustic peristyle garden full of wildflowers and herbs to a sequence of private rooms. The slave gestured me toward a winter dining alcove where I overheard Praetextatus and his host still breakfasting.

'. . . but he recovered, against all expectations.' Praetextatus was speaking.

'And that should have ended the affair. Why be so foolish?'

I stopped to listen. I'd never lost the slave boy's skill of blending into the curtains.

'For the sake of the city, at the risk of their own skins? Perhaps freshened ambition had fed too long on resentment.'

'Resentment doesn't justify their actions.'

'I know, I know,' Praetextatus said. 'It was like a rare wine. Too many thirsty people had got a sip of it. The wrong men couldn't wash it off their palate.'

'Did they approach you?'

'Not directly . . .' Praetextatus gave a rueful laugh. There was the clink of glassware. '. . . reputation for priggish caution protected me. . . . not to be trusted with their plans. By the time I . . . too late.'

'. . . warned them?'

'They didn't listen to me. Just produced another vague omen or flimsy prophecy which fed their folly. I could only keep my own interests well clear.'

'. . . Probus took the same tack?'

'. . . had no choice but to act, to remove all doubts as to his position . . .'

'Poor Aginatius, he—' The host laid a warning hand on Praetextatus' arm as he lifted a dried date to his lips. 'Yes? What is it? Who's out there?'

The two men turned on their couches. I'd barely explained my purpose before houseslaves were dispatched to pack Praetextatus' shaving kit.

I retreated to the *fauces* in discreet silence. But as our reunited party trotted away from the *mutatio*, I committed the scraps of conversation to memory—not enough to make sense, yet too much to discard as small talk.

The mere fact that Probus, the powerful head of the Anician clan, and the embittered Senator Aginatius were both mentioned had stirred my speculation.

Hours later, as we waited to swap mounts in Asa Paulini, I tackled the mystery from an oblique angle.

'You know, Prefect, I did my best to solve the Chilo case, as you suggested, yet—'

'It's not your fault Prefect Maximinus doesn't know when to stop, Numidianus.'

'But Prefect why would anyone try to kill Chilo? To silence him? What did Chilo know?'

He slapped his reins and pulled his heavy hood deeper over his brow. The wind was rising up against us and we had another five miles until we reached Cabilonnum. Praetextatus rode faster now, mumbling into the folds of wool, 'That's over, Numidianus.'

'But if it's truly over, why does Chilo hide away on a farm out here?'

'Because he can't leave for Africa until spring sailing resumes—'

He bit his hasty tongue. 'Forget Chilo, Numidianus. I insist. It was a foolish idea . . .'

He'd only meant to forgive me for failing him. After all, he'd implied only months ago that if I could close the Chilo case in time, I'd earn the credit for stopping Maximinus in his tracks.

Instead, I'd caught him in a secret conference with none other than Chilo himself.

I leaned hard against the pommels of my horse. Praetextatus looked angry I'd guessed the nature of his detour. He could not imagine the true reason I found his words more chilling than any sheets of icy rain. He could not know those were almost the same words Urban Prefect Olybrius had uttered to me in the Theater of Pompey.

This was no coincidence. Valentinian had not been expected to rise from his deathbed in 368. *But he recovered against all expectations.* There *had* been a 'silly plan, a foolish idea' a plot to make sure 'a true Roman' succeeded the dead Pannonian. Yet here I was, racing to persuade that same emperor, so terrified of treason, that he had no reason to suspect a conspiracy in Roma. I must insist that his deputy's purge of Roman vice to eradicate the seeds of treason was a cruel error in judgment.

I was escorting Praetextatus to challenge the most powerful man in the world, to say to his face that he was wrong in policy and practice. And the most respectable pagan Roman of our generation and priestly leader of our embassy, Vettius Agorius Praetextatus, might well know all this to be a lie.

⚖⚖⚖

The battering winds only subsided as we traveled the final stretch of *Cursus* from Tabernae. I knew these roads only too well. I'd watched the young Caesar Julian urging his soldiers to repair barbarian-devastated towns before marching against the Alemanni at Argentoratum in 357 to claim his first victory towards imperial fame.

We were losing the few hours of winter daylight just as the great 'Black Gate' of Treverorum hove into view nestling between protective mountains some miles to our right. The red sandstone from the nearby foothills gave the city a glow at sunset that Roma's gray and white marbles couldn't match.

I expected we'd pick up pace to comfortably settle in some imperial wing before darkness fell. Instead, Praetextatus reined in and slowed to a trot. He pretended sudden interest in stone monuments and *mausolea* lining the road. He dismounted to examine one memorial some seventy-five feet high dedicated to a wealthy family in the cloth trade.

I'd passed this way countless times as an eager postal rider. These grandiose installments and expensive carvings were commonplace to me, particularly this one. But Praetextatus studied it carefully. Why did he look so discomforted by this stone portrait of the 'Family Secundii' in the midst of daily life?

'These are Romans? They sit upright at a table to eat! And these boys at their studies? They wear Gallic shoes. And this patriarch, he's clean-shaven, but he gives money to very roughly-dressed and bearded clients.'

'Such is life here, Prefect—'

'There are many things *in life*, Numidianus. I've seen oddities in Egypt and Antiochia and Hispania *in life* since I was a boy.'

'These are northern customs.'

'Obviously, but why would a Roman of taste choose such souvenirs for posterity? Would he not memorialize his life with more decorum? More refinement? Wouldn't you, Numidianus?'

It was the nicest thing the noble Praetextatus had ever said to me. Such a confidence between a Roma-bred aristocrat and freedman could only happen north of Lugdunum.

We advanced up the right bank of the Mosella and passed a mess of rotting wooden piles—the traces of our ancient predecessors marking their arrival in the land of the hostile Treveri tribes. Soon we passed dozens of warehouses lined with boats in dry dock and wagons groaning with *amphorae* of white wine waiting for export. The dockworkers took little notice of us.

When we reached the formidable stone bridge sitting on six squat black stone pediments, we turned into view of the Lenus-Mars Temple. We proceeded through the city gate and up the *cardus decumanus* towards the great Baths marked by the statue of an Amazon.

Again Praetextatus scowled. 'That's rather good. Not the work of a local, surely?'

'Imported here from Roma, Prefect.'

He sighed. 'Like so much that lends this capital a facsimile of worth.'

Pursing his lips, he pulled his velvet *pilleus* lower over his brow and the fur collar of his cloak higher.

Had he never visited Treverorum before? When he'd famously challenged Valentinian's 364 ruling on pagan ritual sacrifice, he'd been serving as the governor of distant Achaea.

Praetextatus sniffed again as we rode over a sewer grate. We turned due east toward the imperial complex. Here we reached the regular streets, the impressive forum, and far to the western edge of the city walls, an amphitheater for eight thousand spectators built into the eastern city wall. And finally the Aula Palatina, Constantine's great basilica with a church visible at the end of the imperial forum.

I told Venustus, 'That church houses the Christian Savior's Holy Cloak brought back from the East by Constantine's mother Helena.'

Praetextatus muttered: 'What great joy that rotting relic must give them.' He took the prominence of a city with 'a holy relic' as an affront. These Christians rose in power, arbitrated morals, and grew fat on legacies to the Church.

We announced our arrival at the Imperial Palace and demanded an audience with Valentinian. We were told the Emperor was in council with his generals for the day. We were given an hour in two days' time. Praetextatus insisted—no later than the following morning would do. He won.

Then Praetextatus paraded our party through the echoing reception rooms. He embodied, certainly for those brave minutes, everything I'd been raised to admire. There was classical *paideia* in every syllable of his impeccable introduction of Senators Venustus and Minervius to the court stewards. He negotiated with deputies of the *Magister Dispositionum* the exact hour of our audience and requested the attendance of Imperial *Quaestor* Eupraxius with authoritative comportment. He displayed impeccable *dignitas* when his mercenaries were assigned to a barrack nearby and we were assigned bedrooms at the farthest end of the palace.

So far, in the court of a Pannonian emperor who despised education, pagan worship, refined manners, tasteful dress, and simple good breeding, Praetextatus had done well. He gave Venustus and Minervius a confident nod. We'd ridden in silent, near-frozen, tight-lipped haste for over a week. We were less than twenty-fours from cutting Maximinus' campaign of humiliation and blood-shed off at the knees.

It was not until we passed the long wing of the imperial bedchambers that my illustrious companions' demeanor faltered.

'Did you hear that?' Minervius whispered. 'What's that chewing?'

Down the corridor came a clanking sound belonging to fetid cells underneath an arena and a smell as pungent as a sewer.

'I suggest we don't linger,' I said.

I was too late. The scraping of chains across marble lured the curious Venustus to peek past a barricade of heavy curtains marking the Emperor's connubial wing. He turned a white face to Praetextatus.

'It's a beast,' he gasped, 'eating a man's—'

'It's a bear—either Innocence or Goldflake.' I hustled the shocked officials away. 'I'll explain the Emperor's pets in the safety of our rooms.'

CHAPTER 17, THE COURT OF BEARS

—VALENTINIAN'S CONSISTORY—

Next morning, I gathered our party fifteen minutes before our scheduled audience. A jittery Minervius glanced behind the curtain separating the imperial suite.

'The cage is empty,' he whispered to me.

'Because she's on duty.'

Raising the cubs Goldflake and Innocence began as a jest in Valentinian's new court. But when the she-bears were big enough to earn their keep as judicial man-eaters, the joke turned sour. Their foul cages grew ever more ornate as their bellies grew fatter, their fur sleeker, and their palate more 'selective'. Their trainers were no longer comely slave boys dangling decorative chains and ceremonial whips. Only hardened recruits from the bowels of city arenas had the skill to control Valentinian's lumbering killers.

When our contingent reached the echoing anteroom of the *consistorium*, I pulled aside the *magister admissionum* in charge of the timing and supervision of audiences.

'Prefect Praetextatus has come a long way and is not a man to waste anyone's time. Please allow no interruption. The lives of wellborn Roman men and women hang on this.'

'You have exactly a quarter of an hour on my timetable, *Magister Agentium in Rebus*. Make good use of it.'

A scowling *Magister Officiorum* Remigius appeared barely a foot behind me.

'Postpone your audience, Numidianus. Had you shown the courtesy of communicating your visit in advance, I could have warned you, the Emperor's in no mood for any bookish debate.'

'The detention houses of Roma are filled with *honestiores*—men and women both—in shackles. They would be startled to hear their wounds and burns dismissed as bookish, *Magister*.'

I braced my shoulders to assert my height over him. But I panicked inside. By law the Castra was represented on the Emperor's council by the *magister officiorum*. But instead of assisting the Castra's renaissance from the ashes, the Gaul Remigius had been nothing but obstructive and proprietary over access to Valentinian from the day he replaced the Pannonian Ursacius. Remigius might well interfere today out of sheer spite.

Only after proving my personal worth to the ailing Valentinian by untangling the Britannian conspiracy of 368, had I forced open a crack in Remigius' bureaucratic blockade. And as my network of *agentes* graduated up the rungs toward auditing provincial offices, I'd learned that Remigius' personal record was far from spotless.

A hint about 'accounting concerns' had won me a fragile truce. But I couldn't rob this greedy Mogantiacum native of the obeisance we owed his office. So I forwarded to him my *agentes'* audits of vicars, prefects, governors, and administrative offices across the Empire. We inundated Remigius and his treasury counterparts with deskwork on a quarterly basis.

Re-establishing this check on corruption had been the Castra's greatest official success over the previous four years. It also kept Remigius distracted from the true heart of our service, our collection of intelligence.

Praetextatus led us into the *consistorium* behind Remigius, the *Magister Admissionum,* and the *Magister Memoriae*. The gathering around the Emperor included the ambitious Hispanic *Magister Equitum* Flavius Theodosius. And there was the Frankish Merobaudes, that incorruptible veteran. This senior warrior had survived the downfall of his lodestar General Silvanus in 355 to oversee the return of Emperor Julian's corpse from the Sassanids' sandy battlefields.

And oh, divine gods, there at the far end was the over-eager, imperial tutor Ausonius! Was he already promoted to 'adviser' here? He was tossing me a vulgar wink. I'd recommended him to teach the twelve-year-old *Augustus* Gratian.

I ignored the ingratiating Ausonius' welcome. I was no neophyte to these halls. I'd seen too much. I remembered too much.

How different this felt from the *agentes*' audiences before Constantius II! That 'divine' sovereign had sat rigid, carapaced in gold robes and embroidered tunics, his large cow eyes unsmiling, and his ring-encrusted fingers spread in formal stillness on the wide arms of his *cathedra*.

And where were all the scribes and notaries that had recorded Constantius' every sneeze? Where were all those silver and bronze screens and grilles that had hid the chamber ladies encircling the beautiful Macedonian Empress Eusebia as she eavesdropped on proceedings?

And where once the richly-colored mosaics had been scrubbed so clean and smooth, penitents and subordinates could prostrate themselves full length to "worship" Constantius' purple hem, we now tripped on thick rugs and furs tossed in all directions to warm the chilly council chamber.

The old man-high braziers stood cold and empty. No burning incense countered the wintry haze. The Emperor huddled under a coarse blanket pinned over his once-meaty shoulders. He wore a fighting man's tunic and well-worn riding trousers. Supreme power had not improved the demeanor of a man groomed on army discipline and swift punishments. The ferocity of Goldflake and Innocence, caged in the corner, mirrored the growing distemper of their owner.

I'd known the former tribune Valentinian too long to expect the getup of an eastern warlord influenced by Persian fads. But his physical decline shocked me. Valentinian had risen from his deathbed but looked far from well. The Pannonian's eagle features were all the more graven and humorless after illness. His manly stature, regal features, and robust camp-side manners had once recommended him for military success. But not every man raised to become a commander in the field benefits from being draped in purple and encircled by sycophants and rivals.

If the past winter's campaign against the Alemanni had cost the man so much, what good were his generals—Aequitius, Theodosius, Merobaudes and the others in the field? Who could he trust?

There was one old friend in this court I trusted. However, Valentinian's second wife, Justina Flavia Aviana Vettius Picenus was absent this morning. Since the death on the Rhenus front of one of her two brothers, *Tribunus Stabili* Constantianus Vettius, she'd retreated into mourning.

She now had one fewer ally at court and Justina needed allies badly. Her remaining brother, Cerealis Vettius, would be an insufficient bulwark against the diehard Pannonians loyal to Valentinian's discarded first wife Marina Severa.

Justina's place as the new consort could only be secured by bearing an heir to rival Marina Severa's little 'Emperor' Gratian. Beautiful but close to thirty, she was by even our modern standards too old to carry her first child.

No, this morning I couldn't rely on my old friend Justina's sage advice.

Of course *Magister* Remigius was not to be robbed of his little moment. He signaled the *Magister Memoriae* to proceed. We were formally introduced, myself in the most perfunctory style, then Senators Venustus and Minervius and then—

The Emperor shook a weathered hand at me, 'I know Numidianus. I presume this is our very noble—'

Praetextatus' great name and dazzling accretion of civic titles and religious honors were nonetheless read out. I had time to contrast his confident bearing with the battled-scarred indifference of our provincial ruler.

The Emperor's mouth curled to one side as he took in the nobleman's confident posture and everything it implied—the classical education, boundless wealth, impeccable family tree, and noble moderation.

Praetextatus was everything Valentinian envied and despised. Throughout the required protocol, brief as it was, the Emperor signed and handed off three rescripts. He pulled himself out of his chair and wandered over to his pets. He thrust a bare hand between their bars and stroked a muzzle. The bear sniffed his palm, hoping for a treat.

Watching these two opponents, I was torn in spirit. I was raised as an educated Roman, yet throbbing with Numidian desert blood, servant to this court of soldiers defending our weakened borders, yet disgusted by their treatment of the ancient city I loved.

And my new distrust of Praetextatus sat like a cold stone in my stomach. Was a threat to this regime from Roma so unthinkable? I'd seen for myself the Emperor lying on the very banks of the River Styx, the shades of the dead reaching across the black current for him. I'd seen the factions jockeying outside his bedchamber—the Gauls, the Pannonians, the Hispaniards—ready to tip over his deathbed the second his breathing stopped.

Praetextatus began: 'Our delegation comes to correct a judicial abuse terrorizing the Mother of Cities beyond reason and honor and setting an unhealthy precedent for Roman Law in all corners of your great empire.'

'Our long legal tradition is clear in all respects,' he continued. In true Ciceronian fashion, he detailed all the legal arguments he'd just promised to pass over for the sake of economy. '... Constantius II did indeed, in one instance and in one only, approve torture in a case of suspected *magicos apparatus*—but let us take note. That single case addressed suspicion of conspiracy against the very person of the emperor by someone in his presence at court. In contrast, it would be hard to link any cases of frivolous social vices in distant Roma to—'

'This court does not consider adultery frivolous.' The Emperor had abandoned his bears and returned to his chair.

'Neither does adultery constitute treason against the state, *Auguste.*'

'Go on.' But Valentinian had made his point.

'The law is very clear; *honestiores* are not subject to torture unless treason or *laesa maiestas divina*—for Tacitus reminds us, "Emperors are as gods—" are included in the charge. You yourself, *Domine*, ruled in a letter to Prefect Olybrius on July 8, 369, that torture was permitted for cases of *maiestas*, "the same law for one and all," but *no other charges without consultation of the emperor himself.*'

Valentinian shot to his boots. 'I never decreed such a thing!' A bear poked her nose between the bars. Valentinian's anger often heralded a fresh meal.

Praetextatus seemed unfazed: 'With respect, our embassy argues that the *veneficium, magicium,* and *adulterium* cases now before our city courts have not been referred to you, case by case, as you decreed, with one exception—the appeal of the boy Lollianus pressed by his aggrieved father, the esteemed Prefect Lampadius. Otherwise, we maintain that a gross miscarriage of Roman Law is at work.'

'Didn't you hear me? I granted only one ruling, Praetextatus, to distinguish between your beloved pagan rituals and foul black arts! I'm a tolerant man when it comes to religion! But I never sent the decree you just cited!'

'You did, *Auguste*.' Praetextatus actually smiled.

Valentinian went purple, eyebrows bristling. 'I did not! I will not be challenged! I will not be the victim of calumny!'

Our delegation was in grave and sudden danger. Valentinian had just re-framed our appeal into an attack on himself—treason punishable by death.

With a sidelong stare at the bears, Minervius began trembling. Venustus whispered to Praetextatus: 'Take care, Noble Friend. For all our sakes, please take care.'

But Praetextatus folded his arms and didn't flinch. Did he feel protected by Olympian divinities or an intellectual's earthly disdain for our ruler?

'You sent that decree two years ago, *Imperator*.'

'You're lying! I never sent it.'

'Yes, yes, you did, *Auguste*,' said a gentle African baritone.

The Imperial *Quaestor* Eupraxius, the renowned Moor from Caesarensis, stepped forward from a cluster of attendants. I exhaled with deep relief to see the man I'd known years before as the Master of the Rolls now promoted to such legal heights.

The Moor drew a large morsel of dried meat from his long sleeve and tossed it into the bear cage. He nodded to our delegation and approached Valentinian's chair.

'You issued such a decree, *Auguste*.'

'I did not! My authority cannot be called into question!'

'But I drafted it myself at your instruction, '*Nullus omnino ob fidiculas perferendas inconsultis ac nescientibus nobis vel militia auctoramento vel generis aut dignitatis defensione nudetur, excepta tamen maiestatis causa, in qua sola omnibus aequa condicio est.*'

'No person whosoever, without the consultation and knowledge of the Emperor, shall be stripped either of his position in the imperial service or of the defense by his birth and high rank, for the purpose of compelling him to submit to torture with cords, except in the case of high treason, in which there is only one and the same status for all.'

I listened to Eupraxius' sibilant 's' with a tug of homesickness for our shared desert homelands—though the undiluted African in Eupraxius was more pronounced in his high cheekbones and flared nostrils.

He gave a small bow and with a graceful sweep of his arm, cleared the hem of his long cloak to retreat back to safe obscurity.

A long and awkward pause broken only by embarrassed coughs and animal growls followed.

Valentinian's temper tantrum had left him panting but he shared my affection for the African courtier. Canny Eupraxius had been the first to hail Valentinian's Gratian as full *augustus* and undisputed successor over so many rivalrous factions of adult candidates.

The Master of Rolls signaled for a goblet of thinned wine. Valentinian downed it in gulps before relenting.

'Then I will review any cases not directly linked to the charge of *maiestas divinas* as I ruled. I make no changes to the laws on capital punishments but there should be no torture of Roman senators or their households for anything less than treason— unless I say so.'

Praetextatus bowed in thanks to Eupraxius. He wished the Emperor good health.

'I was never better,' Valentinian barked. 'The audiences are over for today. My bears are hungry for lunch.'

The keepers rolled the heavy cage out of the *consistorium*.

We were returning to our rooms when we heard screams from the courtyard below. For a second, I feared it was Eupraxius—his professional integrity condemned as insolence.

But no, our palace attendant explained, an imperial smithy had delivered an iron breastplate artistically embellished according to our sovereign's design. He asked for payment. But Valentinian had fed him to the bears instead, because the finished piece weighed a sliver less than stipulated.

Minervius raced to a high window but I pulled him away. 'It's better not to look,' I said.

⚜⚜⚜

I felt the built-up exhaustion of our journey wash over me. An hour later, I dragged myself, limp and aching, from the hot steam of the baths to my bedchamber. I was ready for early oblivion. The sun had scarcely left the western sky when I was already snoring in the same linen I'd worn to the baths.

'*Magister* Marcus Gregorianus Numidianus?'

Someone called softly outside the door. I decided to 'sleep' through it.

'It's Cerealis Vettius, *Magister*. Do you remember me?'

Sleepy and dull, I answered the door. I remembered an anxious Roman youth with curled hair and smooth cheeks. Sixteen years ago he was fetching his still-virgin sister Justina from my escort to safety back home in Roma. Justina was then a thirteen-year-old empress, already deposed, smuggled home after her dramatic tumble from the dead Usurper Magnentius' throne. Their disgraced father had committed suicide, leaving his three children politically ruined and friendless.

I opened the door to an adult stranger. I invited him into the room, stoked the brazier's faint embers back into light, and lit the iron lamp.

I knew I'd changed from the strapping, ambitious freedman *agens* with the thick bronze curls and a muscular riding seat. I was a limping, middle-aged official now. And Cerealis was a hardened soldier. A rope-like purple scar cut deep from forehead to hairline. It had been badly sewn and possibly infected.

Old Roman blood mixed with the new blood of Constantine Chlorus had once guaranteed the Vettii-Picenii all the chances in the world. They'd been gifted with rare pedigree, fine education, great wealth, and undeniable beauty—but such breeding was meant for careers under a kinder reign than Valentinian's.

Did Cerealis know it was my own Commander Gregorius who'd chosen his sister for marriage to the nearly-barbarian Usurper Magnentius? Was it the fault of our Manlius clan that Cerealis' family had fallen into that political maw? It must have taken the three siblings every ounce of wit and sublimation of cultivation to rise so high in the Pannonian's coarse court.

'Yes, Cerealis, of course I remember you. I was sad to hear of your brother's death in battle.'

'I'm not here to reminisce about Constantianus.'

'No, I thought not. I'll be only a minute.'

He led me along minor passages and narrow staircases to a small chamber at the farthest end of the long palace.

'She sleeps alone now, as she's heavy with child,' he explained.

Justina was waiting in a suite of two rooms. The antechamber was painted in murals of dancing nymphs and woodland animals. In the rear room was a blood-red bedcover against gold-framed brick-red walls with painted figures of black urns and dark green fronds. The effect was elegant, if sanguinary. I had a fleeting impression that I'd been in this suite before. But I didn't recognize the décor.

'At last, Marcus! A legal mission, I hear! I was just telling Anemone here about my ancestress Neratia, the wife of Marcus Antistius Labeo, a renowned jurist who knew the Great Augustus. But why do I tell a fellow Roman family stories three centuries' old?'

'Haven't I seen Neratia's bust in your home in Roma? But those mossy walls are so vulgar, so jammed with venerable Romans, don't try to impress me.'

Justina laughed as the plain-faced Anemone in tightly-braided hair and heavy wools poured us wine.

'You see, Anemone? I rise to imperial consort and still the *magister agentium in rebus* treats me like a little girl. Oh, Marcus, how good to see you again. Forgive me if I don't rise to the occasion. I'm a very pregnant old lady. I will pray to my God, and you must pray to your pantheon of deities, that I survive my coming ordeal in one piece.'

'If all goes well, *Domina*, surely the happy result must be two pieces.'

She laughed too hard. She was starved for jokes.

'Your last letter to me was very vague, Marcus. I hear rumors—'

'All true. Our beloved city faces disaster. Your old society, the *honestiores*, are too idle. They neglect honest devotions in the temples and instead fill their days buying worthless gladiator spells and their nights testing love potions.'

'It's frightening, Marcus.'

'I find it sad. I spent so many years rebuilding the *Schola*, I didn't notice the spirit of Roma rotting into ignorance. The libraries are dusty, *Domina,* and all the bookstores shuttered. Only poison-makers prosper and—'

Justina started trembling! I placed a hand on her shaking arm. 'Are you well, *Domina?*'

'Your talk of potions! Poisons! I'm terrified of someone hurting my baby. Anemone tastes everything first.'

Despite a swollen belly under heavy rose silks, she now paced a little. Then, releasing some pent-up demon, she demanded, 'I need the truth, Marcus, and you would know. Did Constantius' Empress Eusebia sabotage the pregnancies of Julian's wife, Empress Helena?'

'Apodemius suspected she did. Eusebia was childless. She envied Helena's pregnancies. The Castra got a secret report from an informant attending Helena's first failed delivery. But the second miscarriage could have been caused by—but *Domina!* Helena's tragedies are over!'

'So Eusebia was guilty.' Justina's eyes widened. 'And is it true that the child of Constantia, the daughter she bore Caesar Gallus, was deformed and witless?'

'Yes. I saw the poor creature in Antiochia.'

'She wasn't exposed at birth?'

'And you call yourself a Christian, *Domina?* No, Anastasia was hidden away.'

I rose to check her nervous pacing. '*Domina,* sit down. To brood on the bad luck of other imperial women can't be good for your baby.'

'It wasn't all bad luck, Marcus, you just admitted it. There are many who don't want me to bear an heir to compete with Marina Severa's Gratian, starting with that lady herself. This boy will seal my place at Valentinian's side.'

'You're sure it's a boy?'

'I must have a boy, before it's too late. How are your twins?'

'Fine. And their mother is hiding in Ostia, protected by our man Cornelius. But your husband? We saw him this morning. His recovery seems . . . incomplete.'

I helped her stretch out on a sofa. Anemone gathered the priceless rose skirts under a white fur coverlet.

'He's changed, Marcus. His illness robbed him of some mental calm. He fears anything, everything, and everyone.'

'Valentinian must find the balance between reasonable worry and foolish complacence. He has my sympathy.'

'Does he, really? Really?'

'Yes. I came to Treverorum to argue that his fears are unfounded. But on the journey, I believe I overheard Praetextatus allude to a failed project of succession that festered on after your husband's recovery.'

'Well, I'm not surprised. That deathbed vigil was a rather overcrowded event.'

'I heard just enough to know that there *was* a threat to your husband's reign. But it exists no longer. If only loyal men like Praetextatus and Olybrius had trusted me from the beginning—'

'Oh, Marcus, no man with a secret trusts you. They know your *schola*'s motto—'

'Putting the service of empire first?'

She sighed. 'You try so hard not to choose sides or support a faction. You think it's a point of honor.'

'Am I wrong?'

'Yes. You hold yourself above other men—even emperors. You mistake a knot of resentment paralyzing your common sense for an ideal.'

'Resentment?' I bristled.

'Marcus, will you always be a freedman with a wide belt and those shining *campagi* on your feet and yet—'

'Yet what?'

'Yet nursing the soul of a half-Numidian slave.'

'The new imperial consort learns cruelty.'

'No, I'm not cruel—not yet. I work to soften the cruelty of my husband. What he's lost in weight, he's gained in bad temper.'

'At least the fruit of that softening is showing.'

She patted the sky-blue silk girdle supporting her round belly. 'Don't mock me. We both know a wiser ruler would never display all his power—much less abuse it.'

She fixed me with those clear eyes over a flickering lamp flame. 'Let me tell you what happened a few weeks ago during the hunt. One of our pages—a good, strong boy—held the leash of a valuable Spartan hunting hound. The dog got over-excited. It tugged and lunged, but the page held fast.'

'The dog was eager for the starting horn?'

'Too eager. It had been starved on purpose. It turned vicious and sank its fangs into the page's arm. The boy screamed and dropped the leash. So before the signal blew, the dog dashed away and was lost.'

'Valentinian lost his temper? He had the dog put down?'

'No, he had the page put down like a dog. Cudgeled to death before the day was over.'

Her voice had turned as steely as the voice of every female power they say lies behind the throne of every man—be he sandal-maker or emperor.

'Don't judge me, Marcus. I spend every day and half the night begging Valentinian to dampen his rages.'

'Then don't mock my service to the Empire he rules.'

'But you serve with no more sympathy than my girl here. Anemone only obeys me because I'm the Imperial Consort. That's her fate as my slave. But I don't flatter myself. Anemone would sell me in the market tomorrow if our positions were reversed.'

'No, *Domina*, never!'

'Of course you would,' Justina scoffed. 'Any slave would, given half a chance.'

I agreed with Justina. 'One of the victims of Maximinus' purge is a matron whose sins were reported by an embittered slave—'

I shot to my feet, overturning a small brazier, and sending flying red embers into the air. Justina snatched away her rich skirts and Anemone scuttled across the tiles to sweep up the hot coals.

'Marcus, what's wrong?'

'It wasn't Anepsia's slave that that reported on Apollonia. It wasn't Sapaudulus.'

'Who's Sapaudulus?'

'It was Drusilla. Justina, our slave Drusilla is betraying my wife.'

Drusilla had used Flaccus as her go-between for the earrings. Flaccus had entertained Maximinus' two *protectores* at his corner shrine. The direct connection between my bedchamber and the offices of Maximinus and *Notarius* Leo pierced me like a *ballista* dart.

Did Drusilla even realize she was Maximinus' informer? She'd seen her mistress entertain Anepsia and even visited the older woman's house. While serving trays in the garden or dressing hair in our bedroom, she'd overheard careless banter about Roma's social peccadilloes. Willingly or not, she'd talked about Hesychia, Flaviana, Charitas—all of Apollonia's circle—to Flaccus who held her petty theft over her head as blackmail. Maximinus' hounds had only to question our corner *vicomagister* to learn all they needed.

Oh, the gods! How had a *magister* of imperial intelligence failed to detect the most dangerous spy of all, embedded like Cleopatra's asp in the very bosom of his family?

'You're quitting Treverorum already?'

'Apollonia's in danger.'

'But you just said she's safe in Ostia! You ride all this way and stay only two days?'

Justina's petulant note jarred with her regal manner and gold-festooned hems. Flavia Justina Avian Vettius Picenus had been the loneliest and bravest of little girls. Almost thirty, she remained as courageous as she was ambitious and beautiful.

But she was as lonely in Treverorum for true friends as the child bride of the gruff usurper, Commander Magnentius.

'I'm sorry, *Domina*. I'm quitting the city within the hour,' I said. 'By the time they notice I'm gone, I'll be halfway to Divodurum.'

CHAPTER 18, A WIDOW'S LAST GAMBIT

—THE ROAD TO ROMA—

As I raced off, I was indifferent to the challenge of reaching Roma in time and too blinded by panic for Apollonia to enjoy relief over the success of Praetextatus' appeal which now I might be the first to convey.

Once I reached Roma, Maximinus' tortures must stop. The innocent could retain clarity of mind to prepare strong defenses for court. The guilty would face their due punishments, but at least in the process, wouldn't scream out the names of innocent colleagues and friends under the pain of the claws or the agony of the rack.

But as soon as I reached Tabernae, I felt close to collapse. I realized I would never survive the marathon back to Roma without some assistance from my *agentes*.

I needed help to close the miles between Apollonia and myself in record time. I spotted it the next morning: two postal riders, Diorix and Julius Talavus, sitting in low-slanting winter sun over a quick meal before sorting their burdensome sacks for distribution down the Mosella route.

I commandeered them to stow their mail sacks and escort me at top speed, through Lugdunum to Arelate, where I would fling myself on the mercy of two other *circitores* for the last leg to Roma—mailbags be damned. The provincial hubs, church officials, and well-placed society wits located off the postal hubs linked to this main route would have to wait another few weeks for their gossipy packets and court correspondence.

I ordered the *agentes* to give me no quarter. The weather was drier than the week before, but even fair, crisp skies and desperate determination don't transform the stamina of a frantic man over forty. I ordered my boys to drive me like an ageing racehorse wearing blinds.

I suffered many long hours, my lips pressed tight under the wool muffler wrapping my face and my thighs gripped hard around the saddle as I battled my confusions and fears. How had it come to this?

Having refused to ally myself with Maximinus' investigation, I had expected he wouldn't like me or trust me. Perhaps he even despised me as an ex-slave of the Esquiline Hill, given the education he'd scrounged for himself as a citizen in the backwaters of Pannonia.

But had he also envied the affluence I'd earned as a tenacious estate manager resuscitating the Manlius House after the terrible civil war between Magnentius and Constantius II? He'd certainly proved greedy for the rich properties of every landed senator he threw into chains.

'Get some sleep now, *Magister*,' Diorix said.

A few hours later, it was, 'Time to ride again, *Magister*,' from an apologetic Julius.

And as I guzzled down a bladder of chilled *posca* in Ludna or tossed tasteless bowls of hot lentils down my gullet in Octavus before saddling up again, my frantic mind circled like a mill wheel. Around and around—why surveil me? Why entrap me? Why target my innocent wife?

If Maximinus wanted to neutralize his nemesis, it should be the unassailable Praetextatus who'd just braved the Court of Bears to restore Roman citizens' rights. Praetextatus wielded far more money, intellectual clout, and political respect than a dogged *curiosus*. Praetextatus was an enemy to be feared, to be countered...

'Time to change horses, *Magister*. Rest here while I supervise... We'll stop at the *mansio* in Valentia next, if you can hang on a little farther, that is. The wine is better there...'

The boys were so kind, yet so firm in following my strict orders, I almost wept with gratitude as they forced my protesting body back into my saddle after only another two hours' nap.

'We keep going. Keep going,' I mumbled. I had to believe Apollonia was still safe in Ostia. She must be. What harm could

Drusilla do there anyway, far from that viper Flaccus and Leo's *protectores* spies?

Of course Apollonia was safe. It had been brazen of Leo to question her in the first place. After all, I was no powerless Roman has-been, like the senators Abienus or Eumenius. I was no retired councilor to dead emperors like that sobbing Lampadius. To arrest Apollonia on flimsy charges would be an audacious political attack on a working chief of a *schola* reporting directly to Valentinian's court.

I could fight back. I must get there in time. I must . . .

'. . . We'll drop you here, *Magister*. Are you all right? Here's your room, down this way, *Magister*. The riders from Roma should arrive for these sacks by midday. It's been a privilege riding with you. Please, sit down here, *Magister* . . . I said, it's been our privilege escorting you, *Magister* . . .'

Or did Maximinus think that frightening Apollonia was a justified attack? A counter-attack? For what? I'd flattered myself that Maximinus believed he needed me when he first got the Chilo case. And anyway, my refusal had done him little harm, only delayed his purge by a few weeks.

'We should reach Roma tomorrow, if we set off before dawn, *Magister*. I've ordered us a good pitcher and roasted ribs in honey and anchovy paste . . .'

But . . . to encircle my family with spies over days and weeks, to use Flaccus and Drusilla to penetrate my domestic sanctuary from so early last autumn? Did not this extended surveillance betray anxiety from the very outset of Maximinus' climb to unchecked power?

Anxiety over what? Had I still not grasped the depths to which Maximinus might *fear* me—even before I shut my gate against him? He'd gone to unexpected lengths. Drusilla had never stolen anything before, not even as a lively child surrounded by our young scion's toys and treats. Flaccus must have encouraged Drusilla's resentments and promised her rewards for stealing something—anything. And he'd repaid the silly girl by blackmailing her into spying.

So Maximinus had targeted my household as long ago as the earrings' theft last September. Why? What could I do? What did I know?

And if I solved that riddle, might I glimpse the answer to ending the city's hell?

Roma's hilltop roofs and domes beckoned just ahead. I'd assumed I was slowing the pace of my last pair of escorts until I bid the two *circitores* goodbye as they stabled our mounts. I overheard their unmistakable relief at seeing the back of me.

'Jupiter!' one said, 'what could I say? He's the boss, after all. But one more day of that and one of us would've died—either me or the horse.'

Fear must have driven me faster than a demon. And so it had been in 354, as the young Numidianus struggled to keep up with the *Magister* Apodemius, many decades older, racing headlong along the westward *Cursus*. We were on a marathon race from Pola to deliver the red slippers of the beheaded Caesar Gallus to his cousin Emperor Constantius II in Mediolanum.

I chuckled at the memory. There again, the white-haired Apodemius had bested me. The old man had *literally* ridden a horse to death and leapt onto a fresh animal without a backward glance.

The familiar suburbs were giving way to the older villas and crumbling marble mausolea of forgotten families. The city gates were opening to the traffic on the Via Aurelia.

Within an hour, I'd be home.

☙☙☙

But home was empty. I raced through the echoing *fauces* to the *lararium*. There was no cooking smell, no incense, no racket of little boys, no squawk from Cicero on his perch, and no scolding Lavinia. I crossed the main rooms in shock. I searched the emptied servants' quarters in panic.

The slaves, Lavinia, and the twins had vanished. Their clothes, favorite toys, city shoes—all gone. Even Cook had disappeared and left her pots, bowls, and polished utensils stacked in cupboards and cabinets. I'd never seen the work table without some mortar or carving knife at the ready.

The *lararium* gave off the faded scent of stale wax and faded resin but was cold to the touch.

'*Magister*?' A dirt-stained hand clutched my arm. The wiry frame of our gardener seized me in his scarecrow embrace.

'Gavius!'

'Oh, *Magister*! I was to wait 'til you returned. And now it's my sad duty to—' He started sobbing and shaking. And with every wail, the strangling clasp of his sinewy, old arms squeezed more hope out of me.

'What's happened?'

'Drusilla came back without them, *Magister*. Pale and proud and all full of herself, saying the mistress had been caught in some nasty crime. Cook shook her nearly to death before she confessed everything.'

'Gavius, slow down. I can hardly make you out.'

He nodded, but the words were garbled by his sobs. 'The mistress was arrested in Ostia. That's what Drusilla told Cook. And that same night, Drusilla disappeared.'

I felt my soul scream but my voice was cold and slow, like someone else's—the voice of the determined *magister agentium in rebus*.

'Where are my sons? Where's Lavinia?'

'Lavinia kept her head. She bundled everyone up . . . all of 'em, took the whole household to the Manlius oyster farm down in Baiae. Even my little Beata. No one's supposed to know I stayed behind. I've been hiding in the store room behind the servants' quarters. Didn't dare even light a lamp, *Magister*.'

'Where's Cornelius?'

'Cornelius? Cornelius is dead, *Magister*! Cut down defending the mistress! Murdered by gangsters!'

My bad leg buckled under me. I half-fell onto the steps leading down to the still waters of the *pluvius*. Oh, my dear reliable Cornelius! My oldest, truest friend! Such a mean fate for a veteran of so many nobler battles! I'd told myself he would die in Apollonia's defense, but didn't the gods know that was foolish hyperbole meant only as praise?

'Where's Cornelius' woman, Delicia?'

'Stayed in Ostia with his body, *Magister*.'

I'd send her a message immediately. I must settle the burial costs and the memorial plaque. Technically, Cornelius had stayed working for Leo and Aurea on the Esquiline Hill. But we'd all known in our hearts that he'd come to retire there as *dispensator* because of me.

Cornelius and Delicia were a resourceful pair, the retired bargirl and her brusque, scarred old soldier—but Cornelius' pension was meager and money had never stayed in their purses for long. Delicia was beyond returning to her old line of work and I wouldn't wish that life on her again anyway. I expected no argument from Leo and Aurea as to providing Delicia a living out of the ample Manlius income.

I must grieve Cornelius later. Not now.

'And my *agentes*, Avitus and Numa?'

'Raced back to the Castra, *Magister*, swearing your lawyer would get our mistress released by nightfall. But no one has returned to this house.'

'When was this?'

'A day or two after you left, so that makes, oh . . . forgive me, I've lost track now, I'm afraid.' His trembling fingers covered his bleary eyes. His whole body heaved.

'Where's Amosis? At the Castra?'

'No, *Magister*. He sits watch, night and day, like a faithful dog, outside the mistress' detention place. Oh, poor *matrona*—!'

Gavius let out a wail to rend the heart of Minerva herself and fell in a miserable heap at my feet.

'You haven't eaten, have you?'

'Cook left me some cold meat and bread . . .'

I returned to the kitchen and only now noticed his one bowl scraped clean. The pottery platters that usually overflowed with fresh vegetables or fruits were empty. A large jar for dried dates was empty and the vessel of cooking honey licked clean. Unable to cook for himself, old Gavius had survived on raw lentils from a sack kept on a high shelf safe from vermin. The poor man hadn't left the house for so much as a cold snack.

I limped on my walking stick to the grill-shop at the end of our street for a hot stew for Gavius and myself to share in silence.

Then I went to the *lararium* to light the resin and refill the lamps. I prayed to the gods to save my family. But the gods can be slow sometimes. With or without them, I had no time to waste.

☘ ☘ ☘

While I waited for *Quaestor* Clemens, I sent Myron's infirmary slave to attend Gavius until he'd recovered. The lawyer's footsteps soon pounded up the stairs and into my small office, without stopping for permission from Cyrillus.

Seeing me unshaven, unwashed, still in my travel clothes, he knew how desperate I was for news of Apollonia. Our legal delegation to Treverorum could wait. He didn't disappoint me and brandished in his fist what information he had ready.

'The timing of this arrest was no coincidence, Clemens.'

Lavinia's careful disguise with the twins in tow might have fooled Leo's two cloaked *protectores*. But from Drusilla, Maximinus knew of our plans. He knew that I'd left Roma with Praetextatus. He knew Praetextatus was closing in on his free-for-all liquidation of Roma's old families and appropriation of their wealth. He'd panicked.

'Amosis watches over the house from a very visible spot so as to draw attention to himself, while Saturnus has two men spying on the custodian and all his communications with the Notary Leo and Maximinus.'

'We're going to her immediately.' I was already on my feet.

'No, *Magister*, you cannot.'

'What did you say?'

'No one but an advocate can gain access to your wife. You must do nothing to prejudice her trial or for that matter your own position as head of the *Schola* by direct contact with her. All your exchanges must be via a third party, an advocate like myself acting as the Castra attorney or your Manlius family lawyer—whomever you wish.'

'You're saying I can't pay her a private visit?'

'It would be very unwise while you are the boss of the *agentes*. Your authority to carry out arrests must not be abused to interfere with the detention of a family member.'

'But—!'

'Just as your testimony at her trial would be regarded as worthless, possibly detrimental. I recommend you concentrate all your energy in getting the charges dropped.'

'Her trial? On what charges?'

'As accessory to corruption in suppressing information on the concealment of the criminal Senator Abienus. The exact wording cites the following law.'

He flipped through his notes. '*Eos, qui secum alieni criminis reos occulendo sociarunt, par atque ipsos reos poena expectet*: If a person by harboring accused persons, associates himself with the persons who are accused of crimes in which he did not participate, he shall expect the same penalty as the accused.'

'The same penalty! That may apply to the Widow Anepsia but they can't link my wife to her crime like that!'

'Did your wife know of Anepsia's affair with Abienus?'

'She only suspected.'

Clemens winced. 'They'll try to equate her "suspicion" of an illicit relationship to the crime of accessory to concealment. Anepsia's already charged with adultery or *stuprum*. We should expect far worse to come.'

'Apollonia knew nothing of Abienus' concealment! Let me see those.' I grabbed the documents from his trembling hand.

I read for myself, in the *quaestor*'s official script, *litterae caelestes*, the address of my wife's jailer, the date of her arrest, the charge, and the names of two witnesses for the prosecution— Anepsia's traitorous houseslave Sapaudulus and the *vicomagister* Flaccus who could only have heard of the visits to Anepsia's dwelling from Drusilla.

But Anepsia herself had cited Apollonia as a witness for her defense. It was just as I'd feared. Tormented by Notary Leo, Anepsia feared for her life. She was naming Apollonia as a respectable reference against slander. She would argue that Apollonia's visits during the presence of Abienus in her house proved that it was general knowledge in good society that the friendship between the senator and the widow was above board.

In short, Apollonia's impeccable reputation would be exploited to save Anepsia's—but Maximinus had twisted the friendship against them both.

'Your wife is of noble Roman blood, through and through, *Magister*. Ressatus put two of the Castra's best guards on surveillance over the house of detention. They've learned from the slaves of the house that *Domina* Apollonia defends her friend too stoutly for *Notarius* Leo's taste. The more she insists Anepsia was not knowingly in the wrong in sheltering Abienus out of misguided loyalty, the more she seems an accomplice herself.'

Clemens watched me until the silence grew too much.

'Do you know this Flaccus, *Magister*?'

'Yes. His testimony won't stand up. He's not a firsthand witness to anything. He sits at the crossroads of our street tending the old compital shrine. But his worshippers have fallen off. There are no more ritual offerings of *bullae* and girlhood tokens. He barely ekes out a living. Now I know how—that lazy shit sells neighborhood gossip and pilfered trinkets. He fenced some stolen jewelry for one of Apollonia's slaves. She turned on us when her old playmate, the heir Leontus Manlius, grew up and married into a respectable old family.'

'Your own slave girl informed on your house?' Clemens' grip on his *stilus* tightened until his knuckles were white.

'I prefer to think the poor girl was blackmailed into it by Flaccus. And through Flaccus, Maximinus introduced a serpent into our garden. We must find that girl Drusilla. She must tell Flaccus to retract his testimony against Apollonia.'

'Don't waste your time, *Magister*. A bedchamber slave's testimony in favor of her mistress is worthless. Especially as there are slaves in Anepsia's house who witnessed Apollonia's visits. If they vouch otherwise for the prosecution—'

'My wife is innocent, for the gods' sake! To allow one slave's testimony and refuse another's? Can anyone just rewrite Roman Law today? Tell me, where is her defense, Clemens?'

I caught myself pounding the desk. Why lose my temper with my only intermediary?

'I had a quiet word with the *primiscrinius* down at the courts. Her trial date is in three weeks.'

'We'll summon Leontus Manlius from his case in Mediolanum to lead her defense in court.'

Clemens shook his head. 'Again, with all respect to his rhetorical skills, I advise you avoid being seen to use Manlius connections to influence any court. The Ceionii learned a hard lesson when Lampadius leaned on a magistrate to acquit Lollianus. These days, no noble blood is safe. No venerable name carries weight.'

'Then we engage that young lawyer I heard win Proconsul Hymetius' appeal. His rhetoric saved Hymetius from the sword.'

'I shall confer with him immediately, *Magister*, but he may not be necessary. It's clear the Widow Anepsia can't save herself. She's guilty of hiding a fugitive from the state. But she can retract her written testimony that Apollonia knew where Abienus was hiding.'

I'd collapsed back into my chair. 'But Clemens, if I can't get access to my own wife, how can I contact Anepsia? Where is she? Apollonia said she'd obtained a respectable family friend as *guarantor*.'

Clemens sniffed. 'Some family friend. He panicked and withdrew his protection. The magistrate transferred her to the care of a state *apparitor*.'

He handed me Anepsia's detention address with an eyebrow raised in disapproval.

'Why, this is the same house where Hesychia smothered herself! But Clemens, they know me at that house. They're not reliable. Wouldn't that look bad—my pressuring Anepsia?'

Clemens thought for a moment and fiddled with his *stilus* before advising me.

'Leaning on the accused to clear your wife would be totally unacceptable—totally. But as Castra *quaestor*, I remind you, that's not why you would make such a visit, *Magister*.'

'Yes, it is.'

'With respect, *Magister*, no, it's not.'

'Then . . . why would I visit?'

'The Castra is responsible for the terms and conditions of all arrests and detentions of *honestiores*. Suicide is a very unfortunate thing to happen to any custodian. Anepsia's *apparitor* might not want to draw attention to his record by making trouble if and when you investigate the scene of *Domina* Hesychia's suicide for your final report. Anepsia's presence is neither here nor there.'

'So . . . I can visit the house.'

'It's almost an obligation to correct procedure.'

My killing fatigue vanished. I told Cyrillus to order the Castra's curtained *lectica*.

'*Magister*? The Emperor? Praetextatus' delegation?'

'Oh, Clemens, forgive me. Your brief was a complete success. The Moor Eupraxius backed you and gave Valentinian no choice.

From now on, no torture of *honestiores* outside the charge of treason unless the Emperor consents on a case-by-case basis.'

The lawyer smiled with pride, then frowned. 'But won't it take at least a week for Praetextatus to return with a signed rescript to clarify the Emperor's ruling?'

'Perhaps longer. And my word alone is not enough to save Anepsia or my wife.'

⚔⚔⚔

It was a few minutes before dusk and the street torches weren't even lit yet when the Castra bearers stopped outside the house of Anepsia's jailor. I'd hoped to bargain with the official alone. But it was his canny midwife who answered the door, the same shrew who'd sent her decorating bill to the Castra.

'Well, the *Magister Agentium in Rebus* himself,' she said, her eyes squinting through the growing shadows. 'You've come to settle the costs for the last one?'

'Your house repairs are of no interest to the Castra.'

She glanced up and down the street. Her discretion was fine with me. My hood was pulled low over my brow and my insignia was invisible to any casual observer.

'Then why honor my threshold?' She might as well have said 'darken.'

'I must inspect the scene of the suicide for my report,' I said.

'You've already seen the room. Now it's occupied.'

'The widow of Senator Victorinus? She won't be in my way.'

'If she were here—and I'm not admitting she is—she's in no pretty shape to receive handsome callers . . . especially *clarissimi* gentlemen . . . if you see what I mean.'

Her lewd insinuation was beyond sufferance. I pushed past her and slammed straight into her husband blocking my path to that deadly back room.

'You got some court order to show me, *Magister*?'

'The Castra supervises all detentions—and their failures. You know that.'

The *fauces* was too narrow. His bulk stood rooted. 'I think Prefect Maximinus might have something to say about what happens after arrest.'

'As do we. Especially when the sudden death of a lady of spotless character occurs under your watch and begs further investigation.'

The wife gave a cynical snort behind me but the *apparitor* hesitated. In that moment, a frail silhouette appeared in the unlit archway leading into the small foyer behind him.

'Fool! You left her door unbolted!'

'Who is it? Who's come?' The ravaged voice trembled. Anepsia feared her tormenter had returned for more questioning. 'I can take no more.'

'*Magister* Marcus Gregorianus Numidianus, *Domina*.'

She drew back with a start. Now she feared something quite different—my righteous fury and the pain of her guilt.

I raced past and pulling her back into that fatal cell, slammed the door behind us. I caught sight of her face by the flame of the bedside lantern.

I dropped her arm and stepped away.

'Who did that to you, *Domina*. Notary Leo?'

'No. Some brute with a club foot and an iron bar. He laughed.'

Her mouth had swollen into the muzzle of some deep-sea fish, with split lips stiff with bloody crusts.

'Can you see me with the other eye?'

'Just. I've never known such pain. They applied *acetum* to the injury. But they're not finished. They said I would be transferred soon to be strapped across the *eculeus*.'

The 'little horse' would break her spirit before it broke her back. I looked away. Praetextatus' rescript would arrive too late to sway Maximinus' sadists. I didn't have the heart to tell her. Instead, I had to make use of the little time she had left.

'You've confessed to harboring Abienus. But you've falsely claimed it was no secret and made my wife your co-conspirator. I have a right to know what more Maximinus wants of you.'

'Aginatius!' She mumbled. 'He wants Aginatius!'

I sank onto a narrow stool near her cot like a diver sinking into the depths, confused and short of breath.

'Senator Aginatius? Wanted for treason?'

'Yes!' Animated by some sudden hope, she turned her maimed features to me.

'Maximinus lacks evidence against him. But I have a plan, Numidianus, a strategy,' she whispered. 'I'll get myself out of this.'

I detected a fresh frenzy in her. For truth or more lies?

'Listen, Numidianus. I'll get that Pannonian bastard on my side. I'll blame Aginatius for everything. I'll testify that Aginatius subdued me by nefarious spells, then assaulted me.'

'Assaulted?'

'Yes, yes, he *raped* me, in his house.'

'Did he?'

Her story ran dead against Apollonia's shocked account of Senator Aginatius at the mourning party around Victorinus' corpse. Aginatius had not sounded like a frustrated lover or a villain devoured by middle-aged lust to me.

'You see, Numidianus? Then Maximinus will be satisfied!'

'Why?'

'Don't be stupid, Numidianus! Maximinus wants revenge on Aginatius. Surely you know that!' She tossed me a hollow laugh.

How to settle her hysteria? The woman would never survive a trial in this spirit without doing many innocents more damage.

'Anepsia, you gave Maximinus three thousand pounds of silver, your daughter's dowry. Then you gave him half your own inheritance. Then you promised Callista in marriage to Maximinus' son Marcellinus, sight unseen, against your daughter's will. While the rest of Roma has hated this man on sight, you've given all you have to his greed.'

'It's not enough. It's never enough.'

'Why has he turned against you, of all people? Why persecute you now for a lonely widow's fling with poor Abienus?'

'He saw what Victorinus flaunted and he wanted it all—the silver, my girl, the house, the country holdings. But most of all, Maximinus wants Aginatius.'

'But why?'

She slurred in a slow, firm tone, like a drunken mother explaining simple things to a toddler.

'Because Aginatius wrote to Consul Probus over a year ago, while Probus was still here in the city. Aginatius told Probus how the Prefect of the Annona, Maximinus, a nobody, a rude Pannonian parvenu, had insulted the great *Culmen* Probus behind his back.'

'Because Urban Prefect Olybrius had assigned the Chilo case to Maximinus instead of Aginatius?'

'Yes, but I know why.'

'To save his son Alypius.'

She shook her head. 'Because Aginatius had wanted to deal with Chilo more discreetly, keep it all in the family, so to speak. In his letter, Aginatius told Probus that only he, Probus, was powerful enough take Maximinus down for his own good.'

'What did Consul Probus do with this letter?'

'Probus sent the letter straight to Maximinus. Probus betrayed Aginatius. Probus betrayed all of Roma to protect his chances with the Pannonians. Then he took up his new promotion and raced out of Roma for Sirmium on the excuse that a band of Sarmatians were moving toward the Danuvius border.'

There it was again, *Aginatius and a letter*, just as the doomed teenager Lollianus had muttered in his sleep to my guard Defendens. The boy had known of the incendiary letter. He'd heard his elders talk of it, hush it up, cite it, condemn it, or applaud it. It was a letter you'd disavow, run away from, deny ever seeing— if you fell into Maximinus' vengeful hands.

Probus had simply shown Aginatius' attack to its target and sashayed off to greater things. But his family couldn't follow him to safety. Yes, Probus, their *culmen* and powerbroker, the wealthiest of the powerful Anician *gens*, where had he been all these months as his cousins and the cousins of his cousins screamed and wept? He'd been out of Roma, on a convenient prefectural tour of duty for all the months of Maximinus' purge.

There was much that still lay hidden. Why had Aginatius counted on Probus to take down the upstart Maximinus? Had he assumed that Probus was dead set against Valentinian and his Pannonian officials? Quite an error, indeed.

Was it possible that Probus, the third most powerful man in the Empire after the two imperial Valentinian brothers themselves, had been the apex, the capital, the candidate on which the Ceionii and Anicii senators had pinned their hopes of snatching the Empire back from the dying Valentinian?

Was *that* what the inconvenient Chilo had known? Was *that* why Chilo had to be silenced? Was *that* the infamous 'silly idea, foolish plan' dropping off careless Roman lips?

It was like watching the curtain rise on a three-act play of which I had seen only one sketch in rehearsal.

Anepsia's bony hand clutched my arm. 'You've come to help me, Numidianus? Help me bargain for my life? You will tell Maximinus the good news? I'm ready to accuse Senator Aginatius.'

I peeled her claws from my flesh.

'No, *Domina*. I've come to save my wife.'

She slumped back on that lethal pillow and laid a hand over what remained of the beauty that had won her two powerful husbands. 'Of course you have.'

'You know Apollonia's innocent. You entertained her, out of season, in your unheated garden, so as to hide the presence of Abienus inside the house. You hastened her departure so she wouldn't notice anything amiss.'

Anepsia groaned in pain that wasn't only physical. I continued without mercy. 'I need you to write that down with no ambiguity in wording or intention—that my wife is completely innocent.'

'If I write that, will you help me press rape charges against Aginatius?'

'I will do what I can to promote the truth, but only the truth.'

She moaned.

'*Domina*, your case is lost. But there is still time to prove yourself the honorable Roman wife I met in our garden, a matron worthy of Apollonia's friendship, an example of *Romanitas* in the face of certain death.'

'No. First, I accuse Aginatius—'

'First, you'll clear my wife's name.'

'Yes, yes, all right. I'll write it.'

'Write it now.'

'No, no, I'm exhausted and weak. I'll write it after . . . I rest.'

I wasn't hard-hearted enough to hover over her struggle. Her own choice of words would be more convincing than anything I extracted out of her pen by force.

'Then I'll return tomorrow at dawn to collect your written statement.'

She rolled over, turning her back on me. Her bare legs were covered by bruises left by Mucianus' iron rod. Her skirts were smeared with rusty blood. I dreaded to think what that rod had done.

⚔⚔⚔

The next morning Saturnus and I returned before dawn.

'She's gone,' the wife told us with a triumphant smile. 'Took away this morning for the Tullianum. Broke the terms of *custodia libera* by seeing you.'

'Did she leave anything for me?'

'Some lover's souvenir?'

'A paper.'

'She was writing something, but they took all that with'em.'

'Who's they?'

'Your lot still owe us for the paint job.'

She slammed the door in our faces.

When we reached the Castra, I called a staff meeting. It was my first chance to credit *Quaestor* Clemens for Praetextatus' success. It was only a matter of time before Leo's 'interrogations' were curtailed.

But we didn't have time.

I heard the reports of my riders. They'd fanned out as I'd ordered before my departure for Treverorum. The team racing down the westward road had picked up Maximinus' faded trail near the artificial harbor of Portus at the mouth of the Tiberis.

And at last, some divinity had blessed our Castra hunt. Neptune guarding the sea? Or Volturnus the god of the river?

Anyway, it seemed the maritime world didn't bow and scrape to a Pannonian bully official, even one who claimed he ran Roma itself. Hundreds of ships were still in dry dock before resuming spring sailing. The crush of seamen and merchants doing repairs and deals or just cooling their heels around the vast hexagon of concrete docks and warehouses had meant that all the state *mansiones* overflowed.

No *manceps* managing an inn bursting with regular customers dared oust a shipowner or corn merchant from his downy cot to accommodate this stranger, Prefect Maximinus.

And then one landlord had recognized him as the former governor of Sardinia. He had placated the irate traveler by offering him a bed in a room shared by pottery wholesalers.

And true to form, Maximinus had exposed his true nature. He'd demanded the room for himself alone and threatened reprisals, but to no avail. Now more exhausted than before, he'd dragged himself from one establishment to another, his self-control and remaining good sense evaporating, drawing attention and ridicule from all of Portus.

He'd been last seen, unshaven and hollow-eyed, boarding a boat for Sardinia.

My *agentes* delivered more news. Senator Aginatius had been discovered at last, disguised as an estate manager in an abandoned villa, surrounded by his hungry, thirsty slaves whom he ordered to protect him at all hours. They'd all been dragged off in chains and tortured until one slave, close to death, had spilled enough to press charges.

And in addition to treason, Aginatius faced a fresh charge—the rape of Anepsia.

The desperate widow had prepared a paper after all, like the custodian's wife told us. But it was not to retract her claim that Apollonia knew Abienus stayed with her.

She had wasted her last card to save herself with this trumped-up story against Maximinus' political enemy. And I knew this desperate gambit would do her no good at all.

Now Roman Law had failed me. Roman honor and decency had failed me. I did not feel 'one of them.' I felt only contempt for the corruption and ignobility of modern Roman 'society'.

I could rely only on myself and only on others like me, *agentes* without fine birth, great palaces, or gilded family trees.

My officers filed out of my office to get on with their day—reporting road conditions, sorting mail bags, copying sensitive state correspondence, and auditing prefectural accounts. I'd listened, arbitrated, supervised, and served the Empire for three hours.

I told Cyrillus to go to the canteen for his midday meal. I sat behind my desk with my eyes blank and mind burning. How could I answer to the shade of Apodemius? He'd saved Apollonia all through her youth by hiding her under a Vestal's veil. He'd entrusted his most precious possession to me.

What would Apodemius have done now? All he had was intelligence. Weak, arthritic, and 'wispy white-haired,' Apodemius lived by his brains. He would have used any information he had to save his granddaughter.

And then I heard again the dying whispers of the soothsayer Campensis.

CHAPTER 19, BURIED SECRETS

—THE CASTRA PEREGRINA—

I smelled again the Tullianum's stench of dried vomit and blood as if Maximinus' prisoners lay in front of me, half buried alive, rotting into corpses while they still breathed. My mind returned to the pus oozing from the soothsayer's blinded eyes that saw so much:

'Campensis, are you saying Prefect Maximinus is an augur?'

'He tried divination, once upon a time, tried hard. But our wise gods withhold their gifts. Our great divinities know that a man like that misuses whatever they let him see.'

'You must have confused him with someone else, Campensis. Your torturer Prefect Flavius Maximinus is a Christian official in Emperor Valentinian's Christian court.'

'Some Christian! He's a criminal! You doubt my word? You ask that necromancer in Olbia.'

'Necromancer? Necromancy's a foul crime.'

'The Castra knows. . . that old man with the wispy white hair. Ask him . . .'

Ask Apodemius about a necromancer in Olbia, Sardinia. There was another dungeon—the underground repository in the Castra's Temple of Jupiter Redux holding Apodemius' files from the reigns of Constans, Constantius, and Julian. The old man might have traveled to Sardinia, just as he wandered to all corners of the Empire.

When he wasn't sitting through the black hours of night debriefing *agentes* and sorting our reports, Apodemius was quietly slipping from one province to another. He was always listening, recording, and recruiting. He kept reassuring his most obscure informers and his least acknowledged assets, 'You, too, serve the Empire.'

Nothing escaped Apodemius, even when he escaped notice. When I'd first met him, he traveled as a retired Roman nobleman. A year later he appeared as a disreputable North African circus master to recruit me for the Castra. Even when terminally ill, he'd escaped the Castra—garbed as a washerwoman slave—right under my nose. And he'd traveled on his final and fatal mission from Sirmium to Chalcedon disguised as a wealthy Eastern merchant.

I told Cyrillus to fetch Zephyrinus. Myron had supervised our archivist's recuperation well. Zephyrinus seemed more and more like his old self. He entered my inner office carrying an anchovy pastry from the canteen where Cyrillus had found him gossiping about Roma's latest domestic tragedies. It pained me to realize how his ilk had regarded the torture of an adulteress like Anepsia as titillating fodder for the *Acta Diurna* titbits columns. Worse, how many people had heard of Apollonia's arrest?

'How are you feeling, old man?'

'Oh, *Magister*, I've got painful twinges—'

'Good. We're going to disinter Apodemius' file boxes from the Temple.'

'Hold on. What are you looking for?' His tone implied that, along with his senses, he'd recovered some right to limit access to such sensitive dossiers. It was a healthy sign and I hurried him back down the stairs and across the courtyard.

A strong sun warmed the flagstones and lightened the fortress-like atmosphere of the ancient complex. But the Castra's original place of worship survived in cold shadow. It'd been obscured when the Christian chapel was squeezed between the outer wall near the main gate and the tall double doors of the pagan house. The narrow space behind chapel and temple scarcely allowed the passage of one grown man.

The guards from the front gatehouse fetched the Temple's heavy keys, as long as my hand and rusted almost to breaking point. But coaxed with gentle respect, the venerable padlock sprang open at last. The narrow oak doors creaked wide on their ancient hinges.

I hadn't been inside the Temple for some time, not since we raised memorial plaques for the *agentes* Einku and Rufus lost in Sirmium after the great earthquake and flood of 365. Irregular imperial prohibitions on traditional worship had confused and discouraged any *agentes* who might have wished to honor the old gods as before. Half our recruits now attended Father Natalius' Masses in the Chapel.

Zephyrinus held a sleeve over his nose. 'Stinks in here.'

'That's the smell of ancient devotion and the dedication of thousands of worthier men before us.'

'Don't scold, don't scold. You're lucky I'm still here.'

With difficulty, we leveraged up two heavy trapdoors laid in uneven paving stones to one side of the altar platform. We descended worn stone steps. I helped the old librarian navigate the steepest drops.

The guards handed down lamps and heavy torches. I surveyed the stuffy storage space, its moldering contents shifted and shunted, this way and that, as suited the century.

Our beloved temple had been expanded from a small shrine honoring Emperor Severus. And the shrine had been built over a block of army barracks in a *castra* serving the great Octavian Augustus himself. As late as Trajan's day, the Castra had boasted a commandant called the *princeps peregrinorum*—not a *schola magister*.

The army men had made way for the *frumentarii*, military grain distributors who branched out into intelligence and communications operations. But Emperor Diocletian disbanded the *frumentarii* for corruption. And when the first *magister agentium in rebus* under Emperor Constantine reclaimed the Castra for his headquarters, he purged the *frumentarii* from our institutional memory.

'We can't work in the middle of all this junk,' Zephyrinus protested.

'Ancient gossip. You'll love it.'

I took stock. In one dank corner under the beams of the rotting foundation, discarded memorabilia littered our path: a dull-edged *gladius* missing its hilt, abandoned sacrifice utensils, and a clutch of dented bronze plaques propped against a tumble of loose stone.

'Is that a pile of toys, *Magister*?'

'No, they're stone ships carved by soldiers thanking the sea gods for protecting them from shipwrecks.'

I handed the least damaged replica to a guard to clean it up for display at the school. Our cadets should remember the bravery of men who'd served hundreds of years ago.

The guards lit our reading lamps. The miserable repository jumped back to life.

'All right, all right. What are we looking for?' Zephyrinus rubbed his leathery hands. His archivist's blood was heating up.

'We're looking for notes on a necromancer.'

'Necromancy's a dirty crime—eating corpses, wearing their clothes, digging up secrets better off buried. I say leave the dead alone, that's what I say.'

'Last seen in Olbia, Sardinia.'

'Sardinia?' Zephyrinus croaked. 'Nothing happens in that backwater. Probably nothing here but old audits.'

'I cleaned those out when we reopened. But Maximinus was *Corrector* of Sardinia.'

'And the cunt should have stayed there. Every day, the *Acta Diurna* reports he's arrested—'

'Where's Sardinia in this mess?'

The guards helped us drag one trunk off another and shift boxes toward the lamps. They brought down camp chairs, small tables, and cushions for Zephyrinus' stiff joints. They returned to the gate house and we set to our task.

Zephyrinus checked curling leather labels and scraped dust off faded lettering scratched into leather straps. We divided up the years in question and tackled the bundles. It wouldn't take long; there were very few files on Sardinia that had survived my ruthless triage of Apodemius' records in 363.

After a few minutes, it felt like resurrecting the dead *magister* from the ether. His files were a mishmash of salvaged notes sent back from *agentes* riding the *Cursus*, coded scraps from informants signed with cover-names, and summaries in his own spidery handwriting. A few of the records were careful copies, but Apodemius had never much relied on a clerk like Cyrillus.

We sorted notes in faded ink on the cheapest *emporitica* to noble correspondence on expensive *Livia*, and even imperial missives on soft rolls of vellum still dangling broken seals. Some notes were on purse-sized tablets of four or six wood-framed leaves, their dried wax crumbling into my palm and their hinges bent. Sometimes a determined *stilus* had dug so deep with anger or impatience, the nib had damaged the wooden backing.

And as I lifted or set aside one bundle after another, the stinky liniment used by Apodemius' deaf masseur bit my nostrils.

'*Magister*! Here's something!'

Zephyrinus showed me his find.

'It's a report from Terranova. One *circitor* Jovilios is delivering mail from the mainland to the east Sardinian coastal hubs. He reports the *vir perfectissimus praeses provinciae Sardiniae* has launched an inquiry into tax-collection abuse. His aide requests previous audits from our Castra files to establish a base figure for comparison. But Jovilios also hears rumors that the racket goes wider than just one or two collectors and the request might actually be intended to cover some top man's ass.'

'What's the date?'

'361.'

'That's before Maximinus took over.'

After an hour or so, we'd hit a dead end. There was no trace of Maximinus in Sardinia before he was proclaimed *Corrector* of Sardinia, Corsica and Tuscia in 364. Apodemius had died at the stake in Chalcedon in the spring of 362. I knew the very day and exact hour when the dying old man had volunteered to take my place on the executioner's pyre. The time gap killed my theory dead.

Zephyrinus laid his last Sardinian bundle back in its box. We continued, shuffling through other piles, no longer knowing where to focus our efforts. Each passing minute was an hour of torment for Apollonia. Would I rescue her before Leo and his minions came back to question her again?

After a long silence, Zephyrinus folded away a memo on Corsican politics and asked, 'Why was Apodemius talking to a scummy spell-trafficker like Campensis in the first place? What business would drag him into the company of soothsayers and *haruspices*?'

'I don't know. He gleaned intelligence from practically anybody. But he had no time for superstition. He ignored the Church fathers, which I see now was a mistake. He didn't even pay much attention to respectable rituals—including in this temple.'

'Always working on Castra business.'

'Imperial business, Zephyrinus. He monitored the whole empire like his back garden.'

'So for him to meet Campensis, state affairs must have got mixed up with the fortune-telling business.'

'Yes . . .'

I was smiling at a report written by my late friend, Agent Rufus on dangerous road conditions due to brigand ambushes in western Gallia. It looked like he'd scribbled it after too much wine. But the place names and details were clear enough.

The smell of burning lamp wicks grew stronger in the claustrophobic chamber. One of the torches flickered and sputtered out.

'Julian,' I blurted out.

'Emperor Julian?'

'Yes. Julian mixed up state business with magic. Remember his forced restoration of traditional worship? He was ramming it through at high speed, demanding the return of temple treasures looted by the Christians. He was reinstating *haruspices*, consulting soothsayers, and drumming up new rules for worshipping the old cults.'

'I sure don't recall any necromancy!'

'Of course not. But Julian was keen on augurs and magic. Apodemius had us watching Julian closely, myself included. Constantius didn't trust his cousin Julian's sudden rise in Gallia.'

'Julian must've known he was under surveillance. Did Julian trust Apodemius?'

'Are you joking? Apodemius had managed the execution of Julian's half-brother, Caesar Gallus. Killing Apodemius and shutting down our *schola* was Julian's revenge for Gallus.'

'Well, anyway, that narrows it to when Julian took the throne.'

We started sorting the files again, looking from the death of Constantius in November 361 to the death of Apodemius in 362.

'You're exhausted, *Magister*. You'll pass out. You take one more bundle and that's it. Then you go rest.'

The guards revived us with olives and bread. And scrutinizing the remnants squirreled away by the dying spymaster brought that dramatic year back—those long winter weeks of uncertainty, Julian's vengeful arrests of Emperor Constantius' highest officials, and Apodemius' furtive disappearance.

And my meeting Apollonia, hiding with her grandfather in a brothel in Sirmium—the imperial capital in Pannonia.

'Pannonia! Pannonia, Zephyrinus, not Sardinia! Of course! I bet Apodemius met Maximinus' *father* in Pannonia!'

'Forget Sardinia. Concentrate on Pannonia,' he grumbled.

That didn't leave much to search. Apodemius had foreseen the end. He'd used the last months of his life smuggling only critical records from the Castra to the safe care of a trusted old Vestal.

With a shock of recognition, I found a note in Apodemius' faltering handwriting. Then it continued in my own wife's graceful hand:

'... *Carpian tabularis, Pannonia Valeria, haruspex of good repute, dislikes blood-letting* ... *Julian's love of public blood sacrifice, daily slaughter of hundreds of animals reminds Christians of Maximin Daia's Great Persecution. Local Christians afraid they'll be forced to choose between traditional sacrifice or martyrdom. Warn Julian of mounting resentment. Outbreaks of violence.*'

I glanced up. The librarian's sunken cheeks caught the shadows of the little fires flickering in the granite blackness enveloping us.

'It's a start, Zephyrinus. Apodemius was lobbied by Maximinus' soothsayer father to press more moderation on Julian for the sake of political stability.'

'Is there more?'

'Yes ... *they fear influence of Julian's experiments with theurgy, raising spirits from statues. Carpian's lawyer son consulted necromancer Zalmoxis. Father says birds foretell son's death by executioner's sword.*'

'Zalmoxis.'

'Yes. We have a necromancer's name. Then Apodemius lists about a dozen incidents: a riot of Christians near Sopianae, the desecration by pagans of a chapel built over a Cibalae temple ... So Campensis was right.'

'Apodemius writes of "they",' Zephyrinus commented.

'He was collecting intelligence on Julian from the priests.'

The archivist struggled to his feet and started restacking the old packets and dossiers. 'So Maximinus used a necromancer in Pannonia.'

'Then why did Campensis say Olbia?"

Zephyrinus brushed some grit off his tunic. 'Want to bet the necromancer in Pannonia and the necromancer in Olbia are the same bastard?'

'Possibly. If Maximinus used his dark friend to assist his climb up the *Cursus Honorum*—'

Zephyrinus shivered. The late winter sun couldn't penetrate the stony chamber. I too felt the shades of the bloodless dead brush past.

'That burglary that nearly killed you—it looks different now, doesn't it?'

'How so, *Magister*?'

'I've fought off my suspicions long enough. It's always been obvious Maximinus was behind the attack on the archives.'

'He wouldn't dare! For the money?'

'Nothing to do with money. Now I realize, it why it didn't feel right. Even when I immediately suspected Maximinus of the break-in, I fought off jumping to conclusions.'

'Why? He asked for your help up front, didn't he? He made no secret of wanting my files on the great families.'

'And when I refused, he backed off, and I began to suspect him of lying. But now I know what was behind his lying. He never wanted to *study* any family files. He wanted to remove his own.'

'He was hunting for that?'

'Perhaps he knew his father had talked to Apodemius. He had to destroy any record that might kill his rise as a "Christian official" under Valentinian.'

The chamber was too cold for us to remain.

'How ironic! All this time Maximinus must have worried that I knew his nasty secret from the start! You know, he asked me once, was I ever tempted by the dark arts? And there was strange look in his eyes.'

'To test your reaction, *Magister*?'

'Maybe. He certainly tried everything else—cajole me, raid me, sideline me, threaten me, and now frame my wife to silence me. He knows I've gone to see Valentinian in Treverorum. He must be panicked.'

Zephyrinus shuffled back and forth, putting everything back into 'his' order.

'Can that note liberate your wife, *Magister*?'

'No. It's the hearsay of a dead man who burned at the stake. Half is not even in his handwriting. Any magistrate would laugh.'

We collected the discolored cords, fraying twine, rotting sacks and broken seals and secured Apodemius' legacy once more.

I tucked the note under my tunic. I helped Zephyrinus back up the steep steps into the silent temple and called the guards to collect the lamps and torches.

'Go to bed, old man. I'm lucky you recovered.'

'But you look like you escaped from the mines. You can't save your wife without your strength back.'

I thought of Cornelius murdered in Ostia.

'My anger provides all the strength I need. I'm not resting yet.'

'What're you going to do, *Magister*?'

'Find the necromancer Zalmoxis.'

𐊗𐊗𐊗

My inner office filled with *agentes*—sweaty riders just finishing their circuit, men pink and aromatic from the bath, and impatient men pulled away from guard duty or hoisting mail sacks.

'You'll track Maximinus from Portus Augusti across to Sardinia. The trail should lead you to a man named Zalmoxis, a Dacian to judge by the name. Bring him here.'

'What's his trade?' Saturnus had offered me a dozen of his fastest riders, but I wasn't trusting only subordinates. Saturnus himself would lead them out of the city's gates.

'Whatever he professes by day, he's a necromancer by night.'

'Euw!' young Defendens winced. 'I thought that scum was eliminated, *Magister*.'

'I believe he was last in Olbia, here.'

I pointed to the northeastern coastal provincial capital, Olbia-Tempio on my wall map.

'No other lead on him?'

'No, Saturnus. The man who described him to me as "that necromancer in Olbia" died of the Tullianum's tortures.'

The men squirmed with distaste.

'Come on, use your heads as well as your saddles! A parasite like Zalmoxis won't find clients in an open field or volcanic crater.

He'll be preying on pagan Romans in the coastal colonies, near mausolea and cemeteries in the suburbs. Try the other main ports, Turris Libysonis in the west or down south in Caralis and Nora.'

Rubellius half-joked, 'Although, if you're fiddling with a nauseating racket that could get you burned alive, the perfect cover would be hanging around the local church.'

'That's not a bad idea, Rubellius.'

'What's the shipping timing this week?' Saturnus waited for his mail distributors to answer, but I didn't:

'Hire a boat. Now, who knows Sardinia?' I asked.

How I now regretted my neglect of the island! Perhaps reading too many old books to the blind Senator as a slave child had left me with the well-engrained prejudices; apart from its Romanized coastal cities, Sardinia was valued only for its mineral and food exports. But it was still a social dump of middlemen, sailors, brigands, exiles, peasants, and mining slaves.

Tarbus raised his hand. 'I updated the route guide last year. There are four good north-south roads, two coastal and two inland linking Olbia to the southern coast. We're pretty well served by *mansiones* on long stretches between the towns.'

'Backup horses, Tarbus? You'll need to ride relay, as fast as you can manage until you drop.'

'The local horses are slow, *Magister*.'

'It's the land,' Rubellius grumbled. 'Sardinia is all deep gorges, craggy peaks, jagged cliffs. They're bred to climb, not gallop.'

'But our roads are good and even, Tarbus?'

'The *Cursus Clabularis* on the flat stretch across the plateau between Tharros on the west coast down to Caralis is rutted and worn down.'

'No matter, *Agentes*. You should land our Zalmoxis in no time if you stick to traces of the Prefect. Ask in all the baths and *tabernae*.'

They filed out, talking among themselves, dividing up into parties.

'Saturnus?'

'Yes, *Magister*?'

Before you ride out, send me one of those two men you've got surveilling Apollonia's detention house.'

'Figulus or Culeo?'

'Either one. I can't spend a single minute more this far from her. I want him to take me to her.'

I'd never seen that expression on Saturnus' face before. He left without a word.

※※※

Was the urgent mission to Sardinia just a means of distracting my staff? Not at all. But I didn't confess to my officers that I nurtured the ambition to rescue Apollonia while they were gone. They were sure to tell me it was rash—crazy—certain to backfire on the Castra. They'd try to stop me.

Any rescue must be well-planned. I had to know every detail of her detention. I must wait at least the hour it took for Figulus or Culeo to cross the city to fill me in.

There was a tap on my door and Cyrillus poked his head into the office.

'*Magister*, Sabazios is here to see you.'

'Sabazios? My mind's on other matters.'

'Zephyrinus sent him.'

The school's Codes and Signals Master limped in. He was carrying a thick roll in his arms.

'Zephyrinus said you might want to look again at my record of the burglary, *Magister*.'

'I filed your painting with the report. What're those?'

'Zephyrinus says you might want my sketches, too, the ones I used to compose the final painting, *Magister*.'

'I'm waiting for . . . oh, why not?'

With care not to smudge his charcoal strokes, the Thracian veteran unrolled half a dozen pieces of coarse papyrus squares on which he'd recorded what he saw that September morning.

'You see here, *Magister*, this is the position of the displaced items, labelled to assist me later. This is where poor Anthimus lay dying. These are boot prints in the blood, as you asked, but I soon gave up, as our own men had already tracked through it. That's why I didn't feature the tracks in the final rendering.'

'Yes,' I said, rubbing weary eyes that felt caked in wet sand. 'I was foolish to hope for any clue. I wasted your time . . . but . . .'

I felt faint with hunger.

'Well, I was as guilty as any. I tracked the blood myself, here, see? And I sketched my own footprint by mistake.'

'Does any sketch show where the man reading by lantern left everything in disorder?'

'That would be this one. But Zephyrinus says the man took nothing.'

'Because what he was looking for was stored beneath the Temple.'

I paged through his sketches, managing to muster a minute's polite attention from Apollonia's plight. Sabazios' amateurish effort was stylized to imitate the banal murals the average middle-class family plasters across their dining rooms.

'This is your half-foot, here?'

'Yes, *Magister*. What that Frankish axe left me—'

'Sabazios, the Franks cut off your left toes, not your right. Look closely. Your left print would be wide, short, and square, wouldn't it, like your special boot? Here is it.'

He nodded. 'That there is a full boot, so I assumed—'

'But here's a smaller man's normal left boot beside it. This man pressed down on the side of his *right* foot in a distorted curve, here. It's nothing like your stubby, square print.'

Sabazios pulled my desk lamp closer and leaned over the sketch. 'It's a muddle. See why I left it out of my final version?'

I managed an exhausted smile at the veteran coding master.

'Well done, Sabazios.'

'I slipped in the blood. It's corrupted evidence, *Magister*—'

'Shush, Sabazios. You made no mistake. You recorded the footstep of a certain Mucianus, Maximinus' henchman with a right club foot.'

⚖⚖⚖

Someone was shaking my arm.

'*Magister*. Wake up.'

'Myron! Is Apollonia's guard here yet?'

'Not yet.'

'What's keeping him? Has Amosis come?'

'No, not yet. You can't sleep at your desk. Take Amosis' couch. Use one of the barrack cots. No, come to my dispensary where I have clean linens and pillows.'

'I can't sleep. Not until I free Apollonia. I need some men.'

'But you were asleep. Free Apollonia? You can't liberate your wife unless you are *compos mentis*, in full control of your mind and your resources. A short rest first.'

The Greek's tone had changed. He led me like a child across the courtyard, into the gymnasium and upstairs to his clinic. A laundry slave took my tunic and trousers stained with the sweat of my journey back from Treverorum.

Myron brought me a glass of what was left of my own vintage drained away by Zephyrinus' restoration. But I didn't recognize its strange bouquet as I brought the glass to my lips. My head dropped like a marble ball onto the crisp pillow.

I saw Apollonia. She turned her face to me and both her beautiful, brown eyes were maimed and crying pus, like poor Campensis'. She tried to greet me, but her split lips were caked shut with blackened blood like Anepsia's. I reached out for her, but when she tried to lift her arms, they hung useless from her shoulder, limp and broken. Her legs were lacerated by whips and sliced useless like Sericus'. I tried to take her in my arms, but I slipped in her blood and smeared a footprint.

Someone helped me over a chamber pot.

I took some soup and drank more wine. Apollonia had gone. I fell asleep again.

And again. Some wine, some soup, some dreams, and the chamber pot. Myron watching his surgery slave bathe me with warm wet cloths. Durans muttering to Myron, 'He would even destroy the Castra to save her . . .'

And wine again, soup, some flat bread, more dreams. Myron stood near my bed . . . 'Men break over less . . .'

I sipped more soup and was held over the chamber pot once more, then felt the warm wet cloths of Myron's slave wash my limbs. I slept and dreamed. When I heard Myron's voice, I answered him, but could not move my lips . . .

'*Magister?*'

'Who's that?' I struggled to open my eyes. I wanted to get up.

Durans restrained me. The wrestling teacher, an impassable barrier, sat watch over my bed.

I was too groggy to rise. It took many long minutes for my head to clear enough to learn than Myron had drugged me for nine days.

'How dare you!'

'You were planning something fatally foolish, to show yourself to your enemies, to commit a crime, to blunder into the biggest mistake the Castra could suffer.'

'You have no such authority!'

Apparently, I'd made so many feverish announcements that I was going to stage a raid on Apollonia's jailors that I'd more than justified their decision to keep me sedated on Saturnus' instinctive suggestion before departure.

'Eat your lentils,' Myron ordered.

'I must know she's safe!'

'Your men know she's safe, *Magister*. Amosis parades in front of the house like an Egyptian tomcat, his tail in the air, playing decoy. Figulus and Culeo stay vigilant, always listening and corroborating. So far, *Notarius* Leo and his louts are busy with more important victims.'

'How dare you keep me from her!'

'As long as Prefect Maximinus thinks you might still be in Treverorum, advising the Emperor, or still on the road escorting the powerful Praetextatus home, he stays his hand. He is unsure. Reveal yourself here, alone and desperate, and you trigger his sadism.'

'What do you know, Myron? You're only the *medicus*!'

'Forgive me, *Magister*, but you should think more like a Greek. Now drink this pomegranate juice. Here are your clothes, nice and fresh. Rubellius is waiting in your office. Durans, warn Cyrillus the *Magister* is coming to work after his shave.'

Indignant, but at least rested, I felt the spring breeze on my raw cheeks as I crossed the courtyard and climbed to my office, two wobbly steps at a time. Rubellius had raced back to Roma with a coded message from Saturnus in Sardinia. Two of our riders had reached the end of Maximinus' trail in the northwest port, Turris Libysonis—but too late. They'd found the necromancer Zalmoxis—in his grave.

Saturnus' team weren't returning to Olbia alone. They were escorting in utmost secrecy two companions who could only travel at civilian pace. They'd reach the Sardinian coast by tonight and board a waiting boat back to Ostia.

'Don't lose hope, *Magister*,' Durans said.

CHAPTER 20, A WIDOW'S
ACCUSATION

—THE CASTRA PEREGRINA—

Saturnus must have already guessed that the necromancer's death dealt a bitter blow to my hopes for stopping Maximinus. Was he wasting my time on some futile sop or gesture?

I could only guess by the delay that his team's unnamed companions were not professional riders and that their identities were too complicated or sensitive for explanation in brief code. To speed their trip back to the Castra, I dispatched a four-horse covered *raeda* down the Via Ostiensis to the coast. I was tempted to plant myself at the city gates, if only to reduce the suspense I endured.

In the end, I heeded the warnings of my Castra subordinates. My maddened anguish had brought out the mettle of good men. The sound judgment for which I'd recruited them had carried the day. They had joined the *agentes in rebus* swearing to serve the Empire, not to slavishly obey any emperor—or *magister* taking leave of his senses. They'd restrained me for the good of the Castra. Their innate authority was rooted in solid training and common sense, and it outweighed any hierarchy that placed me at the helm. I was left shaken but at the same time, proud of their courage.

I'd now been in Roma just short of two weeks. Apollonia's trial was fast approaching. I must not precipitate anything premature or prejudice the procedure. Better to hide behind the Castra walls. Better to let Maximinus and his men assume I was still delayed with noble Praetextatus and the two senators Venustus and Minervius on the road back from Treverorum. We must use any advantage we had—no matter how slim.

It was Praetextatus only who could deliver the Emperor's written edict against torture, but where was he? What delayed his return? Had he fallen ill on the journey? Was he visiting noble colleagues again—when every minute counted?

Meanwhile, Clemens told Apollonia daily that the Castra had not abandoned her defense and we were watching over her. I was not abandoning her to our feeble courts and the vestiges of Roman Law that cowered in the face of the Pannonian regime.

If we were indeed fighting a serpent like Maximinus, we must tip over the boulder that sheltered him. I'd convinced myself that the necromancer was the lever. Was I wrong?

Clemens and Ressatus burst into my office.

'Your wife's been transferred.'

I shot to my feet. 'Have they moved up her trial?'

'No, *Magister*. But her detention attracted too much attention in that quarter. Your slave has done his job for days on end now, weeping, pacing, even sleeping in the awning over the wine shop facing the *insula* where she's bolted up, cursing her jailor for holding an innocent noblewoman of the city under trumped-up charges.'

Good Amosis was as annoying as a tomcat wailing through a sleepless night.

'This means they'll hurt her—'

Ressatus barred me halfway around my desk. 'Not so fast, *Magister*. She left the house in her own clothes. Her face and arms were unmarked. Her gait was normal.'

Clemens said, 'The trial date hasn't changed but *Magister* Numidianus is right. She's moving closer to danger.'

'Perhaps she turned witness for the state?' Ressatus asked.

I shook my head. 'Never. She won't lie for them. She knew nothing about Anepsia hiding Abienus. But it's not her turn yet. Why is the sand running down so fast?'

'She still has a right to my counsel in court. I'll defend her innocence to the last,' said Clemens. He avoided my eyes.

'It's not going to get to "the last", Clemens. Who followed her? Amosis?'

'Amosis was too busy with his one-man show. He's the talk of the neighborhood. Her custodian tried to remove Amosis from his public vigil but failed. He kept coming back and even Maximinus' thugs have no authority to clear a public street. Pretty soon the whole quarter was talking about the "loyal slave and his mistress".'

'Public mood runs against her? Or for her?'

'For her, thanks to Amosis,' Ressatus said. 'These are humble people in that quarter—*amphorae* wholesalers, rug traders, water clock and balance makers—a noisy neighborhood of small workshops. At first the locals assumed she was just another society whore who deserved every humiliation she got, but her reputation as an honest, modest *matrona* spread up and down the street—thanks to your Egyptian. That's why they removed her under cover of night.'

'Where is she now?'

'Luckily, Figulus was awake—indigestion from bad fish. He woke up Culeo and they followed her to the very northeast corner of Regio VII beyond the Mons Pincius.'

'This is outrageous. As her lawyer, Clemens, you had a right to notification, a right to accompany her. You must know where she's been taken—'

'Well, we know already, *Magister*, but I can't go to her until I get official notice. Otherwise Maximinus will realize Amosis isn't her only watchdog.'

'The boys are watching from a nearby *caupona* in case *Notarius* Leo shows up,' Ressatus said.

'Leo's the interrogator, but he's not the torturer. Tell your guards to watch out for the man with a club foot and his friend with the cleft head. Those two are animals with no mercy. They must not touch her!'

Clemens frowned. Ressatus looked hard at me. 'You're ordering us to pull her out by force, *Magister*?'

I hesitated. They saw the danger I was courting on behalf of my spouse. To order the Castra's *agentes* to forcibly remove a Roman lawfully detained for trial would be tantamount to exposing all of us—my wife, myself, even the *agentes*—to charges of treason. It was a Rubicon for us all.

I took a deep breath. I could not sacrifice all of them. The Castra had too many enemies—in Treverorum in particular. I fought to control my anger.

'All right, Clemens, when do you expect the new address?'

'They must forward it to me today.'

'Good. When you visit her, say this from me. She must tell Maximinus or Leo that she had a vivid dream.'

'A dream?'

'Yes, she dreamt of a dead augur bringing a message for Maximinus—from Sardinia.'

Their faces filled with doubt.

'And what's the message, *Magister*?'

'Just that. The message sounded important, possibly great tidings for his career, but Maximinus must wait until the augur returns to her in untroubled sleep for further news on his behalf. That last bit is most important. He must leave her in peace.'

'You think a dream will keep her safe, *Magister*?'

'It buys us time to think of something better.'

'Or gets her killed,' muttered Clemens as they left my office.

⚼⚼⚼

Through my windows overlooking the courtyard, I heard Saturnus and his team on horseback leading the clumsy rented coach to the gate. It was evening, when the city's curfew on heavy vehicles lifts to allow deliveries for the morning's fresh markets. Two strangers alighted down the wooden steps—a cloaked woman and a boy of about ten or twelve.

Saturnus and his riders ushered them up to my office. Cyrillus ordered food and drink and two beds readied in the barrack.

The two visitors gave me a sense of foreboding. I'd aimed to corner a necromancer in league with Prefect Maximinus. Instead a sallow-faced woman well over thirty scowled at me from under low, thick eyebrows. Her face was livid with Egyptian eye-color and cheek rouge. Her jewelry—that item that identifies the class, age, taste, and origin of any woman in the Empire—was crude and gaudy, just glass stones in tin settings.

'What's your name?'

She stared at me.

'What's her name, Saturnus?'

'This is the necromancer's widow Zia and her son Dotos.'

Her boy wore the cheapest pair of new sandals possible— bought in haste for this journey. Only the gods know what he wore, if anything, underneath his shabby hemp tunic and threadbare wool shawl. He had small green eyes and hair turned rusty and brittle from a miserable diet.

'Give Dotos a blanket, Cyrillus. He's shivering. Take him outside to the bench for his meal.'

'Now, *Domina* Zia—that's the name of a legendary Dacian princess, I believe? I'm sorry your husband is dead—sorrier than you know.'

She sniffed. I took no offense. She was well within her rights to disdain the empty condolences of a strange Roman official.

'Do you know who we are, Zia?'

'Your men said they're officers of the courts.'

'In a way. We distribute imperial messages, collect and audit provincial records, manage the Empire's roads and *mansiones* and *mutationes*—that kind of thing.'

'I've got nothing to do with—'

'You're in the Castra Peregrina, our ancient headquarters. Sometimes the Castra's responsibilities require that we probe deeper into private affairs. That's why you've come to Roma.'

Draining white, she whispered, 'The Castra? You're *curiosi*? You can't arrest me! I'm innocent!'

She started to rise off the stool, but Saturnus gently pushed her back down.

'If you prefer *curiosi*, yes, *Domina* Zia. We make arrests on state charges. But in your case, there's no crime, no charge, and no arrest. You are the guest of the *agentes in rebus*.'

Her noisy bracelets coursed down a forearm as she relaxed a jot. The tray arrived with bowls of tired-looking snacks and tepid lentils left over from the midday meal. Saturnus poured the mother a large glass of undiluted wine. Her hands shook as she guzzled it down too fast.

Saturnus removed his short *sagum*, rain-lashed and mud-crusted from his ride. He took his favorite chair in the corner, settling in shadows cast by freshly-filled lamps.

'Please tell us about yourself, Zia.'

'I am the wife of the dead Zalmoxis. I loved him. I am innocent.'

'Of course you are. How long have you lived in Sardinia?'

'Long enough to hate it. It is more backward than our native home, if that is to be believed. No man honest. No woman decent.'

I smiled. 'Have you ever been to Roma before?'

She glanced down, ashamed to admit how provincial she was.

'You're not our prisoner, *Domina*. After we've talked with you like this, citizen to citizen, you're free to stay a while in Roma, show your boy the sights, and then return home at our expense. Home to Sardinia or home to Pannonia—it's your choice.'

Her face fell. 'Talk? Nothing else?'

'No, *Domina*, we ask only that you tell us what you know of Prefect Flavius Maximinus and his dealings with your husband in the art of divining.'

'Divining?'

She was thinking the Castra didn't know of Zalmoxis' forbidden dealings with corpses. Her other arm released a second rattle of bangles.

'You protested your innocence. Why should we accuse you? We ask about your husband.'

'I thought . . . perhaps . . .'

'We're not prosecutors. We're only curious, right?'

She looked disappointed. 'I had nothing to do with his work.'

'Weren't you married for many years, long enough to raise that handsome boy? Surely you were a great support to Zalmoxis. A quick woman like you would be helpful. How did he make money? Afford such nice trinkets?'

She fingered one of her outsized glass rings. 'He was a . . . middleman.'

Saturnus murmured, 'Well, in a way, he was.'

My premonition of veering off-course was back. I felt like a chariot bumping against the racetrack rails.

'*Domina* Zia, why did you agreed to come here with my men? You weren't coerced, were you?'

'No.' She turned angry. 'Because I thought you would prosecute! That I would be your witness in court!'

Saturnus looked as startled as I was.

'You want to testify as witness for the state against your own dead spouse?'

'No,' she spat out, 'to prosecute that bastard prefect!'

'For coercing Zalmoxis to summon daemons against the laws of decent religion?'

She spat in disgust. 'You fools! For murdering my husband!'

※ ※ ※

280

The Widow Zia said that if the Castra didn't charge Prefect Maximinus of his heinous crime, we were useless, boorish officials of which she'd heard Roma harbored far too many. We were of no use to her. Her journey was in vain. She had no more to say. She gobbled down her meal while we watched, helpless to drag more out of her.

She was very hungry. Two bowls of lentils left her very thirsty. With a kindly smile, Saturnus kept refilling her glass. The boy was asleep, his skeletal form fitting the sink in the downy cushions where Amosis usually napped.

Finally, she wiped her lips clean with the edge of her coarsely woven *palla*. She was a drunk now. How stupid we *agentes* were, for all our bags bulging with important mail!

'Tell us more, please,' Saturnus coaxed.

Zalmoxis, Zia, and Dotos had moved from Pannonia to Sardinia on Maximinus' invitation—no, his insistence. The prefect gave them little payouts, but contrary to his promise that Zalmoxis could establish himself at the rear of Olbia's main temple, Maximinus settled them in the coastal way-station of Portus Tibulae, to protect the new governor's 'Christian reputation', she sneered.

'Zalmoxis was furious. He picked up day work at the public baths down the coast. But he'd been cheated. He'd expected to be Maximinus' official religious adviser. But Maximinus was ashamed of us and terrified his people would realize his Christianity is no thicker than my fingernail.'

'Then why drag your family to Sardinia at all, *Domina*?' You would hardly know Saturnus was interrogating her, his tone was so gentle.

'Because that bastard needed my husband! He believes in the true gods. Oh, yes. He believes real hard, that one. He craves the power of the most secret rituals. He couldn't give them up! He was like a man who sips a wine that gives him true visions. He comes back again and again for more. All his success depended on my husband's counsel from the daemons.'

'Your husband must have been very gifted by the gods, indeed,' I said.

She smirked but said nothing, unable to admit Zalmoxis' fraudulent tricks. And perhaps Zalmoxis didn't even confide his sleight-of-hand to her. He satisfied her simple mind with market stall baubles. If anybody believed hard, perhaps it was Zia herself.

Last December, Maximinus had come to Sardinia and sent for Zalmoxis by word, not risking a written note. Zalmoxis left their tiny home at midnight. He never returned. The next morning, his body was found under a bush, knifed through the heart.

Zia found no weapon. She had no summons in Maximinus' handwriting. The messenger had vanished. She couldn't prove Governor Maximinus—or anyone else—had met her husband that night.

After the woman and child had left for the barrack, Saturnus rose from his corner chair and faced me down over my desk. The desk lamp caught his stern expression.

'Be very careful. Don't believe her too easily. Maximinus' star is rising at court. Why would he take such criminal risks?'

'She believes it.'

'It's what she needs to believe, *Magister*. Bereft of support, far from her Pannonian family, that hag faces a pitiful future. So what does she do? She accuses the richest man she can link to her loss in a vain hope of redress. She wants hush money—that's all. She doesn't even need a conviction to restore her living.'

'But it might be true, Saturnus.'

'You want it to be true, *Magister*.'

'Maximinus traveled to Sardinia in December. Are you saying Zalmoxis' death was a coincidence?'

'Why kill off the oracle that fueled his success?'

'Zia said Zalmoxis was bitter. Suppose—?'

'Focus on what's under our noses. Praetextatus arrives soon, perhaps tomorrow, to rescind the torture. That will pull Leo's claws away from your wife.'

'I wish I could raise the dead myself to bear witness to that murder.'

'Stop. You know only that Zalmoxis is dead. You can't be sure he was murdered. That's just her story.'

'If Maximinus would confess before witnesses . . .'

We'd lost half the night. Spring was coming and the evenings were shrinking as the hours lengthened. Saturnus went off to join his team for a much-deserved rest. I should go home too, but home was an echoing, haunting shell. I stretched my lanky frame out on the much-used cushions of Amosis' bench, my feet hanging over the end, my nostrils filling with the mixed scents of an Egyptian's bath oil and a Pannonian child's dribble.

This was as much my home as any, as long as my true home was wherever Apollonia slept tonight. I prayed that my trick would work; she would escape the tortures of the *eculeus* and iron hooks as long as Maximinus believed her dreams promised secrets for his continued success.

But a fresh fear arose as I dropped off; Maximinus would be keen to hear Apollonia's next dream and the next and the next. I'd sent her no clue as to how to prolong this ruse. And without anything for her to relate, my trick would become a deadly trap.

I gave myself one more day—only one more day—to come up with something better. Apollonia wasn't the only one who needed answers from her dreams. I prayed right there, on Amosis' bench as I fell asleep. And just before dawn, I was visited by the Goddess Fraus, that deity of treachery and fraud who has a woman's face, the body of a snake, and the stinging tail of a scorpion. And this horrible apparition woke me up with a start—and the germ of a crazy plan.

⚐⚐⚐

The next day, Saturnus delivered the actor Roscius to the Castra as soon as dusk fell over his audience filing out of the theater. I heard the two men mounting the steps to the office and ordered Cyrillus to make himself scarce. Roscius might not want too many witnesses.

The thespian wore a fine wool tunic under an embroidered yellow wool cloak heralding spring cheer. The actor's depilated forearms were oiled with thick perfume that mingled with rings of stage sweat.

'Welcome, Roscius. Please take a seat.'

Roscius handed Saturnus his cloak without a nod of thanks, playing a wealthy man greeted by a *dispensator's* slave.

'Do you know who I am, Roscius?'

'Sure. I've seen you around. Everyone in Roma recognizes *Magister Agentium in Rebus* Marcus Gregorianus Numidianus in the street. You're the Boss of the *Curiosi* and this room proves it.'

283

He noticed the wall map, the strongbox for sensitive files, and the wine set. 'Nice. You can see the whole world on that wall. I'm curious myself. Is that my file opened there?'

'Yes. It contains your mother's "profession", your father's gambling debts, and your real name.'

'Names, hah! They call you the "Numidian Hound", know that?'

'If I didn't, I wouldn't be much of a Castra boss.'

'Is my file really that thin? How insulting. I try so very hard.'

'You do know a lot of people above your station, Roscius.'

He sniffed. 'That's hardly difficult. Every citizen worth knowing in this city is above my station.'

'This file says a little more, suggesting I can trust you. Many decent people do—if rumors are reliable.'

'The Castra wishes to recruit me?'

'For one night only. We'll pay you well.'

He gave me a repellent smile. 'Ah, yes, for one night only. A private performance, such as I give in the finest dining rooms of our very best families who like the risqué? That's expensive.'

'I require the performance of your life, more sinister than salacious. You'll play a dead man, returning to predict the future.'

'Oh.' The actor shrugged. He checked the lay of his forehead curls with two fingers. 'That old chestnut. Played it lots.'

'What do you mean?'

'Lucan's *Pharsalia*. Oh, you must have seen it. The one where the witch Erictho summons a dead soldier from Hades to tell Sextus Pompey how the civil war turns out? That's the piece you're thinking of, I'm sure. But please, please don't try it. The trap door to Hades never, never opens on cue.' He rolled his eyes.

Roscius irritated me, but at least he wasn't stupid. In fact, he might be too quick and self-assured for my plan.

'No, Roscius, we'll devise the scenario ourselves.'

'Oh, dear. Amateur sketches always fall flat. Well, what's your plot?'

'The spirit of a murdered *haruspex* returns from the dead to finger his murderer.'

His indulgent smile faded. I wasn't joking. 'Take that show to the courts. Let our glorious Roman Law haggle it out before a real-life magistrate.'

'Glorious Roman Law is letting this city down. Our judges are cowards and toadies. Your performance must be more convincing than any feeble courtroom drama. You must terrify a villain into abandoning his torture of Romans.'

Roscius had been examining his manicure. His head jerked up at my allusion to Maximinus. He lifted his naked arm and swung it slowly in the direction of the Palatine Hill. It was a studied gesture meant to be read fifteen rows above the proscenium but all complaisance had vanished. He looked nervous. He was employing a theatrical pause while he considered his next line which he delivered in a genuine whisper.

'You refer to the Pannonian Acting Urban Prefect? The man arresting the well-born in their fancy townhouses on the slopes around us?'

'Yes, Roscius. Houses that Maximinus confiscates for his moneybox while your admiring patrons and fans, stretched out naked on the *eculeus*, scream in agony.'

'Decent citizens and their wives, I hear.'

'I never said they were decent. But they're *honestiores* and the only audience your theater has left. Without them, your matinees shift from Pompey's elegant stage down to the Circus sand.'

He ran a finger along his eyebrow and checked it for leftover stage makeup.

'And why would I do this?'

'To serve the Empire.'

He suppressed a sour smile.

'So what's your price, Roscius?'

'You both think I'm vicious, don't you?'

'I'm not interested in your morals. I'm interested in your acting skills.'

Saturnus growled. 'You heard the *Magister*. Name your price.'

'You should understand me better, Numidianus. I'm condemned to a life of vice and then despised for being vicious. But it's society that's vicious. I'm bound to this wretched life on stage by law. It was my father's trade—you've already guessed my mother's—and my grandfather's trade and so on. For time immemorial, our fate has been to occupy the lowest rung of free society.'

'I think I understand you. So, do you want the job?'

'Sure, I want the job. I want a job. I want a new life. A new name. A new home, away from this rotting city.'

'Get out of here,' Saturnus said.

'Wait. A job to do what, Roscius?'

'Well, teaching manners so your riders don't climb the social ladder acting like uncouth postmen.'

'Hardly a full-time job.' Saturnus made no effort to hide his disdain.

'That would be only my official job. But I could teach far more useful skills for spies.'

'Such as?'

'Disguise and dissembling. It takes more than Egyptian eye kohl or a false Frankish moustache to keep your man safe from his enemy. I'm sure you teach each boy dialects and accents and road shortcuts and secret codes and all that. But he'll be spotted as a fraud unless—no—watch me.'

Roscius began to walk around my office. He changed his gait half a dozen times. One minute he was an arrogant official, the next a persistent beggar, then a fetching young girl tugging at the long hem of a hand-me-down tunic, then a haggish crone. He stumbled on one leg like a war amputee, then danced on the balls of his feet like one of those holy men east of the Indus.

And he became all these obvious characters without uttering a syllable. To top it off, he straightened up to his fullest height and assuming a wary expression out the side of his eyes, he added a slight limp to his left leg.

In short, Roscius became me, the Numidian Hound, identifiable from fifty feet away.

'It's uncanny,' Saturnus muttered.

'It's all in the mind.' And Roscius began to walk in a weird, rigid manner, like a ghost who has lost the use of his limbs and sight and is propelling himself only by half-remembered gestures and outstretched hands.

'You're hired—for one night,' I told him.

'I'll consider it the inconvenience of an audition,' he said. He knew the Castra had just cast him for bigger parts, but Saturnus was loath to admit him so easily.

'You'll interview the widow of the murdered man today and draft your speech. What else do you need?'

The actor sat back down on the stool and stretched like a cat. 'Oh, the usual—a dirty shroud or wrapping. I'll provide my own chalk for whiting my face. As for setting,' he inhaled, closed his eyes, staging the scene:

'I'll need some kind of Mouth to Hell . . . low lighting, echoing walls, that kind of thing. A cave near a birdless lake would be ideal . . . sulfurous springs rising from the underground—?'

Saturnus exploded. 'Why not hire Pompey's Theater for the night and cast a hundred wood nymphs? The Cloaca Maxima will have to do for you, Roscius. What better place for foul spirits than the biggest sewer in the world, eh, Numidianus?'

'But you'll need lines. Something that puts him at our mercy. We want him frightened out of Roma for good.'

We descended to the barrack where the widow and her boy were resting. She'd slept well and bathed, but was still truculent and confused.

'Describe your husband, *Domina*,' I said.

Zia hardly understood why we interrogated her so closely. Why not drag Maximinus now to court to be tried and beheaded? Roscius took notes and planned his impersonation. But she could not produce more than rudimentary details. Her husband had left the house, saying he had to meet Prefect Maximinus. He often worked at night like that 'when the daemons wandered.' She'd gone to sleep.

In the morning, when Zalmoxis hadn't returned, she alerted her neighbors. Later that morning, dogs found his body lying dead from a single stab wound. A trail of blood suggested he'd been dragged from the porch of the local temple to the thick bush.

'All right, Roscius? It's not much to go on but you must stick to that account. Don't elaborate. Maximinus is bound to spot any detail in the story that contradicts the truth.'

'Especially if he's innocent,' Saturnus warned. 'Making false accusations lands the accuser in court facing the same punishment.'

Roscius looked worried. 'Are you are asking me to play a dead man to someone who knew him very well?'

'That's right.'

He shook his head. 'You have much to learn about the theater, *Magister* Numidianus. I can look like anyone you like, short of a dwarf, so to speak, but how am I to mimic the speech of a man I never met to one who knew him for years?'

We sat in the barrack in silence. The high window sent a streak of sunshine onto a bright square on the flagstone floor. The rude graffiti and erotic cartoons that a dozen *agentes* had scratched into the wall plaster looked cruder than usual in the harsh sunlight.

'You need a medium,' Dotos piped up. 'I've done it before. The daemons always come when I summon them. I know what they want me to say.'

Saturnus shrugged. 'Well, a medium solves the voice problem.'

I took Dotos by the shoulders. 'Can you recite your mother's story? That you both went to bed and your father never returned from his meeting with Prefect Maximinus?'

'I can, if that's what you want.'

'You'll remind Prefect Maximinus that he often consulted your father for the daemons' help from Hades?'

He nodded.

I laid a comforting hand on the child's bony shoulder.

'You're not afraid, Dotos? You must prompt Maximinus until he admits summoning up dead souls. That's enough. We know that much is true. Witnesses must hear him confirm it out loud.'

Saturnus interrupted our conference. 'It'll be impossible to carry off your scheme in the Cloaca Maxima, *Magister*. I've checked. They're doing repairs night and day to finish before the summer *miasma*. It's full of maintenance slaves and drainage engineers. We'll draw attention.'

'That's all right, Saturnus. I've reflected overnight. It's better to draw Maximinus away from anything too familiar, away from Roma altogether. Men believe doubtful things more readily if they've invested energy and time in their own deception.'

'The *Magister*'s right. My biggest applause always comes from the overpriced seats,' Roscius told Saturnus.

And at last, the gods stayed on my side and sent me a better alternative. I spent more than an hour alone in my office drafting my summons from Hades. I chose the oldest vellum in Cyrillus' stock, many times erased and reused, conjuring up the spirit of tired leather and dead men. I hoped the sheer impossibility of the invitation would overwhelm the Pannonia's self-assurance. The widow had said, 'He believes *hard*. He craves the power of the most secret rituals.' If she was wrong about Maximinus' addiction to dark and forbidden ceremonies, we were all dead men.

I wrote, *Prefect Flavius Maximinus, greetings. Do not question how I find you. Such are the powers of the dead. How much better if you'd kept me close, taken me with you to Roma to protect you from your enemies. But I hear the daemons more clearly than ever. Even the Christians know daemons are spirits banished from heaven for unpardonable sins. The daemons are irritated by neglect but can be propitiated by offerings and prayers. So sacrifice with me as before. The grateful daemons will share their visions of your glorious future. Meet me at dusk the day after tomorrow inside the Grotto of the Cimmerian Sibyl at Lake Avernus, the Mouth of Hades itself.*

I ordered Atolitus to drop the sealed letter at Maximinus' office door. 'Wear an unmarked, hooded cloak. Let no one see you.'

Two hours later Rubellius returned from a drinking bout with Maximinus' *protectores*.

'He's cancelled tomorrow's afternoon appointments. He's leaving *Notarius* Leo in charge He won't say where he's going or when he's back. He's taken the bait.'

I tried not to let my voice shake as I shouted, 'We leave before dawn. Warn the men, the child, and Roscius! Round up witnesses, horses, weapons! Saturnus—you'll carry the boy on horseback. No, leave the woman here! Lake Avernus by nightfall tomorrow! He'll be only half a day behind us. Come on! Get ready!'

CHAPTER 21, RAISING THE DEAD

—TO THE GROTTO OF THE SIBYL—

The pre-dawn sky promised clear weather and the Via Appia leading out the Aurelian Walls toward Capua beckoned. The rhythm of a good horse underneath my churning belly soothed my churning stomach. I wasn't riding with the free spirit of my early days as a bachelor *eques* today. For the second time in a month, I was riding out of Roma and away from Apollonia—to save her. And this time, the outcome posed a far bigger gamble.

My breast pounded with that fear mixed with exhilaration when the *cornicen* rises before dawn and trumpets the start of battle. As a slave 'volunteer' on many a battlefront, I'd known what warfare was. Unlike many a slave, I'd survived, again and again.

I'd weathered yet more battles as an *agens*. I'd known the clash of arms, the screams of the fallen, the warm blood foaming into black pools in the cold night. I'd wielded a *spatha* myself and seen the sudden gash, the shock in my victim's staring eyes and the awful mouth forcing out a futile scream.

And each time, I'd beaten down fear. A younger man always does. He whispers under his quickening breath, 'Today I fight with honor. The gods will spare me.'

We older men know the truth, though we don't let our juniors see it. You can bellow from behind your shield in a rising *barritus* and clatter your arms under a snapping pennant, but nothing charms away a middle-aged man's apprehension. We've seen the fickle gods turn their backs on too many noble Romans to believe we're immune. Virtue and bravery count for nothing. The gods do with you what they want.

I needed divine aid more than ever, for I was attacking Maximinus on the gods' own battlefield—the *realm of man's conscience*. Would the gods come to my aid? Or was I the Fates' fool?

Was I even properly armed? My first priority was the terrain. True Romans—even those raised as slaves—enjoy certain advantages over provincial interlopers like Maximinus, no matter how powerful, cruel, or determined. For one thing, we know our own neighborhood through and through.

If Maximinus was addicted to the powers of our ancient religion, if he indeed believed *hard*, then he might have heard of the sacred places where dead spirits ascend to communicate with the living. The ancient Greeks, being Greeks, once held a monopoly on oracles of the underworld, from their homeland to Magna Graecia on our own peninsula: Taenaron, Argolis, Cumae, Herakleia and most important, the *Necromanteion* of Ephyra.

I could be sure that the son of a Pannonian *haruspex* had heard of those illustrious sites. Despite the surge of Christianity across the Empire, many men spoke of them, even if only out of idle curiosity. The temples that housed these morbid openings in the earth were still marked on the Castra's road guides to forewarn our *agentes* to avoid clutches of ghoulish pilgrims or diehard *cultores deorum* clogging the roads passing these dilapidated and spooky tourist traps.

But I was sure Prefect Maximinus hadn't heard of Italia's home-grown and forgotten access to Hades. This was an old grotto at the heart of a circuit of volcanic passages where our city's founder, the hero Aeneas, had followed the Sibyl on his journey to the underworld to seek out his dead father.

Or so they say.

I was staking my life, Apollonia's life, and the future of the Castra on this assumption. For I'd summoned Maximinus to this obscure place of ancient terror, a Mouth to Hades within a day's long ride of the Eternal City. Few pilgrims, pagans, or modern Romans of any kind still visited this deserted place.

I'd only been there once before, almost forty years ago. I was brought along as a reward—or was it a teasing prank?—by the gray-headed *culmen* of the Manlius clan on a social excursion. In those days, the Senator's weakening eyes could still make out more than light and shadow. He'd taken me, with a party of friends, on a day trip from the family's resort property in the Bay of Baiae after an inspection of the estate's oyster beds.

Perhaps it had amused the old man to scare the wits out of his gullible, tousle-headed 'favorite'. Warned where we were going that day, I struggled to hide my panic. I knew what the Sybil of the Grotto was. Hadn't I recited Vergilius out loud, day after day, to the Senator Manlius back in Roma?

No matter that the old man's lips muttered along with my stuttering rendition, no matter than the dust motes of a stifling hot Roman afternoon danced in the study's musty sunshine above my head. Whenever we reached Book VI, the child Numidianus had felt the frozen hand of the Sybil falling on his own skinny shoulder, leading the hero Aeneas down, down, down into the tunnels beneath the deadly Lake Avernus wreathed in sulfurous fumes no passing bird survived.

> '. . . *Spelunca alta fuit vastoque immanis hiatu,*
> *scrupea, tuta lacu nigro nemorumque tenebris . . .*
> Deep was the cave and, downward as it went
> From the wide mouth, a rocky rough descent;
> And here the access a gloomy grove defends,
> And there the unnavigable lake extends,
> Over whose unhappy waters, void of light,
> No bird presumes to steer his airy flight;
> Such deadly . . . such deadly . . .'

'Go on, boy, stop stammering!'

> 'Such deadly stenches from the depths arise,
> And steaming sulfur that infects the skies,
> From hence the Grecian bards their legends make,
> And give the name Avernus to the lake.'

The Senator's pleasure party had reached that very lake and trod up a curving dirt path overarched with trees. It was a very hot day and my new sandals rubbed a watery blister as big as a chickpea into my heel. We were greeted by a priest with a pate shaven to a perspiring gleam. He wore a spotless linen robe and a grim expression.

The Senator's guests and attendants then descended into a long tunnel carved into a cliff. Ahead of us the priest wafted an incense burner to cleanse the stifling air. On a normal morning back in Roma, it would be I who led the fierce-faced Senator Manlius through the crowded *fora*, his bony hand resting on my shoulder, the other gripping a sturdy walking stick.

But on this day, I'd been charged with leading the sacrificial kid goat. The nervous animal bucked too hard for my shaking hands. I was relieved of his lead by an older slave. The shame of that little failure was only the start of my day.

From then on, I crept behind the Senator, my soul trembling at the priest's incantations, my throat gagging on the stink of sulphurous fumes. The corridor narrowed as it wound between dark alcoves and radiating tunnels echoing strange shufflings and rustlings. As we passed one junction, I started at the sudden darting of ghostly silhouettes of daemons and dead men dancing in shadows above our heads.

Another corridor, more rustic concrete than the earlier stone block passages, led us down to third. And yet another descended to a warren of more turnings and forks. The stench of old sacrifice and toxic fumes dizzied me. I clung tighter to the Senator's cloak.

We came to a set of very steep stairs, then a low tunnel, then wooden steps and again a sharp-angled corridor. The glow of oil lamps hung in niches carved into the walls drew us ever forward. The ladies in our group stopped giggling.

We arrived at an abrupt halt, stumbling over each other. One by one, we climbed down a twisting, irregular stairwell into a long and echoing granite lair designated for ritual blood sacrifice. A hole ringed with marble stones in the center of the stone floor gaped open. Below this lowest level, a turbulent spring of black water circled and churned—the River Styx itself.

I cowered behind the adults but could not rip my horror-struck eyes off that hole. At any minute the leering boatman Charon might heave up in the current below, steady his boat with a claw-like hook slung around the marble rim, and claim one of us for permanent oblivion.

So we appeased the great gods. I could not bear to watch, but I heard the ear-splitting braying of our baby goat, the eruption of hot blood, a gush and spill of wet guts into the basin, and then the priests' incantation leading our prayers—for such used to be the way of noble Romans before the Christians forbade it.

I remember little else. I fainted away just after the priest summoned up the dead ghost of a long-lost Manlius ancestor who proclaimed an oracle; our great household would one day betray the living emperor and fall into disgrace, only to achieve slow rebirth through the labors of a faithful bastard slave.

The oracle meant nothing to me that day. It would be another decade before I discovered that I myself was not only a slave, but the Senator's bastard grandson. The old man's day trip had started off as an amusing entertainment undertaken in a spirit of playful homage to lost superstitions. I suspect it ended by shaking the more knowing members of the Manlius household to their very souls.

I do recall that I was excused that night from my duties of pouring wine and passing trays for the guests in the Baiae *triclinium*. And my grandfather and his son, Commander Atticus Manlius Gregorius, soon announced a new plan for little Marcus— I'd start traveling with the Commander's army in the field as soon as I'd dedicated my first downy beard to the gods.

Yes, the oracle of Lake Avernus had changed my life once. Could the spirits save me again?

♔♔♔

'The milestone for Tarracina!'

We were already halfway, at the junction where the *Cursus* met the ancient coastal town. Without the weight of heavy mail sacks, team after team of grateful postal horses had made exceptional time. We soon reached the *mansio* on the southward road to Fundi. There was time for a short meal, a brief drink, then to the *mutatio* Ad Octavium where the horses were the freshest. Then onward, inland on the *Cursus* to Capua, then taking the Via Popilia due south again to the coast, toward Neapolis and our destination, two miles and a bit west of the harbor city of Puteoli.

We'd changed horses eight times and covered one hundred and thirty-five miles in the hours of spring daylight, well within a Castra relay-rider's top target of one hundred and seventy. But this pace was demanding for all but army-trained cavalrymen and Castra veterans. Even after a lifetime of hard riding, this was my third marathon in less than a month.

I hid my exhaustion from the younger men. The widow would never have made it. And her child had fallen asleep in the saddle, cradled in the arms of one *agens*, then another, then a third, for the whole of the trip.

Our poor volunteer thespian had suffered the most. Nearly broken by the relentless pounding, Roscius half-fell, half-stumbled off his last horse. Within sight of all, he dropped his borrowed riding trousers right there on the verge of the *Cursus* and fished out some gooey theatrical concoction for rubbing on his blistered backside. We heard cries of pain no actor could feign. Only a large pitcher of wine would calm Roscius for his coming night under the stars.

We pitched a rough camp well off the road and rested. We could be sure that Maximinus had neither the stamina nor the road support to match our speed. I slept only a few hours on my cloak spread across the thick grass. It was the sleep of my youth, of my days as a slave on the front, of my years on the road as an ambitious *circitor*, determined to beat away the miles in my race to the next postal station.

'Will he believe it?' Saturnus whispered behind me, settling himself nearby.

'Everyone believes it,' I said.

'Not true Christians, *Magister*.'

'Maximinus is not a true Christian. Besides, Emperor Constantius was a true Christian and he ruled it was a capital crime to call forth the dead by magic spells. Didn't that betray a genuine Christian's fear?'

Defendens listened nearby, his expression as apprehensive of Hades' Mouth as the most ardent Republican meddling with the gods of old.

'You're a practicing Christian, Defendens. Which is it?' I asked. 'Do you believe in daemons?'

'Of course, *Magister*. Daemons are spirits banished from Heaven for sins too evil to forgive. The deceitful devils persuade ignorant men to give them honors.'

Saturnus shrugged. 'I still say if Maximinus shows up, it's only out of curiosity to see if Zalmoxis somehow survived his stabbing—not superstition.'

'Christian or pagan, Maximinus believes. He'll come out of fear, curiosity, and ambition.'

Perhaps it was only I who was trying hard to believe.

Our final preparations began at dawn. We set off to find the cliff hidden under overgrown thickets that shielded the volcanic Lake Avernus from the roadside.

By midday I was worried. It was taking far too long to locate the ancient entrance—there were too many other caves and grottoes. Had the Cave of the Sybil been blocked up by Christian busybodies? After another hour or so of frustrated searching, we were running out of time. Was Maximinus traveling with as much haste as we had? Was he coming alone or aided by guides?

Ah, there it was! Saturnus found it, marked by a forgotten path studded with weeds and barely visible behind a thick veil of wild ivy, a narrow, trapezoidal entrance cut into the volcanic cliff overlooking the water. We slashed and hacked the opening free.

Our stage beckoned. Lanterns and torches were pitched and filled to light the worshipper's path to his séance. Now to ready our cast. The final transformations into necromancer and medium took shape. Roscius wielded chalk and white lead paste to disguise Dotos into a ghostly medium.

Then he finished his own disguise. We'd been lucky that the necromancer was not unusually short or tall or deformed. Guided by the widow's description of her husband to our sketching Sabazios, Roscius carried the portrait along with the tricks of his profession in a battered leather sack. He padded himself into a heavyset man closer to forty than thirty with a higher, shaved hairline shooting up from a peak into a startling white-powdered streak. By the gleam of a handheld bronze mirror, he glued on thicker eyebrows. With greasy putty, he extended his nose and then narrowed it by painting stripes of dark theater paint down the sides. He added dark stubble to his chin.

But the dented bronze mirror wasn't his only measure. The most reliable gauge of success was Dotos' reaction. Roscius wasn't satisfied until the boy's green eyes widened with the alarm of recognition.

'Sweep all traces of our boots from the path after we go inside,' I ordered Numa.

Defendens and Numa would hide behind a long stand of thick hemlock shrubs as lookouts over the road.

I led the way into the cave and took Saturnus and Mussidius as my state witnesses. Roscius followed, leading Dotos by the hand as we plunged deeper. Avitus and Atolitus would hide at point halfway into the cave to spy on Maximinus' progress and act as backup stagehands, lighting a wall torch here and there or planting a glowing lantern in a receding alcove to cast lengthening shadows.

We felt our way forward in sober silence. Nothing must detract from the suspension of reality. Nothing must deter the spirits of the underworld from coming to my assistance.

Without a priest to guide me, I was like Aeneas without the Sybil. We wasted at least half an hour or more on wrong turnings or byways that narrowed here to a caved-in dead end or there to a dangerous fall-off over broken walkways. But I was sure that the main route to the gaping hole must have been too significant to abandon to decay.

Drawn by a sudden draft of cool air and the sound of rushing water, I hurried us forward. Maximinus might be on our heels at any moment, already searching the cliffside, noticing telltale tracks overlooked along the grassy path. We found the winding stairwell and scrambled down into the chilly rectangular room.

I left Roscius and the boy to rehearse their paces. With the help of torches, we searched for hiding places in the irregular walls. There were viewing alcoves like small balconies carved overhead and a narrow black tunnel leading on, connecting to a smaller lake nearby. At last we chose our marks and crawled into obscurity, hidden from each other in the shadows.

Suddenly I swelled with doubts. Now that I was a grown man, I found nothing frightening in this setting. Only an innocent slave boy steeped in ancient lore and rousing poetry could have fallen for it. This was ridiculous.

I was about to cancel the whole affair when a faint, but persistent bird whistle sounded from outside the tunnel entrance. And a second alert, the low 'hoo-hoo' of an owl, came from halfway down our descent, in case the whistle signal from Numa couldn't be heard at our depths. Avitus and Atiolitis must conceal themselves quickly.

Prefect Maximinus was approaching? I could hardly believe it. My doubts doubled. From where I perched many feet up the side of one wall on a recessed ledge, all I saw was the stone floor with the deadly circular drop in the center.

For many long minutes we heard only the black water rushing some twenty feet below the hole.

Was I mistaken? Had the whistle been meant for a passing horse? Was the owl merely a lonely bird getting a head start on the evening's mating?

No. Someone was descending through the cave. Was that the sound of bandy legs marching across the buckling planks that bridged one of the muddier tunnels? Not far now. Not long at all. Any minute, the Pannonian would appear underneath the torch lighting the top of the stairwell.

From my hiding place at the far end of the chamber, the prefect looked foreshortened and diminished. He hid his face nearly to the jaw under the hood of that new flame-colored *chlamys* with gold bands.

Until that second, I hadn't known how convinced I'd really been that he would come. Was it really Maximinus? Or had he sent one of his *protectores* ahead to scout out Zalmoxis' summons? The gold-embroidered *orbiculi* emblems on the tunic and the shine of the polished *calcei* in the torchlight—those could belong to any Roman official. But the buckle nestled under a reflecting crescent with the golden grapes gave him away.

The Pannonian surveyed the sacrificial chamber, his intended stopping point beyond which no flames had been laid and no scenery set. With a grunt, he swung a large hemp sack from over his shoulder onto the uneven floor. The sack's contents writhed.

'Zalmoxis!' he bellowed. The caverns and tunnels echoed his summons.

'Zalmoxis!'

He waited. We waited.

'Zalmoxis!'

Kneeling, he unknotted the sack and started back on his heels as a snarling, mangy dog struggled for escape. The prefect grabbed its rope collar just in time, yanking it back under control. He fastened a short leash to the base of the altar basin and pulled until the dog's jowl pressed flat against the stone.

'Zalmoxis! I've brought a sacrifice! A live one!'

The dog sniffed the fetid traces of ancient blood and guts and whimpered. It pointed its muzzle straight at me in the darkness. It had detected my living scent, too. It snarled.

'Zalmoxis! I've come for your counsel!'

The echoing settled down until the only sound came from the rushing 'Styx'.

'I can't wait all day! Receive my sacrifice and deliver your oracle, Zalmoxis! Then we're done with each other.'

The ringed hand that held down the animal trembled. Far across the chamber, Zalmoxis' Dotos watched in the dark for a signal from my ledge. I lifted one finger.

Dotos stepped out of the shadows. Roscius had found a stone alcove halfway down the stairwell. Maximinus must have passed Roscius and the boy hiding only a few feet away as he descended. I was relieved to see Dotos stayed safely above Maximinus' easy reach.

Maximinus peered up. 'But, but—you're not Zalmoxis.'

'No, Prefect. I am the reflection of his son.'

Roscius now stepped forward from the shadows and laid his whitened hand on the boy's head. Dotos said, 'You see? Here I am. This is Zalmoxis who addresses you through the borrowed image and voice of my fatherless son.'

It was chilling. I marveled at them both—but mostly at Dotos. The child was so professional. He didn't flinch at confronting the murderous prefect any more than the practiced actor behind him. And Roscius had nothing to do but glare into space with the dead eyes of the lifeless. Dotos carried the whole show on his thin shoulders.

'Speak for yourself, Zalmoxis!'

'No, Maximinus, I am only a shade now, too weak, too wounded to speak for myself. Hear my boy.'

The fantastic impression suddenly vanished. My stomach emptied, hollowed out by disappointment.

The images of father and son were eerie enough—as long as Maximinus kept his distance. But Dotos didn't *sound* convincing to me. He didn't bellow or thunder. His piping soprano made no impression on the rugged stone walls. He sounded like what he was, a village waif, not a medium from the ether. Even I struggled to make out his next words.

'Do you remember our last meeting, Prefect?'

'It's hardly relevant tonight. What's done is done.'

Was Maximinus playing for time? He sounded confused. He unsheathed a *pugio* to slaughter the dog and perform his sacrifice.

'Before I sacrifice, Zalmoxis, let me examine that shade of your boy. Come down here, where I can touch you.'

'No, we dare not come near, because I remember our last meeting. Don't you?'

The dog snarled again, shying away from the blade. Maximinus left the animal tied and moved a few steps closer to the apparitions.

'Why drag me here, Zalmoxis? I'm a busy man now, an important man.'

'A busy man—thanks to me, Prefect. You profited from my advice.'

The answer was brusque. 'I don't deny I valued your help before. But I was a country lawyer then, a youngster who didn't know any better. I'm told you before, Zalmoxis, I'm with the Christians now. I report to the Emperor himself. He despises traffic with dark souls. I told you that in Sardinia. *I told you, I don't need you anymore!*'

'But that last night you asked the daemons if your father's prophecy has changed. Don't you want their visions anymore?'

What was this? What did Dotos know of any prophecy? Maximinus' eyes darted at the stairwell, now blocked by the ghosts. He was anxious to leave. He retreated back to the basin and started hacking at the dog's knotted leash. Any minute now, he'd eviscerate the poor hound in the cracked basin. But he could not read entrails. I recoiled to think what else he might do to placate the dead.

Dotos' thin voice continued, 'And yet, here you come running at the promise of more predictions! You also asked me that night how long Emperor Valentinian would live.'

By the stairwell's single torch, the boy's sudden wide smile revived the sinister effect—uncanny and unnerving.

But I panicked at Dotos' words. He was veering way off script! Had he forgotten the lines Roscius pounded into his head only last night? Dotos was only supposed to get Maximinus to confirm he consulted Zalmoxis at regular intervals—admitting necromancy was crime enough. Maximinus' evasions were too vehement and confident for my taste. This wasn't working.

'You asked me, would Valentinian die soon—?'

Dotos! Dotos! Shut up about Valentinian's health!

Oh, the gods! I despaired. Dotos was just making stuff up—like all children do. Like my twins' ludicrous stories and wild fantasies—'*Pater*, today I'm a horse. *Pater*, today I can walk on the ceiling by looking down into *Mater*'s hand-mirror.' And sometimes when innocent children try to please those they love, they only make things worse. I'd been crazy to risk everything on an illiterate boy!

'You asked me, who will succeed the Emperor? Do I have a chance?'

Maximinus planted his boots wide now, facing the basin, clutching the whining dog firmly with both hands.

'Those were dangerous questions, Prefect, weren't they?'

'Shut up! I feared the premature ambitions of others—that's all. I sought insight on traitors against Valentinian at court.'

Dotos shook his head from side to side in a slow, deliberate way. If he'd forgotten Roscius' lines, at least his otherworldly poise was improving.

'Why did you ask me who would become Emperor?'

'Someone must succeed Valentinian. Who needs your dark vapors to know that all men die?'

'You don't care about other men. You asked me how high *you* would rise, Flavius Maximinus.'

Maximinus stared up at the boy. The dog sniffed. We held our breath. To his credit, the child waited too.

A worried Saturnus glanced at me from his own alcove not far away. Still standing in place, hands laid on the child in ominous supervision, the silent Roscius' expression widened. We all realized as one.

Dotos had never needed any lines from Roscius. The boy had not gone to bed that night when his mother blew out her bedside lamp. Accustomed to assisting his father's illicit rituals, the little medium had padded along behind, only to witness the murder by moonlight with his own eyes.

His mother Zia had known all along but wanted to keep her child witness safe from the ruthless prefect.

Because Dotos couldn't win. He was challenging a man with the soul of a serpent who was accustomed to waiting long hours under a rock.

Maximinus grew riled, 'Before I sacrifice, tell me the visions you promised.'

'Such dangerous questions cost traitors their heads.'

Maximinus exploded. 'What's your message, Zalmoxis? Tell me the prophecy and let me leave this place!'

The boy began a sing-song chant. He had turned truly daemonic. Was this his father's oracular style once 'the dead' had appeared? We *agentes* had lost control of everything. Evil filled the air.

Dotos' soprano pierced the stony chamber. 'I asked you to take me to Roma, full of rich pagans who need my skills. You refused. You rejected me, Maximinus. Why? I followed you to Sardinia. Why not to Roma?'

'I told you! I'm a Christian now!'

'Take me to Roma. Take me to Roma. Take me to Roma. I will tell the city's finest families how you enjoy it when I devour the flesh of dead men, when I wear their cast-off shrouds, when I lay on their graves, when I deliver their visions.'

'Take you to Roma? You're dead! You'd haunt me forever!'

'I will appear in their great temples. I'll tell them, Prefect Flavius Maximinus listens to the shade of Zalmoxis. And see how his power grows? Why did you stop me?'

'You wouldn't have helped me in Roma! You'd have milked me! Made me your slave until I died!'

'So you stabbed me on the temple porch as the Divinities watched. The gods are angry.'

'I had no choice!'

'And you dragged me to the bushes.'

'You tried to blackmail me. You deserved it!'

'And you denied me a decent burial. You left me to the wild dogs.'

'Tell me the new prophecy for this sacrifice!'

'A rabid cur? Not even a small goat? How profane.'

Dotos spat at the prefect below.

Maximinus stared at the blade in his right hand and the animal quivering underneath his left. The insulted oracle had turned against him.

There was a sudden draft down the tunnel extinguishing all but one torch. At that moment, the dog sensed his chance. He leapt off the basin and scrambled up the steep steps. Dotos blocked his escape but the dog sank his fangs into the boy's leg. Dotos screamed and fell. Roscius dropped to his knees to pull the boy free of the mongrel's jaws.

The delicate spell shattered. If Dotos could be bitten by a dog and rescued by a ghost, these were no phantom shades.

The Prefect bellowed like an angry bull bursting its ropes and escaping the bloody disemboweling of an ancient *taurobolium*.

Maximinus must finish off what he'd started in Pannonia and tried to finish in Sardinia. Kill the boy, then savage his phantom father. He unsheathed his *spatha* and now ready with blades both short and long, made for the actors. Only the maddened, twisting dog blocked his way up the steps. Maximinus grabbed the canine by his rope and flung him, whelping through the air with surprise, straight down the deadly hole. There was a moment's silence, then a splash.

The boy staggered backward, totally exposed to Maximinus' aim. Roscius yanked the child from range, but the unarmed actor was untrained for anything more than mock stage duels. He was helpless against a real attacker. Yet he dodged and braved Maximinus' flashing blades to block the prefect from Dotos.

Saturnus and Mussidius burst from their stony corners and Mussidius gave a piercing whistle. With his *spatha* challenging Maximinus' rear, the giant lured Maximinus back down the stairs, freeing Roscius and the boy to race upward for escape. With difficulty, I'd dropped to the cavern floor and lurched around the gaping well to tackle Maximinus' bulging neck. I yanked back hard but his iron grip on my strangling arm was just as strong.

The Pannonian pushed me back, step by step, toward the hole over the river. I couldn't draw my weapon with my arm locked around him. Gigantic, but clumsy, Mussidius wasn't deft enough to separate us as we thrashed this way and that.

Saturnus circled around the well with weapons drawn to block Maximinus' possible escape down the second tunnel.

A clash of weapons in the blackness above said the battle had shifted. Avitus and Atolitus must have heard the whistle as the fight broke out below, but been blocked from reaching us. Maximinus must have been warier than we assumed. He'd positioned allies along the twisting passageways, allies prepared to finish off more than a dog, if necessary.

I felt the sharp edge of the circular rim under the heel of my teetering boot as my weak leg gave way. I was falling backward. I wasn't letting go of Maximinus. I would carry him with me to our death in the waters racing below. Only my grip around the murderer's waist kept me alive and dangling over cold blackness.

The fight above had reached the top of the stairs. Saturnus and Mussidius were closing in on the well—afraid to tackle Maximinus too hard and send us both plunging to our deaths.

Defendens and Numa finally broke through, scattering the two hellhounds Mucianus and Barbarus with the help of Atolitus and Avitus. I felt a dangerous yank as Mussidius seized his chance and tackled Maximinus. Saturnus reached for my scrabbling legs at the same time, dragging me upward.

With frantic, scraping clutches at the stone floor, I hoisted myself back to safety as Mussidius dragged Maximinus away, still screaming at his minions, 'The boy! Kill the boy!'

Barbarus and Mucianus escaped back up the stairs and raced like hunters after Roscius and Dotos down the twisting dark corridors. I hurried after them with Avitus on my heels, trusting Saturnus and Mussidius to stifle any more murderous commands from the Pannonian. We pounded across the buckling bridge and turned a sharp corner just in time to see Mucianus holding Roscius at bay with his *pugio* and Barbarus swinging his sword to behead the cowering Dotos, trapped against a wall of black granite.

I went after the cripple while Avitus slammed the hilt of his sword down hard on the gladiator's head, deep into where another man's weapon had left that cleft in the skull.

My bad leg slowed me down. I limped around the wrong corner to discover Mucianus poised to run me through with his hand-me-down *spatha*. I jumped back and readied my blade.

'You arrested my wife in Ostia? I panted.

Pent-up fury steadied me—fury at his foul abuse of Roman noblewomen, not goddesses but frail human beings, whom he humiliated, tortured, and killed like animals.

'You killed her guard, Cornelius, in cold blood?'

'That drunken sot?' Mucianus grinned with broken-toothed pleasure at the memory.

A long-dormant bloodlust surged inside me at the sound of Mucianus' cackle. The cripple knew nothing of beloved Cornelius, nothing of what the great-hearted, retired veteran had been to my family or what Cornelius had been to his trusted brothers-in-arms when they overlapped their shields in a battlefield *testudo*.

But I knew. I must repay my dear friend's decades of loyalty and companionship. Give this fiend the privilege of arrest? No, the gods forgive me—but no, no, no.

I plunged my sword deep into the torturer's belly, finished with an upward thrust, and a final wrench of the blade. And then I twisted it with both hands, around and around, and listened to Mucianus groan as I recited, 'This is for Cornelius. And this. And this.'

Was this murder? Execution? Self-defense? I wasn't defending myself. I was defending something deeper and older and finer than myself.

I wrenched my *spatha* out of the bastard's guts and looked around me through the dim light. Around the corner, Avitus stood over Barbarus lying senseless on the ground. We would leave him there to live or die.

Night had fallen outside. Mussidius and Saturnus emerged from the cavern's entrance with Maximinus in tow, followed by Defendens and Numa with our ghosts. The boy's leg wound was not as dangerous as I'd feared. The arrested prefect was short of breath and heaving with exhaustion and shock. He looked up at me, his eyes white against the black Mouth of Hades.

His mind would be racing—how to save himself now, to molt this useless skin, and return in a fresh, sleek guise? How and where could he slither now?

I must think as fast as he did. He'd confessed to a murder, but one very hard to prove in court. He'd brought an illegal blood offering in order to raise a dead man, a crime of necromancy. But the dead man was played by an actor far from dead—not a crime but a farce.

But I was satisfied for one day. We'd heard enough. Whatever the sins of the senators and wives of Roma—and they were legion—Maximinus' crimes were viler still. For the moment, the Pannonian was mine. And for the moment, he surrendered his weapons.

Saturnus held the dog rope ready but the prefect smiled.

'You don't need restraints, Numidianus. 'Nothing would compel me to leave your side. And you will hardly want to leave mine.'

'Leave the ropes for now, Saturnus.'

'And let's hasten back to the city,' Maximinus said.

'You wish to hurry? We all heard you confess to murder. Praetextatus will surely lay charges.'

'Perhaps. Perhaps not, because perhaps you will not press him, Numidianus. Meanwhile, I must be back in time to confirm that *Matrona* Anepsia, Senators Aginatius and Abienus are condemned and executed. You see, I ordered *Notarius* Leo to continue trial proceedings while I was gone. Let's hope we stand this close, side by side, as your wife joins her friends.'

A reptile's blood is cold indeed.

Chapter 22, A Widow's Farewell

—THE VIA APPIA—

Dotos confirmed to Defendens that he had indeed witnessed his father's murder. He expected us to run his father's killer through on the spot. Instead, he watched us take custody of Maximinus and prepare for our ride back to Roma. Disappointed that Maximinus still lived, the boy turned peevish. He was his mother's child.

Roscius' blisters were open and red—mounting a horse was agony. Just past the bridge spanning the Volturnus River at Capua, we commandeered a cushioned *cisium* to carry our two 'ghosts' on a more leisurely journey home. I felt happier knowing they'd soon fall behind by many miles, safely beyond Maximinus' reach.

A stone-faced Maximinus kept at a careful parade trot between Saturnus and myself, frustrating my impatient *agentes* in the rear. He cowered underneath his flowing *chlamys*. His hemp sack lay forgotten in the blackness of the Sibyl's cave.

Over many long years, my political acumen had grown as my physical prowess diminished. The exhilaration of trapping Maximinus soon faded away to common sense as our party swapped horses at Velletri. I still felt vindicated as we approached Roma around noon on the third day—but far from triumphant. As we passed the Tomb of Caecilia Metella three miles out of the city on the Via Appia, I'd begun to rehearse the desperate bargaining that loomed before me.

'What happens when we get back?' Saturnus finally murmured under the cover of clopping hooves passing the Temple of Mars.

'My cards are weak, Saturnus, even with you as witnesses.'

He nodded. 'In the end, we're only Castra *agentes* who claim they overheard a powerful prefect confess a capital crime to a chalk-covered peasant boy in a remote cave. It sounds less credible in full daylight, *Magister*.'

'Maximinus knows we can't arrest him without formal charges laid by a magistrate. Do we dare apply for a warrant with only Dotos as our primary witness?'

'I don't like our futures hanging on corroboration from a child. The Prefect will deny he ever confessed. He'll call us liars. He already tried to silence Dotos in that cave. If we lose in court, we lose our lives.'

'Yes, but at least we've shocked Maximinus. He fears we hold more evidence. He can't risk turning his back without knowing our next move.'

'Which is, *Magister*? Our only weapons were surprise and guilty fear. Now we've used up both. If we don't prevail in proving his crime . . .'

'He'll take revenge on us. I know, Saturnus, I know.'

So far, I hadn't played Fates' Fool. But act too hasty now and we might all be finished. All our charges—of illicit conjuring, soliciting dead spirits for predictions of an emperor's demise and succession, and vicious murder—these might prove as ephemeral as the lingering traces of Dotos' face powder. We prevailed only temporarily over one of the Emperor's most trusted officials through underhanded means. We had no jurisdiction over a man who himself had manipulated Roma's courts. Nothing we said was sure to stick before our spineless and compromised judiciary.

And as fearful of exposure as he might be, Maximinus held one powerful piece on the *latrunculi* board—Apollonia. No victory on behalf of my beloved city would compensate for losing her. He knew that very well.

I had no clear idea how to proceed. We arrived at the Castra to hear that Praetextatus had returned to Roma only a few hours before our arrival through the Porta Capena. His summons for me was waiting at the gate.

The gods had smiled a little longer on us. The excuse to confront our Pannonian captive with the Emperor's revised decree on the use of torture could not have come at a better moment.

—THE PREFECT'S ROPE—

Unshaven and sullen, Maximinus stared at me from under the shadow of his hood. He'd been silent for the entire ride back to Roma. We both understood that the outcome of our standoff depended on which face Vettius Agorius Praetextatus turned to us now. Would he play the Roman nobleman who preferred political caution over challenging the Pannonians ruling the Empire? Or would he prove himself the last devout priest of Roma's religious tradition—appalled and repulsed by Maximinus' necromancy secrets?

I turned to my glowering 'guest.'

'Prefect, I have no authority to detain you before formal charges are laid.'

'A shame. I've grown used to your company, Numidianus,' he sneered.

'Excellent. Then you'll continue with me to the Mons Oppius? Praetextatus' message from Emperor Valentinian is more for you than for me.'

This was the most diplomatic phrasing I could muster. I must be very careful.

His lips tightened. 'By all means, let's hear Praetextatus' business together. It will be my first chance in person to air my grievances against the city's pagans he holds so dear and whom I've shown to be so criminal.'

I ordered two curtained *lecticae* and assigned guards to escort both through the crowded city streets. I could not share a vehicle with this man. He'd already recovered half his previous arrogance. He'd spent the ride from Lake Avernus strategizing his defense and dissecting the high-risk gamble facing him: Who better to hear him out than the most powerful pagan of the Empire? He would deny my story and claim I was framing him. Once he'd discredited my bizarre and desperate accusations, he'd oversee the last hours of Aginatius, Abienus, Anepsia and—I knew that flicker in his eyes—my wife. Later, my Castra subordinates and I would go too.

And so we continued slowly between a protective escort chosen by Ressatus. We rode down the northern side of the Caelian Hill and through the human river of the Subura slums. Then up to the Mons Oppius, through the Horti Vettiani riotous with lush flowering bushes and toward the clusters of clients and petitioners crowding Praetextatus' entrance.

Announced to the noble's *dispensatores*, the great double doors admitted us right away. We strode forward through the *fauces*. Our eyes fixed straight ahead on the end of the tunnel-like corridor. We were like two gladiators entering the arena for combat.

'He will see you shortly,' said a clerk in elaborate robes as he peeled away my escort. Maximinus and I stood there, two combatants poised for single-handed combat, yet jostled and shouldered by dozens of indifferent *clientes*. Some looked confidant and prosperous, others like *togati* hangers-on or obsequious freedmen. Many carried ledgers and accountants' tablets as they waited to discuss their host's estates, far-flung investments, and social and religious obligations.

There were also Praetextatus' 'friends' ready to gossip and mingle, devoting their entire day to a form of subjection-as-recreation. I didn't spot Venustus or Minervius, but I recognized some lesser officials, men with little to do and even less to say now that Roma held no real power. Yet they brandished the costumes, insignia, and batons of complimentary rank and chattered in the language of imperial authority.

A man of Praetextatus' prominence could claim he was a retiree enjoying a life of *otium* and yet never spend a waking hour alone or at leisure. Small wonder he resorted so often to prayer in rural retreat—only then did this society of mediocre minds leave him to our ancient gods.

I didn't envy our host today. Maximinus and I had traveled for days, struggled to near-death, and returned on a dusty road to find ourselves in these rarified halls.

I wore leather riding clothes stained with sweat. When I passed a nervous hand over my chin, I felt the unfamiliar bristles of a beard.

Maximinus still wore the cloak of high station in which he'd preened before me in his temporary office. His torn tunic was stained with blood and filth. I smelled him next to me as one smells a nervous fellow soldier waiting for the blare of battle horns.

We waited at one end of the main reception hall. Its gold-edged walls were hung with *imagines* of illustrious ancestors and the living were pressed together by a stone-faced audience of marble statues and busts on pedestals. The whiff of spring from great tubs of rose bushes, hanging vases of azaleas, and drapes of listeria curtaining the peristyle columns wafted in from freshening gardens.

At last Praetextatus dismissed a gaggle of petitioners and turned to receive us. We were ushered forward. His classical features were drawn and his shoulders bowed by the arduous trip to the northern court. He looked far older than his fifty-five years.

He hid any surprise that I'd answered his summons in the company of Acting Urban Prefect Maximinus, officially higher-ranked than a mere head of department like myself. And though our disheveled appearance was certainly odd, the nobleman's tone stayed as cool as the fountain spray dancing behind him.

'Ah, you got my message, Numidianus. How convenient that you two come together. It's useful to receive Emperor Valentinian's order as one single arm of justice in the pursuit of truth.'

He signaled that one of his dozen secretaries should fetch the imperial vellum on which Valentinian, in the cramped, uneven handwriting of a man raised scribbling battlefield orders, had signed the decree dictated by *Quaestor* Eupraxius. We waited many minutes until the secretary handed it over and retreated to a discreet bench.

'I'm sure you'll read this clarification, Flavius Maximinus, with some relief. A man who came to the city to distribute bread and oil can't enjoy—even *temporarily*—torturing the cream of Roman society.'

Maximinus read in silence. He'd worked as a lawyer. Eupraxius' wording was unambiguous. There would be no more easy torturing of Roman senators out of their old fortunes and fertile estates.

Praetextatus asked, 'Something to report, Numidianus?'

'Yes,' I said. 'I've come directly from the Lake of Avernus, the Grove of the Sybil, where I witnessed Prefect Maximinus attempt criminal rituals of blood sacrifice and necromancy. I heard him confess to a foul murder. I have witnesses.'

The hum of conversation died away in the marbled hall, plastered antechambers, and sheltered alcoves beyond. Only the music of trickling water and the rustle of ivy remained.

'Necromancy? Murder?' Praetextatus repeated under his breath. 'What do you say to this, Prefect?'

Maximinus laughed. But he betrayed his anxiety the moment he lost his lofty court Latin for the rustic accent of his native province.

'Noble *Domine*, I'm a practicing Christian. These *curiosi* only "witnessed" me taking a much-needed break from the pressures of my new office. Sure, I made a tourist's visit to the pagan site. I heard it was once attended by honorable priests like yourself. It was just a provincial's gesture of cultural interest.'

Praetextatus placed his legs a bit apart, as if bracing himself against the both of us. 'What's this talk of killing?'

Maximinus replied, 'Readily explained. I was ambushed one night during a Saturnalia visit to Sardinia. I defended myself in the dark, only to discover I'd killed an embittered sorcerer. He was a slight acquaintance of my late father who was himself a reputable *haruspex*. This attacker had followed me in hope of profiting from my good fortune by means of kidnapping and blackmail.'

Maximinus knew by instinct what all *agentes* are taught—that a lie succeeds best when it hews closest to truth. Praetextatus glanced at me, but I hoped silence would provoke Maximinus into some kind of stumble.

The Pannonian continued: 'Numidianus must explain his own reasons for following me all the way to Avernus. Realizing he intended to put a hostile interpretation on my visit to the Grotto, I come here freely. Would I offer myself up to his fantastic slander if I were guilty?'

Praetextatus asked, 'Who are your witnesses, Numidianus?'

'Two of my officers heard him confess. And I have a first-hand witness to what was no act of self-defense in Sardinia. It was a coldblooded murder, according to the victim's son.'

It seemed wiser to keep Roscius offstage for now. Praetextatus disapproved of the vulgar modern theater.

'Is this son of age?'

'No, he's a child. His unexpected appearance in the Grotto in lieu of the summoned shade of the murdered necromancer prompted Maximinus' startled confession.'

'But . . . then . . . this strange encounter was no coincidence?'

'Of course not. My *agentes* will testify to what they heard and saw—including the preparation of a blood sacrifice to appease the murdered man and worse—to elicit the foretelling of Emperor Valentinian's death and likely successors.'

'Don't blame our senior *curiosus* for his confusion,' Maximinus said. 'The blackmailer's widow and her kid know my position here in Roma. As far as I can make out, they now offer themselves as pawns in some campaign against me.'

Praetextatus was faced with two convoluted tales. His obvious confusion emboldened Maximinus.

'I can't answer for *Magister* Numidianus' motives. But he's been tempted by these peasants to think me capable of treasonous use of fortune-telling and cold-blooded murder. Were I not Numidianus' target, I'd be his apologist. This poor man might believe any lies he's told. He might seize any tale against me as leverage to free his wife, the accomplice of the Widow Anepsia hiding Senator Abienus.'

Praetextatus' eyes narrowed as he stated, 'During my absence in Treverorum, your deputy *Notarius* Leo oversaw the trials of the two senators—no doubt on your instructions. The senators, *Matrona* Anepsia, and their domestic accomplices were executed this morning before dawn.'

He read my shocked expression. 'I'm sorry for your personal involvement, Numidianus. This affair cannot end too soon for anyone who loves this city as we do. I consider it over.'

And with that, Praetextatus chose to cut Roma's losses by leaving my beloved wife as the last bit of fodder caught in the maw of the Chilo investigation. The mosaic beneath my feet—an exquisite rendering of Europa carried off on the bull Zeus—swayed beneath me. Apollonia . . .

'You can't leave things unfinished, Praetextatus,' Maximinus said, growing excited by his easy victory. 'For all you know, Numidianus himself has more than a finger in this pie. Have you asked yourself, whether Numidianus knows more of the dirty affairs around Probus than he admits? Well, who else should know more than the *Magister Agentium in Rebus*? You can't let my investigations end before combing out every last knotty tangle.'

Murmurs and mumbles, alarmed shushing, and strange gasps rose up behind us, like a sea of disturbed waters churning around our straining necks.

Praetextatus caught himself from taking a step forward. The noble's manicured fingers laced themselves around the gold rope cording his waist.

'Dirty affairs around Probus? You refer to our Consul? Excuse me for a moment. I need some fresh air.'

He turned away and slowly circled the garden three times. During this strange pause, I could have sworn even the fountain water froze in mid-air.

Praetextatus returned from his promenade to say, 'I'm sure I do not know what you mean by referring to our consul. Sextus Claudius Petronius Probus is too far away to respond to insinuations. But this sad affair of Senator Aginatius has wound up—save the trial of the *Magister's* wife tomorrow.'

'But, Praetextatus, important questions remain—'

'You've already done well, Flavius Maximinus. It's with regret I see that your moment for well-deserved promotion to greater imperial glory has come only too swiftly.'

Praetextatus signaled for the senior secretary to step forward from his bench.

'I will now dictate a recommendation for you to present in person to the court in Treverorum. Valentinian must read our city's high praise of your recent exertions. No, no, I insist. Why delay? Why allow our city's warm praise of you to cool? While I was at court, I heard that the post of Prefect for Gallia will soon be awarded. You must be on the spot to seize that prize in time. How welcome for a man so lately accused of foul necromancy to rise with untainted reputation even higher among our Christian officials.'

Maximinus heard the hidden threat and now made a fatal blunder. Anyone with a pebble's worth of *Romanitas* in his soul could spot it; the ambitious fool said nothing. He didn't waste another second protesting his innocence. He cared more for his immediate career than his eternal reputation. His grubby Carpi hands grabbed at the escape rope Praetextatus had just offered to lift himself out of his Hades of guilt.

And with that, the goddess Fortuna gave a faint smile. The fountain waters were flowing—of course they'd never really stopped—but the current in the rooms reversed course.

After Maximinus' fatal silence, Praetextatus nodded. 'Good. Please wait for my recommendation in the reception hall with the others. I imagine Numidianus will want to hasten away to his doleful family duties.'

Maximinus' flushed expression drained to stone. He was expelled. He was about to be promoted on vellum but exiled from the ancient Mother of Cities forever. He must leave his rapacious sweep up of our city's wealth and grandeur unfinished. At the last minute, the Empire's foremost pagan had chosen to believe my necromancy and murder accusations after all.

But, how had the brash Maximinus flipped his success to catastrophe? The only thing that had happened was his eager mention of Probus, not only the third most powerful man of the Empire—but its richest. Should Maximinus take down *Culmen* Probus and the Anicians' immeasurable holdings, he would become the West's richest civilian official—an unscrupulous Pannonian millionaire in a court ruled by Pannonians—and possibly Valentinian's successor.

This could never be contemplated. I'd provided just enough leverage for Praetextatus to end the 'Chilo Affair'.

Maximinus humbled himself to wait in the outer foyer. I rode back to the Castra, my mind a storm of confusion.

'*Magister*, your face is white.'

'Her trial is tomorrow, Saturnus,' I moaned.

'You must rest. There's still time.'

'Rest? How could I? *Matrona* Anepsia was executed this morning. All her wiles and bribes couldn't save her once Maximinus decided she was his enemy.'

'Poor Roma's mourning days will never end, *Magister*. How will her daughter survive, married off to the son of her mother's executioner?'

'I don't know, Saturnus. But soon it will be Callista's turn to offer me condolences. I will save her the trouble by offering mine first in person tonight.'

※※※

'This was the chamber where Senator Abienus hid himself,' Callista said. I peered into the dark cubby, a storage space of unpainted walls and a tiled floor stained and cracked by hundreds of heavy *amphorae* dragged or rolled into the kitchen wing.

'He could have stayed there for months, I suppose.'

'But for our betrayal by Sapaudulus,' she said.

We returned through echoing corridors to the public reception room where many months ago, her stepfather Victorinus' body had lain in state. This was the very room where Senator Aginatius had burst in, shouting at the mourners and widow, exposing the dead man for his profitable 'friendship' with Maximinus.

'It must have been a shocking scene. I know it shook my wife.'

'It was more frightening than shocking. My mother hoped Victorinus' death meant the end of all his ugly wheeling and dealing. We were living on dirty money, extorted from old family connections facing spurious charges. I was willing to leave Roma and live shoeless on a farm, but *Mater* was too stubborn.'

'You're wise for someone so young.'

'Sixteen this summer. But I learned a lot watching my mother.'

'You didn't approve of your stepfather negotiating acquittals from Maximinus?'

'It disgusted us both. But *Mater* knew Victorinus was dying. She thought Maximinus would leave us alone. Unfortunately, my stepfather had been too good at bargaining his old friends out of trouble. The Prefect felt shortchanged when their mutual racket ended. We were like fat Umbrian cows that Maximinus wanted to keep milking.'

'So your mother tried to buy him off—with your father's dowry gift, Victorinus' estates, and then—'

'She had nothing left to barter but me. And even after bargaining me away, *Mater* still couldn't save herself.'

And nothing could save Callista from living with this betrayal, even in her future marriage bed.

We retreated to the winter *triclinium*, its worn couches shoved against the walls, leaving us two high-backed wicker chairs and side tables for the diluted wine she offered.

No one attended us. The reception room beyond had been stripped of *imagines* and busts. Callista's future in-laws had ordered her to sell off Victorinus' furniture and slaves to convert her Roman legacy into hard gold. This once-great house would be auctioned off in a matter of weeks.

'Will you join your new husband?'

She nodded. 'With the house sold, I'll have no choice. He's posted somewhere along the Danuvius. Just think, *Magister* Numidianus, only last year I was planning a happier wedding and looking for a new home here, near far better in-laws!'

I laid my hand on her arm. 'Don't pain yourself by looking back. Now I must go. I wish you well. You'll call on the Castra if we can be of some service to you?'

'Your wife wanted to think well of my poor mother,' she said. 'How badly we've repaid her friendship!'

'Anepsia paid dearly herself. No honorable Roman matron should suffer such beatings.'

'Beatings? You saw my mother?'

'Yes. I visited her in *custodia libera*.'

She grasped my two hands and exclaimed, 'How kind of you!'

Above all, we needed truth now.

'It wasn't kindness, *Dominula*. I attempted to wrest a written testament clearing Apollonia from all knowledge of your mother's crimes. And she promised me one. But the only document she handed over in her last hours was an accusation that Senator Aginatius raped her.'

'Aginatius did not rape my mother.'

'I know.'

'She was just so desperate in the end. She knew Maximinus hated Aginatius and wanted him safely dead.'

'Safely? Wasn't it too late for Senator Aginatius to prove Maximinus' blackmail game with your late stepfather?'

Callista's eyes widened. She knew something. She knew more. Was there something else at the core of the enmity between Aginatius and Maximinus? Resentment over the Chilo case? Indignation at crookedly obtained acquittals? Something to do with Aginatius' warning letter to Probus? There must be more.

319

But Callista was a hostage now to the Pannonian's family. She couldn't afford to confide in me. She was quick to deflect my curiosity.

'Yes, come to think of it, you can help, *Magister*, in a small way. *Mater* wrote some farewell letters three days ago.'

'Certainly, *Dominula*. My men will deliver them. After all, that's what my service is supposed to be about.'

She smiled. 'I'm sorry to impose. They're hardly letters of state. But I have no slaves left for errands across the city and I have no energy to deliver them in person. I want to hide away. Sometimes . . . I hope to die.'

She dragged herself to her feet and disappeared down the peristyle walkway into the shadows of early evening. The slap of her slippers faded to nothing. A neighbor's slave kept thumping on a laundry tub in the servants' quarters over the back wall. But little else broke the buzz of cicadas in Anepsia's overgrown garden.

Callista returned and thrust a loose wad of coarse paper into my palm. That money-grubbing landlady had sold her doomed prisoner the cheapest stuff on the market for her final messages to friends. And she'd refused her prisoner any sealing wax or string.

I fingered the loose leaves. 'Did you read them, Callista?'

'No, *Magister*. I spared myself her elegant protestations and well-turned excuses. I want to remember her as she was with my own father—young, happy, beautiful, and respected. She wasn't bad, just proud and weak.'

I left the house happy to be of use to a girl facing such absolute loneliness. She'd distracted me from deep dread of the coming trial, the end of everything I cherished. Callista couldn't even mourn a mother whose bid to save herself included the futile sacrifice of her only child. My own tragedy lay only hours away, but at least I could be proud of my wife's unblemished memory.

By the time I arrived at the Castra, my contempt for Anepsia had softened. I recalled her steely admission, 'You men are brave but we women are resilient. The women of Roma particularly so.' I wasn't impressed with her cynicism, but she wasn't unique. Our modern times seemed too harsh for outmoded ideas of civic honor and private virtue.

After a solitary bath and shave, and a canteen meal with some young *equites* ignorant of my private distress, I retreated to my office.

Now, I must steel myself to sleep only long enough to regain strength to relieve Amosis from his vigil. There could be no further objection to my presence near Apollonia as we faced her trial together. I'd foregone my chance to trade her freedom for withholding accusations against Maximinus. Perhaps I knew such a dirty bargain would not have been her way. In the end, it had not been mine.

Cyrillus' desk lamps were cold and our sensitive reports locked into the safe box. I shrugged off my stifling cloak and heated sealing wax as I sorted Anepsia's letters by urban *regio* or suburban district. Most were addressed to local Romans, but a few of them would travel farther to friends in Constantinopolis or Mediolanum.

Even a weathered *curiosus* like myself, trained to pry, couldn't read her private sentiments; it was painful enough to see Anepsia's educated handwriting reduced to slanting wobbles as she eked out goodbyes by the little eyesight Leo's savagery had left her.

And then I fell on a letter to me. I unfolded it, bracing myself for her defense of what was unforgiveable—snaring my innocent Apollonia in her web of intrigue.

Anepsia must have been in great pain. Her writing was almost illegible:

Domina Apollonia Numidiana, wife of Magister Marcus Gregorianus Numidianus, is completely innocent of all charges against her. She was ignorant of any presence in my house of fugitives or of any immoral activity whatsoever. I freely retract all previous allegations and further, bear witness that any magistrate pursuing the unjust trial of this innocent citizen should impose any intended penalty on her false accusers' heads, as required under Roman Law.

I fell back in my chair. The paper rattled in my hand. A Roman matron through and through, she'd kept her word. Our city was dying on its feet, but its soul was not yet extinguished.

Of course, Anepsia knew better than to entrust this retraction to *Notarius* Leo when she delivered her rape accusations against Aginatius. Anepsia may have been doomed, but she was wise to the

321

devious ways of the Pannonian to the end. She just couldn't have imagined that the obedient Callista would delay delivery of her farewell letters by even a day.

Maximinus would find no credible citizen to rebuild his charge against my wife. Who remained as a witness to my wife's innocent visits but his own future daughter-in-law, the honest Callista?

I stood up and steadied myself on my walking stick. I might weep with relief but no—first I raced to the barrack to wake up Clemens. He must delivery Anepsia's absolution to the magistrate in person tonight.

There would be no trial tomorrow.

CHAPTER 23, DUAL CONFESSIONS

—THE MONS OPPIUS, ROMA—

Y ou tried to buy the Castra's services with false coin, Praetextatus.'

The noble pretended not to hear. He busied himself with instructions to the staff left behind by his absent wife. Aconia Fabia Paulina had departed to Etruria for the summer, taking over a hundred household slaves with her.

Her husband would be joining her in only a week and we two were left alone to dine *al fresco*. The cloud of buzzing clients had dispersed. His senior secretary had retired for the evening. If my host were reluctant to be seen sharing a meal with the Castra's freedman boss, this was the ideal moment to finish any business with discretion.

I persisted, 'You knew all along Roma's two greatest families had been plotting treason.'

'It is hardly treason to plan a favorable succession,' he demurred. His eyes avoided mine in the evening haze. His *pocillator* refilled my glass with fine Falernian wine. Our light meal was an exquisite balance of seasoned grilled vegetables, river fish fried in spiced batter, and seeded flatbreads.

The house echoed to the slap of attendants' slippers down the echoing corridors from the kitchen. The great palace was half-closed for the season and the garden lanterns that lit our supper were few.

Summer's heat pressed down early this year. I'd guessed I had only a week or two more before the city's dangerous fevers rose off the Cloaca Maxima and the fetid Tiberis River sent Praetextatus fleeing to the countryside.

He needed a rest. That impression of age that had startled me last September had settled on the aristocrat for good. Perhaps the departure of Maximinus for the northern court had signaled a truce that allowed him ease at last. His fine, enigmatic features sagged off their noble bones, like sentries shifted off watch.

'You must understand, Numidianus. You'd been absent for some time, first in Britannia and then in New Roma.'

'And along the Danuvius, observing Emperor Valens sign his peace treaty with the Goths' leader Athanaric,' I prompted.

'Yes, well, here in Roma, we faced . . . a situation. In 368, our two greatest families, the Anicii and the Ceionii, had readied themselves for Emperor Valentinian's death. And I still insist, prudent preparation is hardly treason.'

'You call preparation for—?'

'For power, Numidianus. Why not reclaim Roma's rightful place? Valentinian's natural death was the chance to put this city back in control of the Empire she founded and built. That chance may never come again.'

'There was a candidate?'

'Of course, the one true Roman most likely to be standing closest to the Emperor's deathbed amidst all those Pannonians and Gauls.'

'You dismiss the Hispaniards? Our Castra file on the Theodosian family gets fatter each year.'

He had not dismissed the Theodosians. One reason why suddenly occurred to me; any Roman family claiming the throne needed the muscle of a military faction to back them. Had this 'true Roman close to the deathbed' considered allying himself with odd-man-out General Theodosius? But that seemed treason to whisper, even here tonight.

I finished my anchovy toasts and pondered. Surely someone had suggested Praetextatus himself as next emperor. And of course, he'd swatted the idea away. My host enjoying the sweet privacy of his fragrant summer dining room was too comfortable, too rich, too devout, not to mention too proud, to take on such a strenuous risk. But the mere suggestion would have drawn him closer to any plot involving an alternative candidate.

I broke the heavy silence. 'So Consul Probus was their man.'

Praetextatus laid down his knife with a sigh. I'd guessed right.

'Probus wasn't consul then. But he'd served as praetorian prefect and, unlike the rest of us, he's a devout Christian and trusted at court. The Pannonians were facing an Imperial Treasury bankrupted by Julian's Persian adventure. Valentinian was desperate for clever moneymen and the Anicii are rich beyond avarice, rich as Croesus—'

'So a Roman clique behind Probus and his bottomless reserves of gold would cut a deal with the Pannonians and Gauls. How disappointing that the dying emperor struggled back into his boots.'

'To many here, it was. But that should have been the end of it.'

'What happened?'

'Sane and sensible Romans retired to their gardens and baths, took honorary posts from time to time, and tried to forget that they'd ever sniffed the perfume of actual authority.'

'But the whiff of it stuck in a few nostrils. Were they going to kill off Valentinian?'

'Come now, Numidianus. Name a single Brutus in this city with the guts for assassination. But many prayed for a favorable omen, a powerful spell, a magic incantation that might...' He wafted his silver fruit knife through the air.

'And Chilo learned of these febrile fantasies?'

'Yes. He boasted he was ready to pass "treasonous names" to Valentinian. So they planned to kill Chilo—and failed.'

'Rumors reached the court?'

Praetextatus nodded. 'Inevitably. Then Flavius Maximinus arrived. Clearly, he was not one of us. He had no intention of just doling out bread.'

'He drew attention to himself?'

'So I observed him from a safe distance. He formed his disgusting, if profitable. alliance with Victorinus. He kept his ear wrapped around every pillar and column to uncover our pathetic secrets. To test the rumors, he insulted Consul Probus to his face. It was like poking one of the Emperor's bears, but Probus knew he was leaving Roma soon for his new post. He kept his claws sheathed. Frustrated, Maximinus started circling around Olybrius' son Alypius, like a snake winding along an overhanging branch, ready to drop.'

'So Prefect Olybrius made Maximinus an offer—let my son Alypius go into exile and I'll promote you off bakery duty. You take the Chilo case instead of my deputy, Senator Aginatius.'

'Which enraged Aginatius, who wrote a letter to Probus, saying he had enough dirt on the Pannonian to take him down—'

'—the dirt in question being Maximinus' blackmail racket with Victorinus.'

'Oh, Aginatius went further. He also detailed Maximinus' public insults regarding Probus' reputation for "aggressive" property dealing. That was dangerously close to the bone, but Probus is no idiot. He didn't seize the bait.'

'And to me, you couched this tale as an Etruscan fable about hunters and bakers. Why? To protect yourself?'

'Like Probus protected himself. He forwarded Aginatius' letter straight to Maximinus by the hand of an anonymous *baiulus* hired off the street.'

Praetextatus paused as chilled deserts arrived in hammered silver bowls frosted with cold. The kitchen was using up its last ice supply from the imported glacier stored in deep caverns under the city. The frozen spoon stuck to my palate.

He toyed with his honeyed fruit sorbet, so I toyed with mine. The nobleman was willing to divulge more than before but I must not display vulgar inquisitiveness. Too much curiosity might stop up this rare confession, because his story was tinged with shame for the old families' dishonorable superstition and cowardly impotence.

'So ... Consul Probus denied his Anician and Ceionian supporters? He threw Aginatius under the chariot's wheels?'

'As easily as this sorbet slides down my throat.'

'He shot Aginatius to the top of Maximinus' enemies list.'

'Probus had no choice, Numidianus! He'd done nothing wrong in 368 to let his potential for rule be discussed here in private homes. But admit such a thing two years later? He might lose his head!'

'He abandoned his friends and family to the Pannonian.'

'He was wise to placate Maximinus. Since then, Maximinus has terrorized the city and driven families to disgrace, financial ruin, and death. At least I sought to contain the damage.'

'When Olybrius invited me to the Caracalla Baths and asked me to supervise the coming arrests—was that your idea?'

Praetextatus sent our empty bowls back to the kitchen.

'Or course. I knew you'd brought down his rebel brother-in-law in Britannia. You were raised in the Manlius *domus*. You're dogged and honorable. We trusted you to be loyal to the society who made you what you are today.'

What arrogant preening on behalf of Roma! Yes, I'd been a slave to a great senator of the old school, a bastard serving my grandfather in his dusty library. But not one of my promotions, from *eques* to *magister* of the Castra had been earned inside Roma's crumbling walls.

'Trusted me? Hardly! It would have been trusting to explain all this from the start.'

Praetextatus sniffed. 'I couldn't betray the confidence of distinguished families.'

'Of course, Prefect. How could a mere freedman appreciate such a dilemma among *honestiores* of centuries' standing? I should only identify Chilo's would-be assassins to cut short Maximinus' spreading threat. Not their motive.'

'I don't appreciate sarcasm, Numidianus. I knew Olybrius had already identified Chilo's assassins but I did not know Maximinus delayed their executions for his own greedy purposes. I did worry that I'd put you in danger. High-ranking men had tried to silence Chilo. Once you learned the full story, they might have killed you.'

I wiped my lips with his linen hemmed with gold stitching. He was still not straight with me. I'd caught him conferring with Chilo *en route* to Treverorum.

'You still worried more for yourself.'

He frowned. 'I needed someone to ferret out the full truth. Even I was not sure who all the exact culprits were. The city was full of senators who felt the purple had been pulled out from under them. I certainly never guessed Warty Paphius.'

'You feared Maximinus more than you let on.'

'Because the Pannonian was more than half-right—there *had* been a plot to put one of us on the throne. Any rumors reaching Treverorum weren't wrong—just two years' out of date.'

'Why not just explain to the Emperor?'

'Oh, Numidianus, don't play naive with me. You know the man—his vulgar taste in verse, his vicious bears, his barbaric temper. He was raised in a tent. He hates educated men, well-dressed men, pagan men, pedigreed men. He loathes our great city and always will. I saw no point in drawing his anger to myself. His Pannonian hound was bound to catch the Chilo culprits—sooner or later. We wanted you there first, if possible. But he moved too fast for us.'

The sickly aroma of full-blown narcissus wafted in my direction. The throbbing of cicadas filled my ears. An incongruent memory of old battleground horrors flitted through my mind.

'We caught Maximinus admitting to years of necromancy. We heard him plead for a criminal prophesy of Valentinian's death and successor. We saw him try to kill our witness to his murder of a necromancer. Why did you hesitate?'

'Numidianus, you enjoy an uneven reputation—'

'You just called me dogged and honorable—'

'Your authority over the Castra is well-earned, but all men must be careful around the *curiosi*.'

'You didn't believe my accusation?'

He was silent for a telltale moment and I hated him for the words of deliberation that followed. 'I believe you love and serve the Empire, Numidianus. But you're that rare Roman official, like myself, who loves his wife even more. I felt very sorry for you. You seemed to be haggling with Maximinus' reputation for your wife's life. It shows a trace of nobility in you, for all your Numidian roots.'

I bit my tongue. Some things would never change in the minds of men born in golden cribs. I was good enough to serve Praetextatus' empire and useful enough to dine alone with him while his peers and family were gone for the summer. But Aconia Fabia Paulina would never include Apollonia in her intimate circle. Nor would I be asked to dine with Senators Minervius and Venustus when autumn social rounds resumed.

'I'd already sacrificed my chance to haggle on the road back from Lake Avernus.'

'I was just realizing that when Maximinus suggested *I* knew about Probus' so-called dirty affairs. He was closing in on Probus' vast property holdings. Perhaps even on my own estates. You see, Numidianus, when he linked me to Probus, he was declaring to my face that he intended to bring all of us down, the Palatine and Esquiline families—*all of us*. He was going to wipe out the innocent as well as those clinging to purple fantasies. My blood froze. I needed to think.'

I remembered Praetextatus' exasperating saunter around the fountain as Maximinus and I watched and waited.

'So you offered him a recommendation for promotion.'

'And my blood thawed just as quickly, because Maximinus seized his opportunity to escape your slander too fast for a truly innocent man.'

Praetextatus reached for his glass. His manicured fingers trembled in the faint moonlight.

'So you *chose* to believe my account of Lake Avernus?'

'Is it true?'

'Yes! He'd been resorting to necromancy for years. He brought a mangy cur to the Cave of the Sybil for blood sacrifice to appease his murder victim's dead spirit. But he lost his nerve when the phantom of the dead man appeared and spoke through the child.'

Praetextatus blanched and gulped down the rest of his wine.

'Clear the linen,' he muttered to a waiting slave.

He was cutting our leisurely dinner short. His renowned pagan beliefs were too deeply felt for my story of evil not to upset his digestion.

'Please, Prefect, calm yourself. You've confessed the meaning of your fable about the hunter, the baker, and the lawyer to me. As thanks, I now confess my secret to you. The Castra staged a drama with Maximinus our audience of one. The necromancer's spirit did appear, but he was only an actor in chalk and charcoal I hired off the proscenium of Pompey's Theater—the celebrity Roscius. The show turned out more convincing than we'd hoped, because unbeknownst to us, the boy had actually witnessed his father's murder. In a panic, Maximinus tried to silence him with blades right under our noses.'

It was time to leave. Praetextatus did me the honor of accompanying me through the series of courtyards, peristyle gardens, and *atria* all the way to the outermost reception hall. Given the size of his palace, we had some minutes to make our positions clear.

'There's still Notary Leo to deal with,' I said.

'He'll follow his protector out of Roma before too long,' Praetextatus said. 'Those two will continue to rise for a time, but not in this city. That's all that matters to us tonight.'

Praetextatus' *dispensator* handed me my formal cloak, baton of office, and green felt pilleus. Slaves summoned my waiting *lectica* from the outer gardens.

'Prefect, did you know Maximinus' father was an honorable *haruspex* who predicted that his own son would end up dying by the executioner's sword?'

'Where did you hear that, Numidianus?'

'Call it the Castra's art. I've taken measures to make that prophecy even more likely.'

'Be careful. Valentinian's volcanic temper won't permit hearing ill of the men he keeps close. We can only pray that those who truly love Valentinian show him better sense.'

The Castra's sleepy-eyed bearers dropped the vehicle opposite the great oak doors and waited.

'I do pray to the gods, Prefect. I light resin and *cyphi* on our *lararium* to protect us all. But the gods need our help. I've sent a confidential account of Maximinus' disastrous conduct toward Roma to one who's eager to prepare for the future by listening to his elders. In fact, I recommended his tutor, the poet Ausonius, myself.'

'Good gods! You sent a report to Gratian?'

'In secret. Maximinus still plans to eclipse that boy before Valentinian's body is cold. Gratian needs ammunition to defend himself. I offered my report as a sapper's mine planted under a fortress wall, to be ignited only when needed.'

'Gratian will show it to his father!'

'No. He won't. I've spent my whole life observing people, like those slaves watching us from the shadows of your garden. *Augustus* Gratian is only thirteen, but already sensitive to contending forces around him. His ageing tigress of a mother is out of favor and far away while his aristocratic stepmother Justina is about to bear a possible heir with the blood of Constantines.'

'My gods, so the Castra already cultivates the next generation! I'm impressed, but why? I forget, you're the freedman of a famous commander.'

'I am more than that to the noble *gens* of Manlius.'

'I am in your debt,' he said. His smile was a little forced. Since I would never be accepted as his equal, I settled for grudging respect.

'May I call in that debt right now? As the Empire's leading pagan, you might restore the altar in Tullianum Prison. It's a disgrace to our ancient cult. And I suggest you appoint as *vicomagister* one Flaccus who tends the compital shrine in my neighborhood near the Porta Capena.'

'That's no recommendation!' Praetextatus said. 'That's condemnation to a lifetime in those cells, something no Roman court would force on the worst criminal!'

'But this Flaccus is so devout, he'll mistake it for an honor above his station. He is sure to protest,' I said. 'But I thank you for gratifying his prayers all the same.'

I closed the curtains of my *lectica*.

Did I feel remorse at sealing Flaccus' fate? No. I never claimed to be like the Christians, putting forgiveness above all else, turning cheek after cheek after cheek. Perhaps forgiveness is good for some men's souls and when they approach the shores of the River Styx— or whatever heaven Christians attain—their spirits are all the lighter for having forgiven the harms done to them.

And I might even understand that, had I not been the personal target of the Pannonian's venom. Sadly for my soul, I could not meet such a charitable standard when Flaccus' victims had included Apollonia, the light and life of our small family. I never wanted that foul man to enjoy again the soft swing of silk hems and the slap of delicate sandals passing his shrine on the path to our front door. The man was a snake, if a relatively minor snake, and aren't all snakes happier under rocks?

CHAPTER 24, A CITY 'HEALED'

—THE BATHS OF CARACALLA, 371 AD—

I'd never thought of my gentle wife as vindictive, vengeful, or sadistic. She never attended bloody games or sensational matinees. Where the average Roman society lady stretched her neck a few extra inches to catch sight of a vehicle accident or *taberna* brawl, Apollonia turned a sharp corner or pulled her *lectica* curtain shut.

So I was in for a surprise. One morning, her toilet box was open on her dressing table, her silver cosmetic spoons, tweezers, and combs scattered on a face towel streaked with cheek rouge. A new dress of pink linen lay across her coverlet next to a rose *palla* in fine gossamer wool edged with silver leaves.

'Is the mistress going out today?' I asked the gardener's child as I finished breakfast in the garden. Beata was crossing the summer *triclinium* with a spray of fresh hyacinth for my wife's coiffure. She was already five—high time to assume simple tasks. She'd just started running errands for the older slave girl taking Drusilla's place in the bedchambers.

I thought that debriefing Beata first would help me make light of Apollonia's first foray into society since her release.

'Party at the Baths? Market outing with Cook?'

Leo and his wife Aurea were returning any day now from Mediolanum. Our family lawyer's reputation was soaring and I was glad he'd kept clear of the nastiness in Roma. The two young people were to be our honored guests for a welcome-home dinner in a matter of days. I never interfered with the house but surely Apollonia needed to catch up on those preparations.

Beata shook her black curls. 'Can't say, *Magister*.'

I nearly choked on my flat bread. 'Answer me, Beata.'

'Won't, *Magister*.'

'Beata, I am the master of this house.'

'But now I serve in *Matrona*'s quarters,' said the self-important imp. '*Matrona* says I must *never* discuss private-woman stuff with anyone, especially any man—or I'll end up like Drusilla.'

'Your mistress is right, as always,' was all I could reply, as any decent Roman husband would say to his wife's personal slaves. But I had to correct Beata's insolent tone—with kindness, of course.

I took her innocent face between my hands and looked into her wide, black eyes. 'I'm glad you take your first duties so seriously. Gavius will be very proud of his daughter. If you work hard and stay honest, you won't end up like Drusilla. Not unless you fall in love with Atticus or Verus.'

Beata wrinkled her nose. 'The twins? They're just troublemakers, *Magister*. Avitus and Numa once promised to feed them to the Emperor's bears.'

'Did they now?' I'd sent my patient *agentes* back to the Castra with hefty bonuses for their months of private babysitting. Perhaps I hadn't paid them enough. Meanwhile, it was important to get Beata clear on a few things.

'Atticus and Verus are just normal little boys—that's all. But long ago, loving the master's son was the start of Drusilla's troubles. She forgot she was a slave.'

'I won't forget, *Magister*. I never forget. But my father says my mother is now in Christ's paradise where no one is a slave.'

It was the child-like chorus of our modern times. I saw no point in saying her mother, who died in childbirth, was nothing more than a mournful shade beyond the River Styx.

Since her betrayal of our family, we'd recovered Drusilla in flight and offered her a bitter choice: she could work on one of the Manlius' farms or be sold to another master of good reputation from outside the city. She wailed all night in the servants' quarters. Lavinia did nothing to console her. Cook left her hungry. I felt no pity. Apollonia locked the bedroom door against her sobs.

Before dawn, the young woman fled for good.

'Drusilla was terrified of turning brown from working the fields. We can only pray she hasn't thrown herself on that Flaccus, wherever he's gone,' Lavinia said, lighting the morning incense at the *lararium*. 'That scoundrel won't give her much of a life.'

'I know where he's gone, Lavinia. If Drusilla marries Flaccus, she'll be lucky to see much sunlight ever again.'

Lavinia didn't know where Apollonia was going this morning, either. I dawdled over my morning fruit and bread.

My wife emerged from the bedchamber and stood in front of me. She shone in the pink sunshine. Where the loss of our daughter Clarissa had nearly killed her with grief, her ordeal of facing conviction as an accessory to treason had hardened her mettle. Her hair was a mass of fine braids and loops and dangling, embroidered ribbons. Her cheeks flushed at my admiration—but I suspected it was more rouge than womanly emotion.

She looked fierce and radiant. You could model a statue on her—soft shoulders held erect, wide bosom cinched by a fawn belt and purse, under-robe of fine silk swishing as she came to bestow a brisk kiss. Before I could reply, she sped away to our *lectica* parked at the curbside.

I'd picked up something commanding in Apollonia's expression, an unfamiliar mix of confidence and tight-lipped resolution.

I ordered Amosis to gather our things for the brisk walk to the Castra. The daily commute on foot was doing my wounded leg good. I didn't need to use my carved walking stick all the time now, but I still carried it for ceremony and sentiment—and defense.

I would spend the morning reviewing the *agentes*' latest intelligence on instability along the Danuvius and eastward to New Roma. But my thoughts lingered on the mystery of my wife's resurrection from shattered and shocked Roman *matrona* emerging from *custodia libera* into my anxious arms to a flawless exemplar of Olympian beauty.

I might be chief of imperial intelligence, but all I knew for certain was that this was not a woman going to a ladies' lunch—even a lunch thrown by Aconia Fabia Paulina.

𓊽𓊽𓊽

The staff meeting had started with fresh news from the north: The Emperor's move with General Severus across the Rhenus to take King Macrianus' hilltop fortress had failed. During the attack, Roman soldiers had raped and pillaged so loudly that Macrianus had had time to be spirited away in a wagon to safety.

Predictably, Valentinian's bad temper exploded again. Before returning to Treverorum, he'd burned all Alemannus territory within fifty miles. He was now scheming to overthrow Macrianus and install one Fraormarius as king of the Bucinobantes tribe.

It was clear to me that the Alemanni no longer feared our choleric Valentinian or his undisciplined forces. But the Castra could not let news of ever-bolder barbarian rebellions invite scorn or disaster ripple across the Empire. At least there was one bit of success to broadcast. General Theodosius had invaded Alemannia from Raetia and his ruthless surprise tactics had produced results. Hundreds of his barbarian prisoners-of-war were being resettled already on the banks of the Padus River.

Rubellius then delivered the morning's updates on the conditions of roads and postal deliveries throughout Gallia, Hispania, Italia, and even Britannia.

We moved on to reports about the East. From Constantinopolis, Benedictus had sent a bundle of notes covering the eastern coast of the Great Sea down to Egypt and to the west as far as Sirmium.

But each individual summary—whether of unrest over grain supplies south of Antiochia or Gothic harassments inside the Danuvian border—was too incomplete or narrow to obtain a broader analysis. Emperor Valens would be right if he concluded that the Castra's work on behalf of the East raised more questions than it answered. And he certainly knew better than I did the state of his successful alliance with the Armenians that promised a ceasefire with King Shapur's Persians by the end of summer. Emperor Valens hoped to pull back to Antiochia within a few months, wrote Benedictus.

The Eastern mail bag had also included a private letter from Constantinopolis for Apollonia. I left that seal unbroken.

This was a point of honor for me. Even if the *magister agentium in rebus* could spy on the state correspondence of every single Roman citizen from the Emperors Valentinian and Valens down to the lowliest provincial stable manager, there was one Roman whose mail would always be private from her *curiosus* spouse.

And anyway, I recognized the handwriting. I handed it to Amosis to deliver in time for Apollonia's return home and returned to business.

'Saturnus, if the *schola* is to make any meaningful impression on Emperor Valens' court, we can't stretch ourselves this thin between Sirmium and Antiochia.'

'You mentioned recruiting more *agentes* out there.'

'It's obvious Benedictus needs more men.'

He nodded. 'You'll be taking long leave from Roma again so soon, *Magister*?'

'Not just yet. I'm going to transfer half a dozen men from the Castra to Sirmium, as we discussed. And if we step up recruiting on the ground, we'll need to staff a training school in New Roma.'

Saturnus argued with me. The Castra had already operated during my absence for so much of the previous three years, he needed more senior men, not fewer, to support him as my deputy in Roma.

Second, he didn't want to lose good riders covering the routes in the well-developed West for the skimpier road system across the mountains and plains of the East.

And third, he couldn't spare experienced trainers just when the first graduates of the revived cadet school were proving their worth.

The other officers present stayed silent. They might be worrying who would be transferred far from family and friends.

My door burst open and a panting, disheveled *eques* broke the tension. It was Julius Tavalus, hundreds of miles south of his usual circuit. Cyrillus was right behind him. We all saw immediately why my clerk had let the unscheduled rider interrupt us:

Julius Tavalus' boots were filthy and his tunic drenched in sweat. He wore the 'white feather of urgency' in the band of his *petanus*. This priority signal helped a rider cut through the *Cursus* traffic and claim the most powerful horses at *mutationes* along the route. There were very few reasons the feather could be used.

'Tavalus!' I shot to my feet.

'*Magister!*' Tavalus bent over, hands on his knees, and gasped for breath.

'Valentinian's dead?'

He straightened up and beamed. From the bosom of his leather riding tunic, he drew a single roll of fine vellum and thrust it over the desk to my anxious hand. It gave off a familiar scent.

To the Magister Agentium in Rebus and Oldest of Friends, Marcus Gregorianus Numidianus,

Congratulate this dutiful servant of our great empire. May all the citizens of my beloved birthplace, the Eternal City of Roma, share in our imperial joy with prayers and celebration.

I fell back into my chair.

Justina Flavia Aviana Vettius Picenus has given birth to a healthy boy to be known throughout the civilized world as Valentinian II. Thanks be to our Great Lord, Christ the Savior.

Rubellius quipped, 'Well, the old boy's certainly not dead!'

'Excellent good news, considering the death of Valens' boy Galates last fall,' Saturnus said.

I handed Justina's message to Zephyrinus for filing in our archives after commissioning copies for distribution citywide.

'So, *Agentes*, our work is finished for the day in honor of a new imperial son. Tell the canteen the wine is on me. We'll finish these deliberations about Sirmium staffing tomorrow.'

The men filed out in higher spirits than before. For the moment, nobody was leaving Roma for good.

I kept my relief at the news of a safe birth to myself. Most of our riders were too old to remember their mothers' ordeals when bearing or burying young siblings and most were too young to listen to their own wives' moans from the midwife's birthing chair.

Justina was no longer the sober little child handed over to the gruff usurper Magnentius and then handed back, still virgin but wiser beyond her years. She was far too old to be bearing her first child but happily, the infant had arrived.

When Justina had turned her back on all the refinements and inheritance of this city and hardened herself to scrabble for half an empire from a Pannonian marriage bed, she'd betrayed no regret to me. She'd chosen her volatile, cruel warrior. And for her reward, she had someone fresh to rule and raise—Valentinian II. Would the infant resemble the eagle-faced father or the graceful mother?

There seemed no reason to go home to a pair of rowdy boys and an absent mistress for my midday meal. And I felt too old and jaded to join in the ribald toasts of riders and cadets in the canteen.

Amosis was still running Apollonia's letter home, so I headed out alone through the busy streets, heading for the great gardens and vast halls of the Baths of Caracalla. Before the imperial celebrations jammed Roma's *tabernae* with happy drunks, I needed to lose myself in the echoing whispers and splashes of the Baths' cool marble. I wanted to shed the weight of the Castra for an afternoon and scrape away my cares like other men young or old.

I paid a *servus lotus* to guard my clothes and ordered a few snacks. Wrapping myself in a fresh towel, I was heading for the steam room when my name rang out.

'Numidianus!'

There he was again, as if nothing had occurred since last year. Olybrius occupied his favorite alcove. A ray of hot sunshine warmed his hairless legs as his slave trimmed his toenails with a pair of silver scissors.

The retired official's face nestled out of the sun, against a cushion in the shadow of a wide pillar. Only when I took the bench opposite him did I notice his slack yellow jowls. Was Olybrius, who'd claimed a 'convenient illness' last September, actually dying?

'I should be angry with you, *Magister*, but I forgive you instead,' he said. He sipped diluted wine from a chilled blue glass edged in gold.

'I did exactly as you asked. I supervised the arrests for as long as I could. I consider the Chilo matter closed.'

He flicked a delicate face towel into the air in dismissal. 'I mean denying this city the greatest actor of our age.'

'Oh, that.' Roscius' future—as much as the actor could stay discreet—was now less a matter of fans and fame than hard, anonymous work inside the Castra. Come to think of it, he'd been keen to leave Roma himself.

'He told you, *Praefecte*?'

'An unbelievable story! Roscius claims you paid him an enormous retirement fee for playing a dead necromancer in some hellhole under Lake Avernus! Scared that fiend Pannonian into shitting his riding trousers! What an imagination!'

'He's a very good actor but as you suspect, that version is an absurd exaggeration that belongs on the stage.'

'Well, he turned some little incident into high drama. He told me of ghosts dancing on walls and dark, winding passages all the way down to the River Styx! Is it true that lake is haunted?'

'The grotto was very famous once.'

'How do you explain it, Numidianus? Tell me.'

'The sulfurous fumes are real enough. They drive birds away from the skies overhead. And the passages leading down to Hades are real too, but not quite so mythic in origin.'

'So the Sibyl never led Aeneas downward to meet his dead father?'

'Believe what you like, but those cement passages and deep caverns were the work of Republican engineers, part of an underground circuit linking Lake Avernus to smaller lakes and serving as a secret access to a strategic storage site.'

'I never heard that.'

'The circuit lost its military use and became a tourist attraction centuries later. It was a big money-spinner in its day. Pagan priests hid their assistants down the corridors before pilgrims entered the cave. They set up lamps and wooden shadow puppets to project "spirits of the dead" along the walkways and bridges leading to a grotto for sacrifice, with little alcoves all around for worshippers.'

'Sounds like something down at Pompey's Theater,' Olybrius muttered.

'You'd appreciate it.'

'Sometimes I think this old city has forgotten more things than the rest of the world will ever learn, Numidianus.'

His slave started massaging his feet with some pungent oil that burnt my nostrils. I made to leave. Olybrius wasn't letting me go that fast.

'But if I didn't know those details—and I'm a true Roman—how did you know, Numidianus?'

'Because when I was a child, my grandfather Senator Manlius thought a visit to the grotto was a good joke for a holiday outing.'

Olybrius stared. He leaned closer, whispering, '*Your* grandfather? So the rumors are true after all? You carry the noble blood of the *gens* Manlius?'

I stood up. 'Shhhh, Prefect Olybrius. I know you'll carry my secret to your grave for the sake of all concerned. Just take comfort in knowing that the freedman you entrusted last September with such weighty services to the Ceionians and Anicians was more than deserving of the privilege, as my own blood is as old and storied as yours—if not more so.'

I left him sputtering. I had had enough. It was my way of making peace with all of them, calling me a true Roman when it served their purpose and a Numidian freedman to keep me in my place. Impressed or insulted, Olybrius' reaction hardly mattered now. His eyes were bloodshot and his naked stomach a deflated bag of painful-looking knots and bulges. He would carry my bastard's secret across the genuine Styx very soon.

௨௨௨

I arrived home early from the Baths and was surprised to find Apollonia wasn't home yet. The *lararium* sat neglected and cold. I asked Amosis, Lavinia, and Cook where she'd gone. It seems that she'd told the *lectica* bearers to be prepared for a journey across the river to the northern suburbs of the city.

I told Lavinia to put the boys to bed as soon as the sun had set and then light the evening *cyphi* on the altar. I wasn't hungry. The shadows lengthened in the garden. I waited alone on Apollonia's favorite chair and smelled her almond bath oil on the thick summer cushions.

It was nearly dark when I heard the slaves open the front door and my wife dismiss the bearers. Her silhouette appeared in the archway, dark and still.

'We need lamps out here,' I said, rising to kiss her welcome. She turned away from my kiss and sat down on the stone bench.

"No, no lamps. No light.'

'What is it?'

'I feel ashamed, Marcus. Today I've shamed myself. I've shamed you.'

'You couldn't—'

I moved to her side and put my arm around her. Despite the balmy evening, her hand was cold.

'Are you all right? Here, drink some wine.'

She sipped from my glass and shuddered, as though shaking off something vile. Then she took a deep breath.

'This morning we arranged to go together to the execution ground north of the city. There were about a dozen of us—all friends and relatives of Flaviana.'

'Why? What was going on at—?'

'We had demanded a magistrate's formal review of the way Flaviana was dragged naked through the streets. Marcus, I don't care whom she slept with! You knew the proper arrest procedures. Where were you? No matter how she was charged or detained, that humiliating parade through the rabble, beggars tearing the clothes right off her—no Roman noblewoman should ever endure that!'

'I know. I saw it.'

'You *saw* it? And you did nothing?'

'I did everything I could. But it was too late to stop that.'

'Oh, I'm sorry. Why do I blame you? I just feel so . . . dirty.'

'Dirty? Why?'

'Because I watched them punish Flaviana's executioner for dereliction of duty. And I cheered, Marcus, I cheered and I jeered and . . . and I even threw clods of mud at him as he burned to death. I screamed out all my rage for what our city has suffered.'

I took her in my arms as her lost pride gave way to sobs.

'You were right to be angry.'

'No, Marcus. Apodemius didn't raise me to join the same kind of mob that burned down our family home and everyone in it but me. You didn't marry me and . . . give me your trust and . . . our two beautiful boys . . . when now I know, I'll *always* know that I'm no better than those drunks down in the Subura tonight yelling their dirty jokes about Justina and her new baby.'

'Have you eaten?'

She shook her head. I called for a tray and lamps. When the food finally arrived, I studied Apollonia's tear-streaked face by the light. Her new dress was ruined. A strap of her sandal had broken loose. The vengeful senatorial women of the Palatine and Esquiline hills must have rivaled the Harpies today.

'I have to leave Roma again soon for the East. But I promise not to go until you're ready,' I said.

While we pecked at our salad and stewed rabbit in exhausted silence, Lavinia brought the letter from Constantinopolis. Apollonia read it under a palm lamp and then stared over the hyacinths into the dark.

'How's Sybilla?"

'All her news is good. They have a large garden, fresh air, and lots of lively, intelligent dinner guests. But she says the best part is that Drusus has many new students from good families, even if they do insist on speaking Greek.' She allowed herself a rueful smile.

'You miss them, I know.'

'Sybilla would have been ashamed of me today. She would have stopped me from going out, even bolted me in rather than see me lose all dignity, all sense of myself. I've never found a level-headed friend like her since, though the gods know I've tried, Marcus.'

'Most people in Roma keep their friends from childhood. Apodemius made you spend your girlhood in hiding alone.'

'It made me too keen to rejoin society. I withheld my good judgment of other women in hope of catching up with everything I'd missed. I couldn't distinguish sophistication from decadence.'

'Don't be hard on yourself. Things will return to normal.'

'That's the problem! I don't want to return to anything, Marcus! The fig tree we planted never rooted properly. The new ventilation in the kitchen blocks up. And the altar lights keep going out as if the Penates themselves are refusing to make this their home.'

'We'll fix the kitchen vent and the draft over the shrine. You seemed happy to leave our past in the Manlius house to Leo and Aurea.'

'It's rightfully theirs. And we needed a home all our own. But it's not this or that house, Marcus. It's the whole city!'

I could hardly fix the entire Eternal City for her, no matter how much I loved her. We'd both grown up here. It was part of us forever.

'If only the boys could study with Drusus! We'll need a tutor for them this year.'

'When I get to Constantinopolis, I'll ask Drusus to recommend someone—first thing, I promise. And I'll take Sybilla a present from you to show how much you miss—'

'Take me, Marcus! Take *me*!' She crushed Sybilla's letter with excitement. 'Take us all, the boys and Lavinia and Cook and old Gavius and everyone!'

'For how long?'

'For good.'

The hum of the rowdy celebrations down the hill mixed with the shrill buzz of the cicadas in the trees along our garden wall.

'For good?'

'You've said ever since you returned from that miserable Britannia that you have to build up the service in the East—that the East holds the future. The boys will get a better education with Drusus—real working Greek as well as Latin.'

'But you were raised here.'

'I want to be free of my memories.'

'But the Castra's my headquarters.'

'So? You move between the capitals every year anyway, Marcus. I'm used to it by now. What difference does it make to you if we're waiting in Roma for you to return from Constantinopolis or we're in Constantinopolis waiting for you to return from Mediolanum, or Treverorum—or Tripolitania!'

'It would take radical planning—'

'Thank you, Marcus! That's all I ask. Oh, I'm hungry!'

She knew better than to press me any harder. Moving the family from Roma would reduce my time overseeing the Castra. But the city itself was not essential to my work if left to the steady supervision of Saturnus. If anything, Castra routines reduced the time I devoted to the wider Empire—for intelligence-gathering and network-building.

A sudden breeze cooled the garden—carrying the spirits of the dead I would leave behind in Roma—the Senator, the Commander, Apodemius, Cornelius, all the Castra ghosts who haunted the courtyard on my daily crossings between archives, canteen, and office.

And the living? I'd see far less of my beloved Leo and the unborn heirs we hoped would return the Manlius House to its lost glory.

But today was a warning to us both. Apollonia felt degraded by what Roma had reduced her to—and that was over just one day.

I was no better—too proud, too stubborn, and too resentful. Today's petty scene with Olybrius at the Baths was a warning from the gods that Roma's social snobberies and vicious recreations brought out the worst in me. One day might see me sinking to a temptation that made me weep for myself.

As a man reaches his forties, he knows the ways of the world. He should know himself even better. Was I a successful Roman freedman, bred of the city and loyal to its aristocratic hills? Or a Numidian seamstress' son, a despised bastard social-climber, ridiculed for his baton of office and polished shoes and never to be trusted by those who dined off gold plates? Justina had already warned me of my resentments warping my work.

What counted would be seeing my happy wife planning her new garden with Sybilla under a sky free of deadly *miasma* fevers and choking coal smoke. What mattered was hearing my boys reciting their lessons in good Greek and Latin to Drusus' rigorous ears. What outweighed everything was serving the whole Empire, not nursing a dying city.

Praetextatus, Olybrius, and Lampadius, the 'great descendants' of Roma and their ilk, could remember *Magister* Marcus Gregorianus Numidianus as they liked—or not at all. And if I ever wanted to know what such men really thought of me, I could always read their mail.

The End

HISTORICAL NOTES

Ammianus Marcellinus provides much of the background for our *Embers of Empire* adventures. In 1946, gimlet-eyed scholar Erich Auerbach wrote of the Greek soldier-historian:

Ammianus' world is somber; it is full of superstition, blood frenzy, exhaustion, fear of death, and grim and magically rigid gestures. To counterbalance all this there is nothing but the equally somber and pathetic determination to accomplish an ever more difficult, ever more desperate task; to protect the Empire, threatened from without and crumbling within ... Grotesque and sadistic, spectral and superstitious, lusting for power yet constantly trying to conceal the chattering of their teeth—so do we see the men of Ammianus' ruling class and their world.

This is the background for Marcus Gregorianus Numidianus' battle to use his hard-earned freedom from slavery and his classical education to protect the Empire. Whether we mark his world's collapse with the surge of the Tervingi and Greuthungi tribes across the Rhine in 373 or the death of Emperor Valens while battling Goths at Adrianople in 378 or even the Gothic sacking of Rome in 410—the twenty-first century reader knows that the Roman world Numidianus defends is nearing the cliff edge.

Men like Numidianus couldn't imagine that their grandsons might live to see the Western Empire crumbling under impotent imperial figureheads governed by barbarian praetorians. Yet as our protagonist rebuilds the *schola agentium in rebus* that Emperor Julian destroyed, he can't help but notice that the uneducated, the venal, the barbaric, and the irrational are gaining ground over the values of his esteemed grandfather, the senatorial patriarch of the Manlius *gens*.

We have proof that foresight of some kind was not impossible. Ammianus himself was not optimistic about the future. The scholar had already linked deepening greed and political corruption to the Christian Constantine and his three sons. He seems depressed by the failure of his idol Emperor Julian's pagan revival, the rise of Pannonians far cruder than the Constantines, and possibly the succession of religious intolerants like the Theodosians after the disaster in Adrianople.

Ammianus would eventually blame the disaster befalling Valens at the hands of the Goths in 378 on greed; Valens admitted the Goths into the Roman Empire because he wished to reinforce his army while enriching his treasury by commuting the obligation of his citizens to provide recruits into cash payments, (as Timothy D. Barnes sums up Ammianus' opinion.)

And as Auerbach says above, this was already a grim period beset by superstition and festering political intrigues.

In an appreciative essay on Ammianus Marcellinus, J. W. Mackail explains; *these accusations of practicing magic were an outstanding feature of the time. The craving to get into communication with the dead and to force secrets out of dark unseen powers ran like a fever through all classes, especially the intellectuals and the rich. It was condemned alike by the Church and by the civil authority, but it grew nonetheless; and it was held to be public policy to stamp it out by treating it as a capital offense. Such a policy lent itself at once to the trade of the informer.*

The Prefect's Rope explores some of what we know of these irrational fashions and frenzies. By all accounts, even the most educated fourth-century Roman—Christian or pagan—feared the power of the underworld.

In our 'modern' times, it might be hard to appreciate the extent to which sorcery, curses, potions, poisons, and fortune-telling were credited by Roman sophisticates. Notice Marcus Gregorianus Numidianus never says he doesn't fear *veneficium*. On the contrary, our hero reminds himself that any decent Roman avoids the practical as well as political risks of messing around with the dead.

Despite its loss of imperial authority and senatorial power over the fourth century Pannonian regime, Rome was still regarded as the great social center of the Empire. Perhaps the fashion for dark power was a substitute for the political power the city of Rome had long enjoyed and now lost forever?

Prof. Mackail adds: *Civic improvements continued to be made, like the clearing away of the shops clustered round temples or* churches, and the erection of the great obelisk in the Circus. The decoration and machinery of theaters were increasingly elaborate. Public health was scientifically guarded; the precautions taken against infectious diseases, though they probably did not extend beyond the well-to-do classes, read quite like those of modern times. Music was much cultivated; and the manufacture both of organs and of stringed instruments comparable in size to pianos is particularly noted.

But the vast majority of citizens lived only for frivolity and excitement. The public libraries were closed for lack of readers, where they were not perishing from neglect or deliberately destroyed. Frivolous and immoral books on the one hand, spiritualistic and magical treatises on the other, were the only reading of the leisured and educated classes.

Mackail summarizes Rome's fetid and uneasy atmosphere as experienced by Ammianus Marcellinus:

. . . in the fourth century, many new ideas and theories were in the air. It was a time, like the present, in which loss both of hard thinking power and of imagination—which has been suggestively defined as the faculty of seeing and tracing consequences—was accompanied by intense receptivity and by a feverish pursuit of short-cuts alike in thought and in practice.

In other words, 'short-cuts' in analyzing causes and results led to what we today term 'magical thinking.' It certainly left reasonable, educated people vulnerable to irrational fear of what others might do to them by illicit means.

And the lack of education started at the top: Jan Willem Drijvers writes:

Valentinian's and Valens' lack of paideia (classical education) and their incomprehension of rule through honor resulted in a society in which terror and injustice held sway, and those in power behaved like beasts and were predominantly concerned with their own interests rather than with the common good. In Ammianus' view the political culture under Valentinian and Valens, or rather the lack of political culture, was a sign of decline of Roman society. Perhaps it was an even more dangerous indication of decay than the barbarian threats at Rome's frontiers since this deterioration of culture was at the center of power and detrimental to Roman society as a whole.

349

This vacuum at the top led to fatal legal consequences; a key element in the Rome purges of 368-371 was the conflation by Emperor Valentinian of the distant use of magic or poison with the commission of treason against his immediate person. To our way of thinking, these are two very different domains. But not to an emperor who, along with his brother, had survived a suspected joint assassination attempt by poisoning immediately after their imperial ascensions in 364.

This conflation meant Acting Urban Prefect Flavius Maximinus and his henchman Notary Leo (history has lost Leo's full name) were able to add torture (traditionally reserved for cases of treason committed by sub-senatorial classes) to their arsenal when interrogating even the most highborn detainees.

But the legal system and its republican protections had been disintegrating already for some time, notes Mackail:

Under the lesser Antonines Septimius Severus and his son Antoninus Caracalla, trial by jury finally disappeared. That was a more important thing than it may seem. The abuses of corrupt juries were the reason or the pretext; and these abuses were real and grave. But the result was uncontrolled criminal jurisdiction by officials. Legal trial was superseded by administrative process. Death after torture could be inflicted for any crime; and the list of crimes was continuously lengthened.

But beyond that list, the monstrous invention of stellionatus, (cheating, trickery, fraud) covered any act which was not legally criminal. With dreadful monotony in Ammianus comes every few pages a sickening record of tortures and hideous deaths set down almost without comment. Burning alive was the common punishment. There was no redress: 'de fumo in flammam,' 'from smoke to the flames' (or 'frying pan to fire') in an awfully literal sense, was the probable event of any appeal.

Meanwhile, Christopher Kelly says some of Ammianus' account is colored by the ancient historian's clear preference for Emperor Julian whose promise to restore pagan imperial order and unity had been cut short by his untimely death.

'By contrast, his obituaries of Valentinian and Valens emphasize the impossibility of their ever realizing that project.'

Kelly continues: 'Ammianus Marcellinus suggests to the reader through jagged composition, striking juxtaposition, and failure to resolve opposing points of view a more disjointed and fragmentary world. The Roman Empire is breaking up: surrounded by enemies, divided between East and West, split between two rulers. A unified account, a final judgment, a clear-cut conclusion is not possible.'

Experts on Ammianus Marcellinus' Book XXVIII might justifiably quibble that this author has tightened the sequence of recorded events around the Rome 'treason trials.' For the sake of narrative pace, we close our novel without detailing how it was not until *after* Maximinus' promotion from Rome to Treverorum to serve as Praetorian Prefect for Gallia that he engineered the arrests and executions of Aginatius and Anepsia, among others, through the agency of political puppets succeeding him in the Eternal City.

Our truncated timeline is not entirely optional—the historical record is a confusing one. We have tried to include all the real names, charges, convictions, and even omens available, e.g. Hesychia and her suffocating pillow, Flaviana's naked humiliation and the subsequent punishment of her executioner, the senators' plot to kill Chilo, Hymetius' successful appeal, and the failure to save the boy Lollianus by his once-powerful father Lampadius—all these events are documented.

So are the get-out-of-jail cards negotiated for Tarracius Bassus and his pals consulting the gladiator Auchenius as well as Maximinus' jesuitical promise to spare the three accused poisoners the 'flame and the sword'. So is the court scene in Treverorum in which Praetextatus appeals to Valentinian for relief against the greedy 'serpent' Maximinus, prompting the courageous correction of the Emperor's denials by the imperial *quaestor* Eupraxius, the renowned 'Moor of Caesariensis.'

But other identities and relationships are less clear, e.g. was the exiled Alypius the much younger brother or the son of the city boss Olybrius? We'll follow the suggestion of the Italian expert in Late Roman genealogy Rita Lizzi Testa that Alypius was a son.

That said, no episode recounted by Ammianus seems as nightmarishly confused and piecemeal as his version of the terrifying wave of arrests, convictions, and executions that netted Rome's elites. In alluding to these cases, Ammianus sounds uncharacteristically skittish. He even warns us in his preface to his last six books that he has re-ordered or omitted various names and dates for his own safety. Midway through the story, he defends himself, saying the informed reader will see he's taking events and names out of order—omitting some, obscuring others.

Professor E. A. Thompson argues that Ammianus' sudden juggling of facts is because the historian is writing into his own era. Any contemporary might know where the political skeletons are buried. From now on, until the end of these *Res Gestae*, Roman history can no longer sustain a grand narrative. From now on, Kelly concludes, Ammianus' readers, like the Empire's enemies, have crossed the frontiers.

After the claustrophobic 'Roman Noir' atmosphere of *The Prefect's Rope*, it's unlikely we'll focus again on the city elites of fourth-century Rome. Our protagonist Marcus Numidianus is torn by his instinct to protect the pagan Roman society he has always loved from its determined decline into idle vice and superstitious foibles. He fights the creeping recognition that the city in which he grew up, the Rome that weathered the plague and chaos of the third century to find some stability under the Constantines, may not thrive into the fifth.

The words of the young priest Jerome visiting the Tullianum cells—yes, the future St. Jerome who will soon flee to the desert of Chalcis—resonates too strongly in Numidianus' heart to ignore. Protecting the Empire means keeping tandem with an empire finding its future survival in the East—a Christian East.

However, if the fourth century sees the city of Rome left on the margins, it won't prevent certain noble clans from surviving centuries longer.

In particular, don't fret about this story's elusive powerbroker Consul Sextus Claudius Petronius Probus of the Anicii. As the great historian Edward Gibbon notes:

From the reign of Diocletian to the final extinction of the Western empire, that name (Anicia) shone with a luster which was not eclipsed, in the public estimation, by the majesty of the Imperial Purple. The several branches to whom it was communicated, united, by marriage or inheritance, the wealth and titles of the Annian (sic), Petronian, and Olybrian houses; and in each generation the number of consulships was multiplied by a hereditary claim. The Anician family excelled in faith and in riches: they were the first of the Roman senate who embraced Christianity; and it is probable that

Anicius Julian, who was afterwards consul and prefect of the city, atoned for his attachment to the party of Maxentius, by the readiness with which he accepted the religion of Constantine.

Their ample patrimony was increased by the industry of Probus, the chief of the Anician family; who shared with Gratian the honors of the consulship, and exercised four times the high office of Praetorian Prefect. His immense estates were scattered over the wide extent of the Roman world; and though the public might suspect or disapprove the methods by which they had been acquired, the generosity and magnificence of that fortunate statesman deserved the gratitude of his clients and the admiration of strangers. Such was the respect entertained for his memory that the two sons of Probus, in their earliest youth, and at the request of the senate, were associated in the consular dignity; a memorable distinction, without example, in the annals of Rome.

'The marbles of the Anician palace' were a proverbial expression of opulence and splendor; but the nobles and senators of Rome aspired, in due gradation, to imitate that illustrious family.

A branch of the family transferred to the Eastern Roman Empire, establishing itself in Constantinople (where Anicia Juliana, daughter of Western Emperor Anicius Olybrius, was a patron of the arts) and rising in prestige: the scholar and philosopher Boëthius was a member of this family, as was Anicius Faustus Albinus Basilius, the last person other than the Emperor himself to hold the office of consul, in 541 AD.

In the West, on the other side, the Anicii were supporters of the independence of the Western Empire from the Eastern one; they were, therefore, supporters of the Ostrogothic kings of Italy, and as such, celebrated by the king Theodahad.

So the reader might pity the doomed Anepsia, Flaviana, Charitas, and Hesychia, or the three 'stooges' of the Chilo affair, or the feckless Lollianus compiling his silly book on potions.

But don't worry about slippery Consul Probus. When he shopped Senator Aginatius to the ambitious Pannonian, Probus was playing a very long game indeed—one that stretched into the sixth century no less, from Boëthius' library to King Theodahad's banquet table.

PLACES AND GLOSSARY

acetum—disinfecting vinegar, used for wound sterilization
Ad Aras—Aras, Navarre, Spain
adiutor, adiutores—batman or assistant
adulterium—adultery
aedile, aediles—municipal officials responsible for maintenance of public buildings (*anaedēs*) and regulation of public festivals.
aerarium Saturni—official treasury/depository of Ancient Rome
agens, agentes in rebus—imperial officers in charge of roads, postal services, customs regulations, and intelligence gathering in the Late Roman Empire
alarum—danger signal, warning, call to arms
Alpes—the Alps
amiticia—friendship
amphora, amphorae—storage containers, often ceramic or pottery with pointed bottoms and double handles
Ancyra—Ankara, Turkey
Andematunnum—Langres, France
animula noxias—noxious spirits
annona—imperial welfare handout, or tax in coin or produce
annonarium—headquarters of *annona* management
antanagoge—not being able to answer an accusation, making a counter-allegation or counteracting an opponent's proposal with an opposing proposition instead
Antiochia—Antakya, Turkey
apodemus—mouse
apparitor, apparitores—officer who attended magistrates and judges to execute their orders
Aquae Sextiae—Aix-en-Provence, France
arca, arcae—box for scroll
arcanus, arcana—the word *areanus* appears once in Ammianus Marcellinus (28.3.8) and is thought to be a misspelling of *arcanus* and to match a single memorial in Roman Britain to a *miles arcanus*. According to A.M., 'This was an

organization founded in early times, of which I have already said something in the history of Constans . . . (ed. note: in lost Books 1-13). Their official duty was to range backwards and forwards over long distances with information for our generals about disturbances among neighboring nations.' Little else seems to be known about this service but they certainly did exist. The Britannic branch was accused by General Theodosius of suspected betrayal of the Empire in 367 during the Great Conspiracy in Britannia.

Arelate—Arles, France

Argolis—Argolida, Greece

arteria femoralis—femoral artery

Asa Paulini—Anse, France

asper et subagrestis—nasty and aggressive

atrium, atria—open-ceiling'ed central room of house layout

augur, augures—interpreters of omens

augustus, (Auguste, vocative)—honorific for emperor

auriscalpius matronarum—'lady-licker', 'matron-whisperer'

avaritia—greed, avarice

Baiae—Baia, Italy

baiulus—messenger, porter, carrier

ballista—a torsion-powered missile projector/catapult developed over many centuries. By the Late Roman era, the largest *ballista fulminalis* could deliver darts farther than 1,100 meters, e.g. the width of the Danube River.

ballistarius—ballista operator

baltea—straps and buckles, hanging off a Roman belt

Barsino—Barcelona, Spain

Bauli—Bauli, Italy

Bessapara—Pazardjik, Bulgaria

biarchus—a regimental grade between *circitor* and *centenarius,* borrowed from the cavalry by the *Schola of Agentes in Rebus,* who limited themselves to six classes of the cavalry's ten, i.e. *eques, circitor, biarchus, centenarius, ducenarius,* and *princeps.*

Boae—Bua Island, Croatia

Bononia—Bologna, Italy

bruma—winter haze and fog of the shortest day of the year

bucellarii—literally 'biscuit-eaters', private armed militia hired by wealthy individuals or powerful state officials

bulla, bullae—amulet worn by Roman children for protection from the gods

Burdigala—Bordeaux, France

Cabilonnum—Chalon-sur-Saône, France

calceus, calcei—high-cuffed boots originally worn by cavalry riders, later adopted by civilians

caldarium—the hottest room in the sequence of Roman bathing; after the moderately heated *tepidarium*, bathers progressed to the *caldarium* or the *sudatorium* or sauna, before cooling off in the *frigidarium* to relax/swim.

caliga, caligae—heavy hobnailed, boot

calumnia—calumny

Cambodunum—Kempton, Bavaria, Germany

campagi—polished black shoes worn by Late Roman officials

Capua—Santa Maria Capua Vetere, Italy

carcer—jail

cardo—the main north–south-oriented street in Roman cities, military camps, and colonies

cardus decumanus—the east-west-oriented street in Roman street or camp plans

Caralis—Cagliari, Sardinia

carruca—travel carriage with leather roof and suspension straps

Carthago—Carthage, now suburb of Tunis, Tunisia

Castra Peregrina—originally barracks on the Caelian Hill in Rome, Italy built for the *peregrini*, soldiers detached from the provincial armies for special service in Rome. The Castra later became the headquarters for military couriers and then the Empire's secret services, the *frumentarii*, until their disbanding by Emperor Diocletian. They were succeeded by a reformed service, the *agentes in rebus*. The ruins of a part of the Castra and several inscriptions connected with it were found in 1905 under the Convent of the Little Company of Mary, just southeast of S. Stefano Rotondo.

Castulo—near modern Linares, Spain

cathedra—low, wide-seated armchair

caupona—the lowest category of roadside inn/brothel, frequented by thieves and gamblers

causidicus—solicitor

centenarius, (*Centenarie*, vocative tense)—mid-rank of the *agentes in rebus*, after *biarchus* and before *ducenarius* (see *biarchus*)

Ceratae—*mansio* at Beydili, Turkey

Chalcedon—Kadiköy District, Istanbul, Turkey, an Attican Greek colony of 685 BC founded in Bithynia, Asia Minor, named after a stream called the Chalcis. Chalcedon sat directly opposite Byzantium, south of Scutari (modern Üsküdar).

chlamys—military cloak, semi-circular, hip to calf length

cingulum—wide belt, often strutted or jeweled, worn by both fourth-century civil servants and military officers

circitor, circitores—second lowest rank in *agentes in rebus*, after *eques*, (see *biarchus*)

cisium—two-wheeled horse-drawn cart

clarissimus, clarissimi—third rank of imperial official

Clavenna—Chiavenna, Italy

clementia—clemency, mercy

clientes—clients of a sponsor, patron, or benefactor

Cloaca Maxima—the city of Rome's most ancient sewer

codex, codices—paged books bound to a spine, as opposed to scrolls

comes, comites—*comites* wielded posts of every description, from the army to the civil service, while never surrendering their direct links and access to the emperor. They headed major secular departments after Constantine or held military appointments, higher than *dux*, but under a *magister peditum/magister equitum*. On a simpler level, it could mean a local figure's staff.

comitatus—suite of officials, the *comites*, around the emperor

commendatio—letter of recommendation

conditum—wine flavored with flowers or spices, e.g. coriander, anise, pepper, cinnamon

compital—corner shrine

compluvius—opening in *atrium* roof sloping inward to pour rain into the *pluvius*

Comum—Como, Italy

conciliarius—councilor

consistorium—the Emperor's advisory cabinet

consultores—consultants
contubernalis, contubernales—tentmate, eight to a tent
Corduba—Cordoba, Spain
cornicen, cornicenes—horn player
Corona Muralis—crown awarded to first soldier reaching the top
    of an enemy wall
corrector—governor
Cosa—Orbetello, Italy
cruciatis tormentorum—the agony of torture
cucullus—hood of a cloak, hooded cloak
Cularo—Grenoble, France
culmen—chief of a *gens* or clan
cultor/cultores deorum—worshipper of Rome's traditional gods
Cumae (Magna Graecia)—Cuma, Italy
Cunus Areus—the Splügen Pass, Italy, and Switzerland
curiosus, curiosi—insulting slang showing contempt for *agentes*
curriculum vitae—resume or c.v.
Cursus Clabularis—specially engineered roads capable of handling
    heavy cargo traffic
Cursus Publicus—state-managed empire-wide network of roads
    and comfort/layover stations
custodia libera—house arrest or detention under private
    supervision of civil servant or guarantor
custodia militaris—detention under armed guard, originally
    military expanding to more general state detention
cyphi—sweet gallingale, powdered incense or medicinal root
Dableius— near Çayköy, Turkey
Dadastana, Galatia—Kanahisar, Turkey
Danuvius River—Danube River
defensor causarum—defense lawyer
defixiones—prayers and curses for good luck or bad
deprecatio—appeal
Dertoso—Tortosa, Catalonia, Spain
dies Martis—Tuesday
dignitas—dignity
diplomata, diplomatae—imperial travel certificates for use of the
    Cursus Publicus
dispensator—household manager, custodian, majordomo
Divodurum—Metz, France

domesticus, domestici—imperial household servant/guard
domina—lady, term of respect
dominula—girl or very young woman
dominus, (vocative *Domine*)—lord, sir,
domus—household, family
domus culmen—head of a *gens*
donativum, donativa—bonus pay
ducenarius—rank of *agens* after *centenarius,* before *princeps* attached to a top civil servant (see *biarchus*)
dux—provincial governor
Dyrrhachium—Durazzo, Albania
eculeus—'little horse' across which torture victim was stretched
Emporiae— Empúries, Catalonia, Spain
emporitica—variety of Roman paper too coarse for writing and reserved for wrapping uses (derived from the papyrus plant)
epanalepsis—a figure of speech in which the beginning of a clause or sentence is repeated at the end of that same clause or sentence, with words intervening
ephebeum—exercise place for *ephebi*, adolescents
Ephyra— Cichyrus, Greece
epizeuxis—the repetition of a word or phrase in immediate succession, typically within the same sentence, for vehemence or emphasis
eques, equites—lowest rank in the *agentes in rebus,* (see *biarchus*)
evectiones diplomatae (*evectio*)—a license/road warrant to use facilities of the Cursus Publicus network, passport for official travel use, permit to travel by public post
fauces—narrow passage, entryway leading to atrium
fibula, fibulae—pin or brooch fastening a cloak or tunic at the shoulder
fideiussor—private guarantor of arrested citizen out on bail
fiscus—financial house or office
flagellis et verberibus—scourges and whips
Florentia—Florence, Italy
Forum Iulii—Fréjus, France
forum, fora—open main public square in Roman cities
francisca—throwing axe of unique shape used in Frankish warfare
frigidarium—cold water pool/chamber of the baths

frumentarii—the *agentes'* predecessors as imperial information gatherers during the Republican and Principate periods ending with their disbandment by Emperor Diocletian on charges of rampant corruption

frumentationes—workers in grain distribution

Fundi—Fondi, Italy

garum—ubiquitous fish sauce used to season everything

genius—spirit of locale

gens, gentes—clan, family, lineage

Genua—Genoa, Italy

gratia—political connections

gymnasium—exercise hall

harpastum (*harpustum*)—game using ball about the size and solidity of a softball and involving speed, agility, and physical exertion. Little is known about the rules, but it could be violent, with players often ending up on the ground.

haruspex, haruspices—soothsayer

haruspicina—soothsaying

Herakleia (Magna Graecia,)—Policoro, Basilicata, Italy

honesta—honor, honesty

honestior, honestiores—privileged classes of Rome, persons of status and property, senatorial classes, protected by law from interrogation under torture, except in cases of treason

humanitas—humanity

humilior, humiliores—person of lower class or caste of Roman society

imago, imagines—ancestral portraits hanging in the atrium of a noble Roman family home; death masks or busts often labeled with details of the deceased

imperator—emperor

infamia—infamy

infra dignitatem—infra-dig, beneath one's dignity

insigne, insignia—badges or symbols of office

insula, insulae—apartment building

Korinthos—Corinth, Greece

labrum—basin

laconicum—sauna

laetus, laeti—Late Roman term for people from outside the Empire permitted to settle on land granted inside imperial territory on the condition they provide recruits for the Roman military

Lapadaria—La Paderia, Italy

lararium—household shrine for the domestic guardians, the *Lares Familiares*

lares—household gods (see above)

latrunculi—also *ludus latrunculorum* or *latrones*, a 'capture' board game for two players moving cones or 'dogs' around a grid or 'city,' (might resemble chess or draughts)

lectica, lecticae—litter with couch, palanquin, often curtained

lex majestatis—law of treason

libertus—freedman

lictor, lictores—senatorial bodyguards/escorts assigned to imperial officials

Lilybaeum—Marsala, Sicily

litotes—ironic understatement in which an affirmative is expressed by the negative of its contrary

litterae caelestes—formalized Late Roman court handwriting

Livia—a grade of better writing paper, second only to *augustus*

Londinium—London, England

Lucrina—Lucrino, Italy

Ludna—Saint-Georges-de-Reneins, France

Ludus Magnus—Domitian-era wrestling school at the base of the Caelian Hill opposite the Flavian Amphitheater

Lugdunum—Lyon, France

Luna—Luni, Italy

Lutetia—Paris, France

magicium—black magic

magicos apparatus—magic devices, tokens, potions, etc.

magister—head of a government department or *schola*, or general commander

Magister Admissionum—master overseeing imperial audiences

Magister Agentium in Rebus—Master of the *Schola of Agentes in Rebus*, imperial intelligence, postal and road supervision service, reporting to the *Magister Officiorum*

Magister Dispositionum—head of the *Scrinium Dispositionum* and responsible to the *Magister Officiorum* for coordinating the emperor's daily schedule and imperial travel

Magister Equitum—Master of the Horse, a title revived in the Late Roman Empire, when Constantine I established it as one of the supreme military ranks

Magister Memoriae—Master of the Rolls, reporting to the *Magister Officiorum*

Magister Officiorum—a senior imperial officer (in charge of the palatine secretariat,) created under Constantine (306-337) to limit the power of the praetorian prefect, until then an emperor's chief administrative aide.

maiestas divinas—treason against the divine emperor/state

majestatis immunitas—protected from torture

maleficium—black spells

mamillare—strapless brassiere-like undergarment

manceps, mancipes—managers and landlords of state-franchised layover or stopover stations on the *Cursus Publicus*

mansio, mansiones—state-franchised stopovers on the *Cursus Publicus*, relay station, or village providing services and horses

Mare Clausum—winter season closing Mediterranean Sea traffic

Margus River—the Velika (Great) Morava River

Mariana—Mariana Mantuovo, Italy

Mataurum—Ponte Meatauro, Fano, Italy

Mataurus River—Meatauro River

mater—mother

Matisco—Mâcon, France

matrona—matron, respected mistress of a household

Mauretania Tingitana—Roman province at the northwestern tip of North Africa, approximately the northern part of the present-day Moroccan and Spanish possessions Ceuta and Melilla

mausoleum, mausolea—tomb

mea culpa—my fault, sorry

medicus—doctor

Mediolanum—Milan, Italy

memoria—memorial plaques

merum—crude undiluted wine

miasma—summer humid pollution causing feverish illness
misericordia—compassion
mores—morals and standards of the times
Mosella—the Moselle River
mulsum—an aperitif of wine mixed with honey
Mursa—Osijek, Croatia
mutatio, mutationes—relay station on *Cursus Publicus* with fresh horses/services
myrrh—incense made from the resin of a small, thorny tree of the genus Commiphora.
Naissus—Niš, Serbia
Napoli Bay—Naples, Italy
Narbo (Martius), Narbona—Narbonne, France
Neapolis—Naples, Italy
nefarias preces—spells
negotium—business, occupation, 'no leisure,' the opposite of *otium*, leisure
Nemausus—Nimes, France
Nicaea—İznik, Turkey
Niger Lapis— The Lapis Niger or 'Black Stone' is an ancient shrine in the Roman Forum. Together with the associated Vulcanal (a sanctuary to Vulcan) it constitutes the only surviving remnants of the old Comitium, an early assembly area that preceded the Forum and is thought to derive from an archaic cult site of the 7th or 8th century BC.
Nora—Nora, Cagliari, Sardinia
notae Tironianae—shorthand invented by Cicero's slave secretary Tiro, giving rise to the word
notarius, notarii, (vocative case *Notarie*)—notary, high official often used in Late Roman Empire to investigate affairs or execute orders on behalf of court or emperor
numerarius magistri militum—army accountant
nummus, nummi—Late Roman low-value silver-clad coin, continually debased from the monetary reforms of Diocletian
obryzum—fire-tested gold, pure gold
Octavus—Saint-Symphorien-d'Ozon, France
Olbia—Olbia, Sardinia

orbiculus, orbiculi—large embroidered ovals or rounds appliqued to an official's tunic

otium—retirement, leisure (see *negotium*, the non-existence of leisure)

Pachynum—Pachino, Syracuse, Sicily

paideia—Greek concept of classical education and upbringing

Padus River—Po River, Italy

palla/paenula,(ae)—long, hooded circular cloak that became associated with praetorians and other guards over the centuries. For woman, a rectangular shawl or longer cloak

panis gradilis—bread for the poor

pankraton—'all force' combat, a dangerous combination of wrestling and boxing in which everything was permitted except biting, gouging (stabbing your finger into your opponent's eye, nose, or mouth) and attacking the genitals.

Pannonia—Bosnia and northern Serbia

parasitus—pimp

Parcae—the Fates

Parma—Parma, Italy

Patavius—Padua, Italy

pater/paterfamilias—patriarch of the *familia*, the entire household including slaves

patera—a shallow ceramic or metal libation bowl

petanus—non-combat riding helmet

Philippopolis—Plovdiv, Bulgaria

pilleus, (pileus)—brimless flat-topped felt or fur hat of the Late Roman era worn by officers and civilians alike

Pisaurum—Pesaro, Italy

Placentia—Piacenza, Italy

pluvius—pool receiving rainwater through *compluvius* opening in the roof over the *atrium*

pocillator—servant who pours wine

Pola, Istria—Pula, Croatia

Pontifex Vestae

popina—inn offering food and prostitutes

Portus Tibulae—Castelsardo, Sardinia

posca—a refreshing herb-flavored mix of sour wine or water with vinegar concentrate added by travelers to make a refreshing drink

praefectus (vocative *Praefecte*)—chief officer, prefect
Praefectus Annonae—prefect in charge of welfare distribution
Praefectus Urbi—prefect of the city, chief municipal officer
praetor—one of two magistrates under the consul
prenomina—first name
primiscrinius—second-highest ranking official for judicial courts responsible for, among other things, timekeeping of judicial procedures
prolixiores catenae—extended chains
proskynesis—full-length prostration to 'worship the purple' introduced from the Persian custom by Diocletian and stressed in some post-Constantine courts as recognizing the Christian emperor as Christ's vice-regent on earth
protector domesticus, protectores domestici—an elite guard unit of the Late Roman army, who served as bodyguards and staff officers to the emperor
pugio, pugiones—the short, standard-issue military dagger of Late Rome
pusulatum—pure silver in coin
Puteoli—Pozzuoli near Naples, Italy
quaestor—financial, auditing, or legal counselor
Quaestor Sacri Palatii—leading imperial legal expert
raeda—a four-horsed, covered stagecoach hired by their families with much baggage
rescript—written appeals to the emperor on which he appended his decision below the petition with his signature and returned to the appellant
rei publicae utilitas—'the public good' or wellbeing
relatio—recital of evidence
Rhenus or Ripa River—the Rhine
rhetor—teacher of rhetoric
Rhodanus—the Rhône River
rhyton—a drinking container used in ancient Greece in the form of an animal's head or a horn, with the hole for drinking at the lower or pointed end
Roma—Rome, Italy
Romanitas—Roman culture, the qualities of being Roman
sacrae largitones—state treasury
sacrificia funesta—blood sacrifice

saevitia—cruelty
sagum, saga—short riding cloak
Sarguntum—Sagunto, Spain
Saturnalia—seven-day pagan holiday, marking the winter solstice
schola—Late Roman government department
scholares—imperial guards who replaced the disbanded praetorians of earlier Rome
segmenta—embroidered panels or similar elements appliqued onto tunic or cloak
sella, sellae—sedan chair
Senatus Populusque Romanus incendio consumptum restituit—inscription after the fire in 360 AD (translated in text)
senex—geriatric
servus lotus—bath slave
Sicilia—Sicily, Italy
sigillaria—Saturnalia trinkets and figurines, also the last day of Saturnalia festivities
Sirmium—Sremska-Mitrovica, Serbia
solidus, solidi—4.5-gram gold coin issued by Constantine to replace the *aureus*
spatha, spathae—double-bladed sword replacing the shorter *gladius*, standard issue sword of Late Roman military
spectabilis, spectabilii—officials/notables ranked in imperial hierarchy
stabularius—officer or manager of stables
stade, stadia—a *stade* equaled one eighth of a mile
stellionatus—corruption, fraud, deceit, e.g. property double-dealing
stilus, stili—pointed instrument for writing on wax-covered tablets
stola, stolae—women's long over-tunic
stuprum—criminal fornication with a virgin or widow
sudarium—steam room
sulcantibus ungulis—iron claws used in torture
taberna, tabernae—tavern, restaurant
Tabernae—Tawern, France
tablinum—study
tabularium—accounting house
tabularius—accountant
taeneotic—third grade papyrus/paper sold by weight

Taenaron—Cape Matapan, Greece

Tarracina—Terracina, Italy

Tarraco—Tarragona, Catalonia, Spain

Tarvessedum—Campodolcino, Italy

taurobolium—ritual sacrifice over a wooden platform of a flower- and gold-decked bull, leaving the blood to run onto the priest of the Great Mother below, who receives the blood on face, tongue and palate for re-generation and purification.

tepidarium—warm room in the baths that radiated heat from underground flooring

tesserae—mosaic tiles or playing dice from the Greek for 'four sides.'

testudo—battlefield formation in which infantry overlapped their shield into a 'tortoise shell' defense.

Tharros—near San Giovanni di Sinis, Cabras, Oristano, Sardinia

Tiberis—Tiber River

tiro, tirones—beginners, trainees, army cadet, recruits,

togati—clients or hangers-on

Toxandria—area of upper Gaul, covering all or most of modern North Brabant, eastern Antwerp, and the north of Belgian Limburg

Traiana, (Colonia Ulpia Traiana)—Xanten, Germany

Tres Tabernae Cesaris—Saverne, France; 'The Three Shops of Caesar,' sitting at the foot of a pass through the Vosges mountain range in Alsace, France, (not to be confused with the more famous junction, Tres Tabernae, a *mutatio* on the ancient Appian Way, about 18 km from Rome, where St. Paul, was met by a band of Roman Christians (Acts 28:15). The 'shops' refer not to taverns, but to the necessary blacksmith, general store, and refreshment stop.)

Treverorum—Trier, Germany

tribunus—tribune

tribunus stabili—tribune in charge of the stables

triclinium—dining room

Tullum—Toul, France

tunica—woman's undertunic

Turris Lybisonis—Porto Torres, Sardinia

tympanum—a vertical recessed triangular space forming the center of a pediment, typically decorated

Valentia—Valence, France

Velletri—Velitri, Italy

veneficium—the most venal forms of black magic

veritas—truth

via privata—private road off state road, maintained by owners of an estate

via munita—a regular road paved with rectangular blocks of the stone of the surrounding countryside or with polygonal blocks of lava

via terrena—dirt road

vicarius—a Late Roman judge or jurisdictional official, possibly acting in outer dioceses in the place of the *iudex ordinarius*

vicomagister—state priest tending a shrine

vicus—village or in a city, a neighborhood/quarter

vigiles—firemen (In addition to extinguishing fires, the *Vigiles* were the night watch of Rome. Their duties included apprehending thieves and robbers and capturing runaway slaves. The task of guarding the baths was added as a duty of the *Vigiles* during the reign of Alexander Severus when the baths remained open during the night. They dealt with petty crimes and looked for disturbances of the peace while they patrolled the streets. Sedition, riots, and violent crimes were handled by the *Cohortes urbanae* and (to a lesser extent) the Praetorian Guard until their disbandment, though *Vigiles* could provide a supporting role in these situations. The *Vigiles* were considered a paramilitary unit and their organization into cohorts and centuries reflects this.)

vincula, vinculae—shackles, fetters

virgo—virgin

vir clarissimus, viri clarissimi—all senators, category of 'most famous man'

vitis—the fourth-century civilian officer's ceremonial baton based on the baton of a Roman centurion made from a vine staff

volo—shortened form of *voluntarius* for slave volunteering to fight for Roma to earn manumission

Acknowledgments

A special thanks to the site *Lacus Curtius* and its Site Master Bill Thayer for the unabridged version, translation, and footnotes for the *Res Gestae* by Ammianus Marcellinus

Ammianus Marcellinus, *The Later Roman Empire (AD 354-378)*, Penguin Classics, Penguin Books, London, 2014

Barker, Anne, 'Speculations of the Death of Roman Theater,' Wesleyan University, Illinois, 1996

Barnes, Timothy David, *Ammianus Marcellinus and the Representation of Historical Reality*, Cornell University, Ithaca, New York, 1998

Bauman, Richard A., *Crime and Punishment in Ancient Rome*, Routledge, London, and New York, 1996

Bowerstock, G.W., Peter Brown, Oleg Grabar, ed. *Late Antiquity, A Guide to the Postclassical World*, The Belknap Press of Harvard University, Cambridge, 1999

Bradbury, Scott, 'Julian's Pagan Revival and the Decline of Blood Sacrifice,' *Phoenix*, Vol. 49, No. 4 (Winter, 1995), pp. 331-356

Cameron, Averil, *The Later Roman Empire*, Fontana History of the Ancient World, Fontana Press, London, 1993

Chroust, Anton-Hermann, *Legal Profession in Ancient Imperial Rome*, Notre Dame Law Review, Vol 30, issue 4, 1955, pp 534 ff

Curran, John, *Pagan City and Christian Capital: Rome in the Fourth Century*, Clarendon Press, Oxford, 2000

den Boeft, Jan, Jan Willem Drijvers, Daniël den Hengst and Hans C. Teitler, *Philological and Historical Commentary on Ammianus Marcellinus, Book XXVIII*, Vol. 9, Brill, 2009

Dill, Samuel, *Roman Society in the Last Century of the Western Empire*, Macmillan, London, 1899

Drijvers, Jan Willem, 'Decline of Political Culture: Ammianus Marcellinus, Characterization of the Reigns of Valentinian and Valens,' University of Groningen, *Shifting Cultural*

Frontiers in Late Antiquity, Brakke, Deborah Deliyannis and Edward Watts (eds.), Farnham 2012

Drobner, Hubertus R., 'Stretch Yourself on the Rack of Your Heart,' 'Reality, Spirituality, and Emotions in Augustine's Imagery, Augustine on Heart and Life,' Essays edited by John J. O'Keefe and Michael Cameron, *Journal of Religion and Society Supplement Series,* Kripke Center, Supplement 15, 2008

Faas, Patrick, *Around the Roman Table,* Macmillan, London, 1994

Flower, Harriet I., *The Dancing Lares and the Serpent in the Garden, Religion at the Roman Street Corner,* Princeton University Press, 2017

Heather, Peter, 'Senators and Senates,' *Cambridge Ancient History,* Vol. 13, Cambridge University Press, Cambridge, England

Hillner, Julia, *Prison, Punishment and Penance in Late Antiquity,* University of Sheffield, England, 2015

Hughes, Ian, *Imperial Brothers, Valentinian, Valens and the Disaster at Adrianople,* Pen & Sword Books Ltd., Barnsley, England, 2013

Hunt, David, 'Beggars from the Vatican, Ammianus Marcellinus on Roman Christianity,' *Studia Patristica. Vol. XXXIX— Historica, Biblica, Ascetica et Hagiographica,* M. Edwards, P. Parvis, Hubert Young, eds. P. Leuven, Peeters, 2006

Johnson, Paul S., *Economic Evidence and the Changing Nature of Urban Space in Late Antique Rome,* Edicions Universitat Barcelona, 2013

Jones, A. H. M., The Later Roman Empire, 284-602, Vol. 1, John Hopkins University Press, Baltimore, Maryland, 1986

Kahlos, Maijastina, 'Vettius Agorius Praetextatus—Senatorial Life in Between,' *Acta Instituti Romani Finlandiae,* No. 26, Rome, 2002

Kaufman, David B., 'Poisons and Poisoning Among the Romans,' *Classical Philology,* Vol. 27, No. 2 (April, 1932)

Kelly, Christopher, *Ruling the Later Roman Empire,* Harvard University Press, Cambridge, Massachusetts, 2009

Kelly, Christopher, 'Crossing the Frontiers: Imperial Power in the Last Book of Ammianus,' *Ammianus After Julian, The Reign of Valentinian and Valens in Books 26-31 of the Res*

Gestae, J. Den Boeft, J. W. Drijvers, D. den Hengst, H. C. Teitler, eds. Brill, Leiden/Boston, 2007

Lancon, Bertrand, *Rome in Late Antiquity: AD 312-609,* Edinburgh University Press, Edinburgh, 2000

Lee-Stecum, Parshia, 'Dangerous Reputations: Charioteers and Magic in Fourth-Century Rome' *Greece and Rome,* Vol. 53, No. 2, pp. 224-234 Oct, 2006, The Classical Association, Cambridge University Press

Lenski, Noel, *Failure of Empire: Valens and the Roman State in the Fourth Century AD, (Transformation of the Classical Heritage)* University of California Press, 2014

Mackail, J. W., 'Ammianus Marcellinus', *The Journal of Roman Studies,* Vol. 10 (1920) pp 103-118, Cambridge University, Cambridge

Murray, Alexander Callander, *From Roman to Merovingian Gaul, A Reader,* Higher Education University of Toronto Press, Inc., Toronto, 2008

Olszaniec, Szymon, *Prosopographical Studies on the Court Elite in the Roman Empire (4th century AD),* Jacek Wełniak, Małgorzata Stachowska-Wełniak, transl., Nicolaus Copernicus University Press, Torun, Poland, 2013

Potter, David, *The Roman Empire at Bay AD 180-395,* Routledge History of the Ancient World, Routledge, London, 2014

Rich, Anthony, 'Balneae' (Roman section, pp 183-196) of *A Dictionary of Greek and Roman Antiquities* by William Smith, John Murray, London, 1875.

Robinson, O. F., *Penal Practice and Penal Policy in Ancient Rome,* Routledge, New York, 2007

Salzman, Michele Renee, *The Making of a Christian Aristocracy: Social and Religious Change in the Western Roman Empire,* Harvard University Press, Cambridge, Massachusetts, 2009

Sheldon, Rose Mary, *Intelligence Activities in Ancient Rome,* Routledge Press, New York, 2007

Socrates Scholasticus, *Book III,* transl. A.C. Zenos, *Nicene and Post-Nicene Fathers,* Second Series, Vol. 2., ed. Philip Schaff and Henry Wace, Christian Literature Publishing Co., Buffalo, NY, 1890, revised and edited, Kevin Knight, New Advent online edition

Sumner, Graham, *Roman Military Clothing AD 200-400*, Osprey Publishing, Oxford, 2003

Testa, Rita Lizzi, *Senatori, Popolo, Papi: il Governo di Roma al Tempo dei Valentiniani*, Edipuglia, Bari, Italy, 2004

Thompson, E. A. *The Historical Work of Ammianus Marcellinus*, University Press, Cambridge, England, 1947

Trzcionka, Silke, *Magic and the Supernatural in Fourth Century Syria*, Routledge Press, New York, 2007

Watts, Edward J. Watts, *The Final Pagan Generation*, University of California Press, Oakland, California, 2015,

Zozimus, *New History*, Book 3, Green and Chaplin, London, 1814 1814

About the Author

Q. V. Hunter's interest in classical history began with four years of high school Latin followed by university courses in ancient religions. A fascination with Late Antiquity deepened when Hunter moved to a two-hundred-year-old farmhouse near an ancient Roman colony. The farmhouse is easily reached by modern road, but also by the remnants of a Roman road running more directly downhill to the *Colonia Equestris Noviodunum*.

Noviodunum was founded around 50 BCE as a retirement community for Julius Caesar's cavalry veterans. It's listed as the *civitas Equestrium id est Noviodunus* in the *Notitia Galliarum*, (the fourth-century directory listing all seventeen provinces of Roman Gaul.)

Noviodunum became Rome's most important colony along Lake Leman—with a forum, baths, basilica, and amphitheater. Potable water came via an aqueduct running all the way from present-day Divonne, France. Noviodunum belonged to a network of settlements radiating out from Lugdunum (Lyon, France) around the Rhône Valley. Roman colonists were encouraged to supervise the Celtic Helvetii who had been transported to the area against their will after their defeat at the Battle of Bibracte in 58 BC.

Much of Roman Noviodunum was razed during Alemanni invasions in 259-260 AD, well before the period of our story, but it flourishes again today as the Swiss town of Nyon.

Printed in Great Britain
by Amazon